José Calvo Tello

The Novel in the Spanish Silver Age

Digital Humanities Research | Volume 4

Editorial

Digital Humanities is an evolving, cross cutting field within the humanities employing computer based methods. Research in this field, therefore, is an interdisciplinary endeavor that often involves researchers from the humanities as well as from computer science. This collaboration influences the methods applied as well as the theories underlying and informing research within those different fields. These implications need to be addressed according to the traditions of different humanities' disciplines. Therefore, the edition addresses all humanities disciplines in which digital methods are employed. **Digital Humanities Research** furthers publications from all those disciplines addressing the methodological and theoretical implications of the application of digital research in the humanities.

José Calvo Tello, born in 1987, works as a researcher and subject librarian at Göttingen State and University Library. He obtained his doctorate in Humanities from the Julius-Maximilians-Universität Würzburg (Germany) with a thesis about machine learning and other computational methods applied to the Spanish novel. His research is focused on the application and development of computational methods such as machine learning and natural language processing applied to romance literatures and library records.

José Calvo Tello

The Novel in the Spanish Silver Age

A Digital Analysis of Genre Using Machine Learning

[transcript]

Funding: The Early-Career Research Group 'Computational Literary Genre Stylistics' (CLiGS) was funded by the German Federal Ministry of Education and Research (Bundesministerium für Bildung und Forschung) from April 2014 to March 2020 (funding identifiers 01UG1408 and 01UG1508).

Bei dem Werk handelt es sich um die Veröffentlichung einer Dissertation, die an der Graduiertenschule für die Geisteswissenschaften an der Julius-Maximilians-Universität Würzburg abgeschlossen wurde.
Examiners: Prof. Dr. Christof Schöch, Prof. Dr. Fotis Jannidis, Prof. Dr. Angela Schrott

Bibliographic information published by the Deutsche Nationalbibliothek
The Deutsche Nationalbibliothek lists this publication in the Deutsche Nationalbibliografie; detailed bibliographic data are available in the Internet at http://dnb.d-nb.de

Published in 2021 by Bielefeld University Press. An Imprint of transcript Verlag
http://www.bielefeld-university-press.de

Cover layout: Maria Arndt, Bielefeld
Printed by Majuskel Medienproduktion GmbH, Wetzlar
Print-ISBN 978-3-8376-5925-2
PDF-ISBN 978-3-8394-5925-6
https://doi.org/10.14361/9783839459256

Printed on permanent acid-free text paper.

Contents

Acknowledgements

1. Introduction

2. Previous Research and Theoretical Framework

3. Data: Texts and Metadata

4. Feature Engineering: Linguistic Annotation and Transformation

5. Analysis of Subgenre Labels

6. Feature and Labels Selection

7. Analysis of Subgenres

8. Discussion of Tripartite Graph for Genre

9. Conclusion

10. References

11. Appendix

Acknowledgements

Acknowledgements

The fact that I am the only author of this work does not mean that I could have done it without the support of many. This can also be explained as a series of steps in life, and I thank God for those. I never imagined I could be able to write a book of more than 400 pages about literature enjoying most of the process. God does move in mysterious ways.

There are two groups of people that have helped me through this process: the professional and the personal. And these can be structured in concentric circles, moving closer towards me.

The largest groups of professionals I am thankful to, are two communities that have made many steps of this work possible. The first one are the generous contributors of Stack Overflow,[1] from whom I have learned so much, both from their questions and their answers (to me or to other people). The second one are the hardworking editors of ePubLibre,[2] a source from which I have extracted many texts, labels, and summaries. Thanks to both communities.

The second circle is populated by researchers who have offered their time to teach me, debate, or give me personal feedback. I have learned a lot from the workshops of researchers such as Maciej Eder, Jan Rybicki, Mike Kestemont, Frank Fischer, Helena Bermúdez Sabel, and Pablo Ruiz Fabo. I have enjoyed the motivating exchange with Laura Hernández Lorenzo and Daniil Skorinkin, and appreciate deeply the support and collaboration with Elena Martínez Carro, María Concepción Jiménez Fernández, and María Teresa Santa María Fernández. The feedback of several colleagues, especially over the last months, has been very valuable, for example, from Pablo Jauralde Pou, José Teruel Benavente, Brigitte Burrichter, Dolores Romero López, Nanette Rißler-Pipka, Corina Koolen, Peggy Bockwinkel, Hugh Craig,

1 https://stackoverflow.com/.

2 https://www.epublibre.org/.

Sofie Kluge, Nils Reiter, José Luis Losada Palenzuela, Marcus Willand, Janis Pagel, Benjamin Krautter, Jonas Kuhn, and Evelyn Gius. The works of three researchers have always inspired me: John Burrows, Douglas Biber, and Ted Underwood. I would like to thank the three of them not only for their work, but also for their kindness and feedback.

A narrower circle of professionals is constituted by the researchers and staff of the professorship of Digital Humanities at the University of Würzburg. Working in such an interdisciplinary environment has improved my research, with constant contact to people with knowledge in Computer Sciences, Statistics, and numerous fields in the Humanities. Thanks to Steffen Pielström, Julian Schröter, Thorsten Vitt, Keli Du, Leonard Konle, Lukas Weimar, and Thora Hagen.

For five years, the research group CLiGS has been a part of the University of Würzburg, and it has been an honor to be one of its members. I would like to thank the people who have participated in it and from whom I have been able to learn: Ulrike Henny-Krahmer, Daniel Schlör, Robert Hesselbach, Katrin Betz, and Stefanie Popp. Besides, I am thankful to the research assistants (Constanze Ludewig, Lea Kunz, Jakob Stahl), and to my two proofreaders (Nicola Wilton, and especially to Laura Hatry). In addition, thanks to my friends Daniel Marín and Iván Arroyo for their practical help with the e-books.

A narrower group of researchers had an even greater impact: my PhD tutors. I would like to thank Angela Schrott, Fotis Jannidis, and Christof Schöch for always finding time in their busy schedule, for giving me challenging and constructive feedback, and for supporting me financially through this period. By virtue of an intense exchange with Christof, I have been able not only to learn about technology, literature, professional rigor and standards, but also about the kindness and generosity with which he treats his coworkers and the community. He has set an extraordinary example.

But work is just a part of our existence. Life is what happens between the submission of a proposal and the next one. That is why there is an important personal circle with many people that have given me support, especially in the last phase, such as friends (Clemens, Judith, Florian, Armin, Daniel, Renate), my three sisters, and my parents. Thanks to all of them. My children might not know it, but spending time with them helped me put things in the right place and remind me that there are more important things than a research study about Machine Learning and literary genres.

However, the person with the most positive effect on this work is also the love of my life. Thank you for listening, for supporting me, for understanding the life of a researcher, for believing in me during this challenging process. *Sem você não tivesse começado, mas especialmente não tivesse terminado*. This book is dedicated to her.

1. Introduction

1. Introduction

Genres are a contradictory cultural phenomenon. On the one hand, specialists tend not to find consensus about what exactly defines genres (with very few exceptions, like sonnets). In those cases, central questions arise quickly, such as whether it is useful to search for an exact definition, the difficulties of acquiring a closed list of labels, the inadequacy of formal structures (such as taxonomies) to fit real examples, or specific doubts about the status of specific labels: "is 'young-adult novel' really a thing?" On the other hand, everyone interacts on a daily basis with many institutions that use genres: Bookstores, libraries, physical or online shops, or streaming platforms structure their content partially through genre. Netflix highlights new super-hero movies or series in our profile because we keep watching similar content. As readers, we tend to go to the detective novel section of a library or bookstore if we enjoy this genre.

These two contradictory perspectives are especially observable in academic circles. A researcher might be interested in the representations of characters' genders in theater plays of the 18th century, or the way animals are represented in specific short stories of the 19th century. In these cases, genres (theater plays, short stories) are not the main goal of the research, but are used to define the literary corpus of analysis. In other words, the researcher takes for granted that genres are an important manner of structuring culture. However, the effort of obtaining a clear definition or structure of these categories is often unfruitful. Genres seem to be useful, but also fuzzy and opaque.

Literary genres are not only useful to define the corpus we study, they also deserve to be the primary focus of specific research. Literary Studies concentrate their attention on texts, their main instance of analysis. But in most cases, a researcher wants to study more than one work. To define a corpus, the texts need to share specific categories, e.g. they were written by the same person, have been published in the same period, or belong to the same genre. These three categories (authorship, periodization, and genre) are frequently analyzed or used in Literary Studies, although others are also possible (texts which tackle similar topics, are produced in the same region, are published by the same printer, etc.). Among these three categories, genre is the only one that does not concern a factor that is external to the text, such as author or the year of publication. Similar literary works compose genres, and genres organize literary works into groups. Todorov states that "genre is the point of intersection of general poetics and literary history; in this sense, it is a privileged object, which is enough to make it the principal subject of literary studies" (1976, 164), while Wellek and Warren state that "the subject of genre [...] raises central questions for literary history and literary criticism" (1956, 237, originally published in 1942). This is especially relevant in our current situation of massive digitization of cultural heritage and accessibility to quantitative methods. Having a clearer understanding of genres can lead to a better position to study the history of literature, and ultimately the history of cultures (cfr. Garrido Gallardo 1988, 25–26).

The study of genres encounters a very long tradition of discussion, spread across thousands of years, a great number of languages, academic traditions, and many authorities, including Plato, Aristotle, and Goethe. No researcher can encompass all the references about genre. However, some models and structures have created a major impact in this tradition. From the Aristotelian philosophy emerged the model that is most often applied to genre, either explicitly or implicitly. Traditionally, this scholastic model foresees that each text belongs to a genre based on sufficient and necessary conditions. For its part, each genre pertains to a more general genre. Thus, a tree-like taxonomy emerges, similar to those in biology: Texts (as leaves) hang on genres (as branches), and these originate from thicker branches (more general genres). This elegant and somehow intuitive model is thwarted by every attempt of feeding it with real examples. First, many texts belong to more than one genre. Second, there is no consensus about the sufficient and necessary conditions. Third, attempts to identify macro-genres (groups of genres) find little acceptance. For these reasons, other theoretical models have been integrated into the discussion in the last decades, such as the prototype theory and the family resemblance approach. In Chapter 2.3, I will describe these models, structures and perspectives on genre in detail.

A further difficulty around genre is the fact that it is analyzed by dozens of research fields, such as Rhetoric, Linguistics (and several subareas, such as

Corpus Linguistics), Literary Studies, Digital Humanities, Cultural Studies, Media Studies, Sociology, etc. Each field creates its own tradition, composed of a jargon, conferences, and publishing channels, which are unfamiliar to researchers of other traditions. Besides, the differences in languages work as a double wall. First, researchers tend to publish in their own language. Second, the literature they analyze is alien to many other researchers. Four scholars from different countries (for example, Spain, France, Germany, and Russia) working on genre in their national literatures are likely to produce papers that are (in the best-case scenario) only partially understandable to the others, but most likely illegible. Besides, they analyze labels and texts that are mostly unknown to other researchers. The possibilities of sharing knowledge about genre between traditions and languages is therefore very limited.

Considering all these aspects, what is the goal of this research study? This work has several goals, but the ultimate one is to present a theoretical and computational model for genre. This model can be fed with hundreds of real cases from Spanish literature, not only the most canonical works or those that fit the theory. The specific data points are organized in three separate but connected partitions: genre-categories represented by labels, textual instances, and internal characteristics (from linguistic annotation or literary metadata). The interest in the model for Literary Studies and Digital Humanities relies on four aspects. First, it can comprise several observations that until now were seen as unconnected, such as the prototypicality of some texts for specific genres, the variance in the classification results, the description of genres through internal features, or the way that texts and genres interact. Second, the model is able to compute questions about the genres that have found little formalization until now, such as the quantification of the similarity of various genres, or whether there are specific groups of genres (macrogenres). Third, besides its theoretical and computational form, this model can be represented visually, facilitating a shared comprehension between research traditions and languages. Finally, the model for genre here presented is an example of how Digital Humanities (DH) is not restricted to the application of already existing techniques from Computer Science. Much more than that, part of the Digital Humanities activity can be designing new computational methods based on theoretical models that can fit entire real dataset.

This publication pertains to a tradition of academic works that have been applying computational methods to genre for the last decades. In this tradition, researchers of Computational Linguistics and Digital Humanities have been analyzing through computational means whether programs are able to correctly predict the genres given previously by humans (authors, publishers, scholars, etc.). These will be presented in detail in Chapter 2.3. Typically, these papers have used linguistic features, such as the frequencies of the words, and applied algorithms to find statistical patterns that allow differentiating one genre from another. In most cases, these works have shown that genres can be identified to a certain degree, but neither perfectly (some texts are mismatched) nor homogeneously (some genres yield higher classification results than others).

For this research study, I have chosen the period of Spanish literature between the end of the 19th century and the end of Spanish Civil War in 1939, often referred to as the *silver age*, which will be presented in Chapter 2.1. As in other Western literatures, the authors of that time explicitly tried to write against the expectations of traditional genres, venturing new forms. In some cases, they even created ad hoc labels: hypothetically, their own particular genre. The high canonization of many of these writers has led to a research based, in many cases, on one or few authors, reinforcing these overly specific genre-labels. Therefore, I expected the genres of this period to be especially challenging for classification or to be fitted into a single model.

As with any research, its objective needs to be defined and limited. An important aspect of this research study is the fact that it takes a cross-sectional perspective, understanding the period of sixty years of literature as a period, and analyzing it from a synchronic perspective. As I will explain in Chapters 2.3 and 3.1, this is primarily due to the research questions I consider most relevant, but also to the lack of digitized Spanish texts for other periods (see Section 3.1.9). This implies that the concept of genre that is being treated in this research study omits two aspects. First, the historical development of the genres. Second, the communicative intention of the author and their reception by contemporaneous readers. Both aspects have a greater importance in research with longitudinal, diachronic, or historical perspectives (see examples in Section 2.3.4), and their results are captivating, but the data I have access to does not permit this approach, at least not with quantitative methods.

This publication is highly interdisciplinary, applying theories, concepts, and data from Linguistics, Literary Studies, and Digital Humanities. This interdisciplinarity is at the core of the early-career research group where it has been written, called *Computational Literary Genre Stylistics* (CLiGS), at the University of Würzburg, in Germany. But an interdisciplinary research study combining three areas cannot be the concatenation of three publications in each area. One single researcher cannot delve into any of the three areas as much as one researcher focusing on only one aspect could. However, the benefit and difficulty of interdisciplinary works is the fact that they establish a multilateral dialogue between several traditions with one specific goal: In my case, to understand the genres of the novels of this period using computational methods.

As mentioned before, the ultimate goal of this research study is to provide a computational model of literary genre. To develop such a model, four further main goals need to be obtained. The first one is to resolve the question about the representativeness of a data set for the literary texts of this period. Which criteria should literary corpora fulfill to produce representative results about a period? Are they only acceptable when they are big enough? And if so, how big should they be? How do other research areas, like Statistics, solve the question about representativeness of a sample? Are there other methodologies acceptable for the case of literature? These questions lead to the composition of the *Corpus of Novels of the Spanish Silver Age* (CoNSSA), which will be described in detail in Chapter 3.1. In that chapter, I will present a possible method to obtain a statistically representative corpus following criteria from Literary Studies.

A corpus of texts must not necessarily contain information about which texts belong to which genre category. This is why the second main question is what should be the genre palette (the set of labels) that should be analyzed and what should be their source. Should the author be considered as the sole authority of the categories of their works? Is the publisher of the first edition also an acceptable source? What about the publishers of later editions? Do literary scholars know enough to undertake this role? And does the opinion of contemporary users and readers count? If many of them are gathered, will they agree on the labels used and which texts populate which label? In Chapter 5.1, I will evaluate the hypothesis that, even though there are certain differences and nuances, there is a certain agreement between these agents on which texts should populate each genre, and therefore that they consider similar statistical populations for each genre. In Chapters 5.2 and 5.3, I will look closer at the labels from the first edition and whether the term *literary fiction* can be considered a similar label to the rest of subgenres.

However, what if it has been overlooked that certain works share characteristics and that they compose a group that could be identified as a type of novel? In other words, what if there are hidden subgenres? That is my third goal, analyzed in Chapter 6.2: to observe whether it is possible to use unsupervised algorithms (clustering) to identify hidden subgenres. After an evaluation of the method, the resulting clusters will be contrasted against semantic and literary information in order to discuss whether they can be understood as hypothetical subgenres.

The fourth goal is one that occupies several chapters: Apply supervised Machine Learning (classification) in different ways to the categories of genres. As I will describe in Section 2.1.3, many artists and scholars have rejected the idea that genres differentiate the texts of this period. If genre is indeed irrelevant, algorithms should not be able to classify the analyzed corpus. Is this the case or can the algorithms also successfully classify the novels of this period? How well, using which kind of information from the works, and why? These different questions will be answered in several chapters:

1. In this research, I analyze mainly the different genres of the novel, like erotic, adventure, or naturalist novel. These can also be called subgenres (genres of the novel). But before the distinction of types of novels can be addressed, a more basic issue has to be answered: Which texts of this period should be considered novels? As I will show in Chapter 3.3, this cannot be answered undisputedly taking the information from the covers or from manuals of literature. This is why I will first apply classification to a series of cases in which the primary genre is in doubt. For this, I will analyze a version of the diachronic corpus CORDE from the Real Academia Española (RAE).
2. The second question about classification is whether it works or not: Do these quantitative techniques still function in a challenging period like the one analyzed here; and if yes, to what degree? Only slightly better than chance, close to perfect results, or something intermediary? My expectations were that it would achieve better results than chance, but still relatively mediocre. As I will show in Chapters 6.2 and 7.1, the results are surprisingly high, many of them very close to perfect scores.
3. The third question about classification is what exactly leads to the best results. For this, in Chapter 6.2, I carry out an evaluation of the different parameters. As parameters, I consider several possibilities in the process, such as the kind of linguistic annotation, the classification algorithms, the number of features, or the kind of data transformations used. What are the features that allow the best classification of these subgenres of Spanish literature? Do grammatical annotations improve the results? Can se-

mantic information give it a boost? What about textual information such as the number of verses, typography, or the distinction between narrative and direct speech paragraphs? Can a set of features be detected which leads to acceptable results for all subgenres, or are the features always specific to the analyzed category? To what degree does the exact manner of expressing the frequencies influence the results (statistical transformations like relative, logarithmic, binary frequencies, z-scores, or tf-idf scores)? Do these parameters show associations between them, for example, certain algorithms that yield higher results with some transformations? The linguistic tools for annotations will be presented in Chapter 4.1, while Chapter 4.2 describes traditional and new statistical transformations of the frequencies.

4. The fourth question about classification is why literary categories have been mainly classified considering only linguistic information. How can the Digital Humanities and Computational Linguistics communities maintain that to identify literary categories such as the historical novel, the algorithm receives only linguistic features, such as the frequencies of the words? An analysis of literary objects should also have access to literary information, like where and when the action of the novels takes place, what kind of narrator is present, whether the text has a happy ending, or characteristic traits of the protagonist. This manual annotation, which will be referred to as literary metadata, will be presented and discussed in Chapter 3.2. My expectation was that the algorithm should obtain better results when it receives this literary metadata as features. Surprisingly, in Section 7.1.5, I will show that these distinctions bring little improvement for the classification results. However, they are extremely fruitful in the description of genres, tackled in Sections 6.2.6, 6.2.7, 8.7, and the Appendix.
5. The final question about classification is why it work notably better for some categories than for others. Some genres treated in this research study, like *episodios nacionales*, erotic, or dialogue novel obtain constantly higher scores than other categories like social, educational, or realist novel. The exact reasons why this happens are unclear. In Chapter 7.2, I will evaluate a series of hypotheses, resulting in five variables that can account for the majority of the variance of the classification results.

However, the ultimate goal of this research is not only to apply methods on genre, but to produce a single computational model that summarizes the most important characteristics of literary genres. For this model, I will use graph technologies, which will be presented, evaluated, and discussed in Chapter 8. This model is a formal alternative to the scholastic model for genre. To obtain it, the core ideas of prototypes and family resemblance are implemented to define the interaction between text instances, genre categories, and features. The model will be created following an inductive process, i.e. by gathering the observations of each chapter. Different intuitive interpretations of the relative positions of the texts and genres in the graph-based model will be hypothesized and evaluated. Besides, the similarity of genres can be measured. The model offers further possibilities, such as calculating whether there are groups of genres (macro-genres) in the form of communities. Finally, the model will be used to produce empirical descriptions about each subgenre of the novel, with a comprehensive list in the Appendix.

To summarize, the ensemble of research questions outlined above leads to structure of eight main parts, each composed of one or more chapters. After this introduction, a second part tackles the question about previous research in several fields: Literary Studies on the period (Chapter 2.1), computational research on genre (Chapter 2.2), and theory of genre (Chapter 2.3). The third part describes the corpus (Chapter 3.1), its metadata (Chapter 3.2), and the filtering process of novels through classification (Chapter 3.3). The fourth part of this research gives an overview of two further steps relating to the texts: the linguistic annotation (Chapter 4.1), and different ways of transforming the quantitative features (Chapter 4.2). The fifth section deals only with analysis of the labels: a comparison of the institutions (Chapter 5.1), the accuracy of the labels at the first publication (Chapter 5.2), and the specific label of *literary fiction* (Chapter 5.3). The sixth part tackles specific questions about the analysis, more specifically an evaluation of the parameters (Chapter 6.1) and the possibility that some genres have remained hidden until now (Chapter 6.2). The seventh part contains a series of analyses of classification, looking at different ways of applying it (Chapter 7.1), and an analysis of why there is variance in the results (Chapter 7.2). Finally, the eighth part discusses the graph model for genre, which will be used in the Appendix for empirical descriptions of all the analyzed subgenres of the novel.

In addition to this book, there is a group of files that I consider an additional part of this publication. I am referring to a series of Jupyter Notebooks that can be accessed online.[1] These are hybrid documents that can be visualized in a browser and contain several types of cells. In some cells, the researcher can write as if it were a website; in other cells, the researcher can run actual code (for example Python) and the output (either textual, numerical, or visual) is shown and saved in the same document (for further explanations, see VanderPlas 2016 and Dombrowski, Gniady, and Kloster 2019). The majority of the chapters of this book has such a companion Notebook. I have used these to manage the data and extract all the results and visualizations of this research study. They have also been edited for readers who want to delve into specific questions, such as the exact data being analyzed or questions about the parameters. These Notebooks are structured according to the chapters and sections of the text. The previously mentioned online repository also contains the Python functions. In addition, a large proportion of the *Corpus of Novels of the Spanish Silver Age* (CoNSSA) has been published on the online platforms GitHub and Zenodo. Section 3.1.11 gives an overview about which portion of the data (full-text, linguistic features and metadata) can be published in different formats, depending on their current legal status.[2] All these data, files, and scripts allow me to analyze in the following chapters and sections the novel of the Spanish *silver age*.

1 https://github.com/cligs/scripts-ne.

2 https://github.com/cligs/conssa, https://doi.org/10.5281/zenodo.4674257.

2. Previous Research and Theoretical Framework

2.1 *Silver Age*: Genre, Novel, and Subgenre of the Novel

2.1.1 Introduction

This chapter introduces the analyzed period of Spanish literature, called the silver age (edad de plata), and how novels were understood and written at that time. I will point out the different reasons why the analysis of literary genres of this period is challenging: First, authors tried to avoid already existing subgenres and tended to create their own. Second, literary scholars have preferred to study the works of single authors instead of shared genres across this period. The relationship between the novel and other genres will be summarized and I will describe some subgenres that have received more attention from Literary Studies.

2.1.2 Edad de Plata: Silver Age

In the history of Spanish literature, two periods show a rise in the number of important creators and works: first, the Renaissance and the Baroque; second, the decades between the end of the 19th century and the Spanish Civil War (1936-1939). The first one is undisputedly referred to as the *siglo de oro* or *golden age*, following the metaphor used for the periodization of Latin literature. An extension of this label has been used for the second period of splendor: *edad de plata* or *silver age*. Since 1974, José-Carlos Mainer has popularized this term as a generic frame for several generations (*regeneracionistas, modernistas, generación del 98, generación del 14, generación del 27, generación del 36*) and isolated authors (Juan Ramón Jiménez, Ramón Gómez de la Serna). For a discussion of the term *modernist* for this period, see Romero López (1997 and 1998).

The writers of these generations tend to be profusely analyzed focusing on few or only one author. This even happens when one single piece of research treats several authors, who are normally analyzed in separate chapters or sections, like García Nora's classic *La novela española contemporánea* (1963). Here, the researcher directly analyzes specific authors without a general overview of the novel during the period and most chapters revolve around one single author. Another example is the monograph by Landeira (1985), in which he analyzes mainly six authors, using a different chapter for each one of them and a different associated subgenre: Blasco Ibáñez and the naturalist novel; Miguel de Unamuno and the existentialist novel... This isolated analysis of the authors tends to highlight the differences and exceptional features of each of them, minimizing the general patterns among distinct texts that would exist if they practiced similar subgenres. The marked tendency of treating authors disjointedly is probably one of the reasons why this period, compared to the *golden age*, lacks academic institutionalization such as journals, conferences, associations, etc.

This period is contextualized in the international movement of modernism, with particularly strong relations with the artistic situation of the rest of Europe and Latin America (Shaw 2010; Novillo-Corvalán 2017). Some scholars have described this period as: "a cosmopolitan movement in literature" (Lewis 2011, 1) whose "crisis of representation evident in modernism has its roots in other crises: of faith, of reason, of liberalism, of empire" (Lewis 2011, 2). For Calinescu, this crisis takes the form of a rejection of tradition "with increasing violence" that "opened the path of the rebellious *avant-gardes*" (Calinescu 1987, 5). Other authors described these works as "responses to the prevalent cultural and political crisis" (Bru 2009, 9), which strongly influenced the Spanish literature of that time (Romero López 1997, 202–4). Some authors have stated that the aesthetical change that modernism represents ("the Great Divide") is the "greatest of all divisions in the entire history of western man" (Bradbury and McFarlane 1978, 20–21).

In the case of Spain, the chronological boundaries of this period have been in movement and expansion. In the first edition of his manual (1975), Mainer starts analyzing the period between 1902 and 1931, expanding it to 1939 in later editions, and from 1900 to 1939 in his volume of the series *Historia de la Literatura Española* (HdLE, Mainer 2010). Abad Nebot moves the starting point of this period to 1868 (2007), which has been accepted by one of the most active groups concerned with this period, at the Universidad Complutense in Madrid (Romero López 2014).

This project can be considered one of the most central research groups about the silver age with an important focus on digital methods, creating a Web platform for the query of metadata about authors and works, especially from non-canonical authors ("raros y olvidados") called Mnemosine (Romero López 2012). Other DH projects have positioned their research in this period, probably because of their interests in large-scale analysis. Hence, there are several international groups analyzing and editing theater (project GHEDI, led by Santa María Fernández, at UNIR in Madrid), collecting ephemeral publications and bibliography about them (Revistas Culturales 2.0, by Ehrlicher in Tübingen), erotic novels (Virtual Wunderkammer, by Zubiaurre in Berkeley) or more specific projects analyzing the works of a particular creator such as Picasso (by Mallen in Texas), Valle-Inclán (by Santos Zas in Santiago de Compostela) or Galdós (Isasi 2017).

2.1.3 Literary Genre and Novel in this Period

In this section, I use the information and previous research from the area of Literary Studies to create an overview about the novel as well as the genre, which has been constantly questioned and revised. In Mainer's opinion, "the conventional literary genres were resolutely iconoclast" (Mainer, Alvar, and Navarro 1997, 557, my translation), and Buckley refers to an overflow of "the generic boundaries of poetry and prose, novel and short story, drama and cinematic image, [which] create what are in effect new modes of expression" (2008, 45). Longhurst describes the modernist novel in a broader international frame as "incontrovertibly and self-consciously different" (1999, 2). Ródenas de Moya transcribes the opinion of the Spanish poet Guillermo de la Torre: "we all agree on that: that the «literary genres» hardly exist now" (2000, 90, my translation). The best-known defender of the absence of genres in that time was Benedetto Croce, the Italian intellectual who published the *Estetica come scienza dell'espressione e linguistica generale* in 1902 with great impact across Europe and America, a text which I will come back to in Section 2.3.2.1.

Opinions about the specific genre of the novel during this period are similar. Ródenas de Moya (2000, 89–90), Altisent (2008, 2–3), and Longhurst (2008, 41) hypothesize about a hybridization of the novel, mixing itself with other genres like the essay, autobiography, lyrical poetry, cinema, or philosophy. The novelist Antonio Espina uses the word *monstrous* to refer to the novel in an exceptional quote from his work *Luna de copas* where he presents the creation of the novel in a way that could resemble current generative processes such as topic modeling:

> The novel, for the novelist, must be extracted from a series of watertight compartments, in which the ingredients of the novel are inserted in advance. In one compartment the description is placed; in another, the dialogue; in another, the characters, etc., etc. Once this is done, the novelist must close his eyes and take at random, stirring, ingredients from all compartments, throwing handfuls on the chapters. The novel, thus, will be disjointed and monstrous. This is not a defect. (Espina 2004, originally published in 1929, my translation).

Although not so directly, other authors mentioned the necessity of eradicating the novel as the balanced structure of the 19th century or avoiding clear pedagogical aims. Gómez de la Serna writes in *El novelista* "the novel had always been a topic of discussion and it was always supposed to be great work of construction, like a bridge that was at the same time the stair of the heavens" but his protagonist "wanted to make a novel in which life entered without thesis" (Gómez de la Serna 1923, my translation). Bacarisse criticizes the "symmetrical novels like Greek pediments" (1931, my translation). Although these quotes could better resemble the opinion of the latter decades of the *silver age* (modernism, avant-garde), Alonso quotes Valera, one of the fundamental realist writers, who already stated in 1865 that "poetry, and therefore the novel, humiliate themselves when they completely serve science, when they become a plot to demonstrate a thesis" (2010, 494, my translation). In any case, the new forms of novels after the turn of the century received new ways of labeling, the reason why there is an increase of the number of hypothetical subgenres (Ródenas de Moya 2000, 89–90; Aubert 2001, 14; Longhurst 2008, 3).

An important essay about the topic was written by the influential philosopher Ortega y Gasset: *Ideas sobre la novela* (Ortega y Gasset 2009, originally published in 1924). In his work, he postulated the decadence of the novel, not only from an aesthetic point of view but also as far as market data is concerned (Ortega y Gasset 2009, 130).[1] In his opinion, the novel is a genre that needs to be perceived as something else (155), as a "diffuse genre" (158, my translation)

---

1 A year before, T. S. Eliot published a review of Joyce's Ulysses presenting similar ideas that Ortega could have read (Ródenas de Moya 1998, 71). As I will show in 3.1, the information from literary manuals does not show that there were fewer novels in the 1920s, rather the opposite.

that allows other ingredients: "the novel is the literary genre which can contain a greater number of elements alien to art. Almost everything fits in the novel: science, religion, harangue, sociology, aesthetic judgments" (182–83, my translation). In contrast to the essays' initial pessimistic opinions, he ends tracing exceptional expectations for the future of the novel: "the last perfection, which is almost always a perfection of the last hour, is still lacking in the novel" (179, my translation).

2.1.4 The Novel and its Borders

As discussed, the literary genres, and the novel being one of them, show a strong tendency of seeking freedom, heterogeneity, and new forms during this period. In some cases, this leads to a certain proximity to other genres, such as theater, poetry, essay, biography, and beyond. This proximity to other genres can be understood as the origin of specific subgenres of the novel such as the dialogue novel or the lyrical novel. They can either be observed as hyponyms of the novel (types of novels) or as overlaps between the novel and other literary genres (in Section 2.3.3, I will present several ways of structuring several genres). Probably the most evident subgenre that exemplifies the closeness between novels and theater is the dialogue novel, which is defined as a text made up of only (or mainly) dialogue, using the traditional typographical convention of plays:

> Name of the character.- Dialogue (information about movement or details in italics as stage directions).

Although some researchers treat these novels as a phenomenon of the 20th century (Garrido Domínguez 2009, 776; Spang 2009, 1296–97; Jiménez 1998, 20), it should be taken in consideration that previous authors, like Galdós, wrote in this category during the 19th century (Escobar Bonilla 1997). Furthermore, it can be argued that they stem from the classic dialogue genre, which was very common in previous centuries. Lissorgues interprets these novels as a new narrative technique that provides more freedom to the characters and keeps the narrator from assuming his natural role (2001, 71). Besides this subgenre, the influence of the theater has been tracked in other forms, for example as a general characteristic of the prose of the *generación del 98* (Pedraza Jiménez and Rodríguez Cáceres 1986, 115; Rubio Jiménez 1998, 20).

The relation between novel and lyrical poetry is more complex, as the large number of different labels proves: *novela lírica, novela poética, novela poemática, poema en prosa, prosa-poética*, etc. The closeness between these two genres was hypothetically an important feature of the late years of romanticism (Montesinos 1980, 139–42). Even if this imbrication could take a more obvious form in the last decades of the *silver age* (avant-garde) than in the late 19th century (Ródenas de Moya 2000, 89–90; Mainer 2009; Millares 2013, 53), the tendency is probably more visible after the turn of the century with modernism (Ródenas de Moya 2000, 80–81). For Mainer, the classic realist novel is replaced by a "densely poetic and profoundly introspective story" (Mainer 2009, 235, my translation). When talking about lyrical novels, the author Miró is often mentioned (Landeira 1985, 117; Pedraza Jiménez and Rodríguez Cáceres 1991, 125; Lozano Marco 2002), but also others such as Valle-Inclán, Azorín, or Pérez de Ayala (Ródenas de Moya 2000, 81; Villanueva Prieto 1983).

A new group of prose writers emerged in the avant-garde who were identified as authors of lyrical novels: Jarnés (Mainer 2009, 243), Gómez de la Serna (Pedraza Jiménez and Rodríguez Cáceres 1991, 125), or Antonio Espina (Millares 2013, 59). The latter states in his novel *Pájaro Pinto* that "between the novel and the poem there is already an area of interference, truly suggestive" (Espina 2004, originally published in 1927, my translation). For Ródenas de Moya, the lyrical novel became one of the major subgenres of the novel in the latter decades (2000, 72) that even affected prose in general (39).

Besides these groups of prose narrators, whose works moved closer to poetry, there is also a group of mainly poets who wrote some texts exclusively or with large sections in prose. Among them, Juan Ramón Jiménez or Antonio Machado should be mentioned, who wrote entire and long prose texts such as *Platero y yo* (1917) (cfr. Utrera Torremocha 1999, 269–71) or *Juan de Mairena* (1936), respectively. In addition, they also wrote other pieces of works mixing sections of poetry and prose: *Diario de un poeta recién casado* (1916) or *De un cancionero apócrifo* (1933).

The essay is the last genre that I will discuss here, and its proximity to the novel can be located in different aspects. Numerous aspects of the essay are also important features of the novel during the analyzed decades: in the 19th century, many texts and subgenres had the aim to demonstrate an idea (*novelas de tesis*) or the goal of teaching something to the reader, such as historical facts or moral values. After the turn of the century, specific considerations, either concerning the narrator or the character's voices, become more frequent, which often makes them difficult to differentiate from essay fragments. If the topic of an essay is about a person's life, the text could resemble a biography; if this person happens to be the same as the author, then it gets closer to an autobiography. Ródenas de Moya theorizes about the quantitative importance of these two genres in the latter decades of the *silver age* (2000, 96). I have already mentioned some texts reflecting very personal experiences of the authors such as *Platero y yo*. Many others either had a recurrent alter ego (Valle-Inclán: Bradomín; Machado: Mairena; Miró: Sigüenza...), several alter egos (like Baroja with Andrés Hurtado, Silvestre Paradox, Fernando Ossorio), or they themselves appear with their own name in their works (Unamuno, Juan Ramón Jiménez). Azorín even took it one step further and the author (José Martínez Ruiz) decided to identify with his alter ego's name, *Azorín*, which still is the most common way to refer to the author.

2.1.5 Realist and Naturalist Novel

After giving an overview of the novel and its relationship to other major literary genres, I will now summarize different specific subgenres of the novel, in chronological order, starting with the realist and naturalist novel. These two subgenres are rooted in the decade of the 1870s and are often treated together since many Spanish authors worked in both categories during consecutive decades. A typical example for these writers is Galdós, who is considered as the initiator of the new tendencies (Ferreras 1988, 37). Both subgenres share a common European frame in which they evolved with a certain delay in comparison to other national traditions (Ferreras 1988, 12; Lissorgues 2001, 57).

The historical event that is conventionally referred to as the initial phase of the realist novel in Spain is the Revolution of 1868 when the liberal bourgeoisie led the first attempt to create a democratic system in Spain (first as a parliamentary monarchy under Amadeo I, later as the First Republic). That is the reference for the concept of *generación del 68*, to which the most canonical authors of the novel of that time belong: Galdós, Bazán, Clarín, and Valera (Ferreras 1988, 12–13). The literary starting point is normally set two years later, 1870, with the publication of *La fontana de oro* by Galdós (Pedraza Jiménez and Rodríguez Cáceres 1982, 338; Ferreras 1988, 19, 38). Many literary researchers have pointed out that realist novels tried to represent contemporary society (Longhurst 1999, 9): "realists manage to recreate, explain, and thus signify the objective reality of their universe. Coherent totalization means that the totalization is artistic and unitary" (Ferreras 1988, 20, my translation).

In the opinion of Lissorgues (2001, 56), their ethical intention is an important feature of the realist novel, but in a more subtle way than in other subgenres like the historical novel of the first half of the 19th century (Ferreras 1988, 23) or other low-brow novels (*folletín, novela de tesis*). The characters gained depth and authenticity, leaving behind their prototypical roles of the romantic novels. These texts were written, starred, and read by the liberal middle class (Lissorgues 2001, 66). In Alonso's view, many of them showed an optimistic opinion about the future since politics were evolving in their favor (2010, 528). Ferreras, who has worked with traditional methods analyzing a large corpus of novels, suggests that, because their goal was to represent society, the description is an important component of these novels, with a higher degree of detail than before (1988, 13). Another aspect that gained importance was a more descriptive use of language, both in the narrative voice and dialogues (Pedraza Jiménez and Rodríguez Cáceres 1983, 364).

The realist novel reached an important milestone in 1881 with Galdós's text *La desheredada* (*The Disinherited Woman*). Perhaps the failure of the liberal revolution and the resulting restoration of the Monarchy led authors to put in practice what in France had already been a movement for over a decade: naturalism. Writers left their optimistic perspective and placed their focus on physical and social problems, for example alcoholism, poverty, rural despotism (*caciquismo*), or prostitution (Alonso 2010, 537). Although not the initiator, Bazán is the most frequently mentioned representative of naturalism in Spain: in some manuals, her work and the concept of naturalism are even explained in the same section (Pedraza Jiménez and Rodríguez Cáceres 1982, 725), with *Pazos de Ulloa* as the most prototypical novel of Spanish naturalism. Alonso hypothesizes that these novels broadened the literary vocabulary: Scientific terms for specific medical situations and practices appear in the narration. A recurring characteristic is that the protagonist comes from lower classes of society (2010, 559).

Naturalism became mainstream, on one side, with some of the most canonical authors and some of the most important works of the decade (*La Regenta* by Clarín, *Fortunata y Jacinta* by Galdós). On the other side, the movement encountered strong rejection from conservative authors and institutions, becoming a persistent topic for discussion in intellectual media and circles. The Spanish reception of the original French naturalism and its practice has been the focus of several studies which highlight its irregularity, misunderstanding of the precedent, and the Spanish variation of naturalism, sometimes referred to as *naturalisms* (Ferreras 1988, 51; Bretz 1992; Pattison

1965; Landeira 1985, 3; Longhurst 1999, 7–8). Of particular interest is the creation of a catholic version of naturalism (*naturalismo espiritual*, Pattison 1965, 140), where very typical issues of naturalism find a religious answer (often closer to mysticism than to organized religion), such as *Nazarín* (1895) and the novels of *Torquemada* (1889-1895) by Galdós, or *La cristiana* and *La prueba* (both from 1890) by Bazán.

By the end of the decade, the naturalist novel branched off into different continuations (Bretz 1992, 79). First, Galdós was again responsible for a historical milestone with his works *Realidad* and *La incógnita* (both from 1889) (Beyrie and Aubert 2001, 31; Lissorgues 2001, 53). These two novels broke with the realist tendency using meta-literary unsolved references that left the readers to decide whether they should understand the novels as realistic or not. Canonical authors remain partially within these post-realist subgenres, close to the modernist novel, writing non-realistic texts such as *Morsamor* (1889) by Valera, *El saludo de las brujas* (1889) by Bazán, or *El caballera encantado* (1909) by Galdós (Longhurst 1999, 6–7; Beyrie and Aubert 2001, 32). Second, the eroticism of the novels gained importance and became the fundamental aspect of the new erotic novel, one of the most important subgenres of the following decades. Third, there is a more morbid version of the naturalist novel, with Sawa (*La mujer de todo el mundo*, 1885) as its major representative (Pattison 1965, 137–38). These novels are integrated in the decadent style of modernism and are rather peripheral to the canon.

In any case, both realist and naturalist novels endured during the rest of the period: the trend of naturalism returned in the 1910s (with authors like Fernández Flórez or de Burgos) evolving later into the social novel, while younger authors published realist novels (Concha Espina, Zamacois, or Cossío).

2.1.6 Historical and Adventure Novels

In the European tradition, the historical novel has its roots in Walter Scott (Lukács 1955) with novels like *Ivanhoe* (1819-1820) and *Waverley* (1814) as prototypes. They represent the starting point of a genre that spread across Europe and was practiced in different languages (Ferreras 1987, 30–31; Montesinos 1980, 79–80). In the Spanish tradition, this subgenre has been profoundly and meticulously analyzed by Ferreras (1987, 1988). Scott's works arrived in Spain mainly by way of translations, the first one from around 1823 (Pedraza Jiménez and Rodríguez Cáceres 1982, 191). Some of the first examples of Spanish historical novels are *Ramiro, conde de Lucanor* by Rafael Húmara, or *Los bandos de Castilla* by Ramón López Soler (printed in 1830, Ferreras 1987, 37). Already in the next decade the subgenre evolved in Spain with distinctive features, becoming more politicized and developing into one of the major trends in the publishing industry (González García 2005; Ferreras 1987, 32–33). The typical plot of these texts shows the vicissitudes of a hero within a Manichean problematic, in many cases in medieval times, with unrealistic elements (such as wizards or witches), a melodramatic ending, and it often starts with a found manuscript (Ferreras 1987, 69–70; Román Gutiérrez 1988, 144). The goal of these authors is, on the one side, to amuse the reader; on the other side, to address contemporary political topics through historical settings. Therefore, the aim of teaching history stays in the background. During the decade of the 1840s, the importance of the adventures grew, branching off into either historical adventure novels (Pedraza Jiménez and Rodríguez Cáceres 1982, 196; Ferreras 1987, 32–33) or social novels published in the form of serials (*folletín*).

As mentioned before, some decades later, in 1870, a young writer published *La fontana de oro*, set in the Madrid of the 1820s. That was Galdós's first novel (Lissorgues 2001, 57; Beyrie and Aubert 2001, 27), who became the most important author in the following decades. Only three years later, he started his *Episodios nacionales* ('National episodes'), a series of 46 novels published during the rest of his life, narrating different chapters of Spanish history of the 19th century, the majority written in first person, many of them sharing characters or even protagonists (Estévez 2013). The label coined by Galdós (*episodios nacionales*) was published on the cover of each edition and was traditionally used as a kind of subgenre for these texts, treated either as being closely related to the historical novel or as a subtype of it (recently discussed in Isasi 2017, 32–34), but overlapping with other subgenres such as intrigue, picaresque, or adventure novels (Dendle 1992, 29–30). The idea of a long series of historical novels was also projected by later authors such as Costa or Valle-Inclán, who could not fulfill it. Baroja accomplished a similar project some decades later, labeling it *Memorias de un hombre de acción* ('Memories of a man of action'), also with recurring characters, protagonists (mainly Eugenio de Aviraneta), and with a first-person narrative.

Other authors (Bazán, Unamuno, Valle-Inclán, Azorín, Blasco Ibáñez, Concha Espina, Sender) also wrote historical novels without this frame of a series. One of the most common topics of historical novels were wars, especially the Peninsular Napoleonic Wars and the Carlist Wars,[2] but also the First World War or, in later decades, the Spanish campaigns against the revolts in its colonies in present-day Morocco and Western Sahara. Many of these texts are both related to historical or war novels.

As I have already mentioned, adventure novels (*novelas de aventuras*) are understood in the history of literature as a continuation of the first historical novels, with Scott as its common starting point but also with other international examples such as Dumas, Cooper, or Verne (Lara López 2000, 99 and 108). In many of these texts, historical elements disintegrated and unforeseen incidents grew in importance (Ferreras 1987, 32–33). Two of its most fundamental authors were: Manuel Fernández y González, a very prolific author with works like *Allah-Akbar: ¡Dios es grande!* (1849) or *El pastelero de Madrigal* (1862) (Pedraza Jiménez and Rodríguez Cáceres 1982, 230–32; Lara López 2000, 105); and Enrique Pérez Escrich, with texts like *El cura de la aldea* (1863) (Ferreras 1987, 37; Román Gutiérrez 1988, 157). Many of these texts were distributed as serials (*folletines*), modifying the structure of the works to create cliffhangers in each chapter (Ferreras 1987, 61) and they are still kept in the bounds of low-brow literature, seldom included in literary research.

After 1880, some works by Pío Baroja, but also from his brother Ricardo, are often classified as adventure novels. In many cases, they take place in the past or in contemporary times but depict important historical events, using the label *novelas de acción* ('action novels') instead of *novelas de aventuras*. As per Lara López, the adventure novel has its golden period during the first third of the century in pulp magazines finally coining the label *de aventuras*, and evolved after the Civil War towards Western novels (2000, 106 and 120) or started to be labeled as juvenile novels (Martínez de la Hidalga 2000, 46). Its most typical features are the action and physical risk for the protagonist, exotic journeys or setting, and a fast narrative rhythm (Lara López 2000, 98–100).

2 The Carlist Wars took place between 1833 and 1876, and are named after the Carlism movement, who identified Carlos (Carlos V) and his descendants as the rightful heirs (Lawrence 2014).

2.1.7 Comedy Novels

In the later decades of the *silver age*, comedy novels (*novelas humorísticas*) became a trend practiced by a generation of comedy writers (who wrote mainly theater plays) that could be understood as a parallel group to the lyrical and better known *generación del 27 (Burguera Nadal and Fortuño Llorens 1998)*. Some names of this comedy generation are Lara de Gavilán "Tono", Neville, Jardiel Poncela, Mihura or López Rubio. Their works were primarily published during the 1920s. Fernández Flórez was the first author of the *silver age* who dedicated a great deal of his works to humor, with texts like *El malvado Carabel* (1931) or *El hombre que compró un automóvil* (1932) (Echeverría Pazos 1987). Also, Gómez de la Serna used humor as one of the most important aspects of some of his novels, for example in *¡Rebeca!* (1936) (Flores Requejo 2000; Burguera Nadal and Fortuño Llorens 1998, 7). Jardiel Poncela, who wrote mainly theater, used humor in his novels, like in *La "tournée" de Dios* (1932), a narration about an official visit of God to Spain and about everything that goes wrong (Pérez 1993; Pueo Domínguez 1994). Other authors such as Carrere, Ros, or Pemán produced similar novels, continuing the trend beyond the Civil War. Several researchers have observed that aspects like fantasy, autobiography, eroticism, and irrationalism are used to represent intellectual comedy and satire (Echeverría Pazos 1987, 94–96; Pérez 1993, 48). In many cases the stories were absurd with critical traces, as *Relato inmoral* by Fernández Flórez, which addresses the social situation of single mothers.

2.1.8 Erotic Novels

The topics eroticism and sex have already appeared in the description of different subgenres of the period, mainly in the naturalist novel (García Lara 1986, 29). After the 1890s, a section of the naturalist novel evolved into a separated subgenre, the erotic novel, following again the model of the French literature. This type of novels and novellas (*novelas cortas*) has been analyzed in two monographs, each with very different methodologies and aims: while Rivalan Guégo describes a specific and large corpus, analyzing separately particular aspects (2008), the influential work of García Lara takes a rather abstract perspective (1986).

The two most frequently mentioned writers in relation to the erotic novel are Zamacois (*El seductor*, 1902) and Trigo (*Del frío al fuego*, 1906, *Sí, sé por qué*,

1916), although other authors such as Hoyos or Insúa wrote many texts within the subgenre. These novels are not what a reader from the 21st century would classify as erotic: They do describe physical scenes that are not treated in other genres, but "in the evocation of sexual intercourse, most narrators confess their failure in expressive capacity, quite often, one or several dotted lines are interspersed in a narrative that continues only with a temporary indication" (Rivalan Guégo 2008, 197, my translation) or use highly metaphorical descriptions (Rivalan Guégo 2008, 196). The erotic novel has been subjected to enormous criticism, even when authors produced complex texts tackling questions about family, abortion, divorce, or ethical aspects of the female and male roles of the bourgeois catholic Spanish society (Rivalan Guégo 2008, 22). The narrations show a pedagogical aim, with long essay fragments, and their plots end in many cases in dramatic and moralizing ways (García Lara 1980, 216; 1986, 32; Rivalan Guégo 2008, 61). That leads García Lara to use the term "social eroticism" as label (1986, 28). Although the erotic novel achieved a huge success, especially in the male middle classes (García Lara 1980, 215; 1986, 20 and 59), it has been "curiously and hypocritically ignored by the collective memory" (Rivalan Guégo 2008, 21, my translation). It belongs since then to low-brow literature ("infraliteratura," García Lara 1986, 19) and is often treated by researchers rather as a sociological phenomenon than as a literary one (García Lara 1980, 216). A highly canonized author, Baroja, fashions a scene in one of his best-known novels, *El árbol de la ciencia*, in which erotic novels are mentioned:

> One day he was shocked to see that the bookseller had fifteen to twenty volumes with a cover on which a naked woman appeared. They were these types of French-style novels; pornographic novels, clumsy, with a certain psychological varnish made for the use of military, students, and people of little mentality. – Does that sell? Asked Andres the bookseller. -Yes; it is the only thing that sells. (Baroja, originally published in 1911, edition by Caro Baroja 1985, 216, my translation).

The disdain for this subgenre and its readers ("of little mentality") in the quotation is obvious. This can have been prevented the classification of erotic novel in cases of works written by highly canonized authors in which eroticism is central, like *Las sonatas* by Valle-Inclán, *El gran hotel* by Gómez de la Serna, or several of Pérez de Ayala's works. Still, it is generally accepted that some important authors wrote erotic novels, such as Blasco Ibáñez, Dicenta, de Burgos, or Bazán. The two monographs mentioned before point out some of the typical features of these novels: Titles with female names or female references, starred by a middle-class woman, urban contemporary settings (normally Madrid or Paris), often with boat or train trips, and descriptions of interior spaces, underwear, female bodies, and male faces are recurrent (García Lara 1986; Rivalan Guégo 2008). A similar subgenre, intended for female readers, was the *novela rosa*, which has reached even lower steps of the canonical stratification (Álvarez 2000).

2.1.9 Social Novels

Social novels are a major trend during the 19th century, becoming a bestseller and the fundamental genre for many decades of the serials (Pedraza Jiménez and Rodríguez Cáceres 1982, 236–37). Their readers are part of the working class and the authors try to illustrate a clear thesis against social injustice, normally starred by lower-class protagonists in urban settings. It has its origins in the French model of Eugène Sue and *Les Mystères de Paris* (1842-1843). They portray social problems in a simplistic schema of good and bad social groups (Ferreras 1987, 70–71). Its development influenced other subgenres of the same period such as the *costumbrist*, historical, and realist novel. The works of authors who started writing in the period of naturalism like Blasco Ibáñez (*La barraca*, 1898) or Sawa (*Declaración de un vencido*, 1887) are often classified as social novels around the turn of the century.

The label is used some decades later, especially in the 1930s, for some canonized works. In this decade, many authors were followers of pure and abstract art, guided by the idea *art for art's sake*, popularized by Ortega y Gasset (in Spanish: "el arte por el arte") in one of his most influential works *The Dehumanization of Art* (1925). Nevertheless, this tendency found an answer, or reconciled, with a return to social contemporary questions (Castañar 1992, 40; Aubert 2001, 15; Ródenas de Moya 2009, 47). Two of the best representatives of this subgenre are Sender (*Siete domingos rojos*, 1932, *Viaje a la aldea del crimen*, 1934) and Díaz Fernández (*El blocao*, 1928; cfr. Fernández Cifuentes and Gonzalo Santonja 1984, 642), but also authors like Concha Espina, Arderius, Arconada, Benavides, or Salazar were part of it. The setting is typically an urban space in Spain, it takes place during a recent historical incident such as wars or scenes of repression, and the protagonists tend to be a group of people (sometimes movements coming from the left spectrum) or archetypes (Castañar 1992, 306–17). The aim of many of these books was to criticize the system and mobilize lower classes of society and intellectuals (Castañar 1992, 312). This becomes blatantly clear in *Viaje a la aldea del crimen*, in which the author beings the novel recounting that, ultimately, the political responsible for the brutal repression described in the plot was Manuel Azaña, Prime Minister of Spain at the time.

2.1.10 One-Author-Labels: *Nivola*, *Greguería*, and *Episodio Nacional*

In Section 2.1.2, I have observed that researchers of this period have a strong tendency to investigate one specific author independently. This trend is reinforced by the very same authors themselves, who, in many cases, coined their own specific label, similar to their own genres, in many cases without making explicit whether it should really be considered as a different category. The best-known case is Unamuno's *nivola*, a term that was printed on the cover of his most important novel, *Niebla* (1914, 'Mist'). In a fictional preface, one of the characters of the novel, Víctor Goti, claims to be the inventor of the concept of *nivola* and uses it to classify earlier novels by Unamuno (such as *Amor y pedagogía*, 1902). The edition of 1935 presented a third prologue (presenting Unamuno as its author), in which this genre is explained as follows (my translation):

> The novel, the epopee, or the drama impose themselves on the one who believes to be their author. Or the agonists, their supposed creatures, are imposed on him. Thus, Luzbel and Satan, first, and Adam and Eve, later, were imposed on Jehovah. And this one is *nivola*, *opopee* or *trigedy*! [...] My diabolical invention of the *nivola*. [...] This is the mist, this is the *nivola*, this is the legend, this is the eternal life...

In a dialogue with the protagonist of *Niebla* (Augusto), the fictional author of the first prologue (Víctor) mentions the theoretical origin of this new label (my translation):

> I have heard Manuel Machado, the poet, Antonio's brother, who once brought a sonnet to Don Eduardo Benoit, to read it to him, it was written in Alexandrian verse or some other heterodox form. He read it and Don Eduardo said: "But that's not a sonnet!..." "No, sir," said Machado, "it's not a *soneto*, it's a... *sonite*." Well, with my novel, it's not going to be a novel, but ... what did I call it?, *navilo... nebulo*, no, no, *nivola*, that's it, nivola! Then no

> one will have the right to say that it violates the laws of the novel... I invent the genre, and inventing a genre is nothing more than giving it a new name, and I give it the laws that I like. (Unamuno, originally published in 1914, edition by Valdés 1982, 200, my translation).

The fictional text presents a mix of philosophical, playful, and provocative intentions and an explicit intention of "inventing a genre" by two steps: creating a label and assigning some rules. Since the publication of this work by Unamuno, libraries, publishers, and researchers have kept using the label in their descriptions and metadata, some of them arguing in favor of taking it as a genre label (Øveraas 1993, 16; Landeira 1985, 37), so a century after his publication, the label can be found in the very basic information of Wikidata about *Niebla*.

Many other authors coined what I call *one-author-labels*: Labels used as if they designated genres (or subgenres of the novel) that were only fashioned by one single author, such as the discussed example *nivola* of Unamuno. Similar cases were produced by Galdós (*episodio nacional*), Pérez de Ayala (*novela normativa, novela simbólica*), Baroja (*novela de acción*), Azorín (*novela impresionista*), Valle-Inclán (*esperpento*),[3] Blasco-Ibáñez (*novelas valencianas*), or Gómez de la Serna with several ones: *greguería, novela de la nebulosa, novela grande*, or *novela multitudinaria*. Mainer states about this last author that "he freed the genres" (Mainer, Alvar, and Navarro 1997, 596, my translation), while Umbral points out that he is a "writer without genre" who "pretended genres" (1984, 226–29, my translation). These *greguerías* are, along with the *nivolas*, one of the best-known examples. In this case, the texts are composed of sentences in prose, normally quite short, in some cases even lacking a verb, typically amusing, surprising, poetic, or transcendental (Senabre 1984). Although it would not be typically considered as a subtype of the novel, it is often not formally related to any other genre than prose (Ródenas de Moya 2000, 49). Here is a selection of *greguerías* (my translation, in the original they do not form any stanza or paragraph, nor do they need to follow a certain order):

> Slice of watermelon: moon of blood.
> The O is the yawn of the alphabet.
> Eternity envies the mortal.
> The kiss is hunger for immortality.
> The head is the fishbowl of ideas.

3 Rather a new style that he used in different genres: plays and novels.

Currant of kisses.
Time tastes like dry water.
All the birds are maimed.
The Spaniard/Spanish is a soul in pain.[4]

In academia, there is no consensus about which status these one-author-labels should have: Should they be considered mere jokes of the authors or marketing strategies of the publishers? Should they be considered for tasks such as descriptions or classifications? Are they hyponyms of specific subgenres (for example, episodio nacional as a kind of historical novel) or intersections between two subgenres (episodio nacional as a blend of historical and adventure novels)? Are they supposed to constitute a different genre that does not belong to the novel (as the quotes by Unamuno imply)? Normally, the answer depends on the analysis: A researcher who analyzes a particular author tends to consider the label and even argue for its acceptance as genre; a researcher who compares several texts from numerous authors tends to ignore these labels. In this research, I will analyze each label independently, with skepticism about their status as subgenres, but without dismissing the possibility that some of them can exhibit similar properties to other subgenres.

4 The original greguería is ambiguous: "El español es un alma en pena."

2.2 Genre in Digital Humanities: Methods, Features, and Data Representation

2.2.1 Introduction

In this chapter, I present the most important approaches in the fields of Digital Humanities and Computational Linguistics to study genre, focusing on the applied parameters (methods, features, transformations, types of genres), the historical innovations, and the achieved results. First, I will introduce how genres have been integrated in research from the fields of Machine Learning and Digital Humanities. Then, I will describe the historical development of the analysis of this category through different fields, such as Corpus Linguistics, Computational Linguistics, and in more recent years Digital Humanities. In the next section, I will introduce the different types of tasks in Machine Learning (supervised and unsupervised), discussing how they have been applied for genre analysis.

One of the core questions the researcher needs to answer is the way of representing the internal features of the texts. The most frequent representation is the *Bag of Words document model*, in which the frequency of each token or feature in a text is counted and usually standardized by the size of the text (relative frequency of tokens in a text). As I will show, frequencies of tokens yield very high results in classification of genres, especially when its simplicity is considered. There have been two further transformations of the vocabulary widely used in different fields: Computer Science often converts the lexical frequencies into tf-idf values, a way of weighting the importance of each word in a collection. A similar idea follows the conversion of the relative frequencies to z-scores. By that, the standard deviation of the frequency in a corpus is taken into consideration, which is the base of the most successful method in stylometry and authorship attribution: Delta (Burrows 2002). Both transformations and others will be presented in detail in Chapter 4.2.

Besides the algorithms and transformations of the linguistic information, several other topics will be discussed in this chapter, such as the kind and source of the labels gathered, the size of the corpus, the kind of annotation or the level and variance of accuracy achieved for literary or more general genres.

2.2.2 Genre in Computer Science

From the computational point of view, there are several distinctions about how to operationalize the belonging of instances (such as texts) to categories (like genres). I am going to introduce several basic concepts of Machine Learning that will be used throughout this research study.

The first possible case is when the researcher has data, but no labels for it. That would be the case for a corpus without metadata: It only contains texts, but no information about who wrote each text, when it was produced, or to which genre it belongs (to mention some typical categories). The lack of labels requires an *unsupervised* Machine Learning scenario (Alpaydin 2010, 11; Müller and Guido 2016, 133). In this case, algorithms can be used to group or *cluster* the instances that show similarity in their data. For example, if the analyzed corpus contains texts from Argentina and Spain, the algorithm could use the difference of frequencies of words like the pronoun *vos* and *tomar* (with several meanings: 'to drink', 'to take') on the one side, and the pronoun *tú* and *coger* (also with several meanings: 'to take', 'to fuck') on the other, to create two groups (or clusters) of texts. However, the algorithm will not make explicit that one cluster is composed by texts coming from Spain and that the others are from Argentina, just because it does not contain this information (these labels, these metadata). It will be the work of the researcher to interpret these clusters either by looking at the features and comparing it to their knowledge about linguistic particularities of both dialects, or by reading several texts of both and discovering the underlying categorization.

Parallel to the unsupervised tasks there is the *supervised* approach, in which the researcher has data and the labels for the studied category (Alpaydin 2010, 11; Müller and Guido 2016, 27). In my case, these would be the digitized text and the associated labels about the genre of each text. The goal in this case is to analyze whether the labels or output can be predicted from the data. Depending on the type of output, it is divided into:

- Classification: when the output (also called label) is discrete or categorical (like the name of the author, the gender of the protagonist, the genre of the text).
- Regression: when the output represents a numerical continuum (like the monthly income of a person, the degree of canonicity of an author, the year a document was created).

All the articles I will mention in this chapter have understood genre as categorical classes, therefore applying classification to its study. In most of the works about the topic, each text can belong to several genres. That is why it has been treated as a multi-label problem, in which the labels are transformed into binary classes: whether the text belongs to the adventure novel or not; whether the same text belongs to the naturalist novel or not, etc. (see Section 2.3.3.2). However, some articles have preferred to treat genres as a multi-class problem in which each text belongs only to one category (cfr. Kessler, Numberg, and Schütze 1997; Jockers 2013; Hettinger et al. 2016). The model of binary classesdiffers already from the classic scholastic model of taxonomies of genres in which each text hung from a single genre, as a leaf hangs from a single branch, which will be presented in Section 2.3.2.1. Binary genres indicate that every text can belong to any number of classes. Using the binary labels of the genres, Santini (2011) developed a theoretical model for the analysis of genres: the zero-to-multi genre classification scheme. In her work about the genres of the Web, she proposed a scheme that makes explicit that each text can belong to any number of genres, from zero (individuality) to several (hybridism), which will be presented in more detail in the next section.

2.2.3 Genre in Digital Humanities

Genre has been an analytical category in several areas of Digital Humanities, especially those which use text as their primary data. In stylometry, the corpora are normally composed of a single genre (like theater plays) or subgenre (like tragedy) because it is expected that different genres exhibit linguistic differences. Just to mention two milestones of stylometry, Mosteller and Wallace analyzed the federalist papers, a collection of texts with the same genre but from disputed authors (1963), while Burrows proposed Delta using long English poems (2002).[1] For specific purposes, along with periodization, genre is one of the most important criteria for the collection of corpora, and therefore an important aspect to consider.

Other researchers have analyzed the interaction between the author's gender and the genre they wrote in. Besides the linguistic features that distinguish male and female authors, Argamon et al. found that the stylistic markers of gender correlate to a certain degree with the distinction between fictional and non-fictional texts (2003). Koolen analyzed the perceived literary quality and gender in the Dutch society and examined genre as a variable (2018). Her profound and seminal research shows how different genres (*literary fiction*, suspense, romantic, and miscellany) have various ranges of perceived literariness and quality (*literary fiction* on the top, suspense and miscellany in the middle, romantic on the bottom). Besides, she also reveals that the author's gender is unbalanced in the different genres (more male writers in *literary fiction*, only women in romantic) and how these two facts let male authors achieve higher positions in the literary industry.

Some DH methodologies such as the use of graphs for representing social networks of literary characters, have been applied to show and analyze the literary characters, normally either in theater plays (Trilcke et al. 2016; Krautter et al. 2018; Santa María et al. 2018) or narrative texts (Rochat 2014; Jannidis et al. 2016; Isasi 2017). In addition, the genres of other media were analyzed by Machine Learning approaches such as music (Basili, Serafini, and Stellato 2004) or graphic novels (Dunst, Laubrock, and Wildfeuer 2018). All these examples show that, even when genre is not the analyzed phenomenon, it is often an important criterion for defining the research object: The instances of many corpora have a single constant genre.

2.2.4 The Start of Genre Classification

Literary genre is only one specific type of textual genre that has been treated by different research groups (linguists, computational linguists, digital humanists) in the last decade. Previously, the most common case was to analyze journalistic or general corpora. A pioneer in the study of genres applying computational methods is Biber, who started working on this topic in 1988.

1 The original paper of Burrows does not ascribe these poems to any subgenre, such as epic.

He used Common Factor Analysis to distinguish mainly between two different concepts of categorization of texts: genres and text-types. For him, genres are categorizations based on external criteria, while text-types would be classes that are based exclusively on linguistic data. From the point of view of Machine Learning, this concept of genre can be understood as classes in a supervised task that are extracted from a third source like a catalog, while text-types result from clusters based on linguistic features. A discussion of the diachronic development of Biber's terminology can be found in Santini (2004).

One of the first attempts on genre classification is undertaken by Kessler, Numberg, and Schütze (1997). In their study, they analyze various categories, such as genre (editorial, legal, non-fiction, fiction), brow (popular, middle, uppermiddle, high), and narrative (narrative against non-narrative).[2] For that, they use the Brown corpus, working with different supervised algorithms and extracted types of linguistic annotation as features (morphological, syntactic, punctuation, and lexical information). When the task is performed in a multi-class way, they obtain an accuracy of 0.79 (with a baseline of 0.33) using a two-layer neural network. The results achieved a mean of accuracy over 0.9 when the classes are binary. Even when when the structural cues (annotated by NLP tools) obtain slightly better results than the superficial ones (lexical and punctuation), they assess the computational costs as unjustified (Kessler, Numberg, and Schütze 1997, 38). One of the largest caveats of this research is the unexplained massive sampling of the corpus, erasing 40% of the original texts without explaining the criteria. Besides, the three analyzed classes (brow, narrative, and genre) were not theoretically justified, and neither was their association tested. Furthermore, they modified the labels of the corpus (Kessler, Numberg, and Schütze 1997, 5) and did not publish the data, so it is impossible to assess how accurate the whole process was.

From the same year is the work of Sigley (1997), who applies Principal Component Analysis (PCA) (in comparison to the Common Factor Analysis preferred by Biber) to a collection of texts from New Zealand. His first aim is to create a principal component that correlates with the subjective understanding of what characterizes a text as more or less formal. For that, he models a series of tokens, annotating and grouping them with specific linguistic information and applying a z-scores transformation. Finally, he employs PCA and

2 This is exactly what they call the categories and their different possible values.

obtains the different components by calculating the correlation of the principal component to the numerical values from a group of annotators, with a correlation of 0.93^{***}. The results allow him to confirm the utility of the features and the PCA in order to get an index for textual formality. In addition, Sigley visualizes the genres of the used corpora with the two principal components and clusters them in a last step. Sigley's research and the one by Rauber and Müller-Kögler (2001) are two of the few papers that applied clustering methods for genre analysis, at least before the rise of DH after the 2010s. Rauber and Müller-Kögler present a tool that allowed analyzing corpora through Self-Organizing Maps with the idea of using it for browsing digital libraries.

One of the first works about genre classification that deals with texts in a language other than English is Stamatatos, Fakotakis, and Kokkinakis (2000), who examine several genres in a corpus of Modern Greek. Also, following Biber, they consider numerous kinds of linguistic and technical features, for example lexical frequencies, grammatical information, vocabulary richness, and further information from the NLP tools such as whether the tools quit analyzing sentences due to their difficulty. They compare the combination of features with the 30 and 50 most frequent words and use Multiple Regression for analyzing the corpus. Their results show that their combination of features had fewer errors than both for authorship and genre. From the current perspective, this work shows a clear caveat: The frontier of some dozens of most frequent words has been largely overcome and it raises the question whether the chosen features would still yield better results than some thousands of lexical features.

The first article considering Spanish texts for genre classification, to my knowledge is Cerviño Beresi et al. (2004), who apply classification algorithms for journalistic subgenres in a big corpus of Argentinian newspapers. They evaluate various algorithms and the annotation from several lexical stemming tools and report an accuracy between 0.82 and 0.96 for the different binary genres. Nevertheless, they select the 10 (out of 19) genres that achieve higher results in the first sections of the evaluation, a step that can be criticized as cherry picking genres.

The work by Berninger, Kim, and Ross (2008) presents a different approach to the genre problem: They focus on a way of collecting a corpus for genre analysis through student submissions. This is one of the few works that analyzes the inter-annotator agreement about the labels of genres, fairly general in this research (poems, music sheets, curriculum vitae, scientific articles...). The agreement of the different annotators is generally low, varying between 37% and 54% for all genres, although some show higher correspondence (handbooks, CVs) in contrast to others that could be understood at chance level (magazine article, business report, technical manual). In the genre palette they consider poems and books of fiction (probably a concept that is similar to the novel), whose agreement is around 75%, a surprisingly low result for such canonized genres. A possible explanation could be that they try to examine a rather large number of genres (70), causing a low baseline (around 1.4%).

One of the most ambitious works about genre has been carried out by Santini in her PhD, published in 2011, a study that has been largely ignored by DH. She studies Web genres in several corpora, using features of many types: lexical, grammatical, pragmatic, and graphical (the layout of the websites, probably the only research that has used tags as parts of the features). She employs unsupervised, supervised, and rule-based techniques. Over various chapters, she discusses different models of understanding genre (hierarchical, prototype model, family resemblance), creating experiments to answer basic questions about genre that are seldom analyzed in other papers, such as the one about the inter-annotator agreement or whether single-class classification is enough to analyze a genre. She concludes that genres are not mutually exclusive categories, proposing the *zero-to-multi genre classification scheme* in which each text might belong to *n* genres: individualization (a text does not belong to any genre) and hybridism (a text belongs to several genres) are two common characteristics of genres that should be taken into consideration. In her work of 2010, Santini compares the classification of genres of several corpora of websites, using the same features (lexical, grammatical, semantic, and format *facets*) but the genre palette that each corpus supplied. For the different corpora, the results of accuracy lay between 0.42 and 0.94.

Finn and Kushmerick (2006) use the concept *genre* (and describe the state of the art both from the theoretical and the computational approach) to classify different aspects of the text such as its objectivity and the polarity of reviews. These are nowadays clearly related to sentiment analysis and not to genre classification. An interesting aspect of the paper is the fact that instead of mixing different types of features (lexical and grammatical) into the same data frame, they calculate for each one a decision tree, and on top of it, an ensemble decision tree that takes a final decision. One of the later papers on classification that can still be placed in Computational Linguistics is Petrenz and Webber (2011), who suggest another form of evaluating the results of genre classification. In their opinion, genre classification should not only be defined by accuracy but also through *stability* over different topics following the idea that genre should be independent of its theme.

2.2.5 Literary Genre in the Past Years

The two last papers of the previous section show a historical development in the area. In the latter years of the 2000s and the beginning of the 2010s, Computational Linguistics has shifted its interest from genre classification towards other types of textual categorization, especially semantic or topic related (Blei 2012), with a few exceptions such as the application of Deep Learning or the use of the graphical features from the cover (Chiang, Ge, and Wu 2015). However, these years have seen a rising number of works of DH tackling genre through computational methods. Examples are Ramsay with networks and subgenres of Shakespeare (2005), Yu with the evaluation of different parameters in the classification of literary eroticism and sensitivity (2008), or Kestemont et al. who already investigate the influence of genre in stylometry (2012).

A group at the Stanford Literary Lab (Allison, Heuser, Jockers, and Moretti) and Witmore published in 2011 the first Literary Lab Pamphlet, in which they analyze subgenres of the novel using PCA and clustering based on lexical and typographical information. Moretti had already done theoretical work about genres (2005), proposing the hypothesis that literary subgenres could have a certain periodicity in their development. One of the results of the group is that some highly frequent lexical unities are useful markers for genres, but at the same time are hardly interpretable and therefore offer little new knowledge about their studied object: "If all men in an audience wore pink, and all women blue, the colors would differentiate them perfectly, and tell us nothing about them" (18). They use clarifying metaphors about genres, for example, buildings with "distinctive features at every possible scale of analysis: mortar, bricks, and architecture" (8), or compare genres with an iceberg "with a visible portion floating above the water, and a much larger part hidden below, and extending to unknown depths" (25).

Two years later, in 2013, a fundamental text for DH was published: *Macroanalysis* by Jockers. In this seminal work, he analyzes via different techniques several aspects of literature, such as author, genre, and period. For that, he uses both unsupervised methods (such as hierarchical clustering on Euclidean distances, PCA or topic modeling) and supervised methods, employing lexical and typographical information. One of the interesting aspects of his work is that he tries to separate the different factors (period, author, genre, and gender) that can be traced through linguistic features. He even quantifies the influence of each of these categories by comparing the p-values of a linear regression. Due to that, he obtains that the most influential factor is text, followed by author, genre, decade, and the gender of the author (96–99).

The paper of Schöch (2013) can be considered as the starting point of several works and publications about genre coming from Würzburg, including the present publication. The goal of this specific conference-paper is to answer the questions of whether different ranges of tokens can be related to clusters that are associated with authorship or genre. For that, he uses a balanced corpus of tragedies and comedies by Corneille and Molière. He concludes that more clusters show coherent information about genre when more than 1,500 Most Frequents Words (MFWs) are used as features.

One of the most important investigations about genre in the field of DH is a report written by Underwood analyzing a large collection from HathiTrust (2014). Human annotators mark the genre of each page, considering paratexts as one possible class. Underwood uses both lexical (transformed as z-scores) and structural features (extracted from linguistic annotation, typographical information, and calculations such as type/token ratio). Additionally, he prefers logistic regression as algorithm due to its speed and similar accuracy in comparison to other algorithms such as support vector machines. The results show around 0.94 micro-average F1-score for the larger genres, with paratexts being "consistently the hardest problem" (28). In another paper, Underwood (2016, revised in 2019) tests several hypotheses about the historical development of different genres (Gothic, science fiction, and detective). Using logistic regression and lexical information (again transformed in z-scores), he shows that some genres such as science fiction and detective novels are stable over more than 150 years, while others like Gothic disappear after some decades. Besides, he argues that classification is a suitable method to analyze social constructs such as genres, which can be traced using linguistic features. He argues that these aspects of genre could be understood with the models of family resemblances or prototype theory (which I will present in Chapter 2.3 and apply in Chapters 7.2 and 8).

An interesting paper about literary subgenres is Hettinger et al. (2016) in which they classify German novels comparing very different kinds of features: from simple lexical frequencies (transformed as Min-Max), different combinations of parameters for topic modeling, and network features based on the interaction of protagonists (applying several NLP tools). They apply support vector machines and instead of binary classes (as used by other researchers), they compare several genres pairwise. Surprisingly, the outcomes show that the lexical features bring the highest results, not being surpassed by any combination or modification of the other more complex features. In recent years, Jannidis and his team have started to analyze thousands of German low-brow novels from the German National Library (Jannidis, Konle, and Leinen 2019).

Also in 2016, Wilkens published an article in which he used unsupervised methodologies to cluster U.S. American novels evaluating the hypothesis whether high canonical works behave as a *literary fiction* genre. He analyzes a large corpus (nearly 9,000 novels) using several types of features (topic scores, geolocation, very specific lexical information, and metadata about the year, and the gender of the author) and k-means and DBSCAN as algorithms for clustering. Observing the results, he proposes that the label *literary fiction* should be included in genre analysis, especially for highly canonized novels of the 20th century. A clear caveat of this work is the fact that neither the algorithm, nor the features (some of them highly complex, others very disputable like the gender of the author) or parameters are formally evaluated.

León Pacheco (2017) tests genre classification in his bachelor thesis using neuronal artificial networks (multilayer perceptron) in a corpus of 10,000 prose texts in Spanish (of unknown source and edition). The main goal of his work is to establish the differences of using several architectures for Deep Learning (by Amazon and Microsoft). The best outcome is delivered in multiclass classification with 0.39 F1, a surprisingly low result for the size of the corpus and the complexity of the method, but partially explainable because of the fact that only the 100 most frequent words are used.

This study has been written in the frame of the CLiGS projects, whose members have delivered several conference-papers about literary genre since 2015. This practical experience with different techniques gave us the opportunity to work on shared projects exploring several questions, from which, ultimately, my own research benefited. Some of the most relevant to this publication works of the group are about the development of topics over text in different genres (Schöch, Henny, et al. 2016), the neutralization of the authorial signal for genre clustering (Calvo Tello et al. 2017), the use of sentiment analysis for genre classification (Henny-Krahmer 2018), the application of the theory of prototypes in classification tasks (Henny-Krahmer et al. 2018), or the publication of several literary corpora in Romance languages (Schöch et al. 2019).

2.2.6 Conclusions and General Patterns

What are the general patterns of this short history of computational methods for the analysis of genre? First, the great majority of researchers have worked only with English sources, with some exceptions using texts in German, French, Spanish, or Greek. Two important historical developments occurred as far as the type of analyzed texts is concerned. While during the 2000s, genre classification was a common task in Computational Linguistics, the topic has become a trend in DH in the 2010s. Along with this change, in the later period the focus has shifted from broader genres (journalistic texts, Web, corpora) towards literary subgenres, mostly prose. Most works have applied ad hoc palettes of genres, in many cases obtained from authorial works or catalogs. Some papers do not give acceptable reasons about their sampling of the corpus (Kessler, Numberg, and Schütze 1997) or genres (Cerviño Beresi et al. 2004). Very few works have compared the assignation of labels from different sources or annotators (Berninger, Kim, and Ross 2008; Santini 2011). Even though the community might have the feeling that the size of the corpora is increasing, a linear regression of the size of corpora and the year of publication does not show statistical significance, with a median size of the corpus of around 200 texts (further details can be observed in the Jupyter Notebook of this chapter). Apparently, the corpora analyzed in recent years are not larger, but the kind of genres are more specific: While in previous decades it was common to analyze very general genres, currently the focus is on specific literary subgenres.

Clearly, the most useful features are lexical information (either as relative frequencies or transformed in different ways such as z-scores or tf-idf). The only work with differing results is Stamatatos, Fakotakis, and Kokkinakis (2001). However, they apply only 50 lexical features, a number that has been widely surpassed in the last years (as examples, 1,000 in Underwood 2014, 3,000 in Hettinger et al. 2016). Even though there is research which suggests that some of the best features to distinguish genres are punctuation or function words, many researchers still delete stop words, punctuation, or leave the punctuation as part of the tokens. When used, the grammatical information normally brings higher performance to the classification when the information is combined to the lexical one. With regard to transformation, the use of tf-idf, relative frequency, and conversion to z-scores are the most common representations of lexical information. Some papers applied features like indirect information about the annotation process, lexical richness, layout, topic modeling, sentiment analysis, and distribution of characters over the page. Other types of linguistic annotation such as semantic (from dictionaries or techniques such as word embeddings), pragmatic, or literary metadata are infrequent.

The great majority of the cases transform the genre labels into binary classes and report accuracy. Only some papers compare them pairwise and a few inform about the task when undergone as multi-class. Only one paper assigns the information about genre to a smaller unit than the entire text, and that is Underwood (2014) who considers pages, with remarkable results (a similar design will be undertaken in Section 7.1.4).

In relation to the type of task, most works employ supervised methods, with support vector machines as one of the favorite algorithms. In the papers considering unsupervised techniques, cluster analysis (based on a Delta matrix) and PCA are preferred. An interesting fact is that almost no paper used a grid search for the optimization of the parameters: In a few works different combinations are compared, but not every possible combination of parameters is evaluated. Therefore, it has not been properly answered which computational means can yield best classification results for a given corpus, which in my case will be tackled in Chapter 6.2.

With that, the question about the practice of computational analysis of genre has been described. However, a millennial tradition about theory of genre has preceded it, considering several models, structures, and perspectives, which will be presented in the following chapter.

2.3 Theory of Genre

As described in the previous section, there is a tradition of computational research in textual genre which has been undertaken mainly by researchers from Computer Sciences and Computational Linguistics. It is only in the last decade that literary scholars and interdisciplinary teams have analyzed the specific case of literary genre using computational methods, some of them with previous experience in the areas of stylometry and authorship attribution. The analysis of the category of author is much less problematic than the case of genre: In most cases, the author (normally one) that wrote the text is undisputed. In the majority of the periods, cases of co-authorship represent a tiny fraction of the publications. This contrasts with the complexity of the conceptualization of genres in which every step is disputed: Do texts belong to a single subgenre or can they belong to several? How many and which precise labels should be used in the classification? Whose labels should be analyzed – the author's, the library's or the publisher's? Do the texts have to pass a set of necessary and sufficient conditions? Do genres conform to structures as taxonomies? Do they overlap? Can a text belong more to one genre than another? In other words, the classification of texts into genres has several issues much less relevant or even unknown in other literary categories. These issues include hybridism, overlap, ambiguity, lack of a shared palette, and vagueness on how to structure their similarities. This is particularly relevant for the period analyzed here, in which many authors tried to escape the frame of traditional genre categories.

In this chapter, I will present the main abstract distinctions of cultural concepts and give some examples of their application to the notion of genre. The goal is neither to recreate a historical overview of the concept of genre, nor present all possible abstract models or structures. Both goals would be beyond the possibilities of this publication. Instead, I want to describe a selection of models, structures, and perspectives about genres that have had a major impact either in theoretical areas or in computational analysis. These will represent the base for the expectations and limitations of the computational model that will be presented in the discussion (Chapter 8) of this book.

I am aware that some concepts that are presented here are truly basic to Linguistics, Literary Studies, Digital Humanities, or Computer Science, and that some readers could wonder whether such basic explanation are necessary. However, this is necessary in order to make interdisciplinary communication possible.

First, I will present an overview of the basic distinctions of the concepts and definitions. Second, I will describe the three main models (scholastic-structuralist model, hybridism, family resemblance, and prototypes) that a text should comply with in order to belong to a genre. Third, I will discuss the different structures in which genres relate to each other (taxonomies, flat, or gradual structures), and in the last section, I will introduce two perspectives on the analysis of genre: a longitudinal historical perspective with fewer genres being analyzed which looks more closely at a specific source of labels, and a cross-sectional synchronic perspective in which a larger number of labels are analyzed over a shorter period.

This chapter is the third and final chapter on the theoretical frameworks in this book. The previous chapters (Chapters 2.1 and 2.2) have clear international centers of activity and publication (i.e. studies of Spanish literature and the main DH conferences and journals). In contrast, in this chapter, genre theory is discussed in a wide variety of traditions, depending on the academic national tradition, subject and language analyzed. Each combination of these aspects (e.g. French-based Literary Studies in Spanish texts or German-based Linguistics in English texts) has had its own important milestones in the last decades. This research study is highly interdisciplinary, with its main roots in several traditions: Spanish-based Literary Studies in the Spanish language, German-based Literary Studies in the German and Romance languages, German-based linguistics in Romance texts, and international DH research in several languages. Against this background, I have focused on summarizing the most important concepts encountered in these areas during my research, with further concepts omitted due to time constraints.

2.3.1 Basic Distinctions about Concepts and Definitions

In many textual contexts, words like *novel* or *poem* (in Spanish, *novela* and *poema*) can be found, and these can be confirmed in any linguistic corpus. These words are recognized by speakers as *genres*, which are groups of texts with certain particularities. Like any other word, they can be seen as *linguistic symbols* in the traditional term of the linguist Ferdinand de Saussure (Kabatek and Pusch 2011, 39–40; Becker 2013, 32–33). According to de Saussure, linguistic symbols have two components:

1. A linguistic expression, also called *signifier* (French: *signifiant)* or form: for example, the word *novela* in Spanish, *novel* in English, *Roman* in German, etc.
2. The linguistic content, also called *signified* (French: *signifié*) or concept: i.e. the meaning shared by speakers (in the linguistic convention written as 'novel').

In a sense, an important goal of this research study is to analyze what the *signifié* is of *signifiants* such as *adventure* or *erotic novel*: What do speakers mean when they state "this text is an adventure novel"?

To go a step further, I would like to imagine that someone, with an actual book in their hand pronounces a sentence like "I have just read this novel and I like it very much." The person probably uses the word *novel* because they think that the object somehow belongs to this concept and it is therefore acceptable to use the form *novel* when referring to it. This example shows how linguistic communication also relates to external elements or objects in which reality is perceived. This third element, the *referent*, was introduced by Ogden and Richards and, together with *form* and *concept* (*signifiant* and *signifié* in Saussure's terminology), it completes the semiotic triangle (Kabatek and Pusch 2011, 123–24), which is exemplified in Figure 1.[1]

The form is the pronunciation of the word *dog*. The concept of 'dog' is the shared knowledge that the speakers hold about it. Finally, the referent is not a mental visualization of the dog, but a specific instance that can be observed in the external world; in other words, a real dog, in this case called Carlos

1 Even though this model has been criticized and further developed, I prefer to present here the original model because of its influence in several fields. For a critique and more complex semiotic models, see (Raible 1983) and (Blank 2001, 8–9).

Figure 1: Semiotic triangle of dog

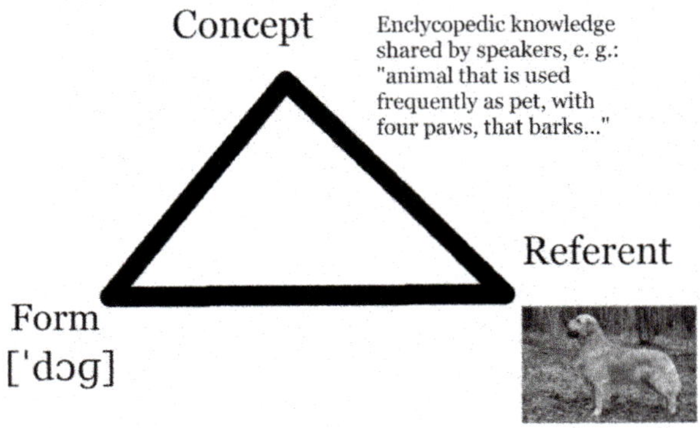

(according to the metadata from Wikipedia) was photographed in 2013.[2] As for the case of the dog, this schema can be applied to literary genres (Figure 2) in which a form like *novel* can be used to label a series of texts in the reality (like a volume of *El Quijote*), based on a series of encyclopedic knowledge that the speakers share.

Another useful differentiation is the classic one of *extension* and *intension*. The intension of any concept is the characteristics that constitute the concept, while the extension is the number of referents that belong to the symbol (Kabatek and Pusch 2011, 124; Pawłowski 1980, 53–54; Escandell Vidal 2012, 23–25). The intension of the symbol *novel* would be the characteristics of the concept 'novel', while the extension would be the number of instances in the world that are novels. A possible inductive analysis of genre would be a study of the intension of, for example, adventure novels (their shared features), by collecting the entire extension of adventure novels and analyzing their characteristics.

In scientific texts, it is common to define the analyzed object in the introductory sections. A definition (e.g., in the traditional example, "a bachelor is a single adult male") is composed of three elements: the *definiendum* or term to be defined ("a bachelor"), the *definiens* or defining concept ("a single

2 https://commons.wikimedia.org/wiki/File:Golden_Retriever_Carlos_(10581910556).jpg.

Figure 2: Semiotic triangle of novel

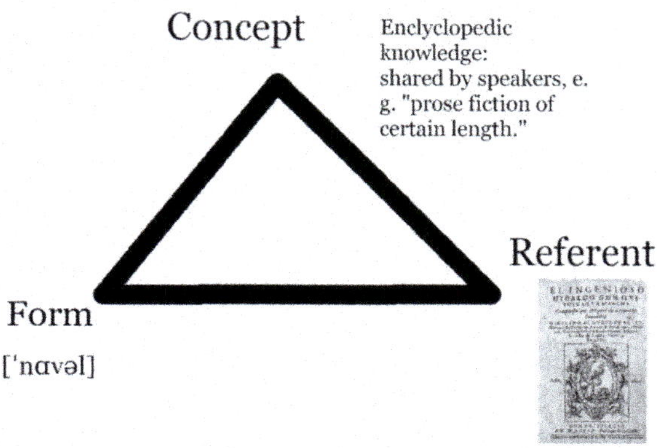

adult male") and a *copula* ("is") which unites the two other elements (Pawłowski 1980, 9–12; Kabatek and Pusch 2011, 35). For example, Encyclopaedia Britannica provides the following definition: "Historical novel, a novel that has as its setting a period of history and that attempts to convey the spirit, manners, and social conditions of a past age [...]". In this example, "historical novel" is the *definiendum*, the first comma is the *copula*, and the rest ("a novel [...] of a past age [...]") is the *definiens*.

An important differentiation in philosophical definitions (but rarely used in linguistics or lexicography) is made between *nominal* and *real definitions*. A nominal definition is a "terminological determination" that "we accept [...] on the basis of an explicit terminological convention or linguistic use" (Pawłowski 1980, 29, my translation). In contrast, a real definition "portrays an empirical generalization" (Pawłowski 1980, 30, my translation). The Humanities, and in particular Literary Studies, have typically not been subjected to empirical methods, partially because of the lack of digitized data and partially because the researchers preferred hermeneutic processes using a smaller range of samples with selected excerpts. From this perspective, I can assume that the definitions by previous scholars of the subgenres discussed in Chapter 2.1 are nominal definitions, since none of them assume an empirical perspective, use shared sets of features, propose hypotheses, or test them (even though some researchers used rigorous methods in a rather larger section of texts, such as the Rivalan Guégo 2008, Ferreras 1988, or Lara López 2000, all cited in Chapter 2.1). One of the goals of this work is to propose a way towards real definitions for the subgenres analyzed, which will be presented in Section 8.7 and put into practice in the Appendix.

2.3.2 Models of Genres

In this section I will introduce four different models that describe the interaction between instances, characteristics and categories: the scholastic-structuralist model, hybridism, family resemblance and prototypes.

2.3.2.1 Classic Scholastic-Structuralist Model

The *definiens* or concept of a linguistic symbol can be split into the two components introduced by Aristotle in the traditional scholastic schema of *genus proximum* and *differentia specifica* (Atkins and Rundell 2008, 414–15). Using the classic example, a bachelor would be a person (*genus proximum*), that is male, adult, and unmarried (*differentia specifica*). This model has been applied in many cases to genres and ultimately results in the development of tree-like structures or taxonomies in which finer concepts (such as the subgenre war novel) have a more general genus (historical novel), repeating the process any number of times (e.g. war novel > historical novel > novel > literary prose texts > literary texts > texts). The application and critique of taxonomies of genres will be discussed in the next section about the structure of genres.

From a logical point of view, the components of a definition can be understood as *necessary and sufficient conditions*. For a person (referent) to be labeled a bachelor (term), they must have several characteristics: It is necessary for them to be male, but this is not sufficient; it is also necessary for the person to be unmarried, but again, this condition alone is not sufficient. Only an unmarried, male adult has the sufficient and necessary conditions to be referred to as a *bachelor*. Likewise, and following the previously given definition, a setting in the past would be a necessary but not sufficient condition for a novel to be a historical novel; it also has to be based on facts.

This classic semantic model was further developed in structuralism, following the example of the phonemes, which are defined by binary values in a series of phonetic features such as vocal, labial, dental, etc. This scheme has been adapted to the area of lexical fields, analyzing, for example, several types of seats (chairs, sofas, stools) and their distinctive features in binary values (with or without backs, legs, arms, etc.). It is traditionally accepted that although this model is able to formally define some concepts (from areas including law or the natural sciences, such as legal institutions, substances, units of measure or living beings), it fails to accurately distinguish cultural and social concepts with blurry borders, for example literary concepts (Vivas 1968; Atkins and Rundell 2008, 416–17; Hempfer 2014).

This rigid process of assigning a categorical label to each referent based on the necessary and sufficient conditions of the concept is, in many contexts, understood as *classification*. In many cases it is accepted that the referent should be labeled with a single term, as any animal belongs to a single genus rather than to several. This concept of classification differs from that of Machine Learning, where distinct features are used to identify the referents sharing a label from those that do not, rather than search for necessary and sufficient conditions. In addition, the computational classification is differentiated into multi-class (each instance belongs to a single class, where each novel belongs to a single subgenre) and multi-label (each instance can belong to several classes, where a novel is classified as both adventure and historical). See Section 2.2.2 for further details.

Which specific genre labels should be classified (understood either from the logical or the computational perspective) is an open question, but in many cases the basic set of possible genres (or genre palette) has its roots again in classic philosophy. Plato is normally the first authority on genres when viewed chronologically, and he applied a three-part distinction, using the relationship between poet and text as criteria: The poet himself talks (dithyramb), lets others speak (tragedy and comedy), and a combination of both (epic, Garrido Gallardo 1988, 10; Zymner 2003, 11). Aristotle's *Poetics* became one of the most influential works of all time in literature (Garrido Gallardo 1988, 9; Genette 1988, 200; García Berrio and Huerta Calvo 1992, 11; Schaeffer 2006, 7). It is a short text with the goal of describing several literary genres which became normative over time (Zymner 2003, 11–12). Aristotle distinguished two main descriptors for genres: the mode of imitation (lexis in Plato, Genette 1988, 190), and the register of the imitation. Garrido Gallardo argues that *Poetics* has a mainly textual-linguistic perspective for differentiating the genres (1988, 17). In any case, this influential text comprised also a three-part schema, in many cases understood as the distinction between drama, epic, and lyric. However, following Gennete, Aristotle actually differentiated between dithyramb, epopee and drama (1988, 186–87).

Finding and consolidating a three-part schema has been a pattern in genre research until the present (Genette 1988, 200), with Bovet being the epitome of the "trinity obsession" (Genette 1988, 222). The classic palette of three main genres has undergone many modifications and further differentiations, such as the addition of the sarcastic by Frye (1957), or the essay by García Berrio and Huerta Calvo (1992).

This lack of definitions with a certain degree of acceptance among scholars, for the great majority of genres in terms of necessary and sufficient conditions, has been used as an argument for doubting whether genres have any ontological existence or aesthetic interest. The strongest opinion against the basic concept of genre was published in 1902 by Benedetto Croce, who accepted the usefulness of genres for practical reasons (e.g. sorting criteria in libraries), but rejected the adequacy of using these terms in aesthetic research or philosophical discussion due to the inability to assign accurate descriptions or laws to these concepts (Zymner 2003, 38–41). Croce's position had influence in authors like Blanchot, Gundolf, Vossler, Spingarn, Hack, or Fubini (see Hempfer 1973, 37). García Berrio and Huerta Calvo noted that Croce's critique mainly focuses on how genres were used for normative purposes for many centuries (1992, 129) and Wellek and Warren explain it as a "reaction against extremes of classical authoritarianism" (1956, 226). As these authors stated, genre research is descriptive, at least since the middle of the 20th century (1956, 234), and therefore, from our current perspective, it is difficult to recreate the intellectual context of Croce's critique.

2.3.2.2 Hybridism

Any researcher looking closely at real data about texts and their genres quickly finds that a text could belong to several groups, even when looking at a single source of information. The idea that the genres overlap or the existence of mixed-genre is frequently present (Chandler 1997, 2; Baßler 2010). However, mixed-genres are normally treated as exceptional cases of hybridism. Besides, it is normally not specified what exactly this hybridism is. A complete schema of this is the three-part unified schema by Hartmann and Guérard, who proposed terms like "lyric-lyric," "lyric-epic," and "lyric-dramatic" (García Berrio and Huerta Calvo 1992, 148). An example of this overlapping of genres in a literary text is to be found in *Hamlet* (for example in the *Folger Digital Text* edition), in which Shakespeare, in the words of Polonius, lists the dramatic genres in isolated terms, pairwise, and all in combinations:

> The best actors in the world, either for tragedy, comedy, history, pastoral, pastoral-comical, historical-pastoral, ‹tragical-historical, tragical-comical-historical-pastoral, [...]›. (Mowat and Werstine 2010).

One of the most important theoretical frames about hybridism in genre is also a specially influential voice in the German-speaking sphere: Goethe. This author distinguished, besides the historical genres such as *novel* or *ballad* (Dichtarten, called poetic classes by Genette 1988, 227), three natural or basic forms (Naturformen or Grundformen, Fricke 2010, 10) – the poetic modes in Genette's terms: epic, lyric, and dramatic. These could be represented in isolation in a text, forming the specific genres (the epic, the lyric, the drama), or in combination to a certain degree, thus making it possible for a novel to be strongly lyrical and slightly epic, or a poem to be both highly dramatic and lyrical. These three categories have sometimes been understood as ahistorical tendencies that appear in several specific historical genres or as the main categories in a hierarchy of the genres (Zymner 2003, 27–28). The idea of a degree of belonging to a form or mode was used later by thinkers such as Petersen (1944), which will be discussed in later sections.

The question about the number of genres that a text might belong to is open. Many works implicitly accept that a text belongs to single genre, particularly if the research takes account of what the author wanted to express with the labels, as will be discussed in the section on longitudinal historical studies (Section 2.3.4.1). On the other hand, there are authors like Derrida (1980) who, in his "law of genre," asserts that texts participate in at least one genre, with the possibility of belonging to additional genres:

> A text cannot belong to no genre, it cannot be without or less a genre. Every text participates in one or several genres, there is no genreless text; there is always a genre and genres, yet such participation never amounts to belonging. (Derrida 1980, 65).

As explained in Section 2.2.4, Santini proposed the *zero-to-multi-genre classification scheme*, in which any text can be related to an open number of genres. A text could belong to no genre (a *genreless text* in Derrida's terms) where the author has individualized the text and where "texts cannot be safely ascribed to any existing genre (zero-assignment)" (Santini 2011, 169). The text could also belong to one or "show several genres at the same time (multi-genre assignment)" (Santini 2011, 169). This work is one of the few that explicitly provides the possibility for texts to not participate in any genre.

2.3.2.3 Family Resemblance and Social Institutions

The inadequacy of the classic scholastic-structuralist model of necessary and sufficient conditions has been discussed not only for literary genres but for many concepts in general, including in the Humanities and Social Sciences, where the borders of the different classes are blurred. To more accurately describe the characteristics of these concepts, other models have been presented.

The family resemblance model was briefly (in only a few paragraphs) proposed by Ludwig Wittgenstein in his *Philosophical Investigations* (originally published in 1953, consulted Schulte's bilingual edition of 2013) to answer a possible critique that the term *language games* (a corner stone of his philosophy) lacked a definition. His response was that there is no possible accurate definition of the word *game* (*Spiel* in German) when observing different kinds of games ("board-games, card-games, ball-games, athletic games," Wittgenstein and Schulte 2013, 36e), highlighting the fact that one must look at the real objects and their particularities: "To repeat: don't think, but look!" There is no trait common to all of them; some are amusing, in some you lose, in some there are several players, in some luck is important:

> […] we see a complicated network of similarities overlapping and criss-crossing: similarities in the large and in the small. I can think of no better expression to characterize these similarities than "family resemblances"; for the various resemblances between members of a family – build, features, colour of eyes, gait, temperament, and so on and so forth – overlap and criss-cross in the same way. – And I shall say: 'games' form a family. (Wittgenstein and Schulte 2013, 36e).

Some researchers have already used family resemblance as a theoretical model for genres. These include Hempfer (who will be discussed later) and Fricke, who applied it to the genre of anecdote, noting that the features in the model cannot all be facultative (in the sense of optional); some of them have to be necessary (2010, 10–11).

In my opinion, there are several weak aspects in Wittgenstein's argument, although these do not affect the pillars of the model. The first is the attempt to produce a single meaning for the word *game*. In a sense, Wittgenstein is rejecting the possibility of polysemy. The dictionary *Duden* lists 12 main definitions for the word *Spiel*, and seven more sub-definitions; the *Oxford Dictionary* has five main definitions for the word *game* and nine sub-definitions; the

Spanish *Diccionario del Español Actual* has 15 main definitions for the word *juego* and 12 sub-definitions. These three examples of lexicographic authorities in the European languages show that there was no attempt to find an ultimate definition for the word *game*, but rather, it was reduced into smaller lexical units and a definition was assigned to each of these.

My second critique is the poor choice of the family metaphor. Familiar relationships between people are not defined by shared physical traits but exclusively by two kinds of relationships: genetic (descendant or ascendant) and political (married to or adopted by). Trying to identify members of a family using superficial features (as for those listed by Wittgenstein) could be practical and to a certain extent functional, but could not be an accurate theoretical model for defining family relationships, especially if marriage or adoption between members of different ethnic groups is not seen as exceptional. I do share the opinion that many concepts lack accurate boundaries or common traits for all the referents, but I do not think that families are a good example of this.

A third problem of the family resemblance model is its brevity and its open interpretation by researchers, as observed in following quote by Pawłowski: "what it is here meant, and obviously *Ludwig Wittgenstein* thought [...]" (1980, 204, my translation). In scholarly discussions it is common for several researchers to comprehend or apply the model in dissimilar ways. For example, the professor of Romance Literature, Klaus Hempfer, claimed that Franz von Kutschera, a professor of Philosophy, failed to understand Wittgenstein's definition of family resemblance (2014, 409). In my opinion, the lack of specific implementation of the family resemblance model in real examples and comprehensive cases prevents a shared and deeper understanding of its potentials and limitations.

Families are not the only social entity that have been used as a metaphor to explain genres in the history of literary research: Genres have also been compared to *social institutions*. Wellek and Warren used the simile of social institutions to explain the specific characteristics of how literary works participate in these groups in different manners:

> The literary kind is an 'institution' – as Church, University, or State is an institution. It exists, not as an animal exists or even as a building, chapel, library or capitol, but as an institution exists. One can work through, express oneself through, existing institutions, create new ones, or get on, so far as possible,

> without sharing in polities or rituals; one can also join, but then reshape, institutions. (Wellek and Warren 1956, 226).

In this model, each literary work would be compared to a single person. Their grouping in genres is not defined by genetics or necessary and sufficient conditions, but by a loose historical association: how they participate in different ways in an institution. The authors do not contrast their model with the family resemblance model, nor do they cite Wittgenstein. However, they do cite Pearson's article, who introduces the term *institutions* for describing genres (1940, 68–71) and who does mention Wittgenstein's model. In any case, the authors specify very few characteristics of social institutions that could be extrapolated to genres, besides their historical mutability and an uncertain assumption about the obligatory participation of each literary work in at least one genre. Díez Taboada provided this simile and gave more examples about the behavior of texts as members of the genre-institutions:

> If genre, then, is an institution, it is logical that in it, in addition to the founder who draws a first model or programmatic work, there will be affiliates that follow to the letter and scrupulously the founder as model, idlers who forget it; reformers who renew it with vigor or adapt it to new historical circumstances; detractors who criticize, contradict or parody it, seeking their limitations; theoreticians who at every moment try to fix, sometimes pedantically, its characteristics; annihilators who fight and finish it, destroying or exhausting it; continuers who pick up the prestige of its name for new realities founded by them, or who in different periods will put new names to things that in the end are so similar that they could be called with the same denomination. (Díez Taboada 1965, 15, my translation).

The use of institutions as a model to understand genres has been used since then in different traditions. Todorov (1976) or Voßkamp (1977) use it mainly to explain the communicative function of genres between the authors and their contemporary readers. Through the label, the author communicates the category of the text and therefore awakens a series of expectations in the reader based on other texts. In many cases, the author actually wants to modify this *horizon of expectations*, a concept coined by Jauß (1970). With this process, labels change over time, becoming associated with other expectations. The historical reconstruction of this communicative process is the central goal of many of these articles which have a longitudinal perspective, which will be addressed in Section 2.3.4.1.

In any case, the social institution metaphor is not tied to this historical reconstruction, nor to the communication between author and readers. This metaphor can also be understood by recognizing that texts participate in genres, as people participate in institutions. The participation is not necessarily defined by the writer, it can also be assigned by other agents, even decades or centuries later. In addition, these institutions do not necessarily have to be observed in their historical context, but may be contrasted against each other.

In essence, the family resemblance and social institution model dispose of the requirement for finding necessary and sufficient conditions and instead propose a loose relationship between their referents (instances) and the concepts (or features in computational terms).

2.3.2.4 Prototype Model

In addition to family resemblance, the other competing model for genres often mentioned in the research is the prototype theory. This model dates back to 1973, when Rosch analyzed the learning process of a group of teenage speakers of the Indonesian language Dani. This group was chosen because its language does not have lexicalized terms for color or basic forms. She conducted two experiments in which the participants were required to learn the names of colors and specific forms, measuring the ratio of error for each element. The results found that central items (e.g. a perfect square) were learned more easily than modifications (e.g. a freehand square or a square with a gap on one side).

Figure 3: Prototype and modification of square used by Rosch (1973, 343)

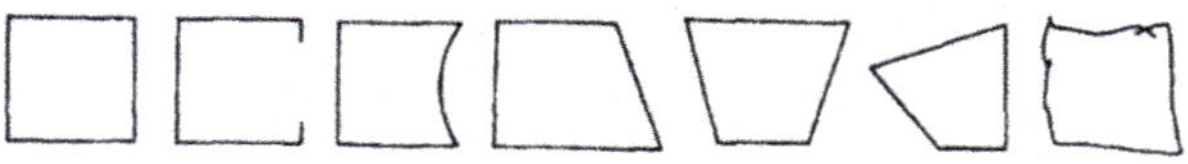

FIG. 2. Basic square and six transformations.

The terms *central*, *focal* or *prototypical* are used synonymously throughout the article. In her conclusion, Rosch proposes that more complex categories (birds or fruits) could have similar cognitive models (349). These were included in the ten categories that she analyzed in a follow-up article (1975) gathering answers from university students. The respondents tended to agree when giving scores for items that were seen as better examples of the different categories: Apples and oranges are more clearly identified as fruits than coconuts or pawpaws; robins or sparrows are more often selected as good examples of birds than emus or penguins. This last category was visualized by Aitchison (2012, 69, originally published in 1987) and has been widely disseminated (even translated, for example into Spanish in Escandell Vidal 2012, 174).

Figure 4: Birdiness rankings by Aitchison (2012, 69)

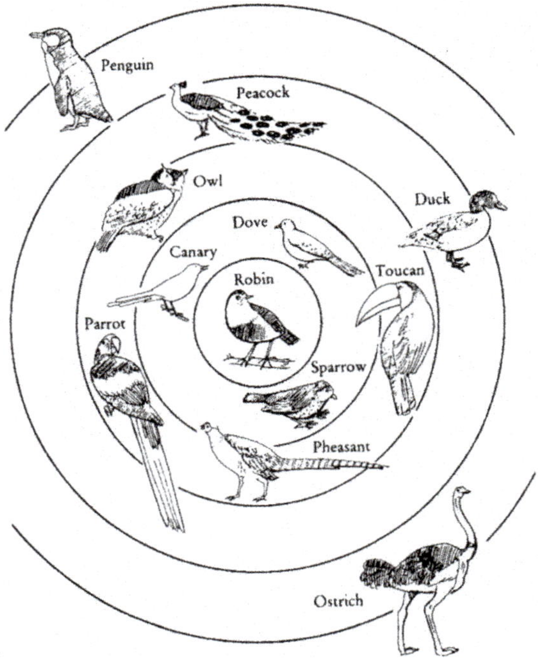

Figure 6.1 Birdiness rankings

Although the illustration of Figure 4 is very efficient in showing that the robin is *birdier* than the penguin, there is an important flaw: The vertical and horizontal axis are not labeled. The peacock and the pheasant appear to be at different poles of the vertical axis, and a similar effect is observed for the toucan and the parrot on the horizontal axis. This leaves the reader wondering what this spatial distribution represents. The reason for the lack of labels is very simple: The two dimensions do not actually mean anything, thus the reader is misled. As with the squares in Rosch's paper of 1973 shown in Figure 3, the birds should have been arranged along an axis (horizontal or vertical), with the robin as the positive extreme (the best exemplar) and the penguin and ostrich at the negative pole (the worst ones). The word *central* appears in Rosch's 1973 paper up to 58 times, many times as a synonym for *focal* or *prototypical*, but was dropped in her paper of 1975. The concept of central has its purpose in the example of the colors, where the wavelength creates a natural arrangement, but not in the other categories.

In summary, in Rosch's prototype model, each item does not belong to the concept in categorical terms (i.e. it does or it does not), but rather in terms of degree (i.e. it belongs clearly to the category or it belongs vaguely to the category).

One of the most comprehensive papers on the application of the family resemblance and prototype theories to genres was written by Hempfer (2014)[3] who initially rejected taxonomies as an accurate model for genres (405–6) and the nominalistic critique against genre as a tautology (409). Hempfer proposed the model of family resemblance to explain the instances (texts) where there is no agreement on a basic set of features in order to belong to a genre (409). To operationalize the ahistorical invariants (archi-texts or modes in Genette), he proposed the model of the prototype (414), remarking that:

> [...] the fundamental difference between the 'classical' concept of class as a means for categorization and the prototype concept therefore consists in the fact that a class tolerates only membership or non-membership, while membership in a prototype category is 'a matter of gradience.' (Hempfer 2014, 411).

In my opinion, the prototype and family resemblance theories are competing models to the classic scholastic-structuralist theory, but they are not mutually exclusive. Both modify different sections of the semiotic triangle:

3 Hempfer had written before a monograph about genres (1973). Although he cites Wittgenstein, he does not refer to the family resemblance as model for genres. Of course, he also does not mention the prototype model since Rosch was publishing her first articles on the topic that same year.

- The family resemblance and social institution models are distinct in that not all the instances referred by a term have to share common traits or necessary and sufficient conditions. Nevertheless, this model says little about the way in which the terms should be defined for each instance.
- The prototype theory highlights that the labeling of a referent or instance is better described in terms of degree than categorically.

Both aspects can be combined to explain the distinct particularities of the genres, as discussed in Chapters 7.1 and 8.

2.3.3 Macro-Models of Genres

The four models presented above (classic scholastic-structuralist, hybridism, family resemblance, and prototypes) define the way that the referents must display a series of conditions defined by the concept in order to be labeled within a specific category. Nevertheless, these models have not established how the different categories relate to each other. Thus, in this section, I am not examining the referents, but only how a category (e.g. adventure novel) relates to other categories (e.g. historical, war novel, etc.). One can intuitively accept that an adventure novel is a type of novel, and that adventure novels and historical novels have more similarities between them than with romantic novels. It could also be argued, that specific subgenres constitute a macro-subgenre (for example, historical and adventure novels). These relationships between genres and subgenres are what I call the *macro-models of genre*,[4] and in this section I will present some of the most common ones.

2.3.3.1 Taxonomy

By far the most frequent macro-model is the taxonomy, which imposes a strict composition in which the concepts (e.g. genres) can be classified in tree-like

4 In previous publications, I have used the concept structure of genres. I now prefer to use the concept macro-model for two reasons. The first is that by using the prefix macro, it is clear that larger components of the model are being treated. The second is that I will use the term structure in Chapter 8 to refer to the formalization of the model, following Weisberg's terminology (2013). Thus, the different possibilities presented in the previous Section 2.3.2 could have been called micro-models of genre. However, it is unusual to find the prototype model presented as a micro-model.

structures. Actually, this macro-model is a consequence of the concepts of *genus proximum* and *differentia specifica* of the scholastic model seen in Section 2.3.2.1: Every node (e.g. *historical novel*) hangs from an upper branch (its *genus proximum*, or in semantic terms, its hypernym, in this case *novel*) and has specific features (its *differentia specifica*) that distinguish it from the other sibling nodes (Fricke 2010b, 8). For example, a historical novel can be a novel in a historical setting with the intention of representing the reality of that time. This macro-model is more or less explicit in many essays, often applied without real examples (Garrido Gallardo 1988, 26). Figure 5 shows the epic-narrative taxonomy as presented by García Berrio and Huerta Calvo (1992, 171).

Figure 5: Taxonomy of narrative-epic genres by García Berrio and Huerta Calvo (1992, 171)

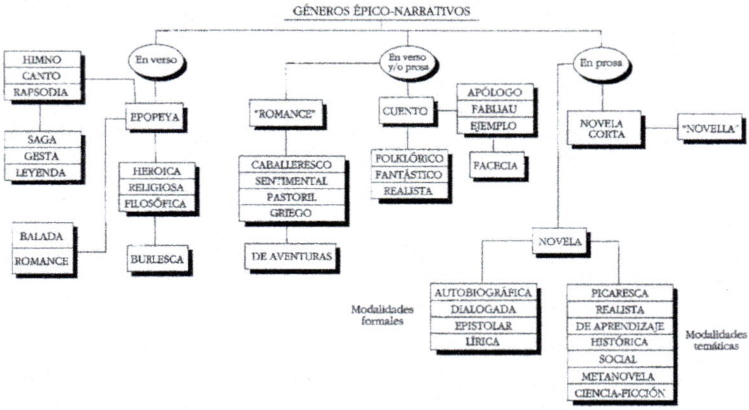

Taxonomy, as a macro-model of the conceptual understanding of the genres similar to the species in biology, is surprisingly frequent, even in our time (Schaeffer 2006, 9). This conception was taken further by authors like Brunetière, who, in 1880, proposed a Darwinian evolution of the genres, in which they would compete against each other (see Petersen 1944, 121 or Schaeffer 2006, 33 for a critique). The idea that genres can be explained with animal similes is also present in Moretti's hypothesis that states that genres tend to survive over a similar span of years as living beings. In his hypothesis, genre would be phenomena that tend to live around 25 years, dying with a "total change of their ecosystem" (2005, 20). This hypothesis has been recently analyzed and rejected by Underwood (2016, 2019).

Genette (1988) proposes a distinction between archi-genres (also called modes, like lyric, epic, and dramatic, but potentially also others) that would contain specific genres, creating taxonomies; the examples that Genette gives are: *épique > novel > roman policier > roman policier "réaliste"*. Although Genette criticizes this, he also followed the three-part schema in his article and defined the source of the speech act as the most fundamental criterion: delivered by the poet, by the characters, or a combination of both (1988, 206).

Vivas (1968) analyzed the reasons why artists and theorists see the concept of genre as useless. He accepted that by the beginning of the 20th century, many artists turned "their backs on the perfected form" of the novel and tried new forms (97). Together with this, other sociological and artistic processes would have affected the role of genre, such as easier access to culture, the influence of idealistic aesthetics, new aesthetic needs of the public to access the artistic object without previous labeling, and the needs of the readers (98–100). He criticized taxonomy as a structure for genres, saying that it "is the absurd extreme to which the notions of classes and genres have been carried sometimes by men suffering from a taxonomic itch" (99–100). These taxonomies are the product of the scholastic model of concepts applied to genre, and therefore to point out their invalidity is to implicitly negate that genres can be explained as *genus proximum* plus *differentia specifica*.

2.3.3.2 Flat Macro-Model

As I have described in Chapter 2.2, the multi-genre assignment is the most typical perspective for computational studies, normally treated as a multi-label classification task: Any text is assigned to one or more labels and the algorithm is trained to classify each text as either being part of a group or not being part of it. This multi-label macro-model is able to fit the fact that normally the sources use several categories for each text rather than a single category. Nevertheless, it is indisputable that some genres are more similar than others: Memoirs, autobiographies, and educational novels are somehow closer to each other than to erotic or adventure novels. This similarity between genres (that can be visualized to a certain degree in the taxonomy) is completely ignored in the traditional multi-label classification task from computational research. For this reason, I consider the multi-label classification task to use a flat macro-model of genres in which any text belongs to one or more genres in a categorical way, without describing whether the genres are very close or very distinct.

2.3.3.3 Gradual Macro-Model

In addition to taxonomy, and the flat macro-model, there is a further type of relationship between genres that has been used at different moments in the story, i.e. in terms of degree. Julius Petersen (1944, originally published in 1939) created a theoretical macro-model for literary genres in which every historical genre (lyrical novel, hymn, story, fable in his examples) had a position in a three-dimensional macro-model. The three dimensions were Goethe's universal modes (dramatic, epic and lyric, see Section 2.3.2.2), and every historical genre was related in terms of degree to two of these modes. He called this macro-model the *compass of the genres*.

In this macro-model, the three modes (dramatic, epic, and lyric, called *Grundformen*, English: 'basic forms') have different levels of degree, with the *Urdichtung* (translatable as 'proto-poetry') at the center of the macro-model (124–25). These three basic modes are combinable pairwise, creating the historical genres (*Zwischengattungen*, 'between-genres'):

> Between poetry and epic are those species whose form is more or less characterized as a monologic report of a state: elegy, epistle, vision, idyll, and lyrical novel. Between epic and drama moves the dialogic report of an action: frame narrative, letter novel, dialogue novel. Between poetry and drama stands the dialogic representation of states: lyrical conversation, heroic, cantata, dramatic idyll, lyrical drama. (Petersen 1944, 123–24, my translation).

In this macro-model, every historical genre is defined not as a subtype of an archi-genre (as in a dendrogram in which hybridism does not fit), but as a combination of two modes or basic forms. This combination is not represented categorically, but rather in degrees, where the closeness of one to another represents the degree of participation. For example, the lyric drama is both dramatic and lyrical and that is why it sits between both modes; but since it is more dramatic than lyrical, it is closer to drama.

The accuracy, utility, or transferability to other languages of this *compass of the genres* has been criticized (for example by Genette 1988), and, in my opinion, its limitations are shared by many other models presented here: precision of the exact values of each genre. The macro-model could be improved by treating it as a multi-dimensional space in which each genre can be de-

Figure 6: Compass of the genres, by Petersen (1944, 125)

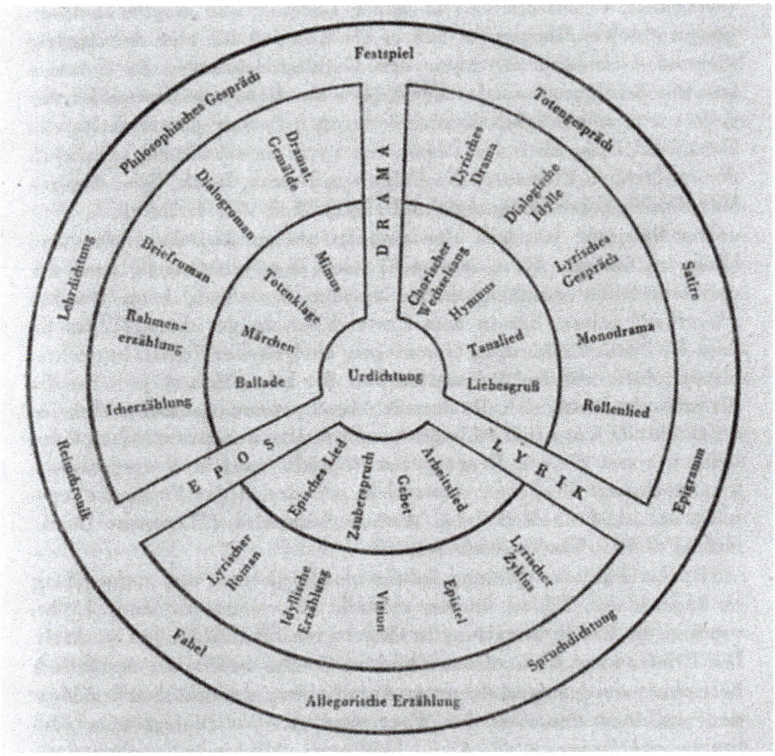

scribed not only in two, but in three, or even more literary modes. Nevertheless, I think this macro-model has many important novelties. First, unlike the flat macro-model of the multi-label classification task, it asserts that some historical genres are closer to others. Second, it accepts hybridism as a core characteristic of historical genres and not an exception, thus moving away from the taxonomic macro-model. Third, it foresees that each genre can be described in terms of degree in a bi-dimensional space. Finally, it places many heterogeneous genres in a single abstract macro-model. The disadvantage of this macro-model is that neither instances (texts) nor the features of these dimensions are represented or clear.

2.3.4 Perspectives on Genres

A further aspect in the research on genres is how the analyzed corpus is defined. Two main perspectives on the studies can be differentiated: longitudinal historical and cross-sectional synchronic. In the following section, I will further describe these two perspectives, giving examples for each of them from Literary Studies, Linguistics, and Digital Humanities.

2.3.4.1 Longitudinal Historical Studies

In longitudinal historical studies, the researcher is interested in reconstructing the historical evolution of specific genres or subgenres. These cases normally cover longer periods (over several decades or centuries), using a handful of categories or fewer as an example. One important aspect is what the author's intention was when using specific labels and what were the expectations of the readers at the time. These highly qualitative labels are time-consuming to collect, and there is little clarity on the exact type of source they should come from: The cover can be interpreted as a rather superficial source that is influenced by the publisher. Besides, for many periods, the number of books that identified a genre on the cover or in the para-text is often small, and therefore the researcher only analyzes a small fraction of the literature of that period.

This longitudinal historical perspective does not relate to any area of research: Both Literary Studies, Linguistics, or Digital Humanities can include the recompilation of data and analysis in this manner, as described below in examples from the different disciplines.

For example, the historical development of genres is a key aspect in an influential work in the German tradition of literary genres by Raible (1980). He summarized five characteristics of literary genres from a semiotic perspective. For him, literary genres are conceptual models that try to reduce the complexity of the texts that are grouped together (322). He described five consequence. First, genres are historical conventions with a normative function. Second, genres show different levels of complexity (e.g. novels can contain short novels, therefore novels are more complex than short novels). Third, in genre, the reader expects specific phenomena in a given order. Fourth, the reader uses the information about the genre to interpret the text (e.g. laugh about or mourn a death depending on whether the text is a tragedy or a parody, 334). Fifth, genres are defined by external text features, such as the goals of the author, the author's situation, and the situations of the readers. Finally, he proposed a methodology for describing literary genres in six dimensions, each one containing several features of the text, and emphasized and encouraged future research in working with specific textual features.

Todorov (1976), on the other hand, suggested that the concept of genre is an important classification method, even though the current genres differed from those in the past: "it is not 'genres' that have disappeared, but the genres of the past, and they have been replaced by others" (1976, 160). In his opinion, "genres exist as institution that [...] function as 'horizons of expectation' for readers, and as 'models of writing' for authors" (1976, 163). He reflected on how the labels of the genres appeared:

> Let us now turn to the other term in the expression 'class of texts': class. It raises a problem only by its simplicity. One can always find a property common to two texts, and therefore put them together in one class. But is there any point in calling the result of such a union a 'genre'? I think that it would be in accord with the current usage of the word and at the same time provide a convenient and operant notion if we agreed to call 'genres' only those classes of texts that have been perceived as such in the course of history. The accounts of this perception are found most often in the discourse on genres (the meta-discursive discourse) and, in a sporadic and indirect fashion, in the texts themselves. (Todorov 1976, 162).

This quote is especially valuable for computational approaches to genres where it is common to find linguistic patterns that can distinguish random groups of texts. Todorov's proposal would mean that the researcher should only use labels that were given either by scholars (i.e. those holding the meta-discursive discourse about genres) or where the text presents itself as something different (e.g. labels on the cover).

A recent study on literary genres with a strong historical perspective was undertaken by Schröter (2019), who analyzed the case of the German *novella*. Schröter states that genres are not based on textual features and that they should be defined in the descriptive language of the Literary Studies (1–2). His analysis of the novella shows that the instances of this category of genre do not show textual or linguistic similarities, and therefore the main goal of this description should be the reconstruction of the label, both in the paratext of the texts or in theoretical works, such as poetics (36). As a consequence, the historical development of the label should be integrated in the concept of the genre by applying the family resemblance model (31–33).

In Digital Humanities, the works with the clearest historical perspective are those from Underwood (particularly 2016 and 2019 which I have already summarized in Section 2.2.5). The main question relating to this publication is Moretti's hypothesis that subgenres tend to last around 30 years. To observe this, Underwood looks more closely at the beginning and end points and the development of genre over two centuries. He uses multi-label classification for several subgenres and plots the probabilities of each text belonging to the category. The early works that show a high probability of belonging to the genre can be understood as pioneers of the genre which share inner features with the rest of the category. The genre shows high probabilities in periods of stability, or a decrease when it is altered. Underwood's results show that while some genres could fit into Moretti's hypothesis, others genres "remained stable for a century and a half" (2016).

A different tradition that mainly focuses on the historical aspect is the German-speaking tradition of Linguistics in the Romance languages: *Diskurstradition*, or *discourse tradition*. The traditional schema of the language proposed by the linguist Coseriu describes three levels: universal (the human capacity of language), historical (the historical languages), and individual (a specific text or discourse). Nevertheless, Coseriu found similar repeated patterns in many languages. Some of these were relatively simple and short (e.g. greeting traditions) and some very complex (e.g. sonnets or detective fiction). For this reason, Coseriu proposed the term *text tradition* (2007, 46, originally published in 1980), later called *discourse tradition* by Koch, who places it in a second historical level of the language, parallel or diagonal to the languages (1997, 44–46). The exact theoretical placement of this second historicity of the language in Coseriu's model has been widely discussed (Kabatek 2007; 2015; Schrott 2015, 120–24). The repetition of linguistic patterns and their modification over time would constitute shared traditions in several languages (Kabatek 2011, 97; Lebsanft and Schrott 2015, 24). This creates a bridge from the linguistic tradition to the literary texts which constitute the most common examples of these studies (Koch 1997, 46–47). An important characteristic of this concept is its aim to cover heterogeneous phenomena in an abstract model:

> The concept of the discourse tradition as a cultural guideline of communicatively appropriate text organization, which was developed in Romance languages, is a central basic concept for a Cultural Linguistics. A characteristic of this concept is its wide range. Thus, under the concept of the dis-

> course tradition very different cultural patterns of speaking and writing can be subsumed: The traditional knowledge of discourse includes communicative habits such as greetings or the opening of a conversation, but textual genres and styles of interaction also act as discourse traditions that model speaking and writing. (Schrott 2015, 115, my translation).

In addition, its primary goal is pluri-linguistic, and this corresponds to the related traditions expressed in several languages, as is the case in European literary traditions. In addition, the discourse tradition is not limited to the historical perspective, as it has been shown to have possible new perspectives in diachronic linguistics (Kabatek 2007, 331–32) and the study of cultural phenomena from a linguistic perspective.

Its great ambition has one clear issue: Since its beginning it has mainly discussed the theoretical framework and characteristics (Schrott 2015, 115), with relatively few works that actually apply it to the specific discourse tradition of several languages for long chronological periods and in defined corpora. A good example of an analysis of the discourse tradition can be found in Schrott (2015, 131–40). Schrott investigates the narrative using *imparfait narratif* in French novels, and directive questions as a form of polite requests in oral communication in French, German, and Spanish.

To fully analyze discourse traditions, it is necessary to have access to diachronic corpora in several languages, across several genres, with explicit metadata and annotation about linguistic and literary phenomena. Besides, the results should be comparable within the variance of periods and languages. This could be achieved by a closer collaboration between Linguistics and Digital Literary Studies, employing shared encoding formats (TEI XML) or annotation sets (such as EAGLES or universal PoS tags) in the different languages, genres, and periods. In this regard, the *European Literary Text Collection* (ELTeC) of the *Distant Reading COST Action* could be the first corpus suitable for analysis about the novel in the European context.

2.3.4.2 Cross-Sectional Synchronic Studies

The other perspective on genre studies are the cross-sectional synchronic studies in which the researcher is interested in analyzing textual groups in a specific period. In these cases, historical development is not of interest because the periods are too short or because there is no expectation for the data to cover complete genre spans. In these cases, it is typical for the researcher to consider a greater number of categories and a larger proportion of texts. This perspective is mainly taken by perspective of Corpus Linguistics, Computational Linguistics, or Digital Humanities, although some works from Literary Studies do seek an ahistorical frame of the genre.

Except for the works by Underwood (2016, 2019) mentioned previously, all the research on genres from Computational Linguistics and Digital Humanities presented in Chapter 2.2 is closer to the cross-sectional synchronic perspective. Some examples include Kessler, Numberg, and Schütze (1997), Stamatatos, Fakotakis, and Kokkinakis (2000), Santini (2011), Jockers (2013), Schöch (2013), Underwood (2014), or Hettinger et al. (2016). In all these cases, the year of publication and the historical development of the genres are of little importance and the analysis plots have no historical axis.

An interesting theoretical contribution comes from Schaeffer (1989, translated into Spanish in 2006), who proposed a historically open understanding of genres, since "the classificatory identity of a text is always open" (Schaeffer 2006, 101–2, my translation). For Schaeffer, labels are assigned in a chaotic process by several authors, creating a "patchwork lexicologique" (1989, 66) and thus the primary work of the researcher should not be in assigning new labels, but rather to "analyze the functionality of the genre names, whatever they are, and try to see to what they are referring to" (Schaeffer 2006, 53, my translation).

Textual phenomena have been studied in the field of Corpus Linguistics from several perspectives that are very similar to what Literary Studies consider genres. An important authority on this topic is Biber, who analyzed how linguistic features are distributed in different genres (or *register* in his terminology, treated mostly synonymously, see Biber 1992, 332) and the correlation between the features using multiple factor analysis. These "bottom-up statistical analyses" (Biber 2014, 7) examine correlations between linguistic features, grouping those linguistic units that tend to correlate and clustering them together in more general patterns, also called dimensions.[5] A score for each dimension can be computed for each text and a mean value calculated for each genre (Biber 2014, 13). "After the statistical analysis is completed, dimensions are interpreted functionally" (Biber 2014, 11). In the following plot

5 This methodology is similar to other methods that group co-occurring or correlating features, such as topic modeling and specifically principal component analysis (PCA), although its typical units, pre-processing steps, visualizations and interpretation tend to differ.

of Figure 7, Dimension 1 is plotted with the means of different genres (vertical axis) in a chronological development (horizontal axis) over the last four centuries for English texts. The successful approach of multiple factor analysis of corpora has been tested by Biber and other researchers across dozens of languages, periods and genres. In a comparative work, Biber proposes two of these dimensions as universal dimensions of textual distinction, regardless of language, period or genre: 1) oral versus literate, and 2) narrative versus non-narrative (2014). There are several aspects from Biber's methodology that would be done differently nowadays, for example applying a shared linguistic tag set of annotations for several languages, using all the linguistic units annotated by the tool, or a more straightforward way of deciding how strongly the features should correlate to be clustered together in a dimension. Nevertheless, in my opinion, Biber pioneered the opening up of a path of statistical methodologies for linguistic features 30 years ago with many important implications for Digital Literary Studies.

Figure 7: Dimension 1 (oral-literate) by genres in chronological development (Biber 2009, 249)

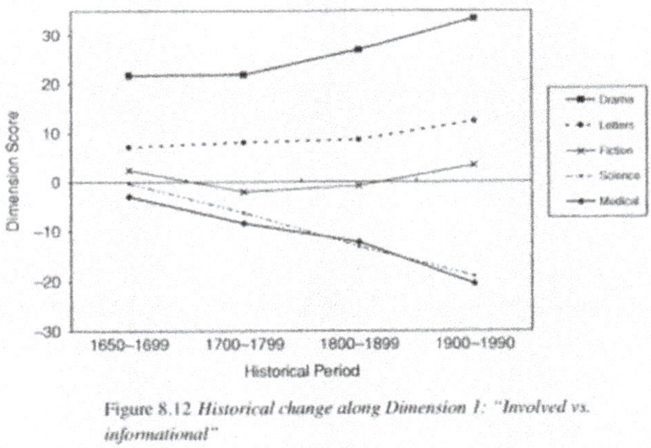

In addition, in the middle of the 1980s, a similar distinction to Biber's second dimension was defined in the German-speaking Romance linguistic tradition: *Nähesprache-Distanzsprache*, or *near-language* and *distant-language*. Koch and Oesterreicher used an already existing distinction made by Söll (1985)

where the medium of a text (written or oral) and its conception are separate phenomena with a certain relationship (Koch and Oesterreicher 1985). A text (e.g. a letter) or many digital formats (e.g. chats) can be written but will contain many of the typical features of oral communication. On the contrary, oral genres, such as academic discourses or sermons, are conceptually created as written texts and therefore show these characteristics. These authors integrate this distinction into the diasystem of Coseriu's Romance linguistics along the terms diatopic, diastratic, and diaphasic.

Figure 8: The near-distant continuum by Koch and Oesterreicher (2011, 13)

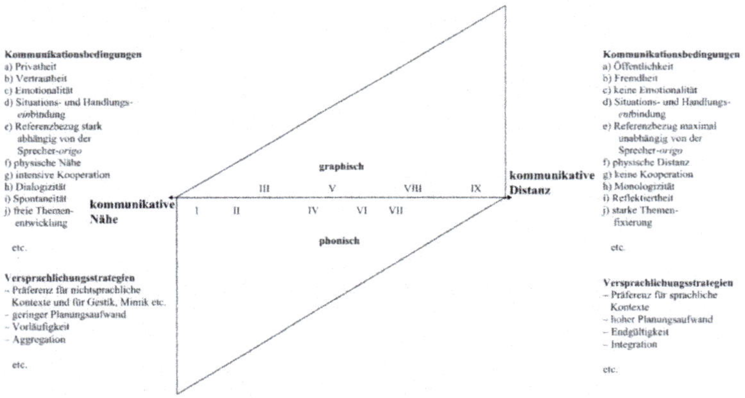

In Figure 8, the horizontal axis represents the communicative distance and the vertical axis can be understood as the frequency of the types of genres that can be found in this position, either in written (above the horizontal axis) or oral medium (below the horizontal axis). The different genres are marked with roman numbers: I) familiar conversation; II) private telephonic conversation; III) private letter; IV) work interview; V) journalistic interview; VI) sermon; VII) scientific conference; VIII) editorial; IX) law text. The model shows that the oral genres are distributed closer to near communication than the written ones, but there is a large overlapping area.

This model has been successfully adopted by many researchers in Romance languages with modifications (for example Dufter and Stark 2003). A clear caveat of the model is its lack of sharpness and standardization of visualization. In the previous figure, the position of the genres on the horizontal axis are not based on any calculation (as in Biber), but are merely hypothetical, and they do not show internal variance in each genre. In addition, the vertical and perpendicular lines are not labeled and are merely drawn to make a perfect diamond. An interesting aspect of this concept is the fact that the researchers presented a comprehensive list of linguistic phenomena in three Romance languages (French, Italian and Spanish) related to the two poles of this communicative dimension and sorted by linguistic levels (Koch and Oesterreicher 2011).

2.3.5 Conclusions

Genres and subgenres are cultural concepts with complex relationships between their main components: categories (labels), instances (texts), and features. Several models have been used or proposed to regulate the interaction between these components. The classic scholastic-structuralist model does not fit many of the characteristics of subgenre, while the family resemblance and prototype models have been proposed and only used in tempting ways. In addition, the fact that some subgenres are more similar to others has not yet found a proper formalization. Genres and subgenres can be analyzed from different perspectives: the longitudinal historical perspective, with a greater focus on the development of a few subgenres and the opinion of the authors, or the cross-sectional perspective, with a focus on many categories over a shorter period.

Any researcher must decide whether they adopt a longitudinal or cross-sectional perspective. A comprehensive analysis combining both is possible but would require an enormous effort in digitizing the texts and extracting their labels. The design of the recompilation of the data and texts in this study uses a cross-sectional perspective. This is partially due to my own interest and partially due to the current situation of the digitization of Spanish literature, which is acceptable in the decades between 1880 and 1920 but shows important deficiencies in earlier and latter periods (see Section 3.1.9 and especially Figure 21).

One of the general aims of this research study is to observe how these different models and macro-models can fit the real data of the subgenres of the Spanish literature of this period, and which computational tasks can be applied. This will be done in Chapters 7.2 and 8. Aspects including hybridism, disagreement among sources, the multiplicity of labels for a single text, or fuzzy descriptions should be treated as characteristics of the genres, finding a suitable place in the model, rather than being understood as exceptions or particularities of specific cases.

3. Data: Texts and Metadata

3.1 Corpus of Novels of the Spanish *Silver Age*: CoNSSA and CoNSSA-canon

3.1.1 Introduction

In this section, I explain the steps taken to design and create the *Corpus of Novels of the Spanish Silver Age* (CoNSSA), which will be analyzed in the rest of the book. First, I discuss different issues regarding the concept of literary corpora, considering the concept of statistical population and how it can be related to literature. Second, I present the criteria for the stratification of the authors and their selection, and finally the selection of the texts. Third, specific steps about the compilation of the corpus are clarified: use of digital sources and my own digitization, encoding process, validation through XML schema and Schematron, enrichment of structure, and human validation.

This data set has been gathered for the first time. That is why one of the last sections is dedicated to the exploration of the corpus through plots and Descriptive Statistics to have a general view about its content and the typical tendencies of the novel of this period. The goal of the description through Statistics and visualization is, on the one hand, to better understand what the ranges and typical tendencies of the novel of this period are. On the other hand, I plot different values over time to comprehend the general evolution of specific phenomena over time, a point of view that, as I have already discussed, is normally abandoned by the research of this period in favor of each author's specificities (see Section 2.1.2). This part (Section 3.1.9) and one in the next chapter (Section 3.2.11) are the only ones in which a historical and not a cross-sectional perspective is adopted.[1] The reason for that is that in these sections the novel is described in general and not in particular subgenres. The corpus is also briefly compared to other existing literary corpora.

1 See Section 2.3.4 for a discussion about the different perspectives about genre analysis.

3.1.2 Literary Corpora

Linguistics has been designing and collecting big amounts of texts in form of digital corpora for decades, evolving into its own subarea: Corpus Linguistics (Sinclair 1991; McEnery and Wilson 2001; Wynne 2004). This field has coined concepts such as *balance* and *representativeness*, created usual representations like *keywords in context* (KWIC), defined units like *tokens* and *types*, or proposed typologies for corpora. Most of these text collections are internally classified in subsections using information either from the text (language, genre, publishing date, form, etc.) or their producers (typically the author's gender and place of birth).

For a few years, different projects of Digital Humanities led by literary scholars have been gathering large numbers of literary texts, mainly in English and German but also in other languages. The goal of these collections is not only to make texts available to the readers, but to analyze them through digital tools and methods such as Machine Learning (classification, clustering, Deep Learning, dimensionality reduction techniques like topic modeling, stylometry, etc.), or graphs and networks.

How should the literary corpora be designed for digital methods? Since 2017, three different publications have shed light onto this question from different perspectives. The first one is a chapter by Schöch (2017) about the compilation of data sets for the Humanities, with many examples about literature. One of the most interesting aspects of this article is the question about how the data set (for example, a corpus of Spanish novels from the 19th century) reflects the actual object of the study (all Spanish novels from the 19th century), also called *population*. In each research the population must be defined considering criteria like time, place, author, form, canonization and general size of the data set. Second, the data set can be either:

- A *representative sample* (with random selection of cases)
- A *balanced set* (with a minimum number of cases for each possible combination of values of the criteria)
- Or an *opportunistic set* (using as many already digitized cases as possible, the usual case)

The second publication, by Percillier (2017), explores specific aspects (such as scanning and OCR processing) of the compilation of literary corpora and its quantitative analysis after the design and the criteria have already been specified.

The third publication comes from the *Review Journal for Digital Editions and Resources* (RIDE). This journal of reviews about scholarly digital editions has published two issues in 2017 and 2018 (number 6 and 7) about text collections. In their preparation, the editors Henny-Krahmer and Neuber (2017) made the criteria available for the reviewers. Its usefulness is beyond the specific frame of this journal, constituting a remarkable check-list for any new literary corpus. In comparison to the already mentioned studies, this text focuses on the importance of the documentation and transparency of the steps and decisions made, the bibliographic identification of the data set, the purpose of the collection, and its re-usability. Like Schöch (2017), they also highlight questions about the preservation and licensing of the data sets.

3.1.3 Statistical Population of Authors

As mentioned above, the first question is the definition of the statistical population: What is the object that the researcher wants to study? In my case: Which are the Spanish literary novels of this period? A population is "the entire set of people, things, or events that the researcher wishes to study" and they have to be "clearly identified on the basis of some trait" (Evans 1996, 15). A population of literature should be defined by institutions that work with literature, such as libraries, publishers, or literary scholars. From these three, only the last marks explicitly specific works as literature, for example, their treatment by manuals, monographs, and papers about literature. For publishers and libraries, literature is just a section of their material, in many cases without explicit differentiation to other textual groups like essays, history, journalistic texts, etc. For that reason, I only use manuals of Spanish literature to define the different populations that will be presented.

An even better possibility would be to use comprehensive bibliographies of the novel of this period, as Henny-Krahmer does with the novels of Cuba, Mexico, and Argentina (2017). In her research, she utilizes mainly three already published national bibliographies for the period she analyzes. As explained in Chapter 2.1, the period of the Spanish literature I analyze in this work has been treated rather disjointedly, tending to analyze either single authors or generational groups. This is probably the reason why analog general bibliographies for the novel of the entire here analyzed period could not be found.

Instead, I decide to use the most comprehensive and finished manual of Spanish literature that covers the period between 1880 and 1939 in a homogeneous way for the population of authors: *Manual de la Literatura Española* (MdLE) by Pedraza Jiménez and Rodríguez Cáceres (1980). The traits for the definition of the population have to be mentioned in the MdLE and must fulfill the following criteria:

- The author must be from Spain.
- The author must have published:
  - novels, that means prose (not written in verse, not to be performed)[2] fictional works,
  - as independent publication (i.e. a book),
  - in Spanish,
  - between 1880 and 1939.

That means that all authors who only wrote theater, poetry, essay, or journalistic texts are excluded from the population. 107 authors fulfill[3] the criteria and for each of them, the following information is gathered: A full and short version of their name, year of birth and death, gender, amount of dedicated pages in the MdLE, the genre (besides the novel) that the author wrote the most in, and links to searches for the author in digital sources such as the Spanish National Library (BNE), ePubLibre, Archive.org, Cervantes Virtual, Wikisource, Gutenberg Project and Google Books.

This data allowed me to analyze the state of the digitization of this period (Calvo Tello 2017). One of the most important results of this work was to observe that both canonization status and year of the death of the author have moderate correlations with the state of the digitization of the author.[4] This information is important because it will have consequences for the collection of the texts and the definition of the corpus.

2 I do include works that were written in dialogue but are treated and understood as novels (for example *La casa de Aizgorri* or *Paradox, Rey* by Baroja, or *La razón de la sinrazón* or *El abuelo* by Galdós). See Section 2.1.4 for a discussion

3 135 authors wrote some kind of prose.

4 It also shows that the most useful projects to collect texts for quantitative research were Cervantes Virtual, Epub Libre and Archive.org.

The chronological criteria to filter authors does not refer to their lifespan, but to whether their works were published between 1880 and 1939. How does that affect the distribution of the different generations in the population? Is there a homogeneous distribution? Are there many authors that are either much younger or much older in comparison to most authors? To explore that, the decades of the authors' birth and death are plotted in Figure 9.

Figure 9: Bar plot of birth of authors

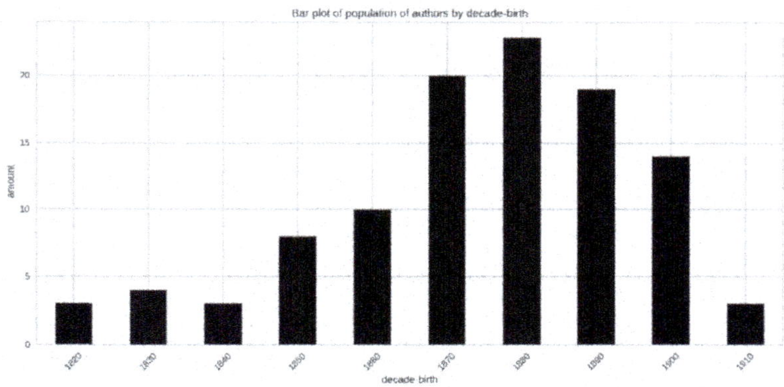

Figure 9 shows that the actual span of dates of birth represents a century, with a distribution skewed to the right with a median[5] of 1881 and a variance, in Interquantile Range (IQR),[6] of 28 years. That means that half of the authors were born between 1853 and 1909. The older authors are over 50 by the year 1880 (the oldest one is José Selgas Carrasco, born in 1822, followed by Juan Valera in 1824), while the youngest author was born in 1917 (Rafael García Serrano). It is surprising that no author born in the 1920s got to publish their first novel before 1939. One of the reasons younger writers might be underrepresented could be explained with the bar plot of Figure 10, with the values of the year of death of the authors:

5 The median is the "middle score in a distribution" and is a better central tendency than the mean in non-Gaussian distribution (Evans 1996, 69–80).

6 "The interquartile range is the range of values that includes the middle 50% of the distribution" (Evans 1996, 83).

Figure 10: Bar plot of deaths over decades

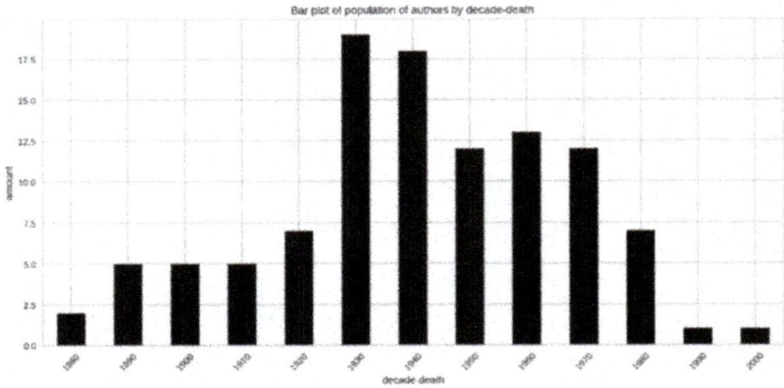

The distribution of Figure 10 resemblances the previous one, with two unexpected high values in the 1930s and 1940s. The median is the year 1945, while the mode[7] of the decades is 1930, with an IQR of 31.5 years, meaning that half of the authors died between 1913 and 1977. Because the average span of life is about 70 years, the decades around 1950 would have been expected to be the ones with the highest values. The reason for this abnormality is arguably the Civil War and its repercussions during the Francoist dictatorship (for example, Miguel Hernández died in prison in 1942). This could also explain why no young writer published novels during the decade of the 1930s: after 1936, the cultural branch could have been affected by the war, a hypothesis that will be tackled later. The span of dates of deaths is even longer than the one of births, covering around 120 years. One interesting aspect is the fact that some authors died shortly after 1880: Selgas Carrasco died in 1882 at 60 years, Rosalía de Castro in 1885 at 48. Therefore, some writers are markedly older than the rest, which means that this population, and therefore the corpus, contains authors related to previous literary periods, and it can be the explanation for some abnormalities observed in Section 8.6.[8]

7 "The most frequently occurring value in a distribution" (Evans 1996, 69).

8 This raises the question if the population should not have two chronological criteria for more homogeneous corpora: one about the author (born after 1839), and another about the works (published between 1880 and 1939).

3.1.4 Statistical Population of Prose

Now that there is a population of authors, the next step is towards a population of texts. Ideally, a population of novels would be the goal now. But as I will clarify, some texts do not show a clear assignment to their main genre: It is unclear whether they are novels, essays, or texts without any general genre (*genreless texts* in Derrida's terminology). That is why, I will first define a population of prose written by the authors defined in the last section. These texts will be analyzed in the following section with the purpose of obtaining a population of novels.

This population is constituted by all prose texts mentioned in the MdLE published between 1880 and 1939 by the authors from the population of authors. From these works, I gather the following information: name of the text, year of publication, main genre[9] (i.e., *novela, cuentos*…), subgenre and dedicated number of pages in the MdLE. This manual contains a total of 1,426 prose works from the authors mentioned in the previous section. From these works, the main genre provided by MdLE is *novela* (English 'novel') with 51% of cases. The next most frequent labels are *ensayo* ('essay') with 15%, *cuentos* ('short stories') with 10%, and *novela corta* ('short novel') with 6%. A group of 62 texts (4% of the population) presents an unclear primary genre, which will be discussed again in the composition of the corpus. Apart from these cases, 14 more labels cover the remaining 34 texts (2% of the population), including, among others: *biografía, crónica, autobiografía, prosa lírica, estampa, greguería, diálogo, memoria, libro infantil, diario, aforismo.*

In the different fields working with corpora, a recurrent criterion for the quality of a text collection is its balance across categories such as genre, decade, author, etc. I have already shown that the prose in the MdLE is extremely skewed: some categories like novel are much more frequent than others, like the essay. Now, I want to examine how do the prose works relate to the different decades. In the following plot of Figure 11, the number of texts of each kind of text is shown by decade. The number of publications analyzed by the MdLE increases constantly. It actually triples from the 1880s to the 1920s, with a remarkable drop in the 1930s, an issue I will address in the next section. What Figure 11 already indicates is the fact that the population of

9 In some cases the MdLE only assigns the genre indirectly, for example, grouping all novels in the same subsections of an author with a reference to the genre in its header.

prose[10] it is not balanced over decades: There are decades with many more texts than others. Trying to create corpora that are balanced chronologically is to distort the object of analysis.

Figure 11: Number of texts over decades differentiating genres

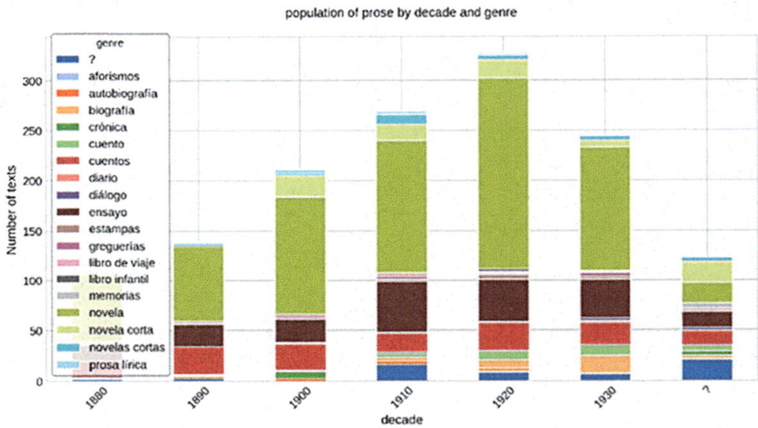

3.1.5 Statistical Population of Novels

From the population of prose, now I am moving to the population of novels: The MdLE contains 727 texts labeled as novels and 62 prose works without any clear information about its genre. That means, the number of novels in the MdLE could be between 727 and 789. In Figure 12, the number of novels treated by the MdLE is plotted over decades. The data of Figure 12 shows a similar distribution of novels over decades as Figure 11, increasing constantly until it reaches its peak in the 1920s: As it happened with the prose, different decades contain very different numbers of novels. The 1930s show again a considerable drop in comparison to the previous decade. I have already mentioned the expected effect that the Civil War could have in the cultural branch, but, is

10 Of course, these values do not represent the total amount of new prose works published over decades, it only exhibits how many works are considered as part of literature, represented by the MdLE.

Figure 12: Bar plot of novels by decades

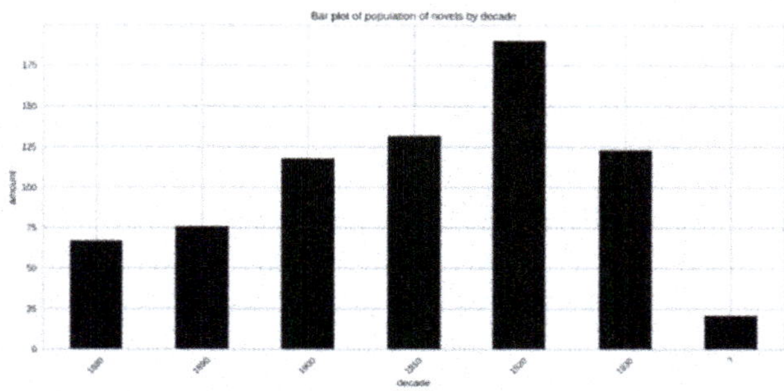

the war the sole explanation? To shed some light on this question, I plot the number of novels per year:

Figure 13: Number of novels over years

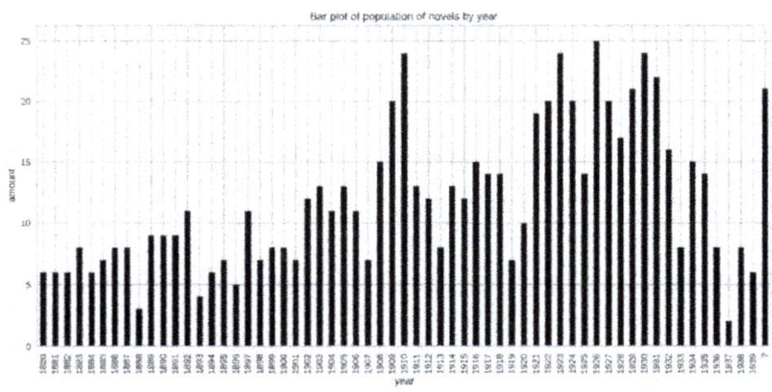

The number of published novels increases constantly until 1910, when one of the highest peaks of the whole period can be observed. The amount stabilizes during the 1910s and increases again at the beginning of the 1920s. What is interesting is that the fall starts before the war breaks out, with decreases between 1933 and 1935. This pattern deteriorates with the start of the war in 1936, with the exceptional low number of only two novels in 1937.[11] Why are there notably fewer novels being published at the beginning of the

11 Martínez Cachero has analyzed the "sterile period of the war" for literature (1984).

1930s than the previous decade? The data gathered for this analysis does not yield a response for that. Ródenas de Moya has defended the idea about the fatigue of the novel in the late years of the Spanish avant-garde (1998, 137; 2000, 67), which could explain the drop at the beginning of the 1930s.[12]The texts marked as novels in the MdLE have been identified. The next step is to observe whether this manual assigns a further label to them, a subgenre, like erotic novel, adventure novel, or naturalist novel.[13] Out of 727, a subgenre label can be identified for 349 cases. In total, this manual uses 88 labels, the most frequent being *novela erótica* (erotic novel) with 38 works (5% of the novel population). This label is followed by five labels between 30 and eight works: *episodio nacional, histórica, naturalista, social, realista, de aventuras*, and *humorística*. The first of this group has been already discussed in the Chapter 2.1 as one of the one-author-labels, similar to historical novels, coined and employed by Galdós. The rest of the labels can be accepted as unproblematic types of novels. After these, there is a long tail of dozens of different labels with very few texts populating them, and many of them are disputable: *de la carne* ('about the flesh'), *de la vida* ('about life'), *sevillanas* ('from Seville'), *sentimental, valenciana* ('from Valencia'), *lírica, de transición* ('of transition'), etc.

At the end of this long tail of the frequency of labels in the MdLE, 65 of the 88 different labels are used for up to three texts. In fact, there are 36 labels that are assigned to a single novel: Either all these are extraordinary single creative works that founded and ended a subgenre, or it is a too differentiated use of labels to categorize texts. That means, the MdLE has a strong tendency to use very specific labels for very few texts with a hand-full of exceptions like erotic, historical, or naturalist novel.

As I have already shown, the several decades contain different numbers of novels. It can now be expected that the different subgenres should be equally distributed throughout the decades in the corpus. Consequently, it should have the same or a similar number of erotic novels, for example, in each decade. But, how is the original data of the population distributed? Does it depart from a balanced situation? To observe this, I plot the most frequent subgenres from the MdLE over decades as a heat map in Figure 14.

---

12 "After 1931, the impression that the novelist renewal enterprise undertaken around 1923 had been ruined took over most of those who had invested their artistic capital in it" (Ródenas de Moya 1998, 137, my translation)

13 In Chapter 3.2 I will present the remaining of the sources, which will be used for the rest of the research study, with its main analysis in Chapter 5.1.

Figure 14: Heat map of correlation between subgenres and decades

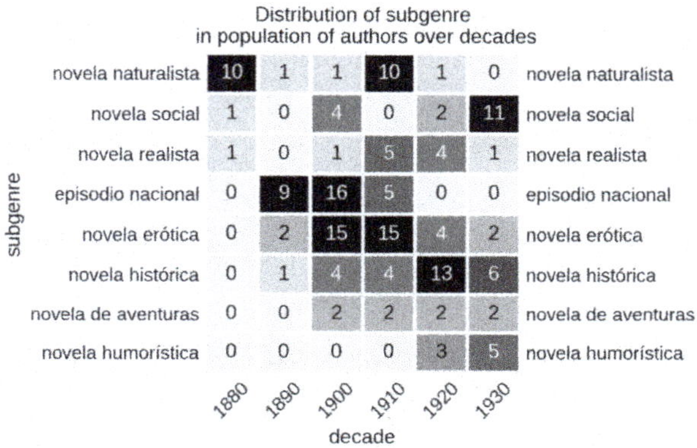

The distribution of subgenres over decades in Figure 14 shows a tendency to contain one or two subgenres that are far more common than the rest during any given decade. This could be expected from labels like naturalist novel, which can be understood as a term that describes a literary period: The naturalist novel would be the novel published at the end of the 19th century. Indeed, naturalist novels are more frequent in the 1880s than in the 1920s or the 1930s, although its frequency in the 1910s is also one of the highest. The most important aspect of this figure is to observe that the naturalist novel does not have a stronger association with a certain decade than the rest. Other subgenres that are not so strongly associated with a literary period do show clear peaks in some decades, such as the social novel in the 1910s, the erotic novel in the 1900s and 1910s, or the historical novel in the 1920s.

The subgenres show correlations with other variables that make it difficult, in many cases even impossible, to balance them and have similar numbers of texts. I have shown why it is not possible to balance subgenres through chronology. As I will discuss at the end of this chapter, this is also the case for the author's gender. This "undesired correlation" (Schöch 2017a, 226) could be seen as an intrinsic phenomenon between categories of literary (or even humanistic) data. Another variable that also shows a strong association with the subgenres is the author, a category that is plotted (only the five most frequent labels) in the heat map of Figure 15.

Figure 15: Heat map of correlation between subgenres and authors

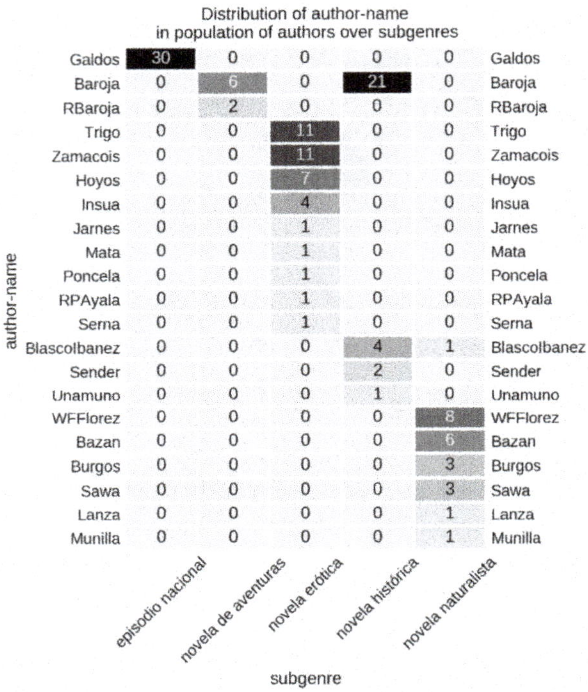

The most common case is to find one or a few authors that are very predominant in the subgenre, with the extreme case of the one-author-label of the *episodio nacional* by Galdós. As Figure 15 shows, the MdLE strongly associates subgenres and authors. Any attempt of trying to balance subgenres and authors would lead to maintain only very few instances, if any at all. The relation between author and genre will be further analyzed in Chapters 5.1, 5.3, and 6.2.

3.1.6 Definition of the Corpora: CoNSSA and CoNSSA-canon

For now, several populations have been discussed and presented. These are the preparatory steps towards a reasoned creation of the corpus. A fundamental decision about the process is the relationship between the statistical population and the actual sample. The standard method in Statistics is *random sampling*, a process that selects instances from a given population by chance (Evans 1996, 197) to "maximize the sample's chance of accurately representing the essential characteristics of the population [...] so that results and conclusions derived from the sample can be validly generalized to the population" (Evans 1996, 22). On this random sample, the researcher can then use Inferential Statistics, "more advanced procedures [than Descriptive Statistics] that enable us to generalize from sample data to population characteristics" (Evans 1996, 26). This method would require to randomly sample a specific number of texts from the population of novels of the MdLE, without considering wether these texts have already been digitized or not. To do that, projects would need to be able to digitize hundreds of texts, regardless of accessibility or difficulty, which is probably one of the reasons why random sampling from a population is extremely rare in the Humanities (digital or not). That is also the reason why I cannot apply it in my research.

The second possible strategy is to create a stratified corpus following the balance of the possible combinations of criteria in the statistical population (Schöch 2017a). This strategy requires to know the criteria that affect the object of study, describe them in the statistical population, and calculate the number of instances in each possible combination of the values. This would have meant in my case the following steps: First, select a number of subgenres that should be studied. Second, obtain the subgenre labels of the entire population. Third, list the criteria that affect the object of study, the subgenre.[14] Forth, obtain these values for the whole population. Fifth, calculate the combination of these values (cells) and get their proportion (i.e., size in the entire population). Sixth, decide a number for the size of the stratified sample. And finally, select (either randomly or in an opportunistic way) the texts that should populate the cells. There are several problems to implement this strategy in the case of my study: It is unclear which subgenres should be considered

14 An open number of aspects like the author's gender, literary genre, canonization, author, year of publication, information about the characters, the plot, the narrator, the setting, etc.

(a question that will be analyzed in Chapter 5.2), which texts are assigned to which subgenre, and whether this assignment should be in categorical terms or in degrees (as in the prototype theory, see Section 2.3.2.4). In addition, it is unknown which criteria affect subgenres and their information to the entire population is inaccessible. And finally, since the classes have strong dependencies as the previous figures showed, it can become impossible to balance all the different aspects.

Since the two standard options seem unfeasible, I decide to follow an alternative two-fold strategy. My goal is to create two different versions of the same corpus, in other words, two samples of the same population, one embedded into the other. To better understand this strategy, I give two examples from different types of instances. The population of Europe can be divided into the different national populations, which itself can be divided into their units: in the case of Germany, the *Bundesländer*. The population of Bavaria, for example, can be divided into their constituent units (cities and regions) and this way we can go deeper until we reach a population so small that a researcher can interview all of its inhabitants, for example, a building. Of course, the smaller the population is, the fewer instances our results will cover and probably the less interesting our outcome will be.

Another example, using now a textual case, is the Bible. This text can be understood as a whole population of verses, chapters, or books the researcher is interested in. Inside, there are two main groups of books: The Old and the New Testament, that the investigator can understand also as populations, populations within a greater population. Inside, there are smaller groups of books like the Gospels, Pentateuch, Paul's letters, that, again, can be seen as a third level of populations. A step further, each book can be seen as a whole population of verses. Depending on their goal, the researcher can choose any population (from the whole Bible to a single book), and then decide whether they wants random samples from it, or get the data from the entire population. In the first case, the researcher would use Inferential Statistics in the sample to get generalizations about the entire population; in the second case, they would use Descriptive Statistics since the entire population is available.

This provides a third possibility for the Humanities[15] besides random and stratified samples: obtain the entire population that can be completely digitized. The fact that for social and medical sciences the study of smaller pop-

15 For other areas, such as medicine there are other possibilities such as random assignment.

ulations is normally not the goal (Evans 1996, 14), can differ for the Humanities. In fields like Literature, Art History, Theology, or Philosophy (and in many cases in Linguistics), the most common goal is to analyze relatively small data sets (not greater than a hundred cases) with instances that had a remarkable impact on culture. The sample would contain all instances of the population; in other words, population and sample are the same and therefore the researchers can use Descriptive Statistics in their data (Evans 1996, 25–26).

For the case of the Spanish novel between 1880 and 1939, the largest population of texts I am considering is the prose works mentioned in the MdLE. I do not argue that this population is the greatest of its kind. Other possibilities could imply trying to obtain all novels mentioned in at least one manual of literature (from a closed list), or even all original novels published in Spain by Spanish authors between 1880 and 1939. These could be seen as the largest population of novels of the period, and despite their great interest, the costs of obtaining them would be too large for a dissertation. Therefore, I am using as a base the largest documented population that I have access to.

From this population of prose works mentioned in the MdLE, I create a smaller population of canonized novels, following the criteria that will be explained in the next section. This smaller population is called *CoNSSA-canon* and it neither contains all the novels of the period, nor all the novels mentioned in the MdLE, but it does contain all the most canonized novels. That is why the CoNSSA-canon is an interesting object of study to analyze this part of the Spanish literature: It can be understood as a corpus that exactly maps one statistical population of canonized novels, and therefore can be analyzed through Descriptive Statistics.

That is the first of the two corpora that my strategy seeks. I design another sample also based on the statistical population of novels in the MdLE, called *CoNSSA*. This one is an opportunistic sample in its size (it contains as many texts as possible) but stratified through authorship, canonization, and decades. The advantage of having CoNSSA and CoNSSA-canon is that I can test hypotheses in both, and see whether a specific tendency is only perceptible in the canonized population, only in the opportunistic sample (and therefore possibly a result of the bias of compilation), or in both; if so, it would be reasonable to think that it is a general pattern of the novels of this period. The population of prose in the MdLE contains CoNSSA, and CoNSSA contains CoNSSA-canon, similarly to the example of the people of Europe of the verses in the Bible. To understand the exact relations and number of texts better, they can be plotted as in Figure 16.

Figure 16: Representation of number of texts in the corpora and populations

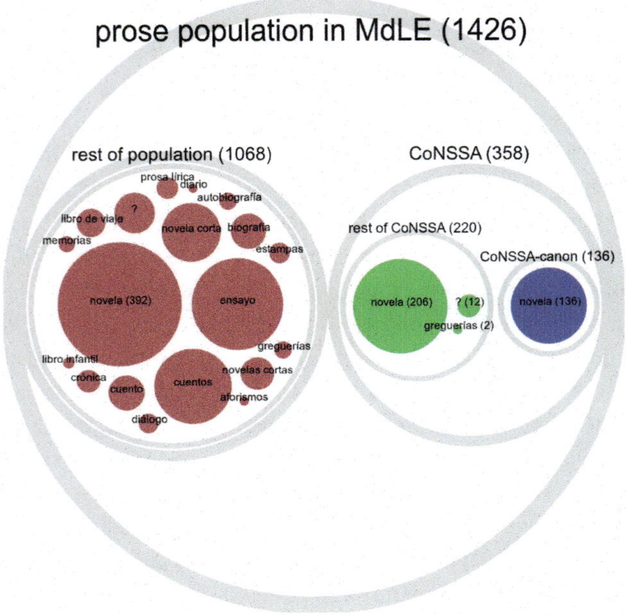

All the texts are contained in the largest population I am considering: the prose population of the MdLE, with 1,426 texts. From this population, I gathered 358 texts, which constitute the corpus CoNSSA, in general an opportunistic corpus with certain stratification, as will be explained in the following section. It contains a total of 344 novels, which constitute around 47.3% of the total of novels in the population of prose. Inside CoNSSA, there are 136 that can be understood as the most canonized novels, which constitute the CoNSSA-canon, a corpus that maps the statistical population of the canonized novels. At the same time, the remaining 206 novels and a group of 14 texts with unclear genre make up the rest of the CoNSSA.

3.1.7 Criteria for Selection

In this section, I want to specify the exact criteria that the texts need to exhibit to be considered part of the canon of the novels, and therefore be eligible to form part of the CoNSSA-canon. Each novel has to fulfill both criteria:

- It must be mentioned in two manuals of Spanish literature (the already mentioned MdLE and the *Historia de la Literatura Española* (HdLE), edited by Mainer, 2010).
- The description in the MdLE must be at least one page long.

These criteria cover a minimal consensus on both, and retain only those works that occupy more space in terms of pages. There are two reasons why the MdLE and not the HdLE appears in both criteria: first, this manual is the most comprehensive; second, it is substantially more structured than the HdLE.[16]Once the definition of CoNSSA-canon is concluded, I design the stratification of CoNSSA. As already mentioned, the canonization has a measurable correlation with the state of digitization of the author (Calvo Tello 2017). Besides, canonization reflects how important the author is for Literary Studies. These are one practical and one theoretical reason to use canonization as the most important criterion of composition of CoNSSA: The corpus contains a larger proportion of the production of the most canonized authors. To formalize that, I need the total number of novels written by each author, plus the canonization status of both author and text. For this, I use again the number of pages used in the MdLE, which is organized in six ranges. To each of these, I assigned a minimum proportion of novel production that the corpus needs to include from each author:

16 While the information about the pages for each novel is to be found in the ToC of the MdLE, the HdLE is rather structured as an essay, going back and forth between different texts, authors, and topics.

Table 1: Number of pages and minimum percentages of each author's work in the corpus

Range	Number of pages in MdLE	Proportion of novel production	Number of Authors in range
1	41 - 180	80 %	13
2	21 -40	60 %	7
3	11 - 20	40 %	8
4	6 -10	20 %	8
5	3 - 5	10 %	17
6	<1 - 2	0 %	33

These percentages are chosen to try to maximize the number of novels in the corpus, considering also the limitations of the project. Authors with fewer than ten pages tend to be digitized very poorly, and the manuals cover the information about their texts scarcely. In fact, most texts of the lower ranges were digitized manually, a costly step in terms of money and time.

There were some extra criteria applied to a few authors for specific historical reasons:

- In the case of authors with an extraordinary large production during this period (Baroja with 55 novels, Galdós with 63), the number of texts collected was limited to 35. This number is still higher than the production of other writers (like Blasco Ibáñez with 31) and avoids a too large proportion of the corpus from only two authors.
- The MdLE analyzes in its volumes of Spanish literature the Nicaraguan author Rubén Darío. He spent a long period of his life in Spain, influencing other authors there remarkably and becoming the most important writer of the modernist movement. For these reasons and the presence in the MdLE, I decided to also collect texts from him. Darío started different prose projects, without ending any of them: *El hombre de oro, El oro de Mallarco, La vida de Rubén Darío.*
- Four authors with extraordinary influence wrote very few texts in prose, that were not published as books: Lorca (*Fray Antonio* and *Historia vulgar*), Miguel Hernández (*La tragedia de Calisto*), Maeztu (*La guerra del Transvaal*) and Ganivet (*Los trabajos del infatigable creador Pío Cid*).

- *Baza de Espadas*, by Valle-Inclán, was not published as a book during its authors life, but only in magazines in 1932, his sole novel in that decade.

All these texts are marked explicitly as exceptions in their metadata and none of them are part of the CoNSSA-canon, which does not contain any exception. Thus, they can be automatically ignored or used for specific purposes.

The 14 works whose genre is unclear also belong exclusively to CoNSSA, and they contain some of the most influential works of this period, such as *La lámpara maravillosa* and *La media noche* by Valle-Inclán, *Platero y yo* and *Diario de un poeta* by Ramón Jiménez, *De un cancionero apócrifo* and *Juan de Mairena* by Antonio Machado, or two editions of the *Greguerías* by Gómez de la Serna. Some of them contain certain chapters belonging clearly to one genre, and others to different ones (such as poetry and prose, like in *De un cancionero apócrifo* or *Diario de un poeta*). But the majority of them represent an intrinsic mix of genres across chapters. The main genre of these works will be analyzed in Chapter 3.3.

Once the number of novels per author was defined, I have to choose which novels of each author should be digitized for the CoNSSA. In this step, I could have just followed practical criteria about the digitized status, or the price of editions. Instead, I tried to define several criteria in order to increase the representativity for the entire production of the author. These criteria are the following:

- Preference for the most canonized texts of each author.
- Representation of the different periods, subgenres, and groups of texts by each author.
- Relative balance of decades over the complete population of novels.

The second criterion seeks to cover the different styles from one and the same author, especially as far as the very prolific ones are concerned. For example, Baroja wrote in different genres (adventures, dialogue, historical, sentimental), grouping them together in different *series* (*La lucha por la vida, La raza, Las ciudades, Memorias de un hombre de acción...*), and his writing stretches over four decades of the analyzed period (1900-1939). The selected texts for the CoNSSA intend to represent all these facets.

In some cases, the previous criteria are not enough to choose one text over another. In those cases, I considered the digitized status and format, favoring the following aspects:

1. Descriptiveness of format (best case: TEI XML)
2. Citations of digitized edition and explanation of their edition
3. Institutionalization of the editing project
4. Full-text documents (for example, one ePUB file instead of several pages in HTML)

Figure 17: Distribution over decades of the population, CoNSSA and CoNSSA-canon

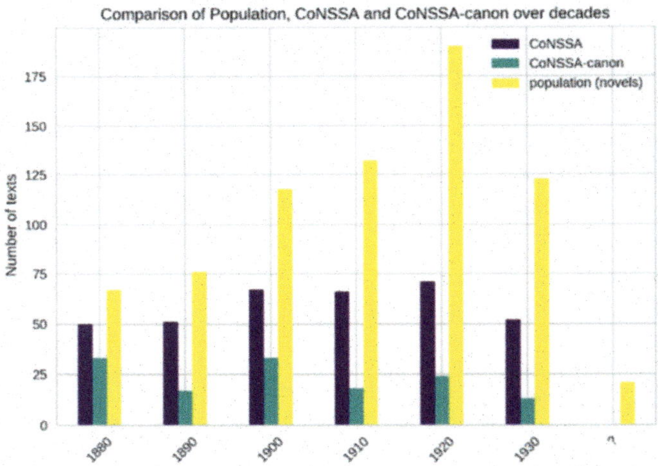

Figure 17 shows the distribution of population of novels in the MdLE, CoNSSA and CoNSSA-canon over decades. The lengths of the bars of CoNSSA-canon and CoNSSA are more similar between them, while the population of novels shows a different tendency, with the highest peak in the 1920s. For its part, the CoNSSA-canon has a peak in the decades of the 1880s and the 1900s. This shows that, while more texts published in the 1920s are treated by Literary Studies, the most influential works were published either in the 1880s or the 1900s. Depending on whether the researcher is using quantitative or qualitative criteria, they will find different shapes of corpora. The distribution of CoNSSA seems closer to the population of novels, though it displays a plateau between 1900 and 1920. The reason for that difference between the total population and the CoNSSA is the difficulty of accessing digitized texts published after 1910, something that will be explained in the following section.

3.1.8 Digitization Steps

The corpus is encoded in XML (as recommended in Percillier 2017) using the Text Encoding Initiate (TEI, recommended in Agenjo 2015; Schöch 2017). The step between the input format (normally HTML or similar) to TEI is implemented in Python scripts using mainly regular expressions. In the cases where no markup is found, I used PDF documents processed with the OCR Software by the company Abbyy (FineReader and Recognition Server). They were then exported as HTML files,[17] joining the rest of the workflow mentioned before.

Once the TEI XML is well-formed, the elements *div* were encoded with a type attribute to distinguish the different levels of text units, with the following possible values:

- *section*: smaller unit than chapter[18]
- *chapter*: most common division of text (mandatory in every file)[19]
- *part*: greater unit than chapters (holonym of chapter)
- *division*: holonym of parts[20]

The Table of Content of the digital source was compared to the digital Table of Content of the XML file (called *outlier* in the program Oxygen XML Editor) to control whether the file has lost spans of text during the conversion. In the cases in which the text was digitized by the project, the PDF was also controlled to avoid mistakes and mark textual elements, such as poems or floating texts.

After that, the metadata of the texts were manually assigned. An abstract of the book is copied (if available, quoting the source), or composed (if I personally read the book) in the *abstract* element of the header. From this infor-

17 To be more specific, headers and footers were not exported, but the CSS information was exported in order to use it for the conversion into TEI.

18 In some cases, it can also contain sections. The divs inside a floatingText were also marked as sections.

19 Normally starting with a header, in many cases sequential.

20 Just in some cases, like the novel El laberinto de las sirenas, by Baroja.

mation, the metadata about the text is assigned, an aspect that will be discussed in Chapter 3.2. A script measured specific area aspects of the text and TEI elements, placing this information in the header as well. Finally, the file was validated using an XML Schema and a Schematron, which is published as GitHub repository.

3.1.9 Description of the Corpus

In this section, several aspects of CoNSSA and CoNSSA-canon will be described. Firstly, because these data sets have been gathered for the first time, so a brief description can be useful to delimit the results of this research and compare it to other corpora. But an even more important reason that will be crucial in Chapter 3.2 is that a description of CoNSSA and CoNSSA-canon offers a sharper picture of the novel of this period. The goal of this research study is to analyze the subgenres of these novels. By knowing what the ranges and central tendencies of the novel during this period are, further ahead, it will be easier to identify whether specific features are just part of the evolution of the novel during the *silver age*, or whether they are specific for a given subgenre.

As already mentioned, the CoNSSA corpus contains 358 texts, with a total of 344 cases clearly belonging to the novel. This data set represents 47% of the population of novels as described in Section 3.1.5. It contains 26.7 million tokens, including 4 million typographical ones. In contrast, CoNSSA-canon contains 137 texts, 19% of the total of the population of novels, with 11.5 million tokens (including 1.8 million typographical ones).

The proportion of the texts per author following its canonization (as described in Table 1) was achieved, as shown in Figure 18.

The more pages the MdLE uses for an author, the higher is the proportion of their works in the corpus. However, for many writers that means 100% of their novels, especially for either those authors with more than 40 pages in the MdLE or who wrote five works or fewer. The median of coverage per author is 86%, with an IQR of 50%. The two data points in the above scatter plot on the right bottom corner are canonized author with a lower proportion than 80%. These exceptionally low values are the unusual cases of Baroja and Galdós, who, as already explained, produced an extraordinary large number of works and their influence in the corpus had to be controlled.In the last section of this chapter, I will report on the difficulty of balance of author's gender in the

Figure 18: Scatter plot of amount of pages (as proxy for canonization) and proportion of novels written by the authors that are in CoNSSA

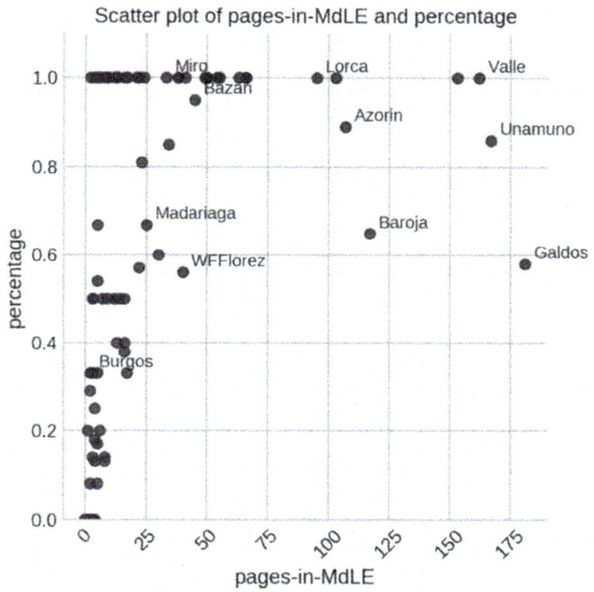

corpus. I have already shown how categories such as subgenres, authors, or decades are not evenly distributed. Actually, there are no reasons to assume that other categories will be distributed equally. That is also the case when the geographical distribution of authors is analyzed. The information about the birth and death of the authors can be plotted over a map of the country to understand its geographical dispersion better, and to know which regions are over or underrepresented. For that, I used the information available in Wikidata (using the identifiers from the Spanish National Library), converted the places of birth and death to geolocations, and plotted them in a map using the DARIAH Geo-Browser.[21] In the next figure, the birthplaces of the authors are shown in orange, and their place of death in purple:

Figure 19: Place of birth (orange) and death (purple) of authors of the corpus. Detail around Spain.

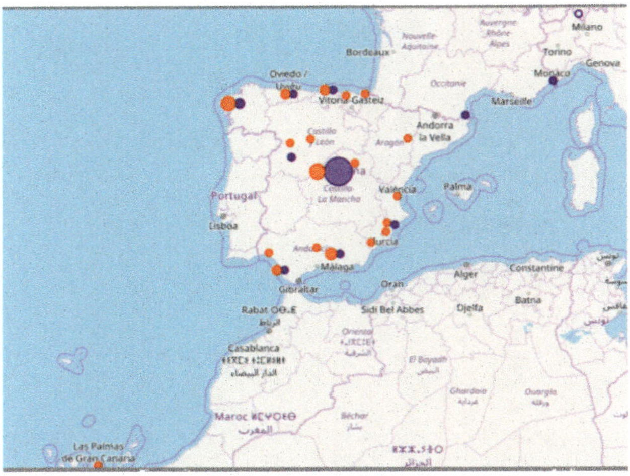

In this map, certain historical phenomena become evident: Madrid is the place where most authors are born, and even more so, where they tend to end their days. On the other side, other regions are clearly underrepresented, especially Catalonia. The geographical places of birth and death are two other examples that demonstrate that almost nothing is balanced in a literary corpus, and that it is reasonable to expect that other sociological variables will behave similarly.[22] What is the distribution of texts per author? Each author has two texts in median, a mode of one, and an IQR of four. That means, half of the authors have between one and six texts in the corpus, being the most typical case a single work. There are 14 exceptionally prolific authors of this

21 Under following link, the data can be visualized interactively in the Geo-Browser: https://geobrowser.de.dariah.eu/?csv1=https://cdstar.de.dariah.eu/dariah/EAEA0-BAFE-5928-4084-0&csv2=https://cdstar.de.dariah.eu/dariah/EAEA0-10BC-53B8-80DA-0.

22 Mainer mentions the fact that most authors came from the middle class, with very few cases of authors who were born in lower social strata (Mainer 2010, 148–49).

period: Azorín, Baroja, Bazán, Blasco Ibáñez, Concha Espina, Galdós, Lanza, Miró, Pereda, Pérez de Ayala, Serna, Valdés, Valle-Inclán, and Fernández Flórez.

Figure 17 with the distribution of the population of novels, CoNSSA, and CoNSSA-canon over decades, shows that it has not been possible to mantain in CoNSSA the high peak during the 1920s that is visible in the population. To explain this failure, Figure 20 shows the association between sources of digitized texts and decades:

Figure 20: Amount of texts over decades, distinguishing source of text

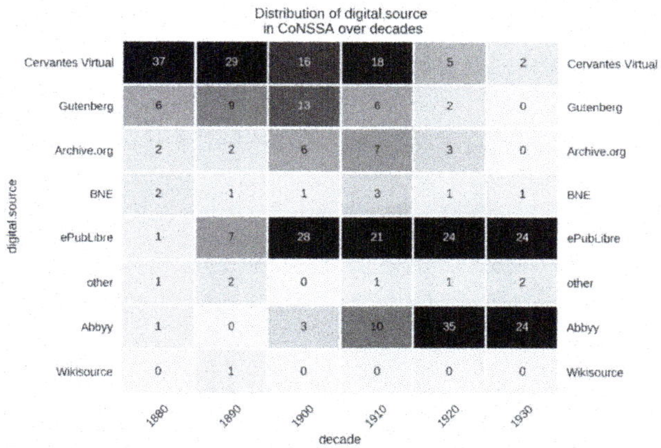

While the great majority of texts of the first decades have been extracted from Cervantes Virtual and Gutenberg Project, those numbers descend notably with time. Already for the 1900s, ePubLibre becomes one of the most important sources, moving towards my own digitization (Abbyy) in the 1920s. Almost all texts of the 1930s come either from ePubLibre or from my own digitization. In order to represent in CoNSSA the high peak of the 1920s that is perceivable in the population, it would have been necessary to digitize another 100 novels, something the project was not able to carry out. A look at the former heat map shows that, for this period of 60 years, the most useful sources change completely: while Cervantes Virtual and Gutenberg Project are enough to analyze the 19th century, they are entirely insufficient for the 20th century. The explanation for this change is, on the one side, the copyright, which in Spain lasts 80 years after the author's death: The industrial rights of writers who died in 1936 expired in 2017. The later a text was published, the more probable is that its author still retains the copyright. On the other side, Gutenberg Project and Cervantes Virtual are projects which started some decades ago, meaning their legal limits are not representative of the current frontier of copyright, but rather of that some decades earlier.

Another aspect that I would like to observe is the standard values of some units of the novels, such as tokens and chapters: What is the expected length of novels of the *silver age*, both in tokens and chapters? What are the central tendencies and how do they typically deviate? Are 19th-century novels longer or shorter than the ones from the 20th century? The length in tokens as a histogram is shown in Figure 21.

Figure 21: Histogram of number of tokens

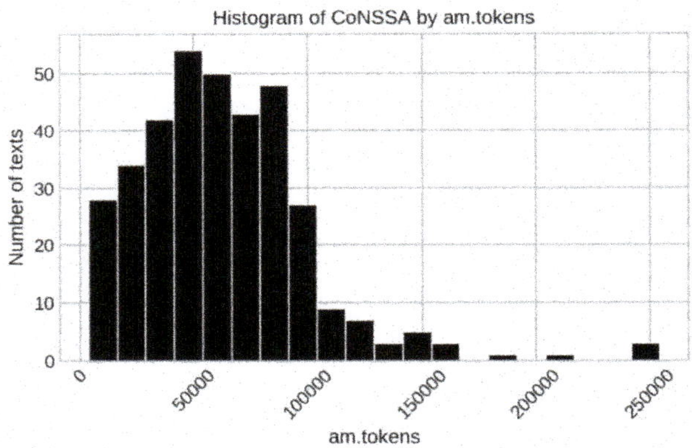

The historgam shows a Poisson distribution with a median around 60,000 tokens and an IQR of 47,000 tokens. To compare these values to known texts of the period, *Juan de Mairena* by Machado (57,000 tokens) or *El árbol de la ciencia* by Baroja (63,000 tokens) are close to this central tendency. The shortest text still labeled as a novel (*Erika ante el invierno*, 1930, by Francisco de Ayala) has less than 4,000 tokens, while the longest (first volume of *Araña Negra*, 1892, by Blasco Ibáñez) has 252,000 tokens.[23] It is not surprising to see that the

23 Overall, there were three novels with extreme values regarding their length: *La Regenta* by Clarín, *Fortunata y Jacinta* by Galdós and *Araña Negra* by Blasco Ibáñez. These three

longest novel was published in the 19th century, while the shortest one is from the 1930s. In fact, novels become overall shorter during this period, which can be observed in the next scatter plot. This tendency takes place both in the CoNSSA (Pearson's r = - 0.24***)[24] and even stronger in the CoNSSA-canon (Pearson's r = - 0.45***). In the case of CoNSSA, the novels become 562 tokens shorter every year on average (that means, that is the slope of the regression analysis) on a regression analysis, while the reduction for the CoNSSA-canon is of 989 characters annually. More details can be found in the Jupyter Notebook.

Figure 22 shows a measurable effect that affects the novel of this period, which can be observed using only basic data such as the novels' year of publication, and the length of the text in tokens: The novels of this period become statistically shorter, with this tendency being even more distinct in the case of the canonized texts. That means, texts belonging to typical subgenres of the 19th century (such as realist or naturalist novels) are expected to be longer than the ones belonging to categories of the end of the period (such as social or comedy novels). Besides the results about the data, this shows how the strategy with the nested corpus can operate: the two versions of the same corpus can be used to evaluate a phenomenon, paying attention to whether it is observable only in the opportunistic and bigger version, or also in the smaller, better controlled canonized population. Ródenas de Moya postulated that prose texts of the later period become shorter over time (2000, 49), but this analysis shows that this process actually starts before the 1930s, and that it is a general pattern in novels.

The entire text is not the only textual unit that becomes shorter in this period. A similar effect is observable at the level of sentences. To measure this, I calculated the median length of sentences of each novel in tokens. After that, I created a data point for each novel and plotted it as a scatter plot in Figure 23.

Figure 23 shows that sentences become shorter during the entire period. In fact, the slope shows that they become one character shorter annually,

---

texts were actually published in different volumes and even each individual volume still constitutes some of the longest novels of the corpus. Considering the particularities of their publication and with the aim of having a more homogeneous length of texts, these three novels are represented in the corpus by their volumes: two for *La Regenta* and *Araña Negra*, and four for *Fortunata y Jacinta*.

24 I follow the convention of the social sciences of using one asterisk if the p-value is smaller than a 5%; two asterisks if < 1% and three asterisks if < 0.1%.

Figure 22: Scatter plot with regression line of length of novels in tokens over years

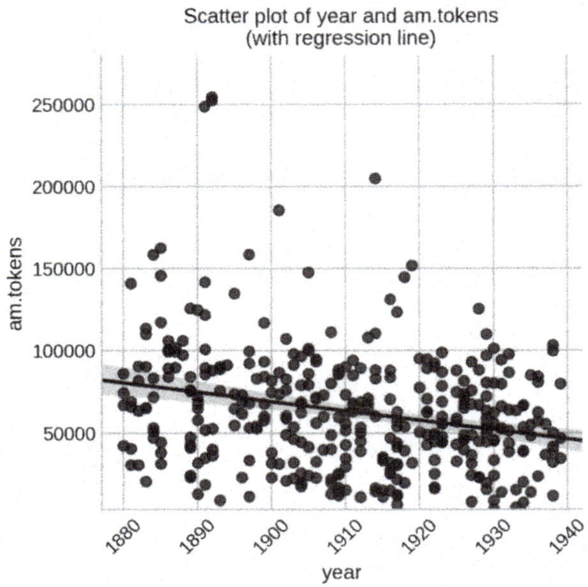

and this happens both in the entire version of the corpus CoNSSA (slope of - 0.97*** characters per year), and in the smaller CoNSSA-canon (slope of - 1.2*** characters per year).

A textual element that has been explicitly annotated in the corpus is poetry. The median number of poems in the novels is one, with an IQR of four. This means that, although there is often no poem at all in a novel, embedded poetry is not an exception but actually the norm. That is an unexpected result that raises further questions: Are these poems original compositions of the author? Are they quotations from other works? If so, from which periods, authors, and languages? Does the style of these poems resemble the poetry published during this period? These questions are beyond the scope of this research, but they highlight the advantages of well-structured corpora and their statistical description.

Figure 23: Scatter plot of the length of sentences (median) over time in CoNSSA

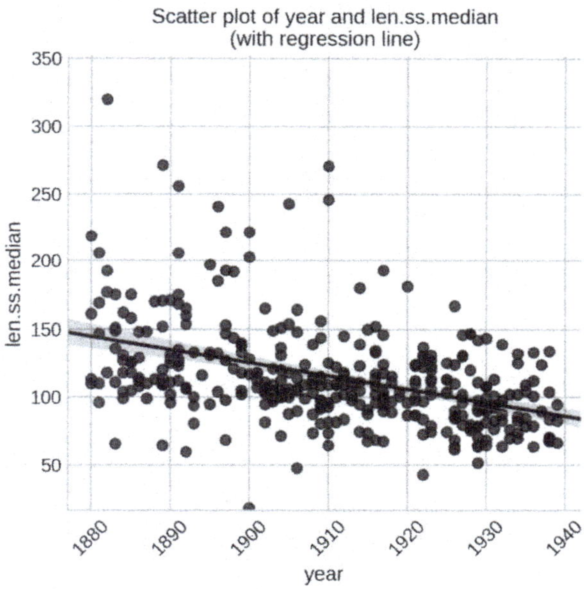

As already mentioned, the corpus contains more than 20 million tokens. If this value is compared to other literary corpora in Spanish, the result can be seen in Figure 24.

As it can be seen in Figure 24, IMPACT (novels of the Golden Age), TESO (theater of the same period) and CoNSSA-canon are quite similar in number of tokens, with sizes around 10 million tokens. The complete version of CoNSSA duplicates that. Two of the corpora created by the Real Academia de la Lengua (RAE), CREA and CORDE, comprise important parts of literary texts.[25] CORDE specifies the exact amount of tokens used for narrative prose: about 31 million. CREA only reports the number of tokens for a broader

25 The last corpus of the Academia, CORPES, does not contain a section of literary text, therefore it does not appear in the illustration.

Figure 24: Number of tokens (millions) in Spanish literary corpora, distinguish format (purple = TEI XML, blue = XHTML; yellow = plain text)

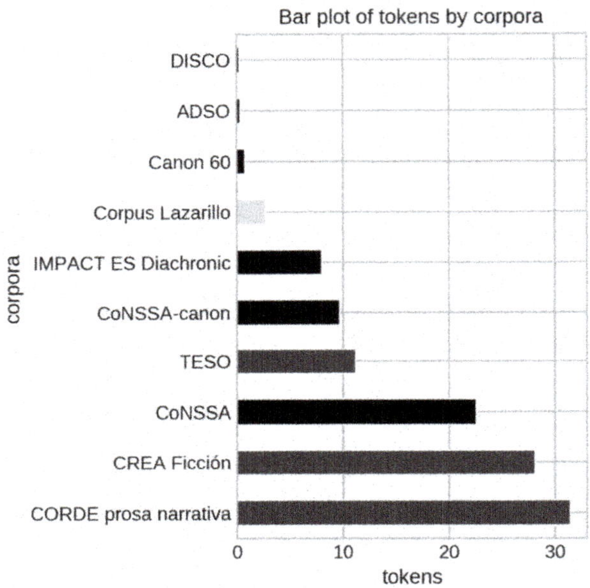

category, that is, fiction: about 28 million. That means that CoNSSA represents around two-thirds of the biggest literary corpora in Spanish. That makes the CoNSSA one of the largest resources of literary texts in Spanish, and the largest corpus for Spanish novels, encoded in TEI XML, as well as for the period between 1880 and 1939.

Thanks to this description of CoNSSA, one of the largest corpora of literary texts in Spanish, a sharper picture of the novel of this period is now available: The basic metadata of texts and authors show strong associations, the mean novel of this period has 60,000 tokens, it tends to have poetry embedded, and both texts and sentences became consistently shorter over this period.

3.1.10 Gender Distribution

One of the expected requirements for corpora in the last decades is a balance between genders: Texts by female and male authors should represent similar or equal proportions of the corpus to be representative for their societies. As I have explained, my corpus follows the statistical population obtained in the MdLE. What does the gender balance look like in this source? From the 107 authors of novels analyzed for the period between 1880 and 1939 by the MdLE, 100 are male and only seven are female: Bazán, de Burgos, de Castro, Chacel, Concha Espina, Mulder, and Sinués. That means that the literary source for the population of authors contains only 6.5% of female authors, leaving 93.5% for male authors. The number of men is clearly overrepresented in this manual.

But what about the female authors that did get into the canon? Are they undervalued in comparison to men? Are they somehow treated as less important authors? To answer that, I again employ the number of pages dedicated to each author as an approximation for canon: The more space literary scholars utilized to discuss an author, the more important she or he is, the more canonized.[26] In Figure 25, the authors are ordered by the number of pages, with the gender encoded in the color of the bar.[27]

Although no female author is in the top ten, Bazán at least makes it in the top twenty. Then there are female authors in the medium range of the canon (de Castro, Chacel, and Concha Espina) and finally some among the less canonized writers (not shown in the figure: de Burgos, Mulder, and Sinués). For both genders, the MdLE has a median of 5 pages.[28] Therefore, the data shows that it is harder for women to get into the canon, but once they do, they are treated similar to men, at least in the MdLE.

For now, I am analyzing the gender distribution in the population of authors, but how does it translate into the population of novels? And how do these values change over time?

In total, male authors wrote 673 novels (92.6%) in contrast to the 54 texts by female ones (7.4%). Figure 26 shows that the total number of works by female authors over the decades remains stable, meaning that the proportion

---

26 Similar quantitative approaches have been already used by different scholars.

27 I set a cutoff of more than three pages in order to get a figure that fits the page, with 64 authors.

28 IQR of 13 for female authors, 21.5 for male.

Figure 25: Amount of pages in MdLE for each author (>4 pages)

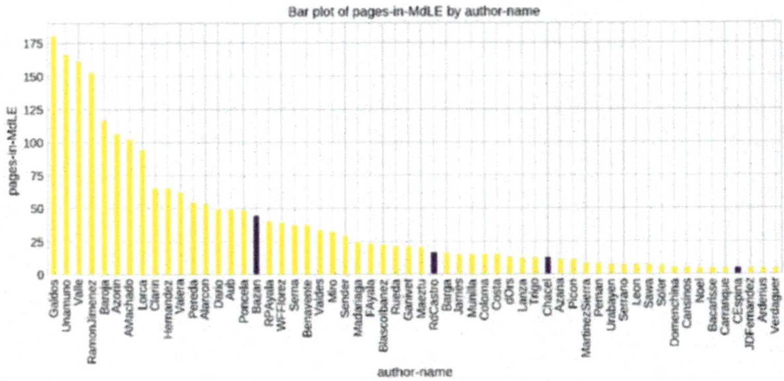

Figure 26: Bar plot of novels over decades differentiating author's gender

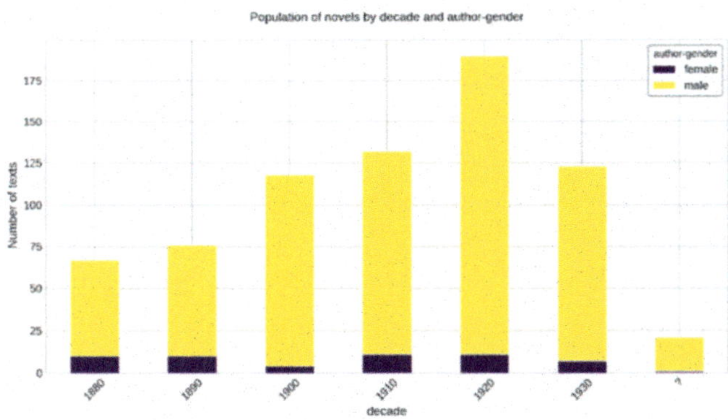

becomes smaller: While in the 1880s female authors write about 15% of the novels, this number drops to 6% in the 1920s and 1930s.[29] The population does not get more balanced in terms of the author's gender in the latter decades, quite the opposite. This is even more surprising if we consider the tremendous

29 These values are strongly affected by the fact that Bazán wrote a large amount of works at the end of the 19th century.

advance in female literacy that took place in those years (de Gabriel Fernández 1997): More women were learning to write and read, but they had fewer chances to get into the literary canon. Since I am using this data as the base for the CoNSSA, it will also underrepresent female authors. In fact, 8.1% of the texts in CoNSSA are written by women, a similar proportion to the one from the MdLE, although slightly higher.

In a recent paper, the researcher Juana María González has studied the journal *Índice literario*, which published reviews of literary works between 1932 and 1936 (González 2021). One of the aspects that she analyzes is the distribution of the authors' gender, arguing that this journal was a progressive publication with women among the publishing board. However, in her study González finds that the number of texts written by women reviewed in this journal is surprisingly low: around 6% in total, 11% in the case of the novels. As it can be observed, the distribution in the MdLE and in the CoNSSA are similar to these results.

There is a clear gender bias, but who exactly is preferring men to women? Who is the source of this injustice? The male and female researchers who wrote the MdLE? I? Researchers of literature in general? Only the ones from Spain? Is it a general problem of Academia? The publishing houses of those decades? Cultural agents who influenced the canonization process? The readers? Their sense of literariness or literary quality (cfr. Koolen 2018)? These questions are definitely beyond the reach of this publication, but one fact is certain: What is currently considered the Spanish novel between 1880 and 1939 is clearly dominated by male authors. Balancing corpora in terms of author's gender is not a question about effort or size of the corpus, but about the concept of population and, ultimately, what is considered literature. Achieving a more balanced scenario of past periods will modify profoundly our concept of literature, a virtuous goal for several cultural actors, including researchers and Academia in general. However, these revisions cannot be expected as by-products of studies of whose main goal has no relation with the author's gender.

3.1.11 Publication of Data

The publication of the data was important for my project and for the entire CliGS project. A section of the CoNSSA was made available in early phases of the project as a part of the *textbox*, a series of corpora in French, Spanish, Italian, and Portuguese. See Schöch et al. (2019) for a description of the corpora and Calvo Tello, Henny-Krahmer, and Schöch (2018) for several comparative analyses.

Similarly to the textbox, the CoNSSA is made available as a GitHub repository.[30] In contrast to the textbox, a section of the texts in the CoNSSA is still under copyright. This restricts the publication of the whole text. For this reason, the CoNSSA has several folders depending on the legal status of the texts. Besides the GitHub repository, the corpus has also been archived in the European platform Zenodo (Nielsen 2013).[31]As the repository states, the texts themselves are in the public domain. They are provided here with the Public Domain Mark Declaration and can be re-used without restrictions. The TEI XML markup and the metadata are published with a Creative Commons Attribution 4.0 International license CC-BY. The repository also contains a suggestion as to how other researchers can reference the corpus.

For those texts whose authors died at least 80 years ago, three versions of the texts are made available: the master format in TEI XML, the annotated format also in TEI XML, and a simpler file that only contains the *body* element saved as plain text. Around 61% of the CoNSSA (217 novels) is published in this manner.

A recent interdisciplinary article with a focus in Germany has proposed a series of extracted features that can be published even when the texts are still protected by copyright (Schöch et al. 2020). Following this article, I have decided to publish not the entire text but a selection of extracted linguistic features for all the texts that can either be published without restriction or that I digitized myself. These files are saved as tables (CSV files). In these files, each row represents a text, and each column a different feature. Among other features, the researchers can find the frequency in the entire text of tokens (tokenized in different manners), semantic annotation, grammatical annotation, entity information, or TEI tags (see Chapter 4.1 for more details). By that, the most relevant features are made available, covering almost 78% of the entire CoNSSA (279 novels).

One part of the CoNSSA that I am able to publish for the entire corpus is the metadata. Given that the metadata consists of formalized information about the texts annotated by myself, it is not copyright protected. The metadata available also contains the information about the source of the digital

30 https://github.com/cligs/conssa/.

31 https://doi.org/10.5281/zenodo.4674257.

text. This means that even in the cases where I am not able to publish neither the entire text nor extracted features, I am providing the source of the digital text. Reconstructing the remaining 22% of the texts is a feasible task for other researchers.

Besides, as time passes, I plan to publish more and more texts when the moving window of 80 years after the author's date of death allows it. For example, the novels of the following authors will be made available freely as part of the CoNSSA in the coming years: José Diaz Fernández (2022), Miguel Hernández (2023), Ricardo León, and Félix Urabayen (2024). On the one hand, this will slowly increase the proportion of the available CoNSSA as years pass by. On the other hand, this means that, with the current strategy, the entire corpus will be in theory only fully available by the end of the 21st century (Francisco de Ayala died in 2009).

3.2 Metadata

3.2.1 Introduction

In the previous chapter, I have presented the definition of the corpus. Why should it contain metadata? What kind of metadata is needed to study the subgenre of novels? How can it be collected and validated? What are the general tendencies of metadata between 1880 and 1939? These four questions lead this chapter. Metadata is knowledge about the text, formalized in a way that it is computationally accessible. In that sense, metadata is the way of connecting non-digital research about literature with digital methods. This information can be incorporated into algorithms and tools in different ways: On the one hand, it can be taken as categories in Machine Learning tasks (either to evaluate methods as I will do in Chapter 6.2 or to classify unlabeled cases, as it will be the case in Chapter 3.3). On the other hand, it can be employed as features to classify more complex categories like genre (see Chapter 7.2), or to analyze its relation with other categories or textual features (see Chapter 8 and the Appendix).

For this purpose, I have annotated CoNSSA with numerous kinds of metadata: information about literary genres and subgenres (which sources have assigned which labels of each text), information about literary phenomena like narrator, setting, type of ending, sociological information about the protagonist, etc.

In the final section of this chapter, the corpus will be briefly described based on this metadata, giving a general overview of specific literary phenomena of the novel of this period.

3.2.2 Metadata, Distant Reading, and Hypotheses Testing

Metadata is at the very core of many textual studies. As Burnard points out "without metadata, the investigator has nothing but disconnected words of unknowable provenance or authenticity" (2004). Even though many researchers or whole areas of research do not adopt the word *metadata*, they employ it as the very basic index. For example, the most standard use case for stylometry, author attribution, needs to assign every text to an author. A subfield of stylometry, stylochronometry, investigates the date of production of the texts, which can be seen as another type of metadata. Library catalogs can be understood as collections of metadata about books (NISO 2004) with a special kind of information: the reference to the place in the library where the book is. Supervised Machine Learning would use metadata, calling it *labels* or only *Y* that represent its classes, while unsupervised methods would apply the available metadata as ground-truth to color and display the results. This metadata can be saved in different ways, one the most basic ones being the name of the file (which is common in stylometry). But other possibilities are also frequent: in simple markup at the beginning of each file, in a structured XML element like in TEI, in a separate table, etc.

Metadata is one of the few elements that can be discussed by non-digital scholars, digital humanists, computational linguists, and computer scientists. However, each of these fields would have different priorities, manners of communicating, and archiving this information. Besides, their interest will differ wildly as far as using this information is concerned. Nonetheless, the different researchers can understand and find it interesting that a novel is written in a third-person voice that is not among the characters of the plot, i.e., a heterodiegetic narrator. The philological interpretation of this fact relating the rest of the literature, the use of this information in clustering or classification tasks, or questions about the optimization of the algorithms would then interest only a section of the researchers mentioned above. That is why I consider metadata the bridge between several fields on the different riverbanks of the digitization.

Actually, metadata can be seen as the computer readable formalization of a cornerstone of Digital Humanities. In 2000, Moretti published "Conjectures on World Literature," in which he coined his influential term of *distant reading*. However, in this article the concept is not related to any digital or computational aim, and there is not a single reference to technology in the entire publication. There, the distance in the reading process is not gained through computers, but only through the use of secondary literature: "it will become 'second hand': a patchwork of other people's research, *without a single direct textual reading*" (Moretti 2000, 57).

In the next chapters of this book, I will analyze dozens of categories in hundreds of texts using thousands of features. Genres are an optimal phenomenon to be analyzed by approaches like distant reading, macro-analysis, or cultural analytics. One can choose to return to a few excerpts of a couple of novels that show how the analysis is observable in the original text. But by doing so, only a tiny fraction of the paragraphs, novels, categories, and features are being used to corroborate the analysis. There is just too much information to find a solid manner of returning to the original text. We need distance when we analyze genres.

Nonetheless, there are at least two weak points on Moretti's argumentation. First, it is unclear how this process should take place exactly, considering that the different researchers tend to disagree regarding the borders of the analyzed phenomenon, its chronological boundaries, their interest, or their epistemological frame. These differences can be understood as bias from the different sources, and later translate into artifacts in the results. Besides, this way of gaining distance does not foresee the possibility for a researcher to include their own reading and understanding of the text. Even though it is clear that a single researcher is not able to undertake close readings for more than a couple of dozens of texts, they might want to cover specific sections of the corpus that are not analyzed by other sources, or to look closer at very specific characteristics.

In this chapter, I argue for distant reading processes through the encoding of metadata, stating explicitly who provides each piece of information: either myself after reading the text, or other researchers. This could be observed as a productive possible path for interdisciplinary collaboration between several researchers: to analyze through digital techniques the qualitative metadata annotated by literary scholars. Formalizing it in that manner, the same researcher and the community can recover the source of information for each single data point. These metadata represent specific literary interpretations that can be used to explain the results. In other words, the researcher is not obliged anymore to return to a tiny fraction of excerpts of the text when discussing the results; they can remain with the metadata, that summarize specific phenomena of the entire corpus. I will follow this strategy – not to return to the original text – in the rest of this research study. In contrast, I will use the metadata in several ways, such as a mean for evaluating the clusters (Chapter

6.2), encoding it as features for classification tasks (Chapter 7.1), explaining the variance of the results (Chapter 7.2), using them to create a unified digital model of the genre (Chapter 8), and describing empirically each analyzed subgenre (Chapter 8 and the Appendix). In this manner, metadata plays a central role in how my research applies, evaluates, and explains Machine Learning applied to the analysis of subgenre.

In fact, the application of metadata has further implications relating the scientific path for the analysis of literature. First, quality metadata allows for an inductive process of statistical description. These are meant to be exploratory attempts that can either better define one phenomenon or observe its development in historical terms. For example, in Section 3.2.11 I will give a short description of what the typical literary characteristics of the novel of this period are. But this is not the only case in this work where I will use this literary metadata. Several Chapters like 5.3, 6.1, 7.1, 8, and the Appendix contain similar inductive descriptions based on the qualitative information gathered from several sources.

The second path that metadata opens is related to the critical rationalism, started by Popper: the falsification of hypotheses. This is a central task in this paradigm, and the role of the researcher is, first, to propose a general explanation of the analyzed phenomenon, and formalize it in two or more variables. Then, it is defined what it could represent in a random process (null model) that could also explain the data. Finally, the researcher measures whether the hypothesis can explain the data statistically better than the null model. This last step is called falsification of a hypothesis. Here, the metadata would represent the formalization of the categories of the analyzed phenomenon.

The alternative to a more formalized procedure is the hermeneutic process of interpreting the results of a digital analysis. For that, the researchers take advantage of their knowledge and reading experience. However, this process has several flaws, such as the tendency to observe meaning and connections in unrelated phenomena (apophenia), select only those results that fit well into the hypothesis, and in general over-interpreting results.

For Digital Humanities, there are two possible goals for the hypotheses. Firstly, the researcher might want to learn about the cultural object, in my case, Spanish literature. In this case, the researcher asks whether the gathered data does behave as a specific hypothesis would anticipate, and if it deviates from the random null model. For example, there is an expectation that as the 20th century progresses, the gender differences in literature become smaller with time. This has been partially analyzed in the Section 3.1.10, but it will be further analyzed in the Section 3.2.11, adding the information about the gender of the protagonists. Another hypothesis about the data that will be evaluated in that section is whether the novels of these period lose specificity regarding their references to reality, taking place more often in unspecific periods, locations. This idea is present in works from Literary Studies (García Lara 1986, 209; Gullón 1994, 199; Aubert 2001, 11; Navajas 2008, 18), and it will be analyzed through the formalization of the uncertainty of the metadata of the value *unknown*. The frequency of this value in the entire schema of the metadata will be compared to what is expected by randomness in a statistical regression model.

Besides the data, the researcher can be interested in the deeper understanding of the method: What exactly is the algorithm doing? How is it working? And why? These are essential questions for unsupervised methods such as clustering, in which texts are grouped based on linguistic features. Do these groups relate to any formalized data that was previously encoded? Or are they just randomly sorted? Metadata will be the way of evaluating the results of the clustering methods in Chapter 6.2. But not only unsupervised methods require explanations, there is also a need to a deeper understanding of the results of classification. For that, I will use metadata and other linguistic measures to evaluate a series of hypotheses in Chapter 7.2 about why some subgenres yield consistently higher results than others.

3.2.3 Typology of Metadata

There have been several proposals to outline a typology of metadata. While the NISO differentiates three main types (descriptive, structural, and administrative; 2004), Burnard signalizes four categories (editorial, analytic, descriptive, and administrative; 2004). The difference between both is probably based on the typical use cases the typologies should cover: more general in the case of NISO, while in Burnard's case it is the environment of corpora and editions in TEI. For this corpus, I will consider three types of metadata:

- *Editorial metadata*: Information about the source of the parts of the corpus.
- *Administrative metadata*: Documentation about the corpus itself.
- *Descriptive metadata*: Classificatory information of several aspects.

While the first two will be tackled together in the next section, descriptive metadata will be explained separately in Section 3.2.5.

Following the TEI Guidelines, I have encoded directly all the metadata about texts and the collections in the TEI *Header*. This strategy provides me with the opportunity to encode various aspects using a shared semantic frame within the DH community. It also offers the possibility to match up easily specific information through attributes, like *@cert* (about the certainty of a specific information) or *@source* (to refer to a specific origin of data).

Each category and possible value of metadata was defined in a hierarchical taxonomy as an TEI XML document, addressing also which type of information they represent (nominal, ordinal, interval, or binary). In the case of ordinal classes, the names of the possible values were also inserted with their numerical position. For example, five values for different types of endings of the novel, varying from zero (clearly sad) to five (clearly happy). This file has been used for several purposes: On the one hand, to validate the metadata of the whole corpus using a Schematron. On the other hand, to recategorize the fields (for example employing the numerical values of ordinal categories, or transforming nominal information into binary fields) for specific visualizations as the ones at the end of this chapter or to employ them as features (see Chapters 7.1 and 8).

3.2.4 Editorial and Administrative Metadata

Each text and author have been identified using the complete name, a short name, and the identifiers of the Spanish National Library (BNE) and the Virtual International Authority File (VIAF). In this way, every text and author can not only be tracked within the corpus, but also as a part of other digital collections. About the sources of the text, I have gathered references regarding three different kinds of editions implicated in the genetic process of each text (all of them encoded inside an element *sourceDesc/bibl* with different *@types*):

- *Edition-first*: The first time the work was published as a book (the date should be between 1880 and 1939).
- *Digital-source*: The digital source. If the text was digitized by the CLiGS, it collects also the year and the exact program used (FineReader, Recognition Server).
- *Print-source*: The printed edition taken as the base for the digital version.

Other administrative information gathered were the editor (*/titleStmt/principal*), the year of the first version of the text as part of the corpus (*/publicationStmt/date*), a private identifier for the project (*/publicationStmt/idno[@type="cligs"]*), the publisher (*/publicationStmt/published*), and the legal status of the text (*/publicationStmt/availability/@status*).

The most important adjustments of the editorial process of the corpus (first draft, validation against schema, modernization) have been encoded in the *revisionDesc* as *changes*. Smaller alterations have been recorded as commits in the GitHub repository. Although the information of the commits is not integrated in the TEI file, the potential of Git for versioning and its capacity to give access to the exact status of the file at any given point in time, led the CLiGS project to not duplicate this information as changes in TEI.

3.2.5 Descriptive Metadata

As I have stated, I consider descriptive metadata those data who represent a categorization of the text considering its internal characteristics. For example, the fact that some sources have labeled a novel as historical novel, or the recognizition of a first-person narrative (autodiegetic narrator). Besides the labels for the subgenres, descriptive metadata have been selected because they are either listed by the history of literature as distinctive features of a subgenre, or their label already reveals the corresponding characteristic. For example, in Section 2.1.8 about erotic novels, different scholars pointed out some typical phenomena of this subgenre, such as middle-class female protagonists in urban contemporary settings. To test if these features really differentiate this subgenre from the rest of the novels, the researcher would need to: select the protagonist, examine their gender and social class and define the temporal and geographical space (for example, Madrid needs to be identified as a city). Finally, the researcher is in the position to compare these descriptive data against other works. Similar examples will be given in the following sections and fully implemented in Chapter 8.

An important aspect for the gathering of the remaining information is a summary of the novel, which has been placed in the element *abstract*. It contains a short summary of the plot of the story and its aim is to give an overview of the entire text. These have been either written by myself after reading the novel, or they have been typed or copied from external sources, such as the MdLE, Wikipedia, or ePubLibre. An explicitly reference to these sources has been kept in an attribute. Thus, the distant reading process can be traced back to the source of interpretation.

Most of the descriptive information has been structured as discrete information into different elements. Many of these categories do not have a specific element in TEI yet, or the possibilities are clearly insufficient. A clear example is the information of the genre. The current TEI Guidelines give different options, one being the attribute *@n (/profileDesc/textDesc/@n)*. This *@n* does not have any specific semantics (its normal use case is a number, but it can contain other elements as well). As I will explain in the following sections, the information about genre that I wanted to collect was much more complex than a single value in an attribute. That is why the members of CLiGS have decided to use the element *keywords* in *textClass*. Each type of metadata can be encoded in a separate term element, defining its class with the *@type* attribute. The structure of the metadata is controlled by tokens separated by a dot, making even similar metadata easy to understand and differentiate, like *author.gender* and *text.characters.protagonist.gender*. The metadata values are validated against a Schematron.

In the corpus, every keyword element has been assigned with a *@cert* attribute with three possible values:

- *High*: In case I read the text.
- *Medium*: In case I could access an abstract (longer than a couple of paragraphs, containing the main information).
- *Low*: All other cases.

Depending on the analysis that I undertake, these values of certainty can be used to filter them, for example, ignoring the data from novels with a low level of certainty. In CoNSSA-canon, all texts have either medium or high certainty. Regardless of the general certainty of the keywords, any term can also have an individual *@cert* attribute, matching up exactly to specific information its degree of certainty.

The metadata about setting, place, and protagonist of the text can be unknown for different reasons: Either the abstract does not contain the data, or the information is not available at all in the whole text. To illustrate the last scenario, I would like to explain one case: in the novel *Aventuras del submarino alemán U*, by Ricardo Baroja, the autodiegetic narrator does not mention his name. The first case of uncertainty ("I do not know it, but probably the information is in the text") has been simply assigned with a question mark; the second case ("I have read the text and I am certain that the information is not there") has been described as *unknown*. A hypothesis about these types of values will be analyzed more closely in the final section of 3.2.11. Most metadata classes also foresee an option called *other*, in cases where the typical values are not acceptable: for example, when assigning gender to protagonists that are objects, like the protagonist carriage of *Memorias de un vagón de ferrocarril* by Zamacois.

3.2.6 Author's Metadata

Apart from his or her name, general information such as gender, year of birth and death, etc. has been gathered about each author. After collecting the BNE identifiers, it has also been possible to obtain further metadata such as the place of birth and death of each author from Wikidata (through Linked Open Data).

Two types of information about the relation between author and text have been collected:

- *Author-text group*: Many authors of this period published some of their works under a shared label. The texts within these groups tend to share more facets than with the rest of the production, like protagonists, settings, topics, periods... Some famous examples are the *Sonatas* by Valle-Inclán, *Novelas contemporáneas* by Galdós, or *La raza* by Baroja. The labels of these groups were often printed as a part of the title, or were assigned by the history of literature.
- *Author-text relation*: The MdLE informed in many cases if (and to what extent) the text reflects the author's life. Because this is a defining feature of genre (autobiography) and subgenre (autobiographic novel), this information (always from the MdLE) was collected with four ordinal possible values: none (default), low, medium, and high.

3.2.7 Text and Genre Metadata

As mentioned before, genre and subgenre categories are more complex than others like authorship or periodization. It is absurd to dispute whether a year existed or not, and there are few cases in which the existence of a person is discussed. In contrast, the discussion of the status of many genres and subgenres is commonplace. While the boundaries of people and years are obvious, it is debatable whether subgenres have boundaries at all. Although a text can technically either belong to several authors (for example in case of multi-authorial texts) or to different years,[1] these are rather exceptional cases. Contrary to that, texts blending various subgenres are rather the norm (see Sections 2.3.3 for a discussion about the macro-models of genres).

The method of encoding information of genre has to be able to capture this complexity. For that, I have defined numerous levels (genre, subgenre) and sources (cover, history of literature, libraries, printing houses), some of them hierarchically:

- *Super-genre*: A general label about whether the text is prose (regardless of specific genres such as short-stories or novels) or other. This value was assigned to mixed if the work has entire chapters of poetry.
- *Genre*: General information about the main genre; the great majority are novels (in Spanish *novela*), but this information can differ in the case of the 14 texts with unknown first genre or the *greguerías*,[2] which will be analyzed in Chapter 3.3.
- *Subtitle*: Part of the title or subtitle that represents some kind of group of texts (*novela, memorias, historia, novela de costumbre...*), with a total of 47 different values.
- *Subtitle from BNE*: Very similar to the previous one but considering all the information of the catalog of the Spanish National Library (64 different values).
- *Subgenre from History of Literature*: The labels that the two histories of literature have assigned to the texts (78 distinct values in the MdLE, 34 in the HdLE). Some examples: *novela naturalista, novela histórica, novela social, novela autobiográfica...*
- *Subgenre from editorials and users*: Labels that printing houses (crawled from Amazon) or digital projects (such as ePubLibre) have used to categorize the texts.

1 For example, an author who started writing a text when she or he was young. She or he finished the first version after a couple of years, she or he published the work with changes several years later and made a new version of it at the end of her or his life.

2 Mentioned as prose texts by, for example, Ródenas de Moya (2000, 49).

- *Own annotation about subgenres*: Labels from a controlled vocabulary of 27 different novel subgenres. These labels were assigned by me after collecting the abstract, encoding the metadata, and reading which labels the other sources used.

The different labels of the various sources will be closely analyzed in Chapters 5.1, 5.2, and 5.3.

3.2.8 Place and Period of the Action

Many subgenre-labels contain information about the place of the action of the plot. There are numerous types of geographical references: *novela americana* (reference to the continent), *novela regional* (to a rural setting), *novela madrileñista* (to the city or town), *novela cosmopolita* (to the size of the place), *novelas del mar* (to the sea, in contrast to the land). These multiple facets of the setting have been encoded using different categories of metadata. Many of these are implied: If the action takes places in Madrid, it means that it also takes place in Spain, which is in Europe, and it means that the sea is far away. Nevertheless, I have explicitly encoded all the fields to use this information in various scenarios.

To assign a value to each metadata, at least half of the novel has to correspond with the value. Otherwise, it was assigned as *mixed*. This specific value is especially interesting because it indirectly represents travel; depending on the geographical level of this value, it can point out travel within Spain (for example *La voluntad* by Azorín), Europe (*El mundo es ansí* by Baroja) or the world (*Genio y figura...* by Valera). These will be observed closely in the descriptions of the subgenres of the Appendix.

Along with the place, information about the period (point and total span) has been gathered. Here is the complete list of the categories:

- *Setting settlement*: Name of the place (city, town, or village) where the action takes place, represented exactly the way it is referred to in the text (*Madrid, París, Valencia, Marineda...*).
- *Setting territory*: Name of the region to which the place belongs, especially interesting for the novels in the rural places, encoded in Spanish (*Castilla, Valencia, Andalucía, Isla de París*).

- *Setting country*: Name of the country to which the place belongs, encoded in English (*Spain, France, Mexico*...).
- *Setting continent*: Name of the continent to which the place belongs, in English (*Europe, America, Asia*...).
- *Setting represented*: Name of the most specific place that is represented in the work, with its name in the real world. For example, what Clarín calls Vetusta in his novels is actually the Spanish town Oviedo; the Marineda of Bazán is A Coruña, etc. If the place is fictional, then the most specific realistic place is assigned.[3]
- *Setting type*: Type of the setting depending on the size of the population, with four ordinal possible values: boat, rural, town (small-city), and big-city.
- *Time period*: Information about the historical period in which the action takes place, with five possible ordinal values: antiquity (<500), middle ages (500-1500), modern times (1500-1800), contemporary (1850-1939), and future (>1939).
- *Time year*: If possible, the exact year in which the action starts. If this information is not available, then only the decade or century is kept (for example: 189? or 18??).
- *Time span*: The period of the action, expressed in days.[4] The certainty of this information is lower than the rest of the metadata. Commonly, the reader cannot be sure about how time passes considering that the references in many cases are vague (*after some weeks, time passed and...*). As Underwood points out "fictional time isn't exact" (2018). In many cases, this information has been deduced by the life of the protagonist or some historical events.

---

3 Maya is fictional, but placed somewhere in Africa; Iberina, in Spain; Liliput, in Australia; while Surlandia is completely out of this Earth.

4 Although the basic unit for the measure of chronological span is days, I always use the next lowest unit of time. That means that, if the action lasts about one month, I encoded 30 days; if it lasts about one year, I have assigned 365 days. Therefore, values such as 35 or 380 are not possible unless the texts specify this as the exact chronological span.

3.2.9 Protagonist Metadata

Another type of literary information with a strong resemblance in the labels is the protagonist. Some subgenres are related to different types of information about the most important character in the novel, like her or his social level (*picaresca, social*), profession (*de guerra, policíaca, taurina*), or the age at the beginning of the action (*picaresca, de educación*). Two other basic pieces of information about protagonists have been gathered: their gender and their name (to document which character has been chosen, particularly pertinent in novels in which this decision is unclear). The specific fields are:

- *Gender*: With two basic values (male and female), *mixed* if there is no clear protagonist but instead a group with mixed genders, and *other* for non-human protagonists.[5]
- *Name*: The longest version of her or his name (surname, if present), with her or his pseudonym in parentheses.
- *Profession*: Categorical values about the profession of the protagonist from a list of 30 general values (*lord, artist, none, business owner, military personnel, religious...*).
- *Social-level*: The social level of the protagonist as three possible ordinal values: low (for characters whose basic needs like nutrition or education are at risk), medium (for characters who need to work, default value), and high (for wealthy characters who do not need to work).[6]
- *Age*: Age of the protagonist from a list of four ordinal values: child, young, adult, and mature. Because these values can change over the course of the text, either the age at the beginning of the novel (in most cases), or the youngest age of the protagonist described in at least one complete chapter

5 I would have encoded other categories such as transgender, but these have been not found in this corpus.

6 This information is affected by the type of setting. A wealthy character in the capital tends to be much wealthier than one from a village. This aspect is even more obvious for some lords from rural areas that have economic problems despite their social position, like in *El mayorazgo de Labraz* by Baroja or *Sonata de invierno* by Valle-Inclán. They are still marked as high social class, because they represent the highest status in comparison to the rest of the characters of the novel.

has been used.[7] The age of the protagonist at the end of the plot can then be calculated adding this value to the time span of the action, explained in the previous section.

3.2.10 Other Literary Metadata

Finally, several literary fields related in different ways to genre have also been collected: data about the narrator, whether or not the action takes place in a realistic world, if the novel has a happy ending, and the canonization of the text measured in different ways.

- *Narrator*: With five possible values: heterodiegetic, autodiegetic, homodiegetic, and two others for texts in other forms, dialogue and epistolary.
- *Representation*: Information about whether the action takes place in a realistic world or not,[8] expressed as three ordinal values: realistic, neutral, and non-realistic. The value *neutral* has been used for texts that leave the decision whether the action is realistic or not up to the reader.
- *Type of ending*: Information about how the text ends, with five ordinal values: negative, partially negative, neutral, partially positive, and positive. The way to assign these values has been to compare the ending of the text with the protagonist's expectations. The neutral texts are those in which the ending is indeterminate (like *Juan de Mairena* by Machado) or in which protagonists do not fulfill their wishes, but clearly marks the beginning

7 Some novels include a flashback to the childhood of the protagonist and represent this period over several chapters, like in *Aventuras, inventos y mixtificaciones de Silvestre Paradox* by Baroja. For shorter flashbacks, the reference to childhood has been ignored.

8 One interesting discussion is what should be considered realistic: Does a novel still take place in a realistic world if angels or the Virgin Mary affect some situations? Does it depend on the encoder's beliefs? What if instead of angels, the creatures are vampires or aliens? The definition of what is realistic cannot be universally defined without cultural bias. Lexicography has already gone through similar discussions about how the cultural and personal values might reflect definitions (Swanepoel 2011; Rodríguez 2013; Lara 2016). I have decided to consider realistic what most of Spanish society of the 19th century could consider realistic, accepting the Christian supernatural beings.

of a new period of their lives (like *La conquista del reino de Maya* by Ganivet, or *Volvoreta* by Fernández Flórez).

- *Quality in history of literature*: Along with the number of pages used in the MdLE, any reference to the quality of the novel in the manual has also been gathered, collected as three possible ordinal values: low, medium, and high.[9]

3.2.11 Description of the Metadata of CoNSSA

In this final section, my goal is to describe the corpus in terms of metadata. By doing so, I want to achieve three different goals: Firstly, I show how already existing knowledge in form of digital metadata (coming from summaries or personal readings) can uncover broader pictures about literature. In other words, metadata is the first step to run distant reading analyses that are not explorations of uncertain tools, but inductive statistical descriptions of literary features. Secondly, I describe the general tendencies of novels of this period. These general patterns of the entire genre can be used to compare specific characteristics of some subgenres: Are urban or contemporary settings specific to the erotic novel, or are they just the most common values in all the novels of that time, regardless the subgenre? Finally, I explore the most noticeable changes of specific literary phenomena over time: For example, are sad endings more common at the beginning of this period and therefore more typical in subgenres of the 19th century like in the realist or naturalist novels?

The first step is then to examine the common values in all novels of the corpus. For that purpose, I apply central tendencies from Descriptive Statistics such as median and mode. Besides, I report the proportion of novels that satisfy these value in CoNSSA. Typically, the novel of the *silver age* is written by a male author (92% of the corpus), with a heterodiegetic narrator (69%), whose protagonist is a male (77%), medium-class (63%) adult (55%), who lives a story that takes place in Europe (90%), Spain (78%). More specifically, in a big city (47%) like Madrid (29%), in contemporary times (94%) of a realistic world (89%) that does not resemble the author's life (72%). The action lasts around

9 It is interesting to see that, typically, the information given was referencing the quality of the work within the author's production ("one of his best works") and not universally ("a good novel") or within the period ("a rather bad novel for this decade").

one year (30%) and it clearly has a sad ending (50%). Although the proportions and deviation change, central tendencies remain similar in both CoNSSA and CoNSSA-canon.

These values are calculated independently from each other, and actually in both versions of the corpus there is one single novel which fulfills all these criteria: *Tristán o el pesimismo* by Valdés. This novel can be seen as the one whose literary characteristics are most similar to the rest; in other words, the least surprising work in terms of its metadata. Deleting the two most strict criteria (the duration of the action and the specific place), 17 other novels fulfill the rest of the criteria, with works by Alarcón, Baroja, Blasco, Francisco de Ayala, Jarnés, Lanza, León, Miró, Munilla, Pemán, Unamuno, and Valle-Inclán (details in the Jupyter Notebook). As a summary, a short empirical definition of the novel of this period can affirm that the story typically takes places in a realistic contemporary Spain, in third person, written and starred by men, with a sad ending.

After looking at the general picture of the novel, I continue investigating the distribution and the development of specific literary metadata during this sixty-year period. As I have shown in Section 3.1.5, some subgenres were rather published in the last decades of the 19th century (naturalist, realist novels), others in the 1900s and 1910s (erotic novel), and a third group in the 1920s and 1930s (social, historical, and comedy novels). That is why the general development of literary patterns are not only interesting per se, they also can shed light on internal characteristics of subgenres.

One field that shows a clear chronological pattern is the information of whether the text resembles the author's life.[10] As described above, the majority of works does not, with 73% of the cases. The number of novels that are somehow autobiographical increases over the analyzed period (Figure 27): While 88% of the texts in the decade of 1880 were clearly not autobiographical, this amount drops to 58% by the 1930s. Similar tendencies are observable in both versions of the corpora, with an even stronger tendency in the canonized one, both reaching high statistical significance when analyzed through linear regression (p-values < 0.001 in both versions).

This tendency is one of the most surprising and solid results of the description and a clear example of the potential of distant reading through metadata of the *silver age*. As Figure 27 shows, autobiographical traces in the

10 Ródenas de Moya pointed out that self-reference (*autorreferencia*) was a tendency in modern art, although this is not undisputed (1998, 93–94).

Figure 27: Autobiographical representation in the corpus over time

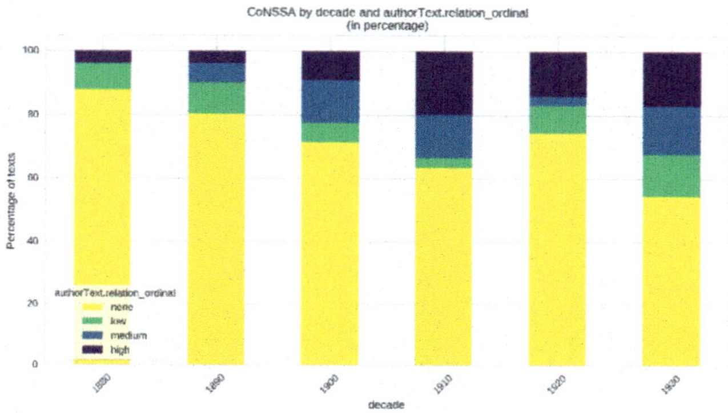

novels were considerably more common in the decades after the 1900s. This could mean that the subgenres which appeared in the last decades are more likely to also be autobiographical than the typical ones for the 19th century.

In the following plots, I explore the space and time of the action of novels. The first case is the geographical distribution of action, plotted on a map. The exact metadata used here is not the name of the place as it appears in the text, but the real-world locations with their actual names they refer to. The geolocation has been gathered using the Python library GeoPy and controlled manually.[11] The visualizations of the map of Figure 28 have been created with the DARIAH Geo-Browser and it can interactively observed.[12]

As already pointed out, Europe, Spain, and Madrid are the most frequent locations in terms of continent, country, and settlement. Only a few other places around the world (USA, Mexico, Argentina, Santo Domingo, South Africa, Morocco, Algeria, Palestine, and unspecified sites in Africa, Australia, and America) are chosen as settings for the novels.

Latin America has surprisingly few cases, which is even more astonishing considering the fact that not one single novel takes places in Cuba, Puerto Rico, or the Philippines. These countries were Spanish colonies until 1898;

---

11 The location of several villages in Spain is approximate.

12 https://geobrowser.de.dariah.eu/?csv1=https://cdstar.de.dariah.eu/dariah/EAEA0-A43B-E9CE-84C6-0.

Figure 28a: Map of the action of the novels in CoNSSA

Figures 28 b, c: Maps of the action of the novels in CoNSSA

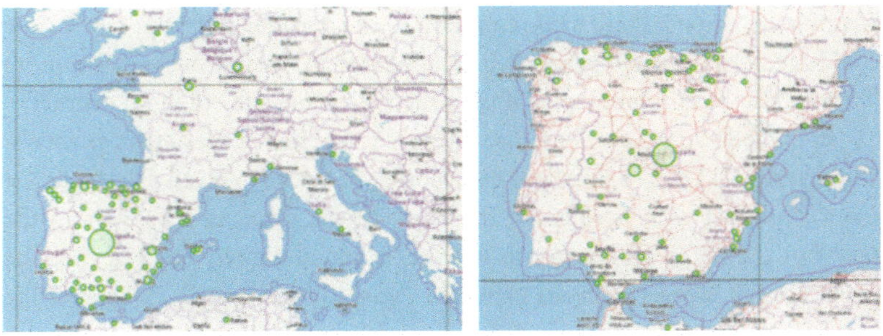

after this year, these territories won their independence in war against the USA. This episode is mentioned in the literature of the time as *el desastre*, 'the disaster', and it had a huge impact on the Spanish society. It was even used to coin the literary *generación del 98*. How is it possible that a war could define an entire generation of authors, and yet the countries involved are so blatantly ignored as possible settings in the novels? Of course, the texts can and do reflect the war in other means different from placing the plot in those regions. However, one would expect that these places would play some role in the novels. The geographical data of the plots do not support the hypothesis that the Spanish-American War marked an important milestone in Spanish literature.

These colonies are not the only place that is clearly underrepresented. Other cases are the Canary Islands, Aragón, Castilla-La Mancha,[13] and particularly Catalonia (cfr. Mainer 2009, 104). In Europe,[14] the novels rather take place in the Western part, especially France.

A tendency only observable in the CoNSSA-canon is the size of the location where the actions occur: Cities are the place where most texts take place during the first decades. The number of urban novels is reduced to the half in the latter decades (Pedraza Jiménez and Rodríguez Cáceres 1983, 340). In the description of different subgenres in 2.1., it has been mentioned that urban settings such as Madrid or Paris are the typical setting of erotic novels. But the data shows that these cities are in any case the most typical setting for the novels, so it would be necessary to analyze if they are statistically more common in erotic novels than in the rest of the novels.

Figure 29: Size of setting in CoNSSA-canon over time

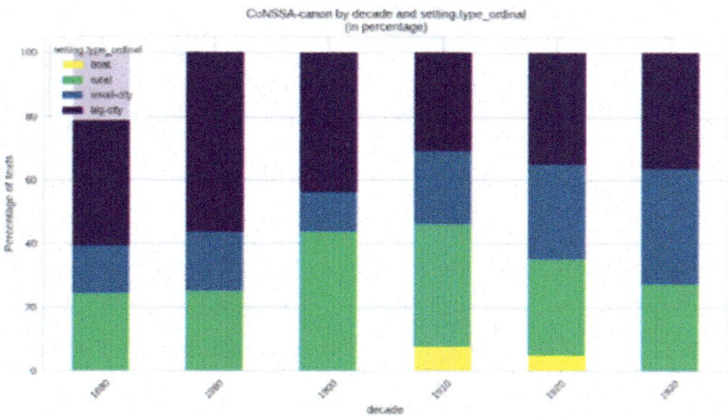

Along with the location, there is information about the historical period in which the action takes place (Figure 30). Both versions of the corpus have around 95% of the texts taking place in contemporary times (1850-1939). Indeed, all the texts of the decade of 1880 are contemporary (cfr. Aubert 2001,

13 The second biggest circle in Spain (southwest of Madrid) is in Castilla la Mancha, around Talavera de la Reina, but it actually represents those novels that do not fix their setting in a specific place in Spain.

14 The circle of the novels that take place in an unspecified site of Europe is set in Luxembourg (where no actual novel takes place).

8). In these years, realism and naturalism were the predominant tendencies. Although contemporary periods remain the most typical cases, its percentage drops until the 1920s. The least contemporary decade is the 1910s, but still 88% of the stories take place in the 19th or 20th century. There is one peculiar value of a novel whose action takes place in the future: *La jirafa sagrada* by Madariaga (published in 1925), a very surprising work with its plot taking place in the distant future, in an African society ruled by women.

Figure 30: Period of the action in CoNSSA over time

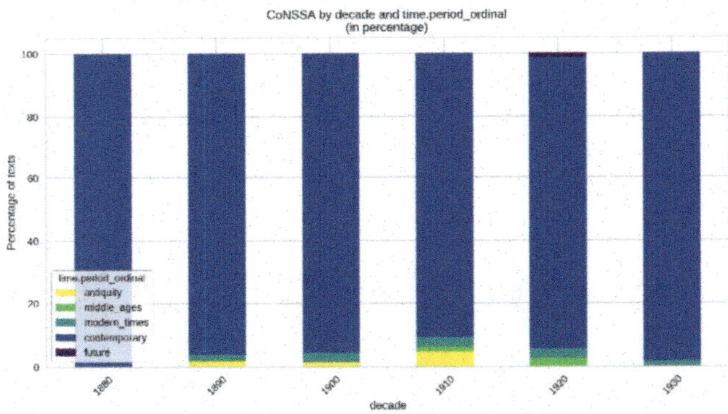

Other information about the period is the span of the action over time, formalized in days. This field is the only one that has been originally encoded as interval, as a value with real numerical value and not only as an ordinal value which expresses its position in a sorted list. Besides its informational nature, this field has a further peculiarity. Most numerical characteristics of a text are originated in a process of counting: How many words are there in a text? How many characters interact in a theater play? For this numerical information, Statistics expects a Poisson distribution. In contrast to these examples, the chronological span is not a counting information and, therefore, there are no clear expectations about how the distribution of this field should be. That is why it is interesting to observe its distribution.[15] Even when the

15 I have deleted the outliers of longer than five years to examine the shape of the most common data. With all the cases, the shape remains similar, with a greater number of outlier on the right.

field is not counting information, the data of Figure 31 does resemble a Poisson distribution. The novels tend to last 365 days both in median and mode, and the data shows a variance of 795 days in IQR. The entire range covers from novels lasting one day (*La media noche* by Valle-Inclán, *La velada en Benicarló* by Azaña) to 70 years (*Abel Sánchez* by Unamuno or *Aviraneta: o la vida de un conspirador* by Baroja).

Figure 31: Distribution of chronological span of the action (in days)

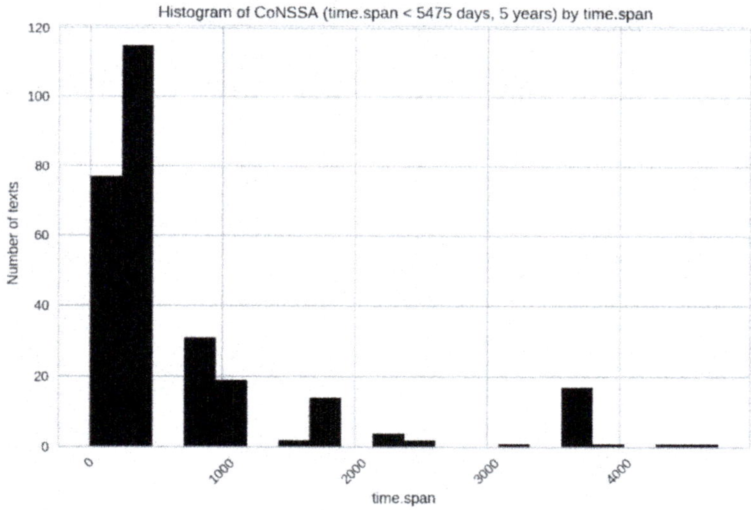

I have already discussed the author's gender in Section 3.1.10. Now, I want to observe the protagonist's gender and its relation to other literary phenomena. As stated above, more texts were written by women in the first decades of this period than in the latter. Does the gender of the protagonist show a similar pattern? Figure 32 shows that it does: While around 39% of novels from the 1880s and the 1890s were starred by a female character, only 14% in the 1920s and the 1930s (with similar results in both versions of the corpus). The distribution of the gender of author and protagonist over time is similar: Women (both as writers and protagonists) are not present in a larger portion of the novels in the later decades, rather the opposite.

I would now like to find out if more correlations between the gender of the protagonist and other social or textual information exist. In Figure 33, each

Figure 32: Protagonist gender over decades

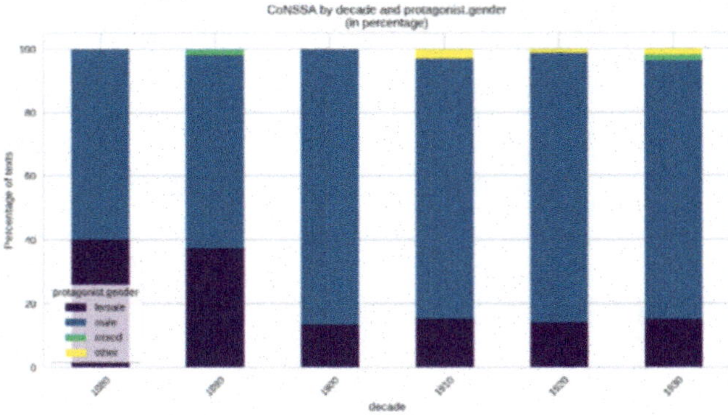

axis stands for distinct ordinal metadata,[16] with the gender differentiated through box plots.

The novels have similar endings for both genders, being slightly more optimistic with women (not in CoNSSA-canon). Women tend to be younger than their male counterparts, have a wider range of social classes (with more cases in the upper than in the lower levels). Besides, they have a stronger tendency to live in cities, and are not meant to appear in boats. One interesting aspect is the fact that male protagonists from lower or upper social classes are outliers (cfr. Johnson 2008, 161).

The last plot, Figure 34, shows the development of the types of endings during these sixty years. As mentioned before, the most common case is a sad ending, which is perceivable through the entire period. The decade with the largest percentage of sad endings is the 1880s (the one dominated by naturalism), with almost 80% of the texts. After the decade of 1910, the number of texts with a neutral ending (neither completely sad nor happy) increases and remains as the second most frequent type of ending. In the canonized version, texts have a tendency to become happier until 1920 (p-value of 0.03 in a linear regression analysis, further details in the Jupyter Notebook), returning to more pessimistic endings later. It is surprising that neither the Spanish

16 With lower or negative values encoded as lower numbers, for example sad endings are encoded as zero, or towns are encoded as two while cities as three.

Figure 33: Box plots differentiating values by the protagonist gender

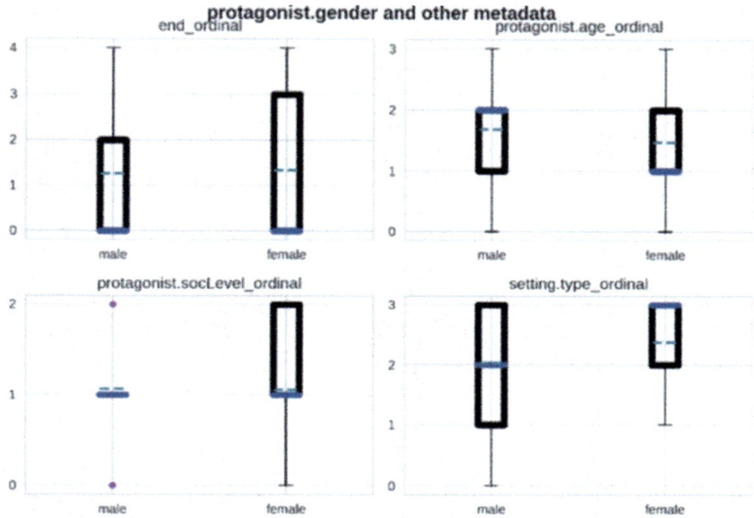

Figure 34: Type of ending over decades

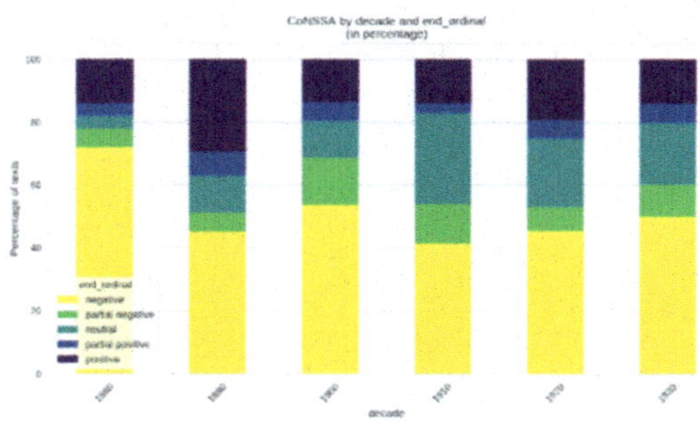

Civil War nor the First World War seem to have a clear effect on the endings of the novels.

The last element I would like to discuss is a specific value given in many categories: *unknown*. As explained in Section 3.2.3, this value represents the same uncertainty in the different metadata types: The information cannot be known by humans using only the text as a source. There is a hypothesis about this period commonly mentioned in which the novels leave the realistic frame, becoming more abstract, and many of its aspects turn fuzzier (García Lara 1986, 209; Gullón 1994, 199; Aubert 2001, 11; Navajas 2008, 18). A change from realist to modernist and avant-garde novels would take place and therefore many actual references to locations or periods get blurred. For example, there are no specific references to places or years in novels such as *Niebla* by Unamuno (cfr. Øveraas 1993, 60). The *unknown* value of metadata could be seen as a formalization of this phenomenon. Thus, if the hypothesis is true, the later decades should contain more *unknown* values. The results do not show statistical significance (p-value of 0.13 in a regression analysis, 0.22 for the canonized version) with a slightly positive slope (p-value 0.004 in CoNSSA and 0.003 in CoNSSA-canon). That means that although texts do show a certain tendency to become fuzzier, there is no empirical data to assert that novels become less specific within this period.

This description has demonstrated the potential of metadata as a solid bridge towards distant reading. In general, the novels of this period are highly realistic, national, contemporary, male-dominated, and end sadly. The development of the analyzed texts of this period shows clear tendencies in both versions of the corpus: Novels become more male-dominated and autobiographical, and slightly less pessimistic. Female protagonists tend to be younger, their stories usually take place in cities and their endings are slightly happier, while male protagonists have a stronger tendency to be part of the medium class and have a wider range of type of settings.

3.3 Filtering the Corpus through Classification: Are all Texts in CoNSSA Novels?

3.3.1 Introduction

In the previous chapters, the criteria for the composition of the corpus and its annotation using metadata have been presented. In Section 3.1.5, a problem has been highlighted: The genre of 10% of the texts of the corpus is unclear and this number includes some of the most important works of this period (by Machado, Ramón Jiménez, Gómez de la Serna, Baroja, etc.). Are these novels, or do they belong to the essay, to journalistic texts, or even to theater or poetry? This question should be answered before moving on to the analysis of subgenres in the rest of the pubilcation. In a manner, this chapter proposes the hypothesis that these 14 texts do belong to the category of novels. To try to falsify this, I apply classification using CORDE as the data set, the largest existing historical corpus for Spanish, created by the Real Academia Española. First, I will evaluate the parameters (transformations of lexical information, algorithms, and number of lexical features) of the classification of the different genres in two different tasks: multi-label (each text belongs to each subgenre or not) and multi-class (each text belongs to a single genre). Next, I will use the prediction function of the best combination of parameters to classify the genre of the texts of disputed genre, both as multi-label and multi-class tasks. Finally, I will discuss the results and modify the corpus for the rest of my research study.

3.3.2 Corpus CORDE: *Bag of Words* and Metadata

As mentioned before, in this chapter I use the largest historical corpus for Spanish: CORDE. In 2002, the Real Academia Española (RAE) launched two corpora: the first with historical texts (*Corpus Diacrónico del Español*, CORDE) and the second with contemporary material (*Corpus de Referencia del Español Actual*, CREA). In the original plan, the contemporary corpus, CREA, would cover the most recent 25 years, while CORDE would assimilate the rest of the texts that could be considered historical (i.e. older than 25 years). Hence, the boundaries of both corpora would move each year. This plan was dropped with the creation of a new corpus, CORPES, covering the 21st century and adding new texts every year. As a result of this, the original corpora were frozen in their development.

In its final version, CORDE contains around 300 million tokens and more than 34,000 texts, with material from the different Spanish-speaking countries (74% coming from Spain), in different genres and topics (which will be explained later in more detail), including an important fraction of literary works. The texts were published or written between the year 759 (with only two instances from the 8th century) and 1974 (Sánchez Sánchez and Domínguez Cintas 2007). Its goal is to offer a representative sample of the language for researchers (Sánchez Sánchez and Domínguez Cintas 2007, 143). The standard use of CORDE and CREA is through two online websites, where the researcher can run queries in the corpora. Although accepted and used as a standard tool by Hispanists (Kabatek and Pusch 2011), some researchers have pointed out several philological problems of the corpus, especially in its medieval section (recently discussed in Rodríguez Molina and Octavio de Toledo y Huerta 2017).

Until recently, the RAE has been reluctant to give access to the full text version of the corpora or other formats of the data, arguing copyright issues relating to the editions of the texts. For this research, I contacted the department of the RAE responsible for these corpora, requesting the frequencies of each document together with any annotation of the document (or metadata). They agreed, and for that I am deeply grateful and hope to give an example of the kind of analysis that could be undertaken if the data was available not only through the browser interface. In fact, some months later, the institution opened the opportunity to request the frequencies and metadata of each text, i.e. that which is used for this research, to the public. The files I received were plain text files (.txt) with specific metadata and the frequencies of each token, exactly in this form:

```
<TITULO>El caballero de Medina</TITULO>
<AUTOR>Cruz, Ramón de la</AUTOR>
<PAIS>España</PAIS>
```

<FECHACRE> 1764 </FECHACRE>
<TEMA>Verso dramático breve: Profano</TEMA>
<MEDIO>Libro</MEDIO>
Número de formas ortográficas: 2951
Número de elementos (tokens): 3940
Número de elementos distintos (types): 1086
400 .
236 ,
153 que
78 y
78 de
...

From this material, the first step is to extract and clean the metadata, differentiating different types of information that have not been separately encoded.[1] The genre and subgenre information is mainly extracted from the first value of the TEMA element (in the previous example, its genre is Verso dramático breve), but also differentiates novels and letters (two genres that are encoded as the second value). Besides, some subgenres are merged due to their small size, such as short and long dramatic verse, combining them in a general *dramatic verse* category. The few steps for the normalization of the genre can be exactly tracked on the Jupyter Notebook of this chapter. At the end, 19 different classes emerge:

> Artes y espectáculos, Biografía-Autobiografía, Ciencias exactas, físicas, naturales y aplicadas, Ciencias sociales y humanidades, Cartas y relaciones, Derecho, Historia y documentos, Novela y otras formas similares, Prensa, Prosa didáctica, Prosa dramática, Prosa lírica, Prosa narrativa breve, Prosa narrativa extensa, Religión, Sociedad, Verso dramático, Verso lírico and Verso narrativo.[2]

Some of these labels do not constitute a genre per se, for e.g. *arts and spectacles* or *religion*, which constitute a group of technical texts on these topics.

In the last chapters, I have described the CoNSSA in several ways. To compare it with CORDE, I plot some categories to obtain an overview of this di-

1 For example, the year of redaction or publication was sometimes encoded as written between two years, before or related to a specific year.

2 It also contains an empty category that seems to be a mistake in the original data.

achronic corpus. In the following figure, the number of texts for each century is differentiated by its category.

Figure 35: Distribution of texts in CORDE by century and genre

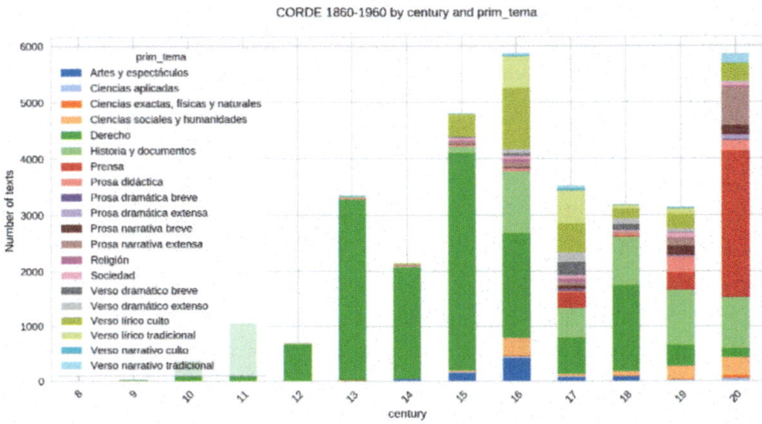

As the documentation of the corpus already points out, the number of texts over centuries is not balanced, but now the detail of this imbalance is clearer: the 8th and 9th centuries only contain a few texts; between the 10th and the 12th century the corpus contains between a few and around a thousand instances; this number increases to between 2,000 and 3,000 for the remainder of the centuries, with exceptionally high values in the 15th, 16th and 20th centuries. Since CORDE claims to be a representative sample of the language and is, in fact, the largest and most comprehensive historical corpus for Spanish, I wonder whether these text numbers per century and genre can be viewed as being representative of the Spanish written language.

In any case, an undesirable effect in the data is again very clear: There is a large imbalance between genres over the centuries. During medieval times, legal texts represent a very large proportion of the texts and remain one of the largest classes until the 19th century. Are researchers of the history of language aware that CORDE is almost exclusively a legal corpus in its medieval section? Or that journals represent around 44% of the materials of the 20th century? In any case, this phenomenon is observable both in CORDE and CoNSSA: It is nearly impossible to have a relatively large sample of texts within a genre over long periods. In the case of CORDE, only three genres having more than a hundred texts offer homogeneous samples over consecutive centuries: historical, legal and high-brow lyrics. For the rest of the genres, the maximum size of the samples is some dozens of texts per century. Genres and subgenres are historical phenomena, and to pretend to balance them over time in corpora is to distort them.

3.3.3 CORDE 1860–1960 + CoNSSA

From the complete CORDE, I extract a section between 1860 and 1960. This represents the boundaries of CoNSSA (1880 and 1939) plus an additional margin of 20 years. There are several reasons for extending the chronological boundaries. First, the data is already available, so it is reasonable to work with more data rather than with less. Second, as discussed in Section 3.1.3, some authors of CoNSSA are representatives of former movements, so some genres could actually find more similarities in earlier publications. Third, some texts analyzed in CoNSSA might have created tendencies that were later practiced by other authors, which argues for an extension of the date of CORDE to some decades after the end of the CoNSSA.

The section of the CORDE between 1860 and 1960 contains 6,587 different texts, including more than 81 million tokens, counting the typographical tokens amongst them. As already mentioned, the works are divided into 19 different categories. These are, as expected, unevenly distributed: While the news category contains 2,310 texts, biographies and autobiographies only cover 13. The chronological distribution of CORDE 1860–1960 is as follows:

The distribution of the number of texts per decade shown in this figure does not resemble any distribution seen until now. Figures 11 and 12 shown in Chapter 3.1 show a peak in the 1920s, with a marked drop in the 1930s. In the case of the section between 1860–1960 of CORDE, these two decades are clear outliers. One of the reasons is the large number of journalistic texts in the 1930s present in the corpus, and a relatively large section of long narrative prose in the 1920s. Were the developers of CORDE consciously attempting to document the prose of a section of the *silver age* (1920s) and the journalistic texts during the Second Republic and the Civil War (1930s) more profusely than other decades? Whatever the reasons for this distribution are, this is the material that the community has been using for decades through the Web interface and this is also the data set I use in this chapter to evaluate and predict the genre of the disputed texts.

Figure 36: Distribution of CORDE 1860-1960 over decades

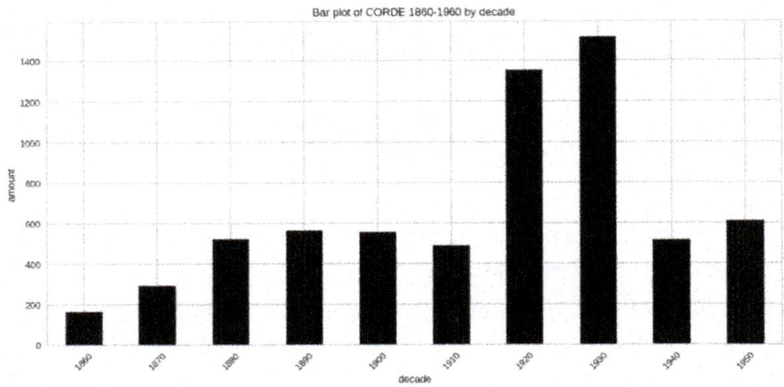

The goal of this chapter is to predict whether a series of specific texts in CoNSSA can be labeled as novels or not. What is interpreted to be a novel can differ from one project to the other. What CORDE labels novels could be different to that of the manual MdLE, i.e. the labeling practice of these sources can differ. Although I consider the labeling of the MdLE more accurate (since it is a manual written by experts in literature), I have the texts from CORDE, a general corpus. Using data and metadata exclusively from the RAE would signify that I am assuming their understanding of the novel. Thus, to avoid this, I merge CORDE with the undisputed novels of CoNSSA, resulting in a new corpus: "CORDE 1860–1960 + CoNSSA." Since many texts are present in both corpora, I control the novels in both corpora by deleting the duplicates. In addition, I delete all the texts from the authors of the 14 genre-disputed texts, so that the algorithm cannot learn the stylistics patterns of Antonio Machado or Juan Ramón Jiménez, for example. In other words, the authorial cue will not influence the results of the prediction. This merged corpus has a total of 6,800 texts (6,456 texts from CORDE and 344 novels from CoNSSA).

3.3.4 Binary Class Evaluation of Parameters

There are several decisions that the researcher must make in classifications, such as the algorithm, type of features (tokens, bigrams, trigrams, etc.), number of features, and the representation of the frequency (relative, z-scores, tf-idf, etc.). Only by knowing which combination of these features yields higher results, can the researcher ensure an optimal outcome. To test all possible combinations, Machine Learning applies *grid search* (Müller and Guido 2016, 262–64) to evaluate the parameters in which the researcher defines the parameters and ranges of possible values. Thus, all possible combinations are tested and the results can then be compared. As mentioned in Chapter 2.2, this step has not been part of the paper analyzing genres through computational means. An extensive evaluation of parameters in the form of a grid search will take place in the Chapter 6.1.

In the grid search of this chapter, the following parameters are evaluated:

- *Number of Most Frequent Words* (MFWs, tokens, including typographical ones): 10, 100, 500, 1,000, 2,000, 3,000, 4,000, 5,000 and 6,000.
- *Algorithms*: support vector machines, k-nearest neighbors, random forest, logistic regression and Gaussian naive Bayes.
- *Transformations of lexical information*: relative frequencies, logarithmic relative frequency (log), z-scores, tf-idf and logarithmic z-scores (log-z-scores).[3]

I apply cross-validation (ten-fold), and for each class the texts are randomly under-sampled to obtain an equal number of positive and negative cases. For example, in the merged corpus there are a total of 483 novels. To evaluate the classification, I select all these novels and the same number of genres belonging to other classes, which are randomly sampled. This means that the sample size of each class varies, but the baseline remains 0.5.

The combination of parameters gives a result of 4,501 possible permutations, making it impossible to report all of them. For this reason, I only highlight the very best results for each genre, as well as general tendencies in the three analyzed parameters. In the following table the best combination of parameters for each genre analyzed are presented. The mean and standard deviation columns summarize the results of the F1-score of the ten values of the cross-validation:

3 This transformations will be presented in detail in Chapter 4.2.

Table 2: Best combination of parameters for each class

genre	mean F1	std F1	text representation	MFW	classifier name	sample size	baseline
Verso dramático	1.00	0.00	relative	6000	Random Forest	34	0.5
Prosa dramática	0.99	0.02	tf-idf	6000	Logistic Regression	176	0.5
Ciencias exactas, físicas, naturales y aplicadas	0.99	0.02	z-scores	3000	SVC	182	0.5
Prosa narrativa extensa	0.98	0.02	log z-scores	6000	SVC	922	0.5
Religión	0.98	0.06	z-scores	3000	SVC	40	0.5
Novela y otras formas similares	**0.98**	**0.01**	**log z-scores**	**6000**	**SVC**	**966**	**0.5**
Derecho	0.98	0.02	log	5000	Logistic Regression	616	0.5
Cartas y relaciones	0.98	0.01	log z-scores	6000	Logistic Regression	2768	0.5
Verso lírico	0.96	0.02	z-scores	5000	Logistic Regression	764	0.5
Verso narrativo	0.96	0.03	z-scores	3000	SVC	380	0.5
Prosa narrativa breve	0.94	0.03	z-scores	6000	Logistic Regression	466	0.5
Ciencias sociales y humanidades	0.94	0.03	log z-scores	3000	SVC	678	0.5
Artes y espectáculos	0.93	0.13	tf-idf	6000	Random Forest	28	0.5
Biografía-Autobiografía	0.93	0.13	tf-idf	10	Gaussian NB	24	0.5

Historia y documentos	0.93	0.07	log z-scores	6000	SVC	206	0.5
Prensa	0.93	0.01	relative	5000	Random Forest	4620	0.5
Prosa lírica	0.91	0.14	tf-idf	500	Logistic Regres-sion	26	0.5
Prosa didác-tica	0.91	0.04	z-scores	6000	Logistic Regres-sion	470	0.5
Sociedad	0.91	0.05	log z-scores	3000	SVC	212	0.5

In general, the best combination of parameters gives results close to perfection. All the genres achieve their best F1-scores between 0.91 and 1.0, all being highly significant in comparison with the baseline of 0.5. Even when two standard deviations are considered, the results are still well above the baseline (the worst case, *Sociedad*, is close to 0.8). The categories with the best results are highly canonical, such as plays both in verse and prose, literary prose texts, novels, letters, or technical texts about science, law, or religion. The cases with the lowest classification values in this evaluation are biographies and autobiographies, news, lyric prose, essays, and technical texts about history, society, and art. Some of these results can be easily explained. Plays, particularly in verse, are easily recognizable, and topics like science, law, and religion have a very particular vocabulary, especially if they are compared to more common themes such as society or art. Still, it is surprising that novels and prose texts are among the most recognizable genres, while news and essays are among the most difficult classes. In Chapter 7.2 it will be analyzed in depth the possible explanations for the variance of the classification in the CoNSSA.

There is a range of values in the most efficient parameters. In some cases, several textual transformations, number of tokens and algorithms lead to higher results. In other words, there is no combination of parameters that always obtains optimal results in the classification. The textual transformations with the majority of best combinations are z-scores and log-z-scores, followed by tf-idf. Two algorithms achieve two-thirds of the best results: support vector machines and logistic regression, followed by random forest. Finally, almost half of the best results have analyzed 6,000 tokens, followed by 3,000 and 5,000.

Until now, I have only reported the very best results, but what are the tendencies both for the different genres and parameters? To answer the first question, I plot the mean F1-scores of the ten best combinations of parameters grouping them by genre.

Figure 37: Box plot with performance for different genres

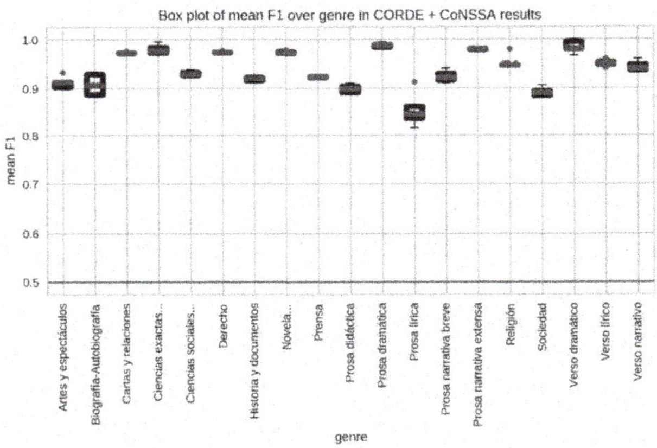

In this figure, each of the 10 best combinations of parameters is a data point, summarized in a box plot showing the median, quartiles and outliers. The baseline is shown as a straight line with a value of 0.5. The previous table contains the best cases; these are also included in the box plot as the highest values, either the upper whiskers or the upper fliers (in cases of outliers). The medians of the box plots have F1-scores between 0.85 and 0.99. This means that not only the very best results for each class are very high, but that other combinations behave similarly. In some cases, the very best combinations of parameters involve outliers (arts, lyrical prose, and religion), meaning that this performance only results from a lucky combination of parameters. Actually, lyrical prose is one of the genres with the lowest median value and a stronger deviation, followed by biography-autobiography. One could argue that lyrical prose mixes form and content in a non-standard manner (narrative prose, lyrical verse), but so too does narrative verse and its recognition is over 0.9. Apparently, when looking at the data in CORDE, it is clearer what a narrative poem should be than what lyrical prose is.

To what degree do the results of the evaluation correlate with the sample size? Are the algorithms only correctly classifying the large genres because they have more data? A regression analysis of the mean F1-score and the sample size from the ten best combinations of parameters gives a value of 0.10 without statistical significance (p-value 0.15, further details in the Jupyter Notebook). This means that the results are not biased by the number of texts as one would expect. The explanation could lie in the fact that small genres are also more homogeneous than large genres and therefore their features are more easily recognizable. Further similar hypotheses will be more closely analyzed in Chapter 7.2.

In the facet grid of Figure 38, the textual results for the different parameters are compared: Textual transformations are rows, algorithms are columns and the number of tokens define the different box plots. In the textual transformations (rows of the facet grid) there are two clear groups: the relative frequency which, as expected, gives the worst results, and the rest (z-scores, logarithmic, log-z-scores, and tf-idf). Even when these four transformations achieve very different values in the highest results, it can now be seen that their performance is actually very similar.

Regarding the algorithms (columns of the facet grid), I have plotted in this figure only the algorithms that show best performance, in order to not make an overly large figure where the labels are hardly readible. Three algorithms (support vector machines, logistic regression, and random forest) achieve in the majority of cases over 0.9. The other algorithms, Gaussian naive Bayes and k-nearest neighbors have clearly lower scores (more details in the Jupyter Notebook). An interesting effect is the combination of transformations and algorithms. Some combinations show clearly higher results than the rest of the columns or rows. For example, the only algorithm that scores over 0.9 using relative frequency is random forest. Similar results are achieved by logistic regression + z-scores or SVM + tf-idf. This means that the combination of the different parameters is not independent and choosing a good classifier and a good transformation could lead to worse results than selecting a mediocre classifier or transformation that achieves high results.

Figure 38: Box plots showing the performance of different parameters

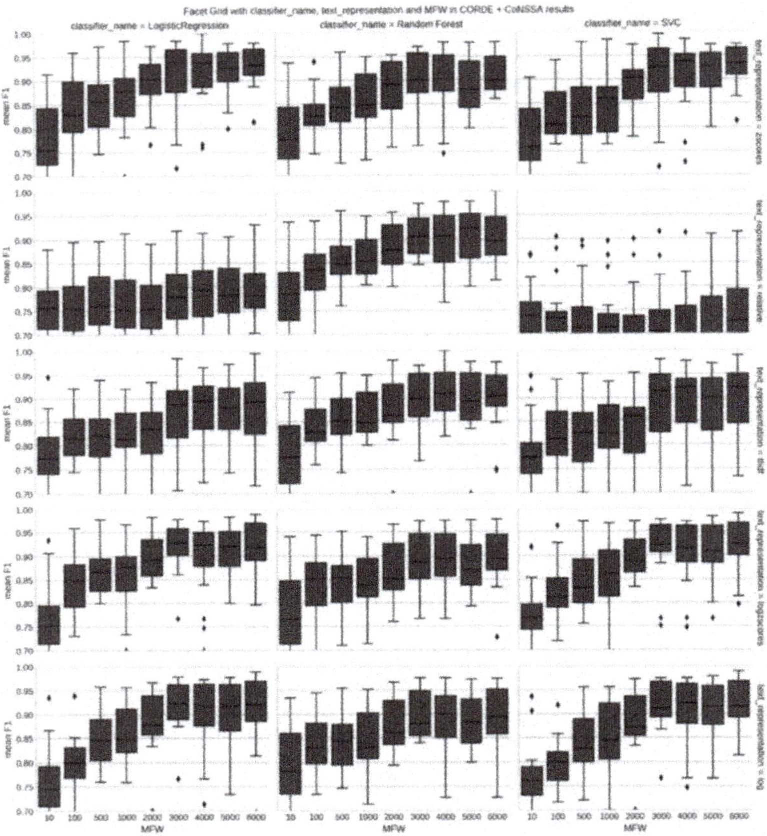

3.3.5 Multi-Class Evaluation of Parameters

Parallel to the binary evaluation, I also evaluate the classification of CORDE 1860–1960 + CoNSSA using multi-class classification. In this case, I do not pass the texts divided into two groups for each genre (either it belongs to the genre or not). Instead, every text (6,800) gets assigned one single label out of 19 possible values. In this way, the algorithm has to choose a single genre for each text. I choose not to under-sample in this scenario because, as already mentioned, the sizes of the classes are extremely unbalanced. If all the classes are required to have an equal sample size, only 3% of the corpus would be used. There are two reasons why I think the results will not be affected by the decision of not undersampling. First, I have already calculated that performance does not correlate with sample size in the binary classification. Second, my interest lies in the category novel in particular, and its sample size is more in the middle range, similar to many others (such as lyrical prose, social science). This makes it difficult for the algorithm to favor this genre over the rest. In this composition, the baseline is not 0.5 as in the binary evaluation. Instead, I use the majority class baseline, which corresponds to the proportion of the largest category in the corpus; in this case this is news, with a proportion of 0.34. Even if the baseline is lower and consequently easier to exceed, the task is more difficult because now the algorithm has 19 different options to choose for each text, instead of the two binary values.

The best results of this multi-class evaluation are achieved by support vector machines using 5,000 MFW transformed as log-z-scores. Calculating the mean of the F1-macro[4] for cross-validation, the best performance achieves a 0.57 (and a standard deviation of 0.04), which is statistically highly significant over the baseline of 0.34. In comparison to the binary classification, the logarithmic frequency, log-z-scores, and z-scores show clearly better results than the tf-idf for the multi-class classification. With regard to the algorithm, support vector machines clearly yields the highest results and the MFW in this case are quite stable between 2,000 and 6,000.

It is important to highlight the large difference between the results for the binary classification (with F1-scores between 0.91 and 1.0) and the multi-class evaluation, with its best results around 0.57 F1-macro. How should be this difference interpreted? On the one hand, the binary classification yields clearly higher results, leading one to believe that it is more accurate. However, the binary task is easier since the algorithm has only two possible values. On the other hand, the multi-class task more accurately fits the data, since CORDE gives only one label per text. Still, as I will show in Chapter 5.1, when more than one source is used, they tend to give several labels. Having only one label per text might simply be hiding the more complex nature of genres. Because there are good arguments for both tasks, I will run both of them in the following section, first as binary and subsequently as multi-class.

4 This variant of the F1-score "computes the unweighted per-class f-scores. This gives equal weight to all classes, no matter what their size is" (Müller and Guido 2016, 301).

To summarize the binary and multi-class evaluations, the classification of the genres of CORDE 1860–1960 + CoNSSA achieves very good results as a binary task, clearly exceeding the baseline for all genres with a high significance with a mean of 0.95 F1-scores over the different genres. When classified as multi-class, the results are also above the baseline, but the results are markedly lower, with best results around 0.57 F1-macro. The parameters that achieved higher results were z-scores and log-z-score transformations of lexical frequencies, support vector machines, logistic regression and random forest algorithms, and between 3,000 and 6,000 most frequent words.

3.3.6 Binary Prediction of Genre of Disputed Texts

Now that the model has been trained, the next step is to apply it to the texts where there is no certainty on whether they are novels or not. The most basic way to do this is to choose the best combination of parameters and predict the genre of each text once. However, this strategy presents different shortcomings. First, the corpus is under-sampled every time, so every time the algorithm is actually learning what the features of the genres are from different cases; consequently, the algorithm can choose a different genre every time. Second, some Machine Learning algorithms, such as random forest, are not deterministic because randomness is involved at some point, i.e. with equal input, the output can differ.

To obtain more robust results, I decide to run a combination of parameters, not for the very best, but rather the 10 highest combinations for each genre, and run each of these 10 times. In this way, I make 100 predictions on whether each text belongs or does not belong to each subgenre. This can be translated into a percentage of the number of times that each instance is classified with a specific genre or not. In total, the genre of each text is predicted 1,900 times (100 predictions * 19 genres).[5] The highest values for each text are highlighted in the table below in bold.[6]

5 For this reason, the rows of the following table are not required to add up to 100. They could actually vary between 0 and 1,900.

6 The texts are referred in the table through short versions of the title. Their complete titles are used in the rest of the text.

Table 3: Number of predictions in prose texts with unclear genre as multi-label task

	Title	**Author name**	**Ciencias sociales**	**Historia y documentos**	**Novela**	**Prosa didáctica**	**Sociedad**	**Verso lírico**
ne0023	Lampara Maravillosa	Valle	0	0	**80**	20	0	0
ne0037	Media Noche	Valle	0	0	**90**	0	0	10
ne0115	Aviraneta	Baroja	0	40	**60**	0	0	0
ne0127	Platero	Ramon-Jimenez	0	0	**50**	0	0	**50**
ne0132	Finlandesas	Ganivet	10			40	**50**	
ne0149	Bandido	AEspina	0	0	**90**	0	10	0

In the 14 cases analyzed, only three texts have been distinctly classified as novels: *Aviraneta: o la vida de un conspirador* by Baroja, *Luis Candelas, el bandido de Madrid* by Antonio Espina, and *La novela de un novelista* by Valdés. In contrast, four texts are clearly rejected as novels: *La lámpara maravillosa* (by Valle-Inclán, social science), *Juan de Mairena* (by Machado, essay), *Cartas finlandesas* (by Ganivet, autobiography-biography), and *Diario de un poeta recién casado* (by Ramón Jiménez, lyrical verse). The column of novels shows that all the texts have been classified as this genre at least 10 times, except for *La lámpara maravillosa* by Valle-Inclán. The most interesting fact is that this text is actually not clearly recognized as part of any genre, something that is also observable in the other text by Valle-Inclán, *La media noche*. This is also the case for the *Greguerías* (Gómez de la Serna), *Tomás Rueda* (Azorín), and *De un cancionero apócrifo* (Machado). For each subgenre, the algorithm has two options:

Either the text belongs to this genre, or it does not. At the end, I expect one genre to have been clearly chosen as the most representative of each text following the intuitive idea that every text must belong to a genre, (cfr. Petrenz and Webber 2011, 385), and that there are not *genreless* texts (Derrida 1980). Of course, the algorithm can decide otherwise, and in fact this is what happened with these texts: The majority of the predictions classify these texts as "not part of this genre," ultimately meaning they do not clearly belong to any. In a way, the Machine Learning prediction and CORDE confirm that these texts are unique works that do not fit into any traditional category, or at least not in the genres that I modeled using the metadata of the CORDE.

However, not all cases are problematic. There is a text that is clearly classified as belonging to two genres: *Aviraneta: o la vida de un conspirador* (by Baroja) is classified 80% as a novel and 70% as biography-autobiography. A similar situation is the case for *La vida de Rubén Darío* (by Darío), which is similarly classified as novel, history, and biography. In general, biography-autobiography is, after the novel, the genre in which most of the texts are recognized. This shows that the sizes of the categories do not seem to affect the results. The size of biography-autobiography is only 5% in comparison to the novel, and is still often used for the prediction. There are also some genres that are always predicted as negative, such as narrative verse, journalistic text, hard science, and lyrical prose. I expected this last genre to be assigned to some unclear instances, like *Greguerías* or *Platero y yo*, but this is not the case. This might be explained by the low results from the evaluation of this category.

The case of the highly canonized text *Platero y yo* (by Ramón Jiménez) is particularly interesting. This text is recognized 50% of the time as lyrical verse, which formally it is not: The text is written in prose and contains only a few verses. Of course, I have given to the algorithm only the vocabulary of the text, what is using for the predictions. Other textual cues would better recognize the formal aspect of the text (such as layout, encoding elements or position on the page). The second class *Platero y yo* is ascribed to is autobiography (30%). Although it is traditionally not treated or read as one, experts could agree on this genre more easily since the protagonist is identified as the author. Finally, it is recognized 20% of the times as a novel. In general, the prediction gives an interesting summary about the genre of *Platero y yo*: it does not completely fit in any genre, its vocabulary is similar to lyrical verse (even though it is not), and it resembles both the autobiography-biography and novel.

The two editions of the *Greguerías* also show unexpected classifications: the novel, arts, and dramatic prose, all of them with values below 40%. Traditionally these texts are understood as closer to lyrical prose, lyrical verse, and short stories, genres that are completely ignored by the prediction (except for the last with only 10%). The algorithm seems to agree with Umbral (see Section 2.1.10.), who said that Gómez de la Serna was a "writer without genre" (1984, 226–29).

I expected the text of *Juan de Mairena* to be predicted by the algorithm as novel; however, this is not the case. Although it is classified 20% of the time as a novel, it is actually one of the few cases in which 100% of the time another genre is chosen: the essay. The prediction suggests that this text is an essay. This can be tinged by the reader: The essay is held not by the author but by a fictional character.

3.3.7 Multi-Class Prediction of Genre of Disputed Texts

In the previous section, I have shown how, in many cases, the algorithm refuses to relate the text to any category. But what happens if it does not have this option? What if the algorithm is forced to choose between one of the genres for each text? Here, I inspect more closely the six cases that did not have a majority in belonging to any genre with the multi-label classification. As for the binary prediction, I use the 10 best results of the evaluation and run each one 10 times. This produces 100 predictions for each text, resulting in percentage values in the following table.

Table 4: Number of predictions in prose texts with unclear genre as multi-class task

	Title	Author name	Ciencias sociales	Historia y documentos	Novela	Prosa didáctica	Sociedad	Verso lírico
ne0023	Lampara Maravillosa	Valle	0	0	**80**	20	0	0
ne0037	Media Noche	Valle	0	0	**90**	0	0	10

neo115	Aviraneta	Baroja	0	40	**60**	0	0	0
neo127	Platero	RamonJimenez	0	0	**50**	0	0	**50**
neo132	Finlandesas	Ganivet	10	0	0	40	**50**	0
neo149	Bandido	AEspina	0	0	**90**	0	10	0
neo172	Greguerias	Serna	0	0	**80**	0	20	0
neo173	Greguerias completas	Serna	0	0	**80**	0	20	0
neo177	Mairena	AMachado	20	0	0	**80**	0	0
neo184	Diario Poeta	RamonJimenez	0	0	0	0	0	**100**
neo217	Cancionero	AMachado	0	0	0	**100**	0	0
neo218	Vida Dario	Dario	0	**100**	0	0	0	0
neo291	Tomas	Azorin	0	0	**100**	0	0	0
neo329	NovelaNovelista	Valdes	0	0	**100**	0	0	0

The cases that have been already clearly classified as novels remain within this genre in the multi-class task. In general, these results are very similar to those obtained by the binary task, only simpler: fewer genres and more instances with the highest possible values. Two of the texts whose genre is still unclear are now clearly predicted as novels: *Tomás Rueda* (Azorín) and *La media noche* (Valle-Inclán). Also, the *Greguerías* have a clear majority classification as novel (80%) in comparison to the second genre, society (20%). In comparison, the text of *De un cancionero apócrifo* is now clearly ascribed to the essay. Finally, *Platero y yo* is classified 50% as a novel and 50% as lyrical verse, a text that seems to reject being simplistically ascribed to a genre.

3.3.8 Conclusions and Modification of the Corpus

In this chapter I have answered the question of whether 14 texts in CoNSSA are novels or not. For this, I have used the frequencies and metadata of the largest diachronic corpus in Spanish, CORDE, together with the undisputed novels of CoNSSA. First, I have evaluated the classification (as binary and multi-class tasks), fine-tuning three different parameters: transformation of the lexical frequency, algorithms, and the number of tokens. The results have shown that the binary classification achieves very good results, while the multi-class classification correctly assigns about the half of the texts.

After the evaluation, I have used the best combinations of parameters several times to predict the genre of the discussed texts. The results, particularly the binary prediction, give a markedly more complex picture about genre compared to the naive notion that each text belongs to only a single genre. Although some texts do belong to a single genre, others seem to be either clearly part of several, only partially part of several, while some seem to reject being classified at all.

The binary classification undisputedly recognizes three texts as novels: *Aviraneta: o la vida de un conspirador* by Baroja, *Luis Candelas, el bandido de Madrid* by Antonio Espina, and *La novela de un novelista* by Valdés. In this classification, four other texts were clearly rejected as novels: *La lámpara maravillosa* by Valle-Inclán, *Cartas finlandesas* by Ganivet, *Juan de Mairena* by Machado, *Diario de un poeta recién casado* by Ramón Jiménez, and *La vida de Rubén Darío* by Darío. A third group (*La media noche* by Valle-Inclán, *Platero y yo* by Ramón Jiménez, both texts of *Greguerías* by Serna, *De un cancionero apócrifo* by Machado, and *Tomás Rueda* by Azorín) were not classified as being part of any subgenre in the majority of the cases. This is an interesting and unexpected result that can be explained in different ways. On the one hand, it could be argued that the set of 19 genres filtered from the CORDE does not cover all the possible genres. There are many literary genres that have not been considered, such as sonnet or tragedy. However, these should be understood as part of the basic genres that are in the model (lyrical verse and plays). It is remarkable that two of the still-disputed texts are labeled with one of the one-author-labels: *greguerías*. These results seem to point out that the *greguerías* do not fit in any of analyzed genres. This, however, does not necessarily imply that they truly constitute their own genre. Other genres, like aphorism, are not part of CORDE and could have obtained better results. In any case, the hypothesis that *greguerías* would be classified as short stories or lyrical verse has been falsified by the use of classification and lexical frequencies.

In Section 3.3.7 I have chosen to go one step further and force the algorithm to classify the disputed texts in a multi-class task. This way, it is not possible for the texts to be assigned to no genre. Of the six texts whose genre was still unclear, the multi-class prediction ascribed *La media noche,* the two editions of the *Greguerías,* and *Tomás Rueda* to the novel. In contrast, *De un cancionero apócrifo* was clearly classified as essay. But the assignment of one text is still unclear: *Platero y yo* by Ramón Jiménez was equally classified as a novel and as lyrical verse. It is noteworthy to observe how the data reject simplistic classification, even when the algorithms are forced to do so.

How do these results affect the composition of the corpus? The most important outcomes of this chapter are now translated into metadata that are saved in the TEI XML files, which will be used in later chapters to filter CoNSSA. For this, I create a new metadata class about genre: *genre.analyzed*. All the texts that have been labeled by the manuals of literature as novels continue with this value in the new class. The seven texts that have been clearly classified as either novels or not novels by the binary classification are now annotated as such, with a high certainty attribute:

```
<term type="text.genre.analyzed" certain="high">novela</term>
```

The four texts that have been recognized as novels only by the multi-class prediction are also marked as novels, but in this case with a medium certainty. Finally, the problematic case of *Platero y yo* is also assigned to the novel, but with a low certainty. In this manner, both the general results and the nuances of the recurrence of the decisions are formally documented. Finally, CoNSSA now considers eight more texts as novels, while six texts are annotated as not being novels and will be ignored in the rest of the chapters.

In the steps of the current chapter, I have analyzed the specific boundaries of the novels using Machine Learning with the aim of filtering the corpora. The use of digital methods does not necessarily imply simplistic results when the data is ambivalent or does not fit in the modeled categories. My corpus contained 14 texts with a disputed main genre, but in the MdLE there are at least 62 similar cases for this period. Besides, I only used the lexical frequency in CORDE and their set of genres. Further analysis of these works could be carried out if more texts and metadata were available.

4. Feature Engineering:
Linguistic Annotation and Transformation

4.1 Grammatical, Lexical, Semantic, and Textual Annotation

4.1.1 Introduction

Numerous textual layers can be identified between the very basic information of lexical frequency and the very complex information of genre. Several units, including tokens, sentences, paragraphs or chapters, can be analyzed from different linguistic perspectives, such as grammar, lexis, semantics, pragmatics, or text linguistics.

Language is often conceptualized as a system of layers, one on top of the other, which is frequently used to structure the content of manuals about linguistics (Garrido Medina 2009; Kabatek and Pusch 2011), Natural Language Processing (Carstensen et al. 2009), or literary style (Leech and Short 2007). An extended schema for the analysis of textual semantics (in German *textsemantische Analyse*) has been proposed by Gardt (2012, 2013). In his proposal, he defines three large groups of textual components (Gardt 2012, 64–66):

1. *Communicative-pragmatic frame*: Includes information about the producer, the reader, the situation, and the medium. These aspects are covered by the basic metadata explained in Chapter 3.2.
2. *Macrostructure*: Includes data about the genre and text type, pictures in the text, development of themes, and textual units. Apart from the pictures, these elements are discussed in the information about genre (Section 3.2.7 and Chapter 5.1), and some transformations of the data (Section 4.2.3.4).
3. *Microstructure*: In which the several linguistic layers are represented.

This last area of Gardt's schema is the one that is covered in this chapter and at least one formalization from each layer is considered here. To be more specific, from the text I extract characteristics from the following layers: layout, morphology, lexicology, phraseology, semantics, forms of argumentation, syntax, and punctuation. The only basic linguistic areas that are not covered are phonetics and phonology, which would be important aspects when considering lyrical genres, but there are no reasons for considering that they would have large impact in the identification of subgenres of the novel.

In this chapter, I present the features that have been annotated in the corpus and discuss the hypotheses on why they could be important cues for the classification of specific subgenres. Additionally, I cite the specific tool that has been employed. The specific annotated features are punctuation, lexical units (tokens, idioms), and grammatical, semantic (entities, *lexnames* of WordNet, catalogs of the dictionary DUE by María Moliner), pragmatic (DPDE, refranario.com), and textual (TEI-tags) features. All these layers will be properly evaluated and analyzed in Chapter 6.1.

4.1.2 Format of Annotation

One could argue that the format of the linguistic and textual annotation is irrelevant since it is only the step between the annotation tools and the algorithm for the analysis. In my opinion, the format does influence numerous aspects, such as the evaluation of errors, the facilitation of specific features, the exchange of documents, and historical archiving. For these reasons, in this section I want to discuss and justify the decisions that have been made.

The different communities using computational methods for cultural objects have strong traditions and preferences for formats. The editorial community works with TEI XML. This format has been partially applied by Corpus Linguists, in many cases using standoff markup for linguistic annotation. However, linguists often also develop their own XML implementation. In contrast, Computational Linguists and researchers from Computer Science prefer JSON, UIMA Type System in XMI files, or just CSV spreadsheets. Some of the most advanced researchers in the field operate with other formats, such as Linked Open Data. The DH community working on Digital Literary Studies has not yet embraced a single format for linguistic annotation.

I have decided to keep the textual and linguistic annotation in TEI XML for several reasons. The first is to maintain the same format in which the original text and metadata have been saved. This allows for a simpler workflow, in which the same technologies and libraries (xPath, lxml, XSLT) can be applied to extract several components. This implies the second reason, i.e., a single file can contain the entire data of each novel: original text, literary and subgenre metadata, as well as linguistic annotation. The possibility of the information being misplaced or lost during the analysis and in later steps is more remote than if the annotation is placed in separate files. A further reason, related to the first, is the fact that a family of technologies related to XML (x-technologies) have been around for several decades and are well documented. Indeed, some of these technologies are exclusively applied to the evaluation and control of the encoded data, in terms of well-formless, the use of specific elements and attributes through schemata, or specific values through Schematron. In addition, TEI XML is still the best option for the interchange of the data because many communities have either adopted it as the standard format (DH, Corpus Linguistics) or are able to work with it (Computational Linguistics, Computer Science). For archival purposes, TEI XML is a format more likely to be understood and considered in future decades than CSV formats (in which the names of the fields represented as columns are normally not standardized and are consequently easily unintelligible), or ad hoc XML representations.

A final reason is the possibility of directly mapping the several textual and linguistic layers into nesting XML elements. This allows an intuitive representation of the annotation at different levels and facilitates the possibility of creating combined features that merge into a single unit of data. As I will show in the next paragraphs, some traits that will be applied are to combine information from examples from the paragraph (whether it is a narrative or direct speech) and from the semantics of the word. Since in TEI XML the paragraph contains the words, these features are easily tractable. Filtering aspects by the position of the text is also possible, only taking, for example, the semantic features that appear in the first and last chapter of the novels.

As is common in TEI, there are several options for encoding linguistic annotation. Nevertheless, two of these are preferred for the annotation: attributes in specific elements or standoff markup linking a specific unit (normally tokens). The standoff markup within XML (not TEI) can be found in the *Text Corpus Format* (TCF), an XML implementation for corpora defined by the European linguistic infrastructure project, CLARIN. In this format, the original source is first encoded as text; in a second element, the tokens are unambiguously identified; finally, the different linguistic annotations of the consequent elements are saved, referring to the identifier of the token. As I will explain in the next subsections, I want to use several NLP tools and linguistic resources that annotate different linguistic layers for my corpus.

These annotations do not have to agree on the tokenization. Consequently, the idea of standoff markup for identifying tokens and then adding annotation in other elements does not seem ideal.

I choose to encode the annotation of each tool in parallel elements as TCF would do. In contrast to this format, I retain the text of the tokens in each element. For this, I customize the TEI schema of the project, creating the element *anno* (for 'annotation') as a third option of the element choice, which normally contains *orig* ('origin') and *reg* ('regularization') with their exact same properties. In the next example, the annotation contains a very simple paragraph in direct speech with only one sentence: "— Por ejemplo tú." First, the primary text is to be found in the *orig* element. Following this, several *anno* elements contain the annotation from several tools and flavors. To keep the example short, I have used the ellipsis to represent further attributes or elements:

```
<p>
<seg type="direct-speech">
<s>
<choice>
<orig>—Por ejemplo tú.</orig>
<anno source="freeling" type="tokens">
<w cligs:form="—" lemma="-" cligs:tag="Fg" cligs:pos="punctuation"
type="hyphen" />
<w cligs:form="Por" lemma="por" cligs:tag="SP" cligs:pos="adposition"
type="preposition"/>
<w cligs:form="ejemplo" lemma="ejemplo" cligs:tag="NCMS000" cligs:pos="noun"
type="common" cligs:gen="masculine" cligs:num="singular" cligs:wn="05820620-
n"/>
<w cligs:form="tú" lemma="tú" cligs:tag="PP2CSN0" cligs:pos="pronoun"
type="personal" cligs:person="2" cligs:gen="common" cligs:num="singular"
cligs:case="nominative"/>
<w cligs:form="." lemma="." cligs:tag="Fp" cligs:pos="punctuation" type="pe-
riod"/>
</anno>
<anno source="freeling" type="multiwords">
<w cligs:form="—" lemma="-" tag="Fg" pos="punctuation" type="hyphen"/>
<w cligs:form="Por_ejemplo" lemma="por_ejemplo" cligs:tag="RG" cligs:pos="ad-
verb" type="general" cligs:wn="00159040-r" cligs:wnlex="adv.all"/>
```

```
<w cligs:form="tú" lemma="tú" cligs:tag="PP2CSN0" cligs:pos="pronoun"
type="personal" cligs:person="2" cligs:gen="common" cligs:num="singular"
cligs:case="nominative"/>
<w cligs:form="." lemma="." cligs:tag="Fp" cligs:pos="punctuation" type="pe-
riod"/>
</anno>
<anno source="dpde" type="dis-part" />
<anno source="refranario" type="dis-part" />
</choice>
</s>
</seg>
</p>
```

One can observe that the two annotations of the tool FreeLing agree on three tokens ("—", "*tú*", ".") but disagree on the words "por ejemplo": Depending on a parameter in FreeLing, the tool will consider it either a single lexical unit or two. A standoff markup solution identifying different layers of tokens and units would have been possible, but the extraction of specific features could have been more error-prone.

There are two disadvantages of this way of annotating. First is its verbosity: In the previous example, the information on three tokens is repeated. However, other solutions would have led to similar redundancies, only in different standoff elements or files. The second disadvantage is the opacity of one annotation towards the rest. In this format, the idiom recognized by FreeLing, "por ejemplo," does not contain the information that it is composed of a preposition and a noun. If the sentence had contained proverbs, these would not be annotated with their semantic or grammatical characteristics. Of course, these aspects are irrelevant for the specific goal of this research about subgenres, but can be of importance in other projects with specific linguistic questions about these compositional units.

4.1.3 Vocabulary and Punctuation

As already pointed out in Chapter 2.2, the majority of research on genre has used lexical information to classify or cluster the texts. Almost all papers that have evaluated the performance of different types of features suggest that vocabulary is the most useful information, sometimes improved by linguistic annotation.

What exactly comprises a token is still open for discussion. The particular case of punctuation is usually treated in three different ways: One can keep it as a token, delete it, or maintain it together with the previous or following lexical token. Normally, these decisions are not explicitly explained and in the section on feature evaluation the reader only has a mere glimpse into it. In different tests, I have observed that some punctuation characters (like exclamation marks) can be some of the best markers for genre distinction, which is the reason why I decide to include all punctuation characters as separate tokens.

A more complex question is whether tokens are the best way of modeling the lexical information that current linguistic tools can give us. Lexicology and lexicography consider units like *echar de menos* ('miss') or *por ejemplo* ('for example') as lexicalized units or idioms whose meaning is not (or at least not entirely) derived from its components. The tool FreeLing offers two different basic units of analysis: tokens or *multiwords* (i.e. idioms). As previously explained, both of these have been annotated in the corpus with the goal of testing whether a more sophisticated understanding of lexical information can improve the results, or if tokens remain the best type of features.

4.1.4 Grammatical Annotation

Grammatical features are usually information added to the classification of genres that improve the accuracy of results (Kessler, Numberg, and Schütze 1997; Stamatatos, Fakotakis, and Kokkinakis 2001; Santini 2011; Allison et al. 2011). For this kind of annotation, I have applied the tool FreeLing which is developed and maintained by Lluís Padró at the Universitat Politècnica de Catalunya (Padró and Stanislovsky 2012). Besides typical steps like tokenization, sentence splitting, PoS (Part of Speech) tagging or lemmatization, this resource has several functions for Spanish texts, such as Named Entity Recognition, WordNet-based sense annotation, or syntactical parsing. The tool utilizes the EAGLES tag set and offers several output formats (CSV, JSON). The research group wrote scripts that take the XML output of FreeLing and converted it into TEI XML.

4.1.5 Entities

The paper by Hettinger et al. (2016) uses networks of characters as features in the novels after a great deal of work in the preparation of thousands of texts, with the results that these features were close to or even lower than the baseline. The observed outcomes are highly relevant and unexpected, since it is very intuitive to presume the hypothesis that the constellations of characters behave very differently in adventure, romantic, or social novels. In general, researchers are not modeling entities (or proper names) as specific features. Instead, it is more common to delete them through culling options, or to just ignore them due to their relatively low frequency within the entire corpus.

To test the hypothesis of whether entities are important features for genre classification without involving the steep and probably unfruitful path followed by Hettinger et al., I consider proper nouns a different kind of feature in comparison to the rest of the lexical units. Standard lexical units (nouns, verbs, adjectives, etc.) have at least one meaning, while proper nouns do not mean anything, they only refer to entities. The fact that the protagonist is called *José* or *Carlos* should not have any great impact on the subgenre of the text. However, other characteristics of proper names can influence the category of the text. In some subgenres like the educational novel, a higher frequency of fewer names (the protagonist and a close circle) is more common than in, for example, war novels. In these, several constellations of changing characters are expected which would have a medium range of frequency. For this reason, the order of frequency of proper nouns referring to people was annotated. The most common proper name of a person in each novel can then be modeled as NEC_PERS_0 (NameEntityCategory_Person_Rank0), regardless of the specific name of the character and, consequently, its presence as frequency can be compared across texts. Other characteristics about the names can be discussed, such as whether the names of the protagonists are typical for the society (which is more likely in subgenres like realist or naturalist novel), archaic (historical novels), or unusual (fantasy novel). This path has not been explored in this work, although I expect these characteristics to correlate strongly with other features of the text.

I have stated that the individual name of a character should not play a role. Nevertheless, this can differ for cases like *Juan*, which is the most frequent protagonist's name of the corpus and, in addition, is a name that is more expected in romantic and erotic novels because of the impact of *Don Juan Tenorio*. Other cases, such as *Dios* ('God') or *Jesús*, question whether these names bring a specific meaning and not only a reference. In any case, the names of the protagonists have also been encoded as metadata, with this information kept apart from the rest of the linguistic information and is thus able to be passed as features (see Section 7.1.5).

In this section, I have only considered the proper names that refer to people. FreeLing also classifies entities of other types, such as places and others. These geographical references are kept in the text as part of the rest of the text. Words like *Madrid* or *España* do not have the same kind of meaning as *pan* ('bread') or *madre* ('mother'). However, the names of places do bring a large amount of universal information that can be important for the text, e.g., references to cities in Spain can be good indicators for *regionalist*, realist, and historical novels, while names of other countries are more likely expected to be adventure or war novels.

4.1.6 Semantic Annotation

Semantics is one linguistic layer that has escaped suitable formalization in NLP until recently. In the last years, several methodologies have been developed following the distributional hypothesis by Firth and condensed in the following attributed sentence: "You shall know a word by the company it keeps" (Eisenstein 2019, 334). In this area, several approaches and specific technologies have been developed such as *word embeddings* (like *word2vec*, Mikolov et al. 2013) or *latent semantic analysis* (like *topic modeling*, Blei 2012). The theoretical advantages of distributional models are that these methods are language-independent, and do not require preexisting semantic tools such as dictionaries.

However, there are four notorious arguments against the implementation of these techniques for this corpus. First, great difficulties are encountered in properly evaluating these techniques. What exactly should a "good topic" look like? What should be the exact similarity between two words? Normally, there are several strategies for the evaluation of such a model, such as intrinsic (comparison to previously annotated human intuition, a costly process), extrinsic (application of the output for a further classification task, an indirect manner of evaluation), or the comparison between several distributional models (a method that can easily be criticized as being circular, Eisenstein 2019, 347–49). The second argument for rejecting these techniques is that they have been applied mainly to data sets that are much larger than CoNSSA. Its application to smaller data sets remains an area of research (Altszyler et al. 2017; Antoniak and Mimno 2018), with the previously mentioned difficulties in the evaluation. The third reason is that different publications that evaluated both topic modeling and lexical frequencies have not found that the first performed better (Hettinger et al. 2016; Henny-Krahmer et al. 2018).

Finally, the fourth argument states that these distributional semantic models have a similar disadvantage as the use of lexical frequencies in comparison to more comprehensible semantic information: the difficulty of interpretation. What does it mean that 1,000 lexical and typographical features are the best discriminators for a genre? How can humans relate these numerous fields to specific definitions of genres? How is this different to using topics, when they are composed by probabilities of thousands of lexical units?

Because of these reasons, I decided to annotate the corpus with semantic features that support the interpretation of the features. For this, I have chosen two very different projects, both of them with lexical information annotated manually. The first are the lexical names in WordNet, a set of 45 semantic areas such as *body, plant, cognition, emotion, perception*, etc. Each group of synonyms in WordNet (synsets) is related to one of these lexical names.

The second semantic resource comes from the classic Spanish dictionary, *Diccionario de uso del español* (DUE), originally published in 1966 by María Moliner. This extraordinary lexicographic work contains many innovative aspects (for the time and even for today) in its content and format. Examples are the lexical order of entries besides the alphabetical order, different layers of semantic disambiguation, collocations, examples, and semantic catalogs. These catalogs are found in specific lexical units that can be seen as the most basic form of important semantic fields, such as *plants, clothes, boats, illness, music, time, writing, army*, etc. The lexical units of the dictionary are related to at least one of these "homogeneous and differentiated semantic groups" (Moliner 1966, XI). The motivation for this belonging are relations of synonymy, antonymy, hiperonymy (abstraction of), hyponymy (case of), holonymy (section of), or meronymy (part of) (Moliner 1966, X). For example, words like *caffeine, cappuccino, pot*, or *café* are somehow semantically related to the concept of coffee, so they appear in the catalog for the word *coffee*. Thus, all of them share a semantic trait, even when they do not belong to the same etymological family. In total, the dictionary contains 1,788 catalogs, some of them with references to hundreds of lexical units (such as *plants, clothes*, or *boats*), while many relate to some dozens.

A digital version of the dictionary in e-book format has been converted to XML and the catalogs have been transformed to a data frame in which each heading of the catalogs relates to its vocabulary. These files have been used to annotate each lemma of substantives, verbs, and adjectives to one or more catalogs.

4.1.7 Pragmatic and Textual Annotation

Besides grammatical and semantic annotation, I want to apply other resources that should cover other layers of linguistic information. The first level is related to the different textual types that are contained in the novel, such as the number of chapters, paragraphs, verses, or their length. This can be easily and accurately operationalized through the TEI-tags of these elements. In this way, the format of the corpus is translated into features that will be passed to the algorithm. Other researchers have used similar but more basic information about the layout for the classification tasks for genres. While Santini used HTML tags as features (2011), Underwood tackled this information indirectly through the proportion of characters for each line and each page (2014).

The second layer of this type is a pragmatic one, annotated through the *Diccionario de partículas discursivas del español* (DPDE). This resource was created by the linguistic research group Val.Es.Co at the Universidad de Valencia (Briz, Pons Bordería, and Portolés 2008) and built through entries written by many linguists. The dictionary inspects lexical units such as *hasta cierto punto* ('to a certain degree'), *mejor dicho* ('or to put it another way'), *por así decir* ('as it were'), etc. They only overlap to a certain degree with the multiwords detected by FreeLing, since this tool considers the majority of the previous examples merely a sequence of independent tokens. In contrast, the DPDE does not contain idioms in general but pragmatic units which are "linguistic elements that guide the interpretation of the discourse; using words in current approaches, they have a more procedural than conceptual character" ("Introducción," my translation). Before I run the analysis, I expect these units to be good indicators for a series of reasons. First, they are connectors between sentences but also markers of argumentation that are more likely to be found in genres like philosophical or historical novels. In addition, they could be good markers for direct speech that tries to imitate oral communication (realist and naturalist novels), in comparison to direct speech in genres like educational or autobiographic novels, where the style of the direct speech can be closer to narrative passages.

The third linguistic unit that has been annotated are proverbs (*refranes* in Spanish). Proverbs can be defined as complete sentences with a lexicalized meaning and without possible flexion. These linguistic units have been the focus of several analyses in other periods and genres (Combet 1996; Oddo Bonnet 2011; Lojendio Quintero 2011; Gálvez Vidal 2014). For this research, the underlying hypothesis is that some subgenres, like the realist, *regionalist*, or naturalist novel, contain more of these sentences than the rest (Pedraza Jiménez and Rodríguez Cáceres 1983, 366–67; Jaime Gómez and Jaime Lorén 1997; Jaime Lorén and Jaime Gómez 2004). For this, I have relied on the dictionary *refranario.com*, a tool I have developed through an NLP company (Calvo Tello and Castillo 2011). This resource contains structured information about the 356 most basic proverbs in Spanish. These have been annotated in CoNSSA with the aim of knowing whether features about proverbs (total number of proverbs in the text, frequency of specific proverbs) can be a marker for specific genres such as realist, naturalist, or erotic novels. Furthermore, since neither standard NLP tools nor the dictionaries tend to consider this information, there is little research about quantitative analysis on them.

A final linguistic textual layer has been annotated: the difference between narrative and direct speech passages. The reason for this is that direct speech should be a good indicator for several subgenres: In some there is an expectation of a lower proportion (social, erotic, historical novels, *greguerías*), while in others it should account for a larger section (realist, comedy, adventure). This has already been measured by some subgenres of the French novel (Schöch, Schlör, et al. 2016). Besides the general proportion in the entire works, I want to observe whether the presence of specific linguistic data in narrative or direct speech also makes a difference in the classification results. Does direct speech follow distinct purposes in philosophical and realist novels? In more operationzalized terms, do the semantic or pragmatic features help to differentiate the subgenres when they are isolated by their relation to narration or direct speech? These kinds of composed narratological-linguistic features will be evaluated in Chapter 6.1.

In the last years, various papers have employed several approaches to automatically identify direct speech in literary texts, such as rule-based classification, classic Machine Learning, or Deep Learning (Brunner 2015; Schöch, Schlör, et al. 2016; Jannidis et al. 2018). This task is highly dependent on the typographical rules applied in the original: For some languages and periods, direct speech can be formalized in rules using exclusively typographical features, while in other periods the readers have to apply their understanding of the text to distinguish them from each other. The Spanish novels from the analyzed period do have clear typographical rules. Therefore, I decide to use a rule-based approach and annotate it in TEI elements, as presented above.

4.2 Transformations of Lexical Data and Linguistic Annotation

4.2.1 Introduction

In the previous chapter, a set of linguistic annotation layers were introduced. The Machine Learning tasks require an even more specific operationalization of each of these in every text. Normally, the first step is to count each feature in the entire document. This is the basis of the so-called *Bag of Words document model* (BoW), or the more general *Bag of Features*. The information about the position in the text of the words (beginning of the text, end of a sentence) is ignored, and at least a second step is applied, namely a division through the entire length of the document to obtain the relative frequency, a typical measure, for example, in Corpus Linguistics.

The same model and transformation could be used for other annotations: relative frequency of direct speech in the text, relative frequency of each TEI-tag, etc. Further transformations are usual in different areas: z-score transformation in stylometry, tf-idf or binary frequency in Computer Sciences, or logarithmic transformations in Statistics. The different fields tend to consider only their typical traditions and neither consider nor evaluate other options. This can be observed given that from all the papers about computational analysis mentioned in Chapter 2.2, none evaluated different transformations, and in many of them the researchers provide neither their decisions nor their reasons.[1] The target group of this chapter is researchers who are active in DH and come from different areas which have common interests with my research: Computer Science, Computational Linguistics, Literary Studies, and Linguis-

1 Some authors were contacted personally by email and needed to check their code to confirm the transformation they had used.

tics. By that, the goal of this chapter is to obtain common knowledge about an aspect that has been overlooked until now.

So, if the different communities only use their typical transformation and ignore the rest, why do I dedicate an entire chapter to exploring this? First, because this in an interdisciplinary work and part of it should be to contrast theories and practices in several areas and, if possible, evaluate which could bring more benefit to the research goal. Second, one specific transformation could bring major advantages to the classification of genre; perhaps a traditional transformation in one of the fields, or perhaps a new modification or concatenation. This is what happened when the stylometrist John Burrows applied a transformation to textual frequency that was standard in Statistics (z-scores) but had been rarely used in Literary Studies or Linguistics. This led to one of the most important milestones of stylometry in particular, and Digital Humanities in general: the textual distance Delta (Burrows 2002). The evaluation in Chapter 6.1 will show that none of these transformations will have the same importance for genres as z-scores had for stylometric analysis of authorship. However, some of them will clearly yield higher results than others. In addition to analyzing the accuracy of the transformations, the reason why some lead to a better classification will also be analyzed. A series of characteristics of these transformations will be evaluated in Section 6.1.4 to explore the possible causes of this difference. These characteristics are described in this chapter in detail. For example, some of these transformations still contain information about frequency (relative or logarithmic frequency), others transform the numerical differences into categorical information (binary), while yet others transform the data in a way that no longer correlates with the original frequency (tf-idf or z-scores).

In any case, why do these fields transform the original frequencies from the texts? Compared to other kinds of information (like colors in pictures or characteristics in living beings), linguistic data tends to follow a particular distribution known as a Zipfian distribution. This was explained by the researcher Zipf, who in the 1930s stated (1932) the empirical law that the rank *n* of a word in this distribution multiplied by its frequency gives a constant (Carstensen et al. 2009, 230). The correlation between the rank and the frequency of each word is, in theory, a perfect line with a slope of -45° when both variables are log-transformed (Lestrade 2017). This law means that the most frequent word of any corpus will be twice as frequent as the second one, and three times as frequent as the third one. This distribution is “about as prevalent in social sciences as Gaussian distributions are in the natural sciences" (Pustet 2004).

This raises the question of what the theoretical criteria are that the transformations should present in order to deliver higher results in the classification. It is thought that a transformation that modifies a Zipfian distribution towards a Gaussian one would be desirable, since many of the algorithms expect a Gaussian by design. Another aspect is the span of the values: While some transformations are expressed in a narrow variance of possible values (for example z-scores typically have values between -3 and 3), others range between zero to several thousands. Another characteristic that is expected to bring advantages is that each unit still contains nuances about their frequency in the original text, while these are completely removed with a binary frequency (becoming a black-and-white transformation, either it is in the text or it is not). Besides, it is expected that losing the correlation to the original frequency will be also an advantage as happened with two very successful transformations in stylometry (z-scores) and Computer Science (tf-idf).

The six transformation described here are often recommended for text classification.[2] Many of the transformations I will present are seldom used in the Humanities, and sometimes applied without a real understanding of their implications. For this reason, I will introduce, plot, describe, and explain each of them, relating their characteristics to the specific data of some words of two novels. Thus, readers without experience of this type of transformation can still relate the results from their own reading experience. In Section 4.2.3 I will propose new transformations based on the variations of specific decisions or concatenations: mean and standard deviation over the file and z-scores compared to several corpora.

4.2.2 Classic Transformation of Frequency of Features

4.2.2.1 Term Frequency

The most basic representations of the frequency of words are the *term frequency*, *total frequency*, or *raw frequency*. All of these relate to the number of times each word appears in every text. This basic representation is seldom

2 Other less frequently used transformations are trinarization (in contrast to binarization), MinMax, and calculation of Zeta values.

used because of its dependency on the length of the text: The larger a text is, the higher the term frequency will be. In the following figure, there are four different plots, each showing several aspects of this representation of data in two novels: *Los pazos de Ulloa*, by Bazán, and *Tirano Banderas*, by Valle-Inclán.

Figure 39: Plots showing raw frequency in two novels

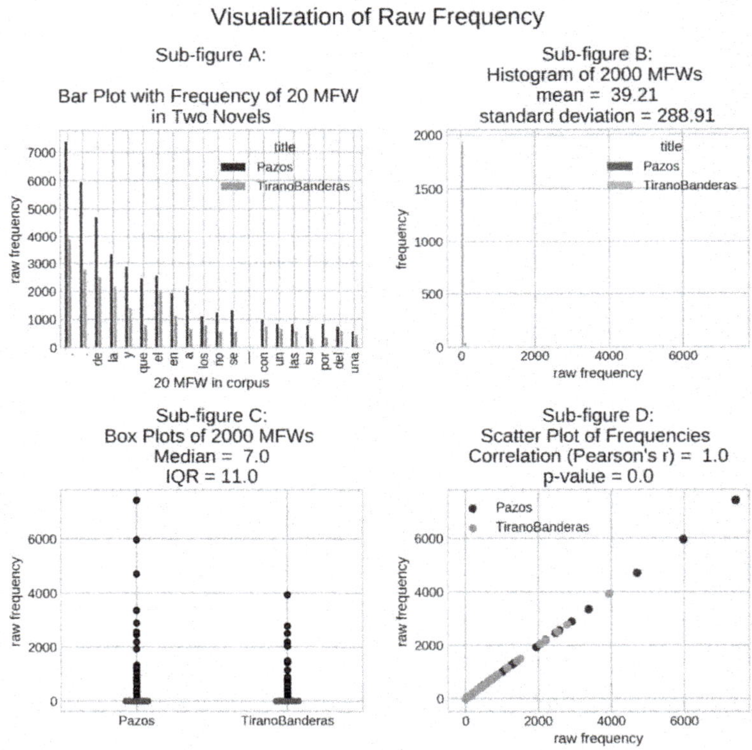

The first plot (Sub-figure A) shows the frequencies of the 20 top tokens (from the typographical character for the comma to the word *una*) and their frequency in the two novels. As is observed, there are more than 7,000 commas in the first text, and around 4,000 in the second (a much shorter novel).

This plot shows an important characteristic of counting and transforming tokens in a corpus: The words are counted in each text, but the counting process takes the entire corpus into consideration. The 13th token (—, an em dash) is an example of this, with both texts containing it zero times. There are different typographical signs to introduce dialogue in Spanish. The digital editions that were used as the base for these two texts did not use the em dash (traditionally understood as more correct), but rather the hyphen (-). The em dash is still in the top 20 MFWs of the corpus, even though it does not appear at all in these particular texts. The distribution of frequencies takes this item into account only because of the other texts, measuring these cases as zeros and therefore adding a zero to the general distribution of the novels. The concept of Bag of Words is a useful metaphor, but it gives the false idea that each text is considered in isolation and that each text is understood as a bag containing tokens which are counted. Actually, all tokens are counted for each bag, even though many of them do not appear. This is what causes one of the most important and problematic features of linguistic data, i.e., its sparse nature. The majority of the words do not appear in the majority of the texts; in other words, the majority of the items are counted zero times in many texts. It also implies that the sparseness and the size of a corpus should correlate with each other: The larger the corpus is, the more types it will contain, and therefore the sparser the distribution will be.

The second plot (Sub-figure B) shows the histograms of the 2,000 MFWs of both novels, with the horizontal axis representing several bins of the possible values of the relative frequency, and the vertical axis, the number of times that this value is represented in the original values.[3] The top of the diagram also shows information about the mean (39.21 occurrences) and the standard deviation (288.91) of *Los pazos de Ulloa*. The distribution shows a very skewed shape with many values close to zero. This means that many words are very infrequent or are not present at all in this text. A very large scale is observed on the x-axis, with a minimum value of zero and a maximum of 7,000.

In Sub-figure C, each text is represented by a box plot. In this transformation, the box plots are flat and very close to zero. This flatness is caused by the skewed distribution I have discussed in the previous paragraph. The median (7.0) and the variance expressed as IQR (11.0) are shown at the top of the plot. The median is a better central tendency than the mean when the data does not follow a Gaussian distribution, as is the case in textual frequencies. The points (fliers) represent outliers in the distribution describing data

3 In other words, the frequency of the relative frequency, as it appears in the label of the axis.

points with extreme values. The highest is the most frequent token, which is the comma, as was observed in the Sub-figure A.

Finally, Sub-figure D is a scatter plot that compares the original distribution of both novels (term or raw frequency) with the analyzed distribution. Since I am currently analyzing the term frequency, both axes represent the same values in this figure, but this will change in the following transformations. At the top, I report the results of a correlation test (Pearson's r) in terms of strength, together with the p-value to consider whether the correlation has statistical value or not.

The total frequency is the base for the rest of transformation, and is useful when sharing data of projects that are still protected by copyright. For example, the corpus CORDE by the RAE has published the absolute frequency of each token in the entire corpus, data that researchers can take and transform further, and similar data per file was used for the analysis of Chapter 3.3. To my knowledge, there is no research question that would benefit from using total frequency in comparison to the rest of the transformation. The data depends to a large extent on the length of the text, greatly varying the maximum value of each corpus and each text.

4.2.2.2 Term-Document Frequency

The first transformation is applied to contrast the term frequency with the length of the text: The frequency of each type is divided by the length of the text. In the case of *Los pazos de Ulloa*, the raw frequency of every token is divided by the total length of the text (102,686 tokens). The result is its *relative frequency* in a document, also called the *term-document frequency*. In Corpus Linguistics, this is probably still the most frequently used representation of data and it is often used in other fields.

The four sub-figures previously discussed contain in Figure 40 data of the relative frequency. In Sub-figure A with the bar plots, some tokens from *Tirano Banderas* (represented by the purple bars) have greater values than *Los pazos de Ulloa* (blue). Relative frequencies enable the comparison regardless of the total length and show that the token *el* has a greater relative frequency in *Tirano Banderas* than in *Los pazos de Ulloa*, even though the first novel is shorter. Of course, the data that had a zero total frequency remains the same.

The histogram (Sub-figure B) represents the same very skewed distribution as the previous transformation, with around 1,900 tokens very close to zero. What has changed drastically in comparison to the total frequency is

Figure 40: Plots showing relative frequency in two novels

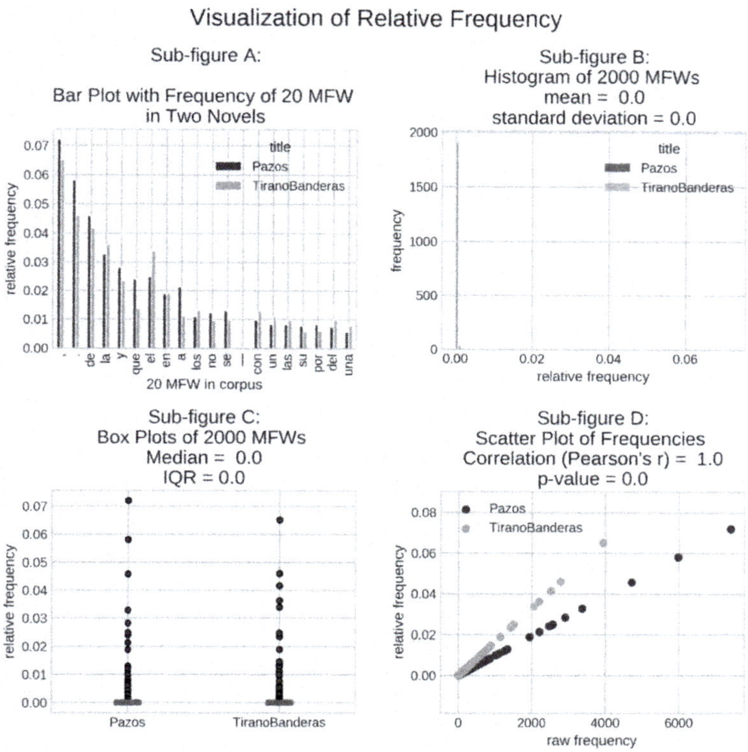

the horizontal axis: Now the data has a maximum value of 0.07. If this data is multiplied by 100, it becomes the percentage of the text. For example, in both texts, commas represent around 7% of all tokens of the text. In Sub-figure D, a perfect linear correlation between the total and the relative frequencies is observed, although the slope varies with the total length of the entire text.

The relative frequency is useful for comparing specific tokens in different texts. One of the disadvantages is that extreme skewness makes some features much more prominent than others. While the majority of real data is close to zero, there are many outliers with high values. Besides, there is no definition of the range. In one text, the most frequent token could represent 10% of the text, while in another text it represents only 2%.

4.2.2.3 Logarithmic Term Frequency

A further step the data can be subjected to is a logarithmic transformation (also called *log transformation*), which is often used in statistical analysis. Logarithms were proposed by John Napier in 1624 and were a useful method for the calculation of large numbers before the era of computers, allowing the transformation of a complex calculation into a simpler one (for example multiplications into additions; Jackson 2016, 42). Nowadays, they are still used for the visualization and transformation of data that follows an exponential rather than a linear growth. For example, the Richter magnitude scale for earthquakes has a logarithmic relation between magnitude (from one to nine) and the equivalent seismic energy. An earthquake of magnitude one on the Richter scale represents around 100 kg of seismic energy. A magnitude of two does not equate to double the seismic energy, but rather ten times more. The scale grows exponentially and so an earthquake of magnitude nine represents a billion (10^9) kg of seismic energy (Jackson 2016, 42–43). A further statistical use of the logarithms lies in attempting to transform a skew distribution into a Gaussian distribution (Haslwanter 2016, 115).

Frequency in language can also be understood as an exponential growth, and therefore one could argue in favor of transforming it logarithmically.

The most frequent words remain those with the highest logarithmic values, but now the differences in Figure 41 are not as great as they were in the raw or relative frequency plots. Originally, the word *de* ('of') was around 500% more frequent than *con* ('with'). After a log transformation, the difference is only 14%. Now all the most frequent words have a logarithmic value above six, without any great difference whether they appear 7,000 or *only* 500 times. The distribution (observed in the histogram of Sub-figure B) is still skewed to the left but much less than in the previous transformations (but without a normal distribution, as one could have expected from Haslwanter 2016). The logarithm of zero is minus infinite, and therefore the words that do not appear in the text should have this value. To avoid infinite values, it is common to replace them with the lowest value of the rest of the data. That is why the words with zero frequency retain a log frequency of zero.

A major difference to the previous transformation is observed in the box plots (Sub-figure C). Now the boxes and the whiskers are recognizable and represent the majority of the data. The mean and the median are very close, as well as the standard deviation and the IQR. The scatter plot (Sub-figure D) shows the typical curved shape of a logarithm, with a moderate correla-

Figure 41: Plots showing logarithmic frequency in two novels

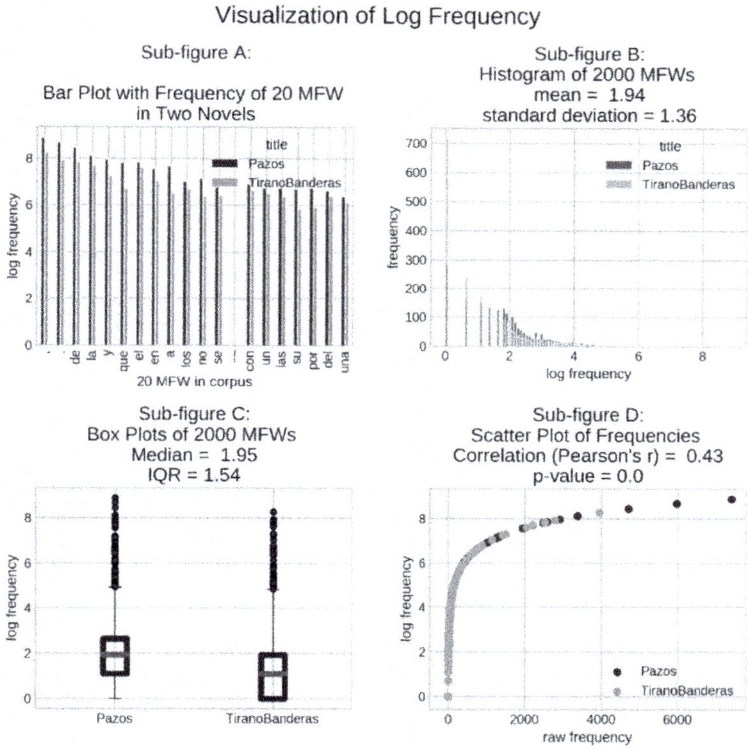

tion between the raw frequency and log frequency. This fourth Sub-figure D clearly shows how the words with a term frequency between zero and 500 occurrences are now distributed between zero and six, with the most frequent words having values up to nine.

This logarithmic transformation was applied directly to the raw data. This is why, in Sub-figure A of the previous diagram, all the words of *Los pazos de Ulloa* have greater values than *Tirano Banderas*: The frequencies were not relative to the total length of the text. The normalization of the frequencies by the length of the text not only changes the comparison of the data, the logarithm of fractions between zero and one now have negative values. A log transformation of the relative frequencies sets the most frequent close to zero with the rest having lower negative values, which can be seen in Figure 42. In Sub-figure A, the tokens of *Tirano Banderas* manage to surpass those from *Los pazos de Ulloa*. In addition to this, the sign, and the specific values of the scale (now from -12 to -2), the rest of the characteristics remain almost identical.

Figure 42: Plots showing relative logarithmic frequency in two novels

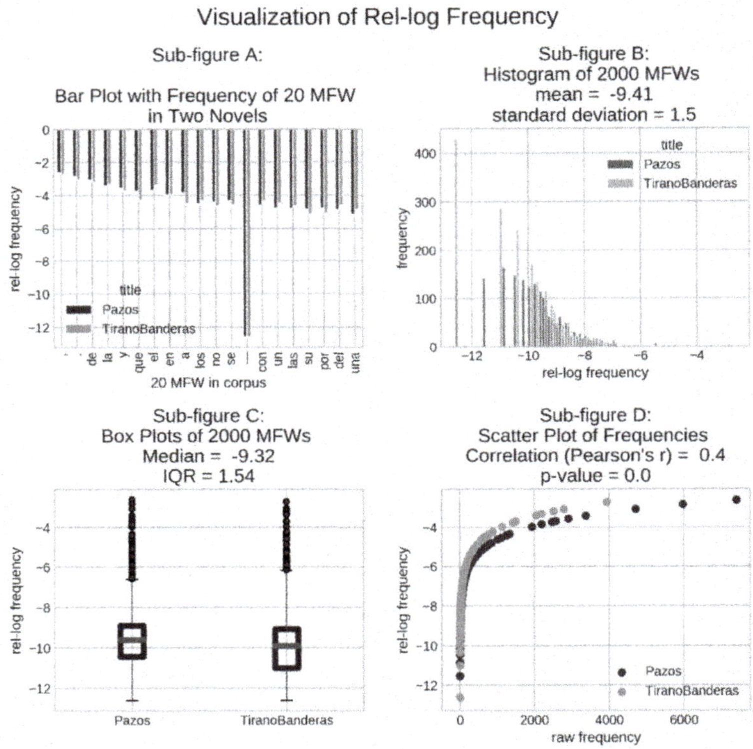

An important decision about the logarithmic transformation is its base. The examples above were natural logarithms using the transcendental number *e*, which is close to 2.718. There are at least two other often-applied bases: two and ten. Regardless of the base, the results are almost identical, with one exception: the size of the scale. The larger the base is, the shorter the logarithmic scale will be. While the values of the logarithm for a base of two are distributed between zero and 13, those using a base of ten are distributed between zero and four, which can be observed in more detail in the Jupyter Notebook. If an even larger base is used, such as 1,000, the logarithmic axis encompasses only one (from zero to one and from -1.5 to -0.5 in cases where relative frequencies are used). It could be argued that having a narrower scale will mean that the Machine Learning algorithms treat each feature equally. Consequently, a base of ten or larger could be more beneficial.

4.2.2.4 Tf-idf: Term Frequency-Inverse Document Frequency

Tf-idf is an often-used transformation in areas of Computer Science, such as Information Retrieval and Machine Learning. It comprises the *term frequency* (or *raw frequency*, already explained in 4.2.2.1), and the *inverse document frequency* or *idf*. The idea behind this transformation is that the words (or features) that appear in fewer documents are more informative than those that appear in the majority of them. Each feature in the entire corpus gets an *idf* weighting that is used to multiply the term frequency of each feature of all the texts.

Even when treated as a straight forward transformation without variants, both parts (*tf* and *idf*) actually have several parameters that are often not explicitly mentioned. This is already observed in Formulas 1 and 2 that two recent publications have used as an explanation:

Formula 1

$$tfidf_{(w,d)} = tf \lg\left(\frac{N+1}{N_w+1}\right)+1$$

(Müller and Guido 2016, 338)

It is not only the notation that is different, but in Müller and Guido plus one is added three times on the *idf* side, having a large impact on the final values. There are, in fact, many decisions involved in the real practice of cal-

Formula 2

$$tfidf_{(t,d)} = tf_{t,d} \times \lg\left(\frac{N}{df_t}\right)$$

(Klinke 2017, 275)

culating tf-idf, i.e., should the input be total, relative, logarithmic (based on two, *e*, or ten), or binary frequencies? Manning and Schütze (1999) summarize three steps in which several parameters can be applied, explaining tf-idf as a "family of weighting schemes." This is also observed in the implementation of tf-idf: In the Python library scikit-learn, where its function for this (*Tfidf-Transformer)* has four parameters, some of them with several possible values.

For these reasons, I have decided to implement tf-idf (Formula 3) with Pandas functions in order to exactly comprehend the steps undertaken, following a simplification of the formula by Müller and Guido (2016).[4]

In this section, I report the results of this formalization of tf-idf and apply it to the relative frequencies (rel-tfidf), without further transformation or normalization.

In Sub-figure A of Figure 43, the tokens that have the highest total frequency now have negative values: Because they appear in all the documents, they are unimportant for tf-idf. The features that had a total frequency of zero retain a tf-idf value of zero, since any number multiplied by zero stays zero. The words with the highest values in *Los pazos de Ulloa* are now *Nucha, Julián, Perucho, Sabel, Pazos,* etc. All these are the names of the protagonists and places of the action, words that are especially frequent in this novel and extremely rare in the rest of the corpus. The distribution of the data in Sub-figure B now shows negative and positive values, with many of them around zero, but some

4 The plus one in both parts of the fraction of the idf prevent the division by zero, having little impact on the final result.

Formula 3

$$tfidf_{(w,d)} = tf \times \lg\left(\frac{N+1}{N_w+1}\right)$$

bins are visible in the histogram (in contrast to the plots with the term frequency). Mean, median, standard deviation, and IQR all have values of zero, meaning that the majority of the data has a distribution very close to zero, as can be seen in the fat box plots. Finally, in Sub-figure D, the tf-idf has a weak negative correlation with the raw frequency: The more frequent a word is, the lower its tf-idf tends to be, while the less frequent it is, the higher its tf-idf becomes.

Tf-idf is probably the most frequent transformation of lexical data used in Computer Science, and it delivers good results for very different tasks. The most important disadvantage is the fact that the parameters are seldom mentioned or taken into account.

4.2.2.5 Binary Frequency

A different type of transformation, a very basic one, is to calculate the binary frequency. In this representation, the information about whether a feature has a low or a high frequency is erased. Yet this transformation gives surprisingly good results in some tasks in Computer Science (Eisenstein 2019, 92). After the transformation, the vector only includes whether the feature appears in the document or not.

The bars in Sub-figure A of Figure 44 show that all tokens do appear in both texts, with the exception of the em dash. There are only two bins in the

Figure 43: Plots showing rel-tfidf values in two novels

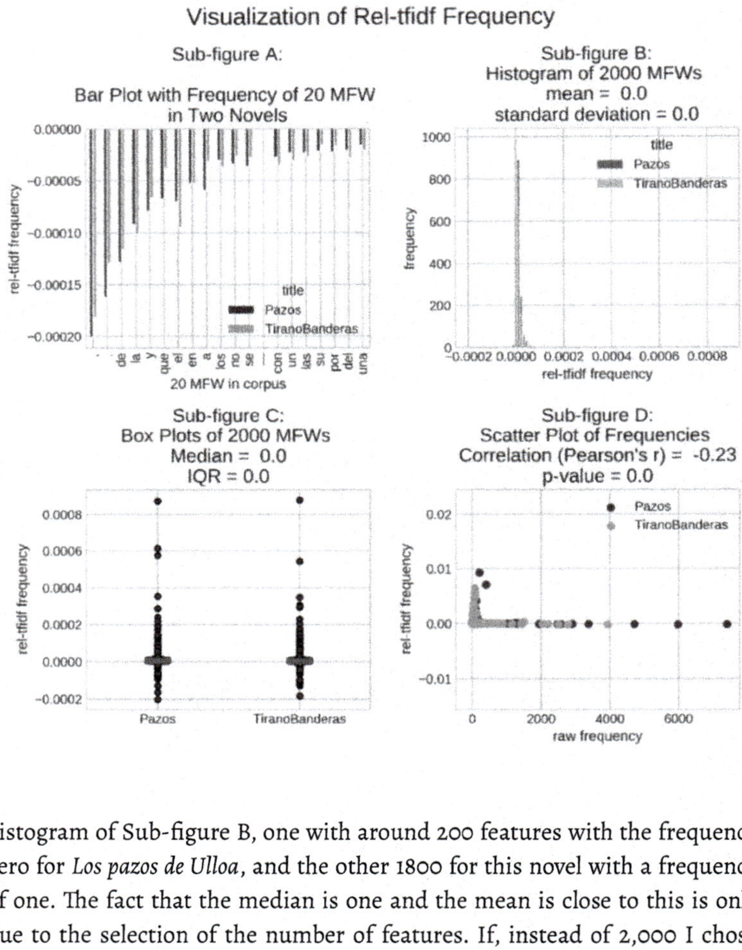

histogram of Sub-figure B, one with around 200 features with the frequency zero for *Los pazos de Ulloa*, and the other 1800 for this novel with a frequency of one. The fact that the median is one and the mean is close to this is only due to the selection of the number of features. If, instead of 2,000 I chose 5,000, the majority would not appear in the text and therefore both central tendencies would be zero or almost zero. The correlation test does not show a statistical significance between the transformations.

Comparing Figure 44 with the previous plots, it becomes clear that binary frequency is a peculiar transformation. Not only the information about the position is lost after the composition of the Bag of Words, but also any information about the degree of the frequency. An advantage is the fact that the

Figure 44: Plots showing binary frequency in two novels

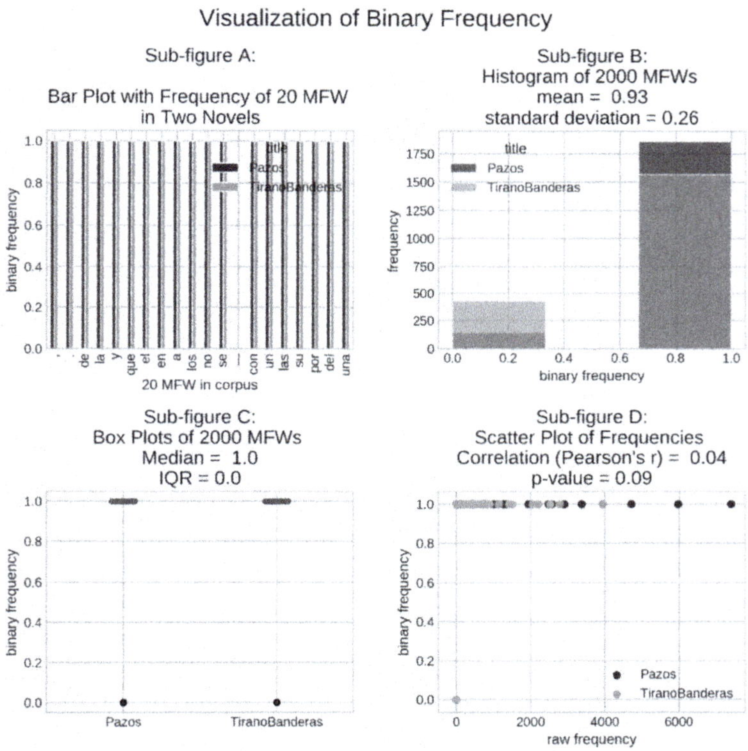

algorithms can compute binary vectors faster than larger ranges of possible values.

4.2.2.6 Z-Scores: Standard Term-Document Frequency in Corpus

In Statistics, a z-score transformation is a standard normalization of the data (Evans 1996, 105–8). In the stylometric community these are mainly known as one step in calculating the Delta matrix (Burrows 2002). The idea behind z-score transformation is to normalize the data in comparison to the rest of the corpus. Is the frequency of a specific feature in a specific text typical in the corpus, or is it instead exceptionally high or low in comparison to the rest of the data set? To answer this, the mean in the corpus is subtracted from each value, and then divided by the standard deviation in the corpus (Formula 4).

Formula 4

$$z = \frac{X - \bar{X}}{S}$$

The z-scores of lexical information are usually calculated from the relative frequency (rel-zscores).

The features can now have positive and negative values, as it can be seen in Sub-figure A of Figure 45 with values from minus one to six. These scores are standard deviations of the mean of the corpus. For example, the token *el* in the text *Tirano Banderas* has a z-score of three, meaning that its frequency is three standard deviations higher than what is expected in this corpus. The shape of the histogram (Sub-figure B) is close to a Poisson distribution, with the peak very close to the mean (-0.02). This moderate skewness is also observed in the box plots (Sub-figure C), which have many positive outliers. These are words with a very high frequency in comparison to the rest of the corpus, such as *tenebrosísima* ('very gloomy'), *zahumadas* (uncertain meaning) or *ahúmes* ('you smoke') for *Los pazos de Ulloa*, which are all words that only appear in this specific text in the entire corpus. In the fourth plot it can be observed that this transformation has no correlation[5] with the total frequency.

Among the six transformations already discussed, only two have managed to assign the highest scores to tokens which were not the most frequent: tf-idf and z-scores. In tf-idf, the highest values were words such as *Nucha* or *Julián*, while the highest z-scores are tokens such as *tenebrosísima* or *ahúmes*.

5 Very weak and without statistical significance.

Figure 45: Plots showing relative z-score frequency in two novels

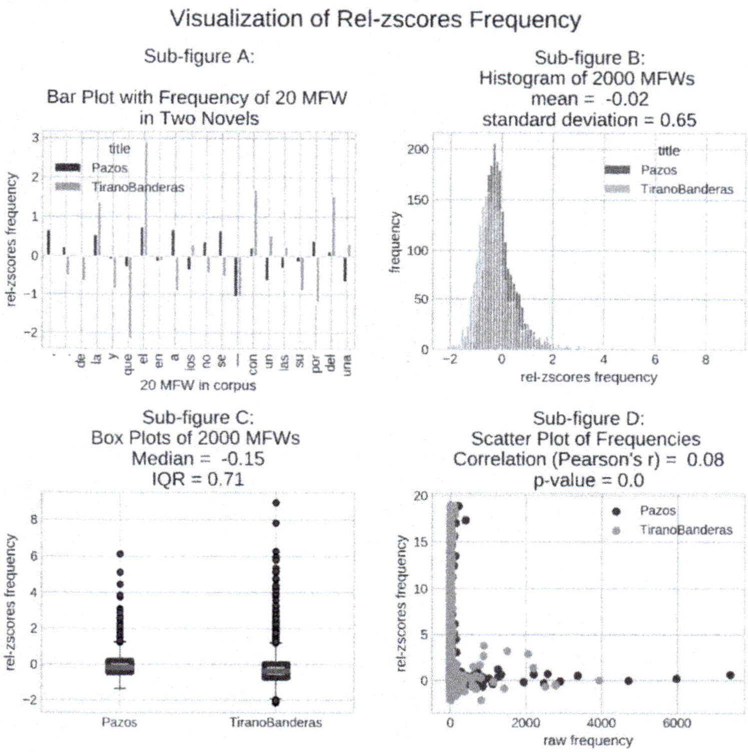

Why do these transformations deviate and what causes this? These four features appear in the *Los pazos de Ulloa* and are very infrequent in the rest of the corpus. The difference is that a feature can only have a high tf-idf if its original frequency was high, such as the names of the protagonists (*Nucha, Julián*). As already pointed out, the tf-idf still correlates with the original term frequency. On the contrary, the z-score transformation does not correlate with the original, and therefore it is able to assign high values, even when the feature occurs only once in the text (such as *zahumadas or ahúmes*, which are extremely rare words in Spanish). The specific names of the protagonist are expected to not be so informative for genre classification, and therefore I expect z-scores to be a better transformation than tf-idf for this task.

4.2.3 Variants

In this section I want to present six variants, each of them altering specific decisions of the previous transformations. All of them are conceptually motivated in an attempt to obtain the desired characteristics mentioned in the introduction to this chapter. The first two are concatenations of a previously explored steps. The third and fourth differ from the classic Bag of Words document model, attempting to capture whether the frequency of the features is stable across the chapters of the text. The two final proposals are variants of the z-score, using either larger corpora (CORDE) or authorial subsets of the corpus for comparison.

4.2.3.1 Rel-Log10-Zscores

The already analyzed transformations (relative, log, z-scores, tf-idf, binary) could potentially be concatenated in a large number of combinations, especially if duplications are possible (for example if the logarithm is calculated in several steps). I have tested many of them trying to find one that would normalize the entire Bag of Words in a text (the entire vector of each text), but without success. Still, two motivated concatenations are worth closer observation. The first one adds three steps: relative frequency, logarithmic, and z-score transformation.

The aim of this transformation is to obtain comparable data between texts (relative frequency), avoid skewness in the distribution (logarithmic frequency on base 10), and weight the features in terms of their standard deviation in the corpus (z-scores).

The plots of Figure 46 resemble those with only the z-score transformation, but with an important difference: While the histogram in Figure 45 shows a Poisson distribution, the concatenation of these three steps is now showing (with 2,000 MFW) in Sub-figure B a less skew bimodal distribution (it shows two peaks). A less skewed distribution of the data can be beneficial for the analysis since many statistical tests expect a Gaussian distribution, which is very rare in the Humanities. One of the peaks of the bimodal distribution is populated by many words that share a similar frequent frequency, while the other only contains all the words that have a zero frequency in each novel.

Figure 46: Plots showing relative log10 z-scores in two novels

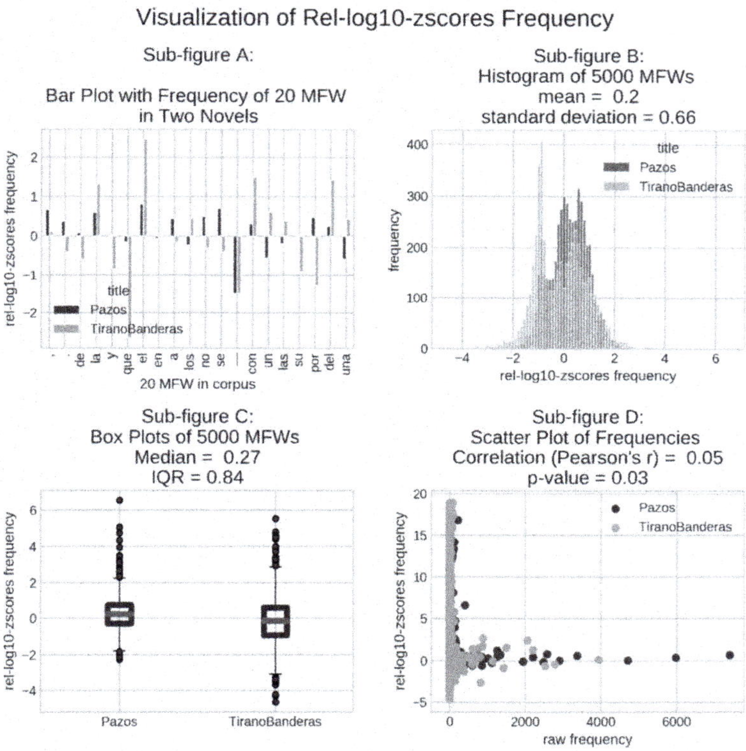

4.2.3.2 Rel-Tfidf-Zscores

The second concatenation applies the two weightings that are most used in different fields with the same data: tf-idf (Computer Science) and z-scores (stylometry). The idea behind this is to prevent the correlation between the raw frequency and the tf-idf, or in other words, to use the tf-idf weighting, and then democratize the values through z-scores.

The results of Figure 47 appear very similar to those for the z-score transformation, again with a distribution closer to Poisson. Apparently, the tf-idf transformation has not had a great impact on the final results of this concatenation. This can be caused by the correlation between tf-idf and rela-

Figure 47: Plots showing relative tf-idf z-scores in two novels

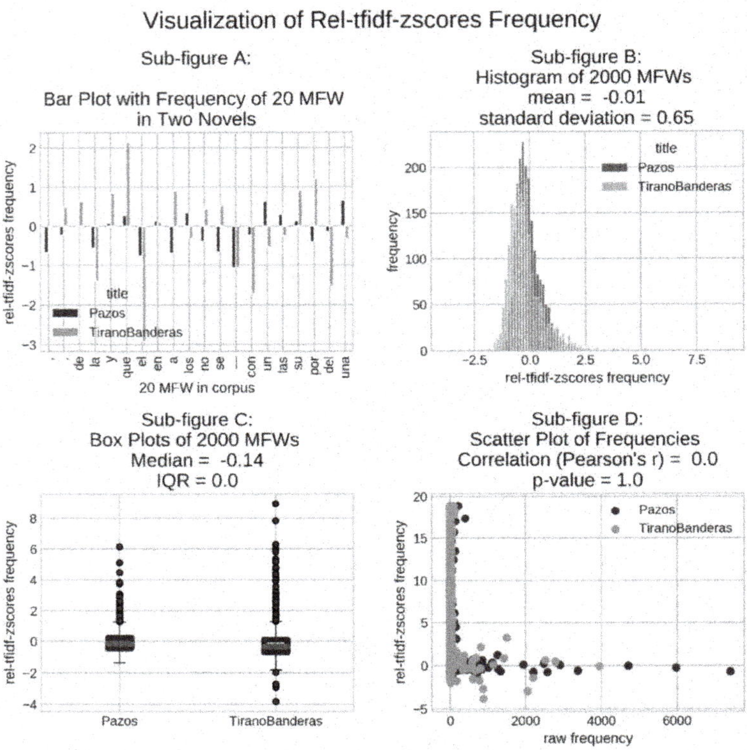

tive frequency. A possible variation of this would be to transpose the steps: rel-zscore-tfidf. However, that would be harder to defend because the tf-idf is specifically proposed for the frequencies of words. In contrast, a z-score transformation is independent of the type of data, and therefore it is legitimate to apply it after the tf-idf weighting.

4.2.3.3 Term Mean Frequency in Chapters

Until now all variants are based on the Bag of Words document model in which the frequency expresses the number of times the feature appears in the document. In a way, the BoW model can be understood as the sum of the frequencies in all sections of the text. A word can have a stable frequency throughout the entire text or be very frequent (or infrequent) in specific sections. Since the BoW is only the sum, the differences in the distribution throughout the text are neglected. For example, if a theme becomes very predominant at the end of the text (for example, the death of a character), or if it is treated briefly in many chapters (work of the protagonist), both of them will appear to have similar frequencies in the BoW, even though their distributions are very different.

A formalization that captures the frequency of each feature in different sections of the document could bring a less skewed distribution of the data, in other words, more stable information about the frequency throughout the entire document. To obtain this, the text should be structured into different sections (chapters, paragraphs, sentences, chunks), calculating the average frequency for each feature in the entire document. How frequent are commas throughout the chapters of *Los pazos de Ulloa* on average? At the end, the output would be a very similar document-term frequency, however, not based on the sum of frequencies, but rather on their mean.

The plots of Figure 48 are very similar to those of relative frequency (Figure 40), even showing an almost perfect correlation with the raw frequency in Sub-figure D. In other words, even when the model is no longer based on BoW, the data is almost identical. However, splitting the novel into smaller units allows other measures to be tested. For example, instead of the mean, the median over chapters can be calculated, although, again, the results are almost identical (details in the Jupyter Notebook). In the next sections, further possibilities will be presented.

An important parameter for this type of transformation is the definition of textual boundary. I choose to use chapters and not other possibilities, such as paragraphs, sentences, or chunks of texts. In Section 3.1.8, I have explained the ways that the chapters were encoded, and in Section 7.1.4 I will use them as boundaries for classification tasks. Chapters are a middle unit of text inside the novel, with several dozen in each novel, yet containing thousands of tokens. They are normally defined by the author and also referred to by traditional scholars in their research. In this manner, I can still follow the exact calculation back to the text as the reader receives it and link the results to academic research. In contrast to chunks of text, chapters have the disadvantage of having unequal lengths. This is why, before the mean is calculated, the relative frequencies in each chapter need to be obtained, as I have done for the previous figure. The possibility of using smaller units than chapters,

Figure 48: Plots showing relative mean frequencies over chapters in two novels

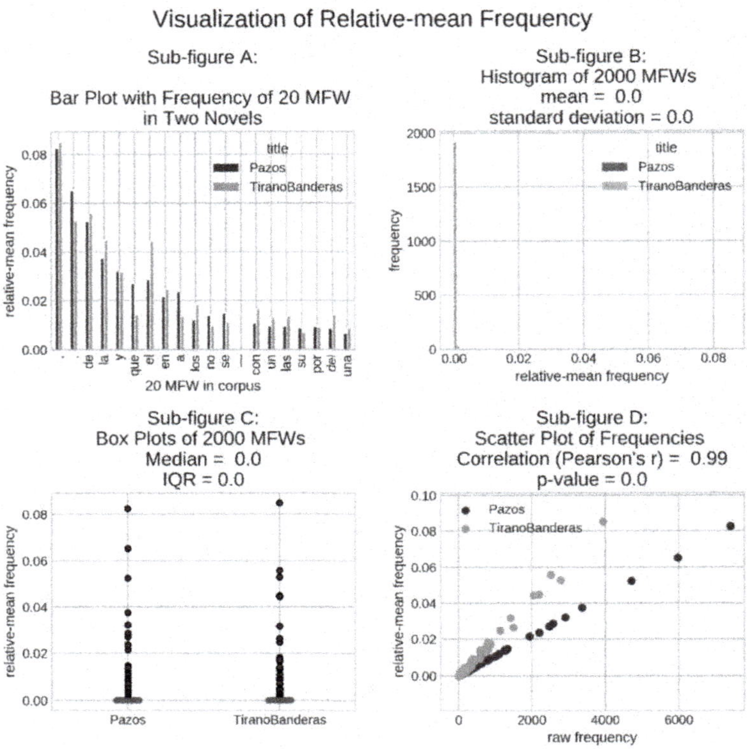

such as paragraphs or sentences, is worth testing. Yet it should be taken into account that dividing the corpus into chapters results in data frames with several thousands of rows and hundreds of thousands of columns, which is costly in terms of time processing. Using paragraphs or sentences would drastically increase the number of rows with very sparse information.

4.2.3.4 Term Standard Deviation Frequency in Chapters

I have already explored two possibilities of using chapters: the sum (term frequency) and mean (term mean frequency). For the term mean frequency, the goal of observing whether each word is homogeneously frequent throughout the text, or only in specific sections, was not achieved. Although it is very frequent to report only the mean of a series of values, it is considered bad practice when these are not presented alongside the information about the dispersion (Gries 2008b, 117). To formalize this, a series of dispersion measures have been proposed by corpus linguists (see Gries 2008a and 2009 for a discussion on several implementations), although their application in DH and Machine Learning tasks is very limited. One of the most intuitive operationalizations of dispersion is the standard deviation of textual units such as chapters. If a token has a high standard deviation across the chapters of a novel, it means that it is very frequent in some sections, and rare in others. For example, in a novel with a narrative perspective that changes from third to first person, the pronouns *I* and *he/she* should have a high standard deviation. In contrast, the first-person pronouns of a novel with a narrator in the first person should have a low standard deviation, even if they are very frequent.

In Sub-figure A of Figure 49, the data shows that *Los pazos de Ulloa* has a much lower standard deviation for the most frequent words than *Tirano Banderas*. This is not surprising: The first novel describes a story with very stable topics and characters, while the second has many changes of perspective and characters. The distribution shown in Sub-figure B is very skewed (although not as much as other transformations) and it is strongly correlated with the raw frequency (Sub-figure D): The more frequent a word is, the higher its variance can be. Both the skewness and the correlation could be mitigated by further transformations, such as logarithm or z-score standardization. To my knowledge, the standard deviation over chapters has not been applied in literary research, and could be a simple operationalization of how heterogeneous a text is.

4.2.3.5 Language-Zscores

In Section 4.2.2.6, I have presented z-scores as the way to standardize the frequency in comparison to what is expected in the entire corpus. In this sense, it results in a *corpus-centric* comparison: It is highly dependent on the corpus used, and could be called *sample-zscores* or *corpus-zscores*. The frequency of a word in a text does not depend on the rest of the corpus, but its z-score does, since the mean frequency in the corpus and its standard deviation are included in the calculations. Adding or deleting one text affects the value of all features in every document.

Figure 49: Plots showing standard deviation over chapters in two novels

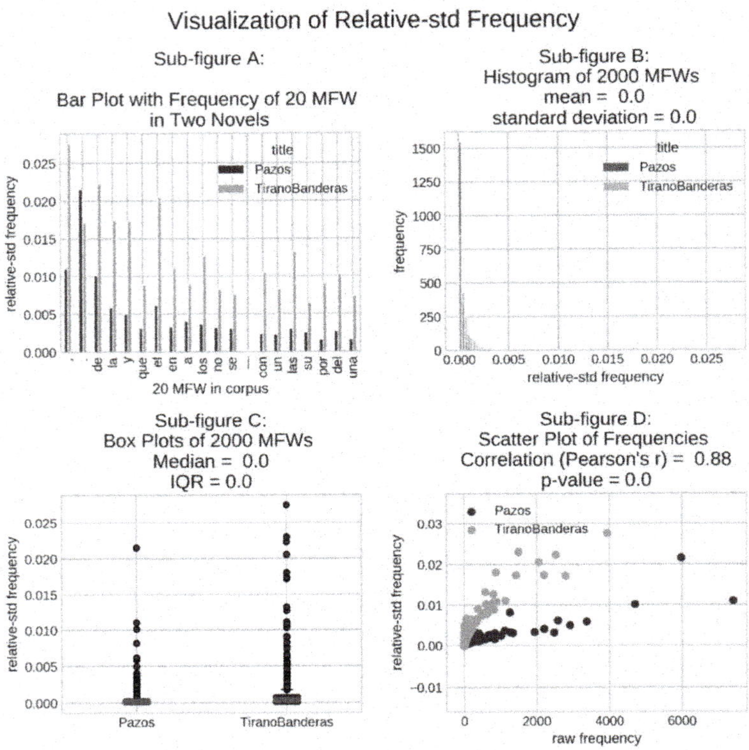

Instead of comparing the frequencies to the rest of the collection, other corpora or subsets could be the base of the standardization. For example, the data could be compared to what is expected in the language, obtaining z-scores that are comparable across different corpora. Rather than calculating the *corpus-zscores*, in this section I calculate the *population-zscore* or *language-zscore*. In Statistics, the mean of the sample (X) and its standard deviation (S) used in 4.2.2.6 are now replaced in Formula 5 with the parameters of the population μ and σ.

More specifically, I compare the relative frequencies in each text to the mean frequency and the standard deviation in an external corpus that claims to be representative of the language as discussed in Section 3.3.2: CORDE

Formula 5

$$z = \frac{X - \mu}{\sigma}$$

(Sánchez Sánchez and Domínguez Cintas 2007). Since this corpus is actually not the population of the language, but the greatest corpus I have access to, it can be modified with the Formula 6:

Formula 6

$$z_{language} = \frac{X_{CoNSSA} - \mu_{CORDE}}{\sigma_{CORDE}}$$

Not surprisingly, the data again resembles the results of the *corpus-zscores*, with the difference being that the values are closer to zero (Sub-figure B of Figure 50). The bar plot in Sub-figure A shows that both novels have similar values, with a few exceptions where the direction is different. This is probably caused by the fact that two novels are being compared to a very general corpus. The two texts are very distinct in their style, nevertheless, in comparison to other genres contained in CORDE (theater in verse, philosophical essay, etc.), they also share many similarities. Thus, it is very likely that this transformation will not deliver the best results for the classification of subgenres of

Figure 50: Plots showing rel-language-zscores in two novels

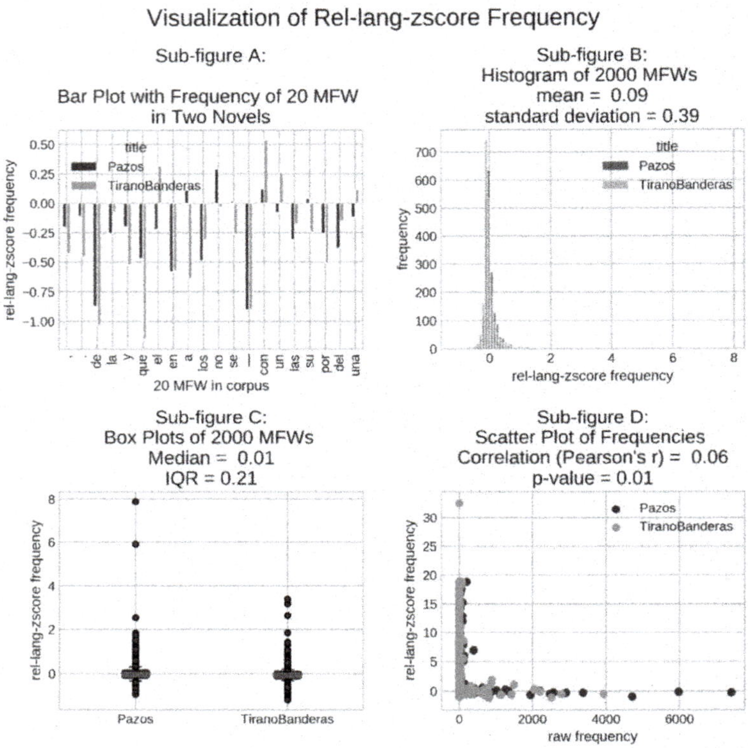

novels, which will be evaluated in Chapter 6.1. However, this transformation could be a path worth pursuing in order to obtain more comparable results in several corpora.

4.2.3.6 Authorial-Zscores

A final modification is tested by simultaneously applying the strategies about structured information in the chapters and the z-scores with a different corpus for comparison. The frequencies of the tokens are very useful discriminators of authorship, and therefore using them could reinforce the correlation of the classes of author and genre in the classification (Hettinger et al. 2016).

For example, Bazán wrote many naturalist novels; in a subgenre task, the classifier might use her lexical frequency distribution (her authorial cue or signal) to classify naturalist novels. In previous research, I have attempted to penalize the authorial similarity between texts after calculating the Delta distances (Calvo Tello et al. 2017). This transformation has a similar goal, but works with the original frequency of features before adding them into the Delta matrix.

The goal of this transformation is to standardize the frequencies of each text using the frequencies in all the works of the same author. The word *de* ('of') has a relative frequency of 0.045 in *Los pazos de Ulloa*; considering that this text was written by Bazán, how expectable is this value? Is this frequency high or low *in her novels*? To calculate this *authorial-zscores*, the frequency of each text is standardized by a subset of novels written by the author:

Formula 7

$$z_{authorial} = \frac{X - \bar{X}_{author}}{S_{author}}$$

The bar plot of Sub-figure A of Figure 51 shows that the z-score of *de* ('of') in *Los pazos de Ulloa* is 0.25 z-scores, meaning it is slightly higher than expected for Bazán. On the other hand, the word *el* ('the') almost reaches a 0.75 z-score, meaning that this word occurs very frequently in this text, considering the author's style. The distribution is skewed to the left, although not as much as for the corpus-zscores. The data points are distributed below -0.5 and a few cases over 1.5., and in general it resembles a Gaussian distribution.

To make the calculation of authorial-zscores possible, every writer must be represented by more than one text in the data set. But, as seen in Section 3.1.9, many authors have written only one novel, making this requirement unrealistic for literary works. For this reason, I have decided to work with

Figure 51: Plots showing authorial-zscores in two novels

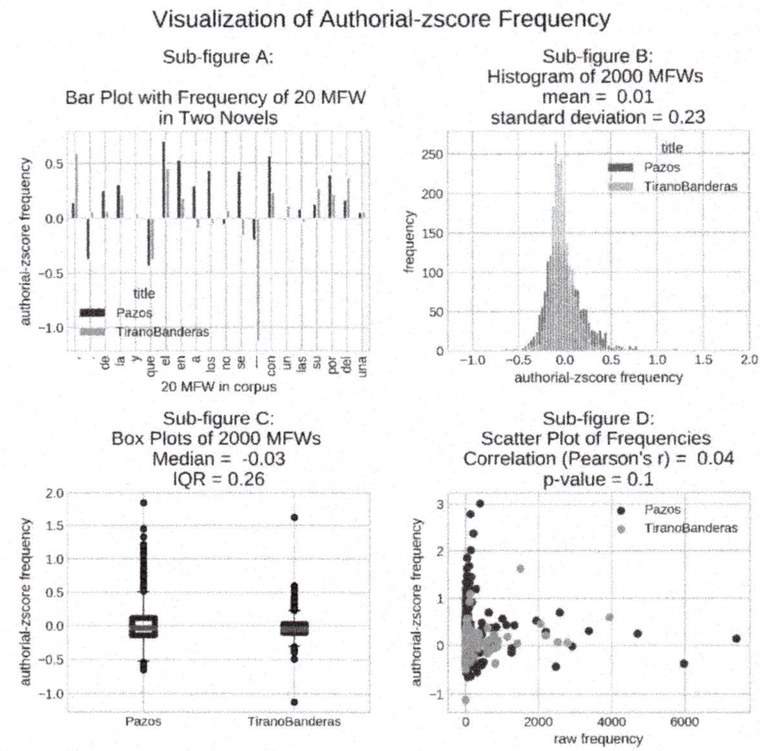

chapters as the base and to calculate the mean and the standard deviation from these. This step will always allow the inclusion of the entire corpus.[6]

The general goal of the transformation is to neutralize the authorial cue at the lexical level. It is particularly interesting because, at the level of tokens, it interconnects standard concepts of Literary Studies (chapter, novel, author) and Statistics (mean, standard deviation, z-score). In Chapter 6.2, I will apply this transformation to cluster the texts in order to identify hidden subgenres

6 Actually, the only case in which it would not be possible to include an author would be if the author wrote a single novel, with one single chapter, something possible in theory but unlikely, and this did not happen in CoNSSA.

that have not been identified until now. In addition, all these transformations will be evaluated in Chapter 6.1.

5. Analysis of Subgenre Labels

5.1 Evaluation of Consistent Subgenres

5.1.1 Introduction

The source and the palette of the labels of genres and subgenres represent a major challenge for different reasons. Labels like *novela épica* and *novela de guerra* ('epic novel', 'war novel') can be understood as synonyms. A war novel can be labeled a historical novel, while many historical novels are labeled as war novels, i.e. they can be understood as part of a taxonomy (see Section 2.3.3.1). Each source (covers, manuals of Literary Studies, printing houses, catalogs, manuals, editorial projects) applies its own set of labels for their own specific purposes, making it difficult to compare data. In other words, irregularity and scarcity are common in the information I want to use as categories. So the question arises: Which labels should be used for classification?

To answer that, several sources of information (manuals of literature, catalogs, metadata from printing houses, own annotation) have been gathered. Four specific questions will be responded to in this chapter: 1) Which labels can be understood as synonyms? 2) If the different sources are understood as annotators, how close are they to each other? 3) Can the subgenres be expressed in a standard way (through multilingual standard schemata)? 4) And, most importantly, which labels can be understood as being consistent among different sources?

5.1.2 Data and Sources

As observed in Chapter 2.2 about the computational analysis of genre, each research project has adopted a source of labels (metadata from the corpus, publishers, manuals, own annotation), but without further explanations of whether this is the best reference, and without any reassurance concerning the reliability of the labels. No project used labels from several sources and only two dealt with the problem of whether different annotators or sources would label text in a consistent way, with the result that both of them achieved a general agreement of around 50% (Berninger, Kim, and Ross 2008; Santini 2011). These publications suggest that using a single reference for the labels is highly questionable. Any researcher involved in the process of annotating this information is aware of the uncertainty and subjectivity of many of the assignments.

For this reason, I have collected the information on the genre of each text from a number of sources. These represent diverse traditions and aims about genre labeling, and all of them have been used in previous computational research on genre. The majority of the references marked the texts many decades after their first publication (with the exception of the information on the cover, which will be treated more carefully in Chapter 5.2), therefore this data set cannot be applied to a historical analysis. These sources were not collected following opportunistic criteria, but rather to represent distinct areas that make use of genre labeling: publishers, researchers in the history of literature, communities of readers and own annotation. The exact sources are:

1. *Genre of the subtitle*: This is the digitized text when its subtitle (sometimes its title) contains any reference that can be understood as a genre: *episodio nacional, historia, novela, novela de costumbres, memoria,* etc. These have been extracted manually, either from the title of the text or from the cover of the digitized document.
2. *Genre of subtitles at the Spanish National Library* (BNE): The different historical editions could change their subtitles over time. For example, in different editions, *Los majos de Cádiz* by Valdés was labeled as a historical or a *costumbrist* novel. Using the textual identifiers of the BNE, all the titles were queried through SPARQL, and the labels were manually extracted from this output. In the majority of cases, the source should overlap with the previous one, and in fact they could have been made out as a single source. One reason why I am keeping them apart is to evaluate them separately. Another reason is to obtain knowledge for other researchers to use on whether it is sufficient to gather the information from the digitized text or not and if there are advantages in querying national libraries for this information.

3. *Manual of History of Literature MdLE*: I read and manually collected the subgenres that the history of literature by (Pedraza Jiménez and Rodríguez Cáceres 1980-2016) used for each text of the corpus.
4. *Manual of History of Literature HdLE*: I followed the same strategy with this second manual by Mainer and Pontón (2010).
5. *ePubLibre*: This community of users and publishing projects ascribed several labels to each text, providing this information on their website and in each e-book.
6. *Amazon*: The publishing houses have the option of assigning metadata to each book. The catalog of Amazon was crawled for similar titles and authors and manually controlled for whether the text was actually in the corpus. If it was, I collected all the labels assigned by the publishers.
7. *Wikidata*: This project hosted by the Wikimedia Foundation allows the query of specific information using Linked Open Data (LOD) SPARQL (through BNE identifiers). From these sources, the field about subgenres was extracted.
8. *DBpedia*: This is a similar project, but hosted by the Free University of Berlin and the University of Leipzig. It automatically structures information from Wikipedia, in this specific case from the Spanish Wikipedia. The subgenre labels were retrieved with LOD SPARQL queries.
9. *Subgenre by CLiGS*: I assigned each text with several subgenres, also explicitly marking which I could consider the most prominent genre. This model enables the selection of either all genres from the source or only the most predominant. I labeled each text after reading the annotation of other sources and encoded the metadata as explained in Chapter 3.2.

There are different reasons why I chose these references. The most frequent sources in the computational analysis of genre are the own annotation, the information from the cover or from an already existing corpus. I am interested in finding out how accurate each strategy is, and whether each of them has a similar understanding of subgenre. Crawling Amazon and querying Wikidata or DBpedia are two other methods that, even if they have not been applied to genres until now, fall within the typical DH tasks; it is arguable whether other projects will do the same in the near future. Using the information from the manuals of literature is a way of linking the classic Literary Studies with DH and is probably what feels like the most accurate information about subgenre.

The sources listed above can be classified by the type of actor labeling the texts: publishers (subtitle and Amazon), researchers in literature (HdLE and MdLE), users and readers (Wikidata, DBpedia and ePubLibre), and DH annotator (own annotation). Besides these, I have tried to collect genre information from the metadata of other institutions, such as Cervantes Virtual, the Gutenberg Project or labels given by the BNE, only to find that they do not assign this information. It is noteworthy that such important institutions working with literary texts have declined to undertake the task of categorising them in subgenres.

5.1.3 Exploration of Sources

How many labels considered the sources for each text on average? How many different labels were used for them? How many books did they label? Which are the scarcest sources? Which are the most common labels for the corpus? These are the questions I will answer in the following section, with the goal of obtaining an initial overview of how these sources labeled the analyzed corpus.

To achieve this I calculate different values for each source, which are shown in the table below.

Table 5: Summary of tendencies in sources

	different labels	labeled texts	ratio	mean labels texts	std labels texts	most common label
Wikidata	4	5	1.25	1	0	*novela naturalista*
subtitle BNE	57	97	1.7	1.07	0.3	*episodio nacional*
DBpedia	5	9	1.8	1	0	*novela realista*
subtitle	41	82	2	1.02	0.22	*episodio nacional*
MdLE	77	218	2.83	1.01	0.14	*novela naturalista*
Amazon	77	219	2.84	3.21	2.69	*ficción clásica*
HdLE	33	104	3.15	1	0	*novela naturalista*
ePubLibre	16	187	11.69	1.35	0.53	*drama*
own Annotation	30	358	11.93	3.49	1.37	*realist*

The first column shows how many different labels the sources used, from 4 by Wikidata to 77 by Amazon and MdLE. This data should be viewed in relation to the number of texts assigned, from 5 texts by Wikidata to the entire corpus by my own annotation. It is remarkable that the sources which work with a larger number of labeled texts, MdLE (218) and Amazon (219), only cover around 60% of the 358 texts of the corpus. Nowadays, not all texts can be purchased on Amazon, and not all publishers enrich their books with metadata, but all the texts in the corpus are referred to and described in the MdLE, and yet, in around 40% of the texts, no mention of any relation to subgenre can be found. Even if the aim of the manual is not to specify the subgenre in each text, it could be seen as a sign that many texts are not clearly part of any subgenre, i.e. a *zero assignment* in Santini's terms (2011) and *genreless texts* in Derrida's (1980). The next source with a wide coverage is ePubLibre with 187 texts, a source that assigns at least one genre (or topic) to its texts. The next three sources (subtitle, subtitle BNE and HdLE) have less than a third of the corpus, with around 100 labeled texts. Finally, the two LOD sources (Wikidata and DBpedia) cover a very small proportion of the corpus.

The number of different labels and the total number of texts can be expressed as a ratio of texts covered by each label (fourth column of the previous table). In this manner, the comparison between two sources that each assigned 100 texts, the first one using ten different labels (ratio of ten) and the second one using 100 labels (ratio of 1), is very clear. A higher ratio means that there are more texts covered by fewer subgenres, which is desirable situation. A ratio of 1 means that the source used a different label for every assigned text, which would be useless for classification purposes. This hypothetical illustration is almost the case for Wikidata, with a ratio of 1.25. In general, the ratio of the majority of the sources varies between 1 and 3, with a median of 2.8, i.e. every third book belongs to a different subgenre. Only two sources clearly diverge from this tendency: ePubLibre and my own annotation, with ratios close to 12. In my opinion, the reason why these sources respond differently to the rest is the fact that both strictly control their palettes of subgenres. Each new text has to be designated an already existing label in their schema or database, while the creation of new labels should be argued and furthermore, should be contrasted against the rest of the texts. In the remaining sources, any new label can be added at any time, thus enhancing the variety.

Finally, I want to find out whether the sources tend to assign one single subgenre or several subgenres to each text. For this, I calculate the mean number of subgenres per source and the standard deviation, ignoring the zeros (fifth and sixth columns). While some sources (Wikidata, DBpedia and HdLE) apply a single label to each text (with a standard deviation of 0), the rest are above 1, with a mean of 1.6 and a standard deviation of 0.6. Consequently, the most common case is that the sources consider between one or two genres per text. Two sources clearly surpass this outcome (CLiGS and Amazon) and assign up to 5 labels, which is still within the margins of the standard deviation. This shows that human institutions do not follow the naive idea that each text belongs to only one subgenre, as in the taxonomies (Section 2.3.2.1), but rather to multiple subgenres.

The final column of the table reveals the most common label used by the different sources, which offers a glimpse into the concept of subgenre applied by the sources. Ignoring the specific linguistic forms, five labels appear: *naturalist* (Wikidata, MdLE and HdLE), *realist* (DBpedia and CLiGS), *episodio nacional* (subtitle and subtitle BNE), *drama* (ePubLibre), and *classic fiction* (Amazon). Both naturalist and realist are typical historical labels of subgenres of the novel and it is interesting that very different types of sources (literary manuals, LOD sources and my own annotation) agree on using them often. *Episodio nacional* is already a one-author label (Section 2.1.10) that is only very common because this author published many of these texts and the concept appeared on the cover. The two other labels are very distinct. *Drama* ePubLibre probably expresses that the texts contain sad plots or endings, and not that the texts are thought of as theater plays (as in the case of dialogue novels). But what do publishers mean by *classic fiction*? As I will explain in Chapter 5.3, this is the historical variant of *literary fiction*, a concept that has entered the studies of literature and DH (Wilkens 2016; Koolen 2018) and in that chapter I will analyze it more closely.

This first exploration of the sources has already revealed some patterns. First, none of the sources (except my own annotation) apply subgenre information to all the texts. Second, the sources show a tendency towards assigning multiple labels to the same texts. These two facts are arguments for the zero-to-multi genre classification scheme proposed by Santini (2011). On the question of how useful the sources are, Wikidata and DBpedia yield the poorest coverage and ratio. The label from the cover (a common strategy for extracting genre information in DH papers) has a mediocre rating for coverage and a poor rating for the ratio. On the other hand, the most convenient sources (that are not own annotation) are Amazon, ePubLibre and MdLE, three very disparate sources observing the phenomenon of genre from very distinctive perspectives.

5.1.4 Exploration of Labels

Until now, I have considered the labels in their different sources, but what if the labels from all sources are observed together? In this case, an entire list emerges of 3,097 units assigned to the whole corpus, with 256 different labels, a first *subgenre palette*. The size of this number divided by the size of the corpus gives a ratio of 1.4 texts per label: In theory, one could encounter two subgenres in every third novel. This ratio would make working with supervised Machine Learning tasks impossible because of the split between training and test set. In addition, this would be a very insufficient classification, not only for computers, but also for humans.

As one would expect, the distribution of the frequency of the labels is extremely skewed. The four most common labels (*realist, sentimental, social, ficción clásica*) are used for more than 100 texts, a dozen are applied between 150 and 50 times (*philosophical, ficción contemporánea, naturalist, historical, literatura y ficción, bildungsroman, drama, antologías, memoir, realista*), followed by a long tail of labels with very few texts, with 112 *hapax labels* (used for a single text, more details in the Jupyter Notebook).

Some sources cover a wider range of the corpus, so the preferred labels of these sources are among the most common labels. For this reason, it is interesting to observe the number of sources that use each label. Do different traditions agree on specific labels, and if yes, on which? To respond adequately to this question, I do not calculate the total texts that were assigned to each label, but the total number of sources that used the label. Even when I consider nine different sources, the highest number of sources agreeing on specific labels is only four, and this happens exclusively with the four following labels: *nivola, historia, novela de guerra,* and *memorias*. Only one of these four (*novel de guerra*) is understood as a clear literary subgenre. The complete distribution of these values is shown in the diagram of Figure 52.

Figure 52: Number of sources for each token-label

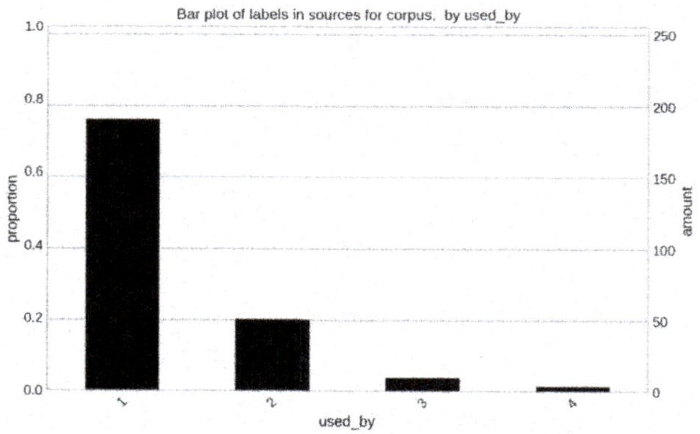

There are 191 labels used by one single source, representing 75%. This is followed by 50 labels (20%) that are employed by two sources, and then only 5% which are applied by three or four sources. As is observed, the labels carry two ad hoc characteristics: They are both used for only a few texts and by a few or just one source.

5.1.5 Semantic Mapping of Labels, Description and Standardization trough Thema

One of the reasons for the disagreement of the sources is the superficial variance of the labels, as is self-evident in the example of adventure novels, referred to by multiple labels as *acción y aventura, adventure, adventure novel, aventuras, novela de aventuras,* or *war-adventure*. Another example is the naturalist novel, sometimes denoted with adjectives (*naturalist*), sometimes with substantives (*naturalism*) and also in different languages (*novela naturalista, naturalist novel*). Other relations go beyond the etymological root and are based on basic semantics, like *novela de amor* and *novela romántica*, or *novela bélica, novela de guerra* and *novela militar*.

These labels have been extracted by the sources for now without further treatment. I call this state *token-labels*. They are exactly as they were in the different sources, *raw*, without any linguistic treatment or interpretation. The problem is that all these sources worked with different goals, without using a shared frame, guidelines or palette. To enable the comparison, an adaption is necessary. For this, I consider *semantic-labels*, which group the morphological, lexical and multilingual variances and do not express any semantic differences, and map these to the token-label.

In this manner, the meaning of each token-label is mapped to at least one semantic-label in Spanish to cover its meaning. In the case where the token-labels clearly refer to two semantic aspects (such as *rural drama* or *humorist poetry*), both are encoded as separate semantic-labels. I avoid losing semantic specificity and I only simplify clear morphological, lexical and multilingual variety, differentiating several semantic-labels in cases of doubt or where interpretation is needed. For example, it is arguable whether *novela de acción* and *novela de aventuras* are part of the same genre or if they should be considered as different genres (other examples are *sátira-humor* or *intriga-policíaca*). In all these cases, I choose to consider them as separate semantic-labels and to retain semantic precision.

The result of this mapping is a new palette of semantic-labels composed of 110 terms. This means a reduction of 57% of the size of the original palette of token-labels (which originally consisted of 256 strings), and yet still yields a ratio of 3.25 texts for each different semantic genre. The distribution of the semantic-labels over assigned texts is similar to the token-labels seen before, only less skewed: While 112 token-labels were used for a single text, 33 semantic-labels are also *hapax labels*. On the other hand, the number of labels used by a single source drops from 75% in the case of token-labels to 49% for semantic-labels, with the following distribution shown in Figure 53.

Figure 53: Number of sources for each semantic-label

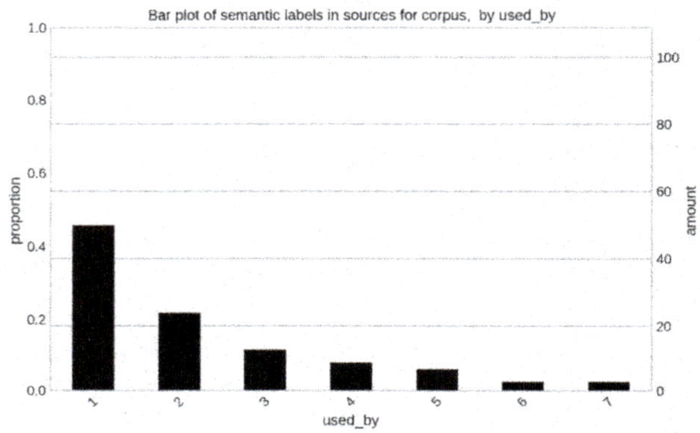

A positive effect of the semantic mapping is a notable increase in the agreement between the sources: To a certain degree, the linguistic differences are superficial and not semantic. Around half of the semantic-labels (54.55%) are used by more than one source, leaving the other half as genres considered by only a single source. There are now three semantic-labels (*humor, realista, guerra*) applied by up to seven sources, a very high result when taking into account that two of the nine original sources only labeled five texts (DBpedia and Wikidata).

There is a certain correlation between the number of sources applying the labels and the number of texts the labels are used for (correlation of 0.37^{***} on a regression analysis, further details in the Jupyter Notebook). This means that, to a certain degree, the more texts a label is used for, the more sources adopt it. For example, the semantic-label *realista* is at the top of both the number of sources (7) and the number of assigned texts (223). But there are two clear exceptions. There are two labels that are used by a single source and yet extensively assigned – *ficción* and *literatura* – the two semantic components of *literary fiction*, a frequent label on Amazon. In their metadata, publishers express that these texts belong to *literary fiction*, a concept that no other source has considered and that bundles genre and canonicity. This will be analyzed in Chapter 5.3.

A further step in semantic mapping would be to express the labels in a way that can be shared between other researchers and institutions working in other languages or periods. In other words, it would be necessary to declare the subgenres in a shared palette of subgenres. There are several projects working on similar questions, such as the POSTDATA project at the UNED, formulating a shared set of concepts for the European tradition of poetry through Linked Open Data technologies. In this field of DH, I have searched for Linked Open Vocabularies (LOVs)[1] that would contain subgenres of the novel. A number of LOVs include the concept of novel, without a finer distinction or with only a couple of subgenres, such as the vocabularies of the DBpedia, FABIO, SIO or RDA Registry. Thereafter, I have searched for further controlled vocabularies using different technologies.[2] Several controlled vocabularies used by European libraries contain the category of novel, again without further specification. Following Underwood (2016), who has used the metadata on genre provided by the Library of Congress, I have considered this classification system,[3] but again there is no information available beneath the novel level. Libraries have apparently rejected the classification of types of novels. To my knowledge, neither computational researchers nor public libraries have created a system of subgenre classification.

I have decided to consider another field that is familiar with subgenres: publishers. With the editorial market becoming increasingly digital (either in the form of e-books or through digital shops for printed books), publishers are aware that they need to share information about subgenres to facilitate the searching of books by customers. Different attempts have been made, such as the *BISAC Subject Codes*, led by the US-based Book Industry Study Group,[4] the UK-based *BIC Standard Subject Categories* by the Book Industry Communication,[5] and the UK-based but internationally developed *Thema subject category scheme* (*Thema*) by EDItEUR.[6] The development of BIC has been frozen in favor of a better acceptance of Thema. There are various reasons why Thema has unmistakable advantages over BISAC: The categories of Thema can be fully

1 On the portal created by the Universidad Politécnica of Madrid <https://lov.linkeddata.es/dataset/lov/>.

2 I searched on the portal of the Basel University *Bartoc* <https://bartoc.org/>.

3 https://www.loc.gov/catdir/cpso/lcco/.

4 https://bisg.org/page/BISACSubjectCodes.

5 http://www.bic.org.uk/7/bic-standard-subject-categories/.

6 https://www.editeur.org/151/Thema/.

downloaded for free, they have been translated into more than a dozen languages (including Spanish), and are developed internationally. This has been progressing since 2013 with frequent new releases.[7] As they explain in their documentation:

> *Thema* is intended as a multilingual subject classification scheme for book content, for use with digital and physical products, for all sectors of the global book, audio-book and e-book trade, and for both online and physical 'bricks and mortar' retail sectors. It consists of several thousand hierarchically-arranged subject categories and qualifiers, each with a descriptive heading (in many languages) and a language-independent code. (Willows et al. 2018).

I consider Thema to be the best proposal for a controlled list of genres and subgenres, even when its main purpose is not the study of literature but the commerce of texts. I manually map each semantic-label to the closest subject in Thema when one is found. From the 109 different semantic-labels, I locate fitting Thema subjects for 61, leaving 47 without a standardized correspondence. This means that I manage to standardize 56.5% of the semantic-labels.[8]

5.1.6 Analysis of Inter-Source Agreement

The fact that two sources employ the same semantic-label does not imply that they assign it to the same texts, that they consider the same extension of the category. Two manuals of Spanish literature might understand what an erotic novel could be in a completely different way, and therefore use the label for disjointed or only partially overlapping sections of the corpus. Accepting the several sources is discussed in the research, for example, whether the labels of the covers can be considered as subgenres for a further analysis (Bortrel 2001, 38–45). If this is the case, I expect the covers to assign dissimilar information to the rest of the sources.

7 I have worked with the release of April 2018.

8 I have evaluated whether the frequency of the labels (by sources and for texts) is related to the presence of the label in Thema or not. Apparently, it is not the case that only the least frequent labels are not in Thema. Further information can be found in the Jupyter Notebook.

Before I analyze which of the specific labels show consistent assignment among different sources, I want to observe how similarly each source labels texts with subgenres. The reason for this analysis is to explore whether the nine sources are similar to each other, if they form clear clusters or whether particular sources label in characteristic ways. I have a series of expectations on their behavior:

1. Sources of the same type (from the cover, from the literature researchers, from the communities of users) assign subgenre labels in a similar way, and therefore, they will cluster together.
2. Since the labels from the covers (of the digitized texts and from the National Library) are the only historical source, I expect them to cluster together, relatively apart from the rest.
3. Since the manuals of literature and the publishers have very different interests, I anticipate these sources to be very dissimilar.
4. The labels given by the communities of users (ePubLibre, Wikidata, DBpedia) will be an intermediary source, similar to both the publishers and the manuals of literature.

Evaluating these expectations will provide knowledge about whether these nine sources are rather alike or dissimilar and whether some of them overlap completely with other sources. In addition, because there is so little investigation into the kind of information given by different sources of labels, the conclusions can be extrapolated to future works using similar sources.

There are several possibilities for measuring whether two humans agree on a specific decision and to what degree. The simplest metric is to calculate the number of agreed cases, called *raw agreement*. While simple and intuitive, the raw agreement percentage does not take into account that a certain agreement could be caused by randomness or the totality of possible choices that should be considered (it is easier to agree when there are two possible answers than when there are more). The raw agreement is a particularly bad indicator for scarce information (Artstein 2017, 299–300), as is the case for genre labels. There is a series of common metrics in Computer Science that consider randomness in their calculation, such as Kappa (with variants like Fleiss or Cohen) and Krippendorff's Alpha (Artstein 2017). They assign values between minus one and one, with zero representing an arbitrary assignment. The major advantage of Alpha over Kappa is that it is more reliable for numerical labels, while the mean of the Kappa across annotators should be equivalent to Alpha. Scikit-Learn offers a function for calculating Cohen's Kappa, and several Python implementations of Alpha are available.[9] Since subgenres are nominal information and Scikit-Learn is a trustworthy library, I decided to use Kappa as the metric.

To measure the agreement, a loop runs over the sources, selects a pair of the sources each time and calculates their agreement (for example, between MdLE and Wikidata, then MdLE and ePubLibre, etc.). But what happens if MdLE assigns the label *historical* to a novel and ePubLibre chooses two labels, *historical* and *romantic*, for the same novel? If the Kappa was calculated for these two sources, this would be understood as disagreement. But they are not strictly disagreeing, one source is merely giving more information than the other. Due to the fact that the majority of the sources actually allocate multiple labels, the agreement of a pair of sources has to be computed for each label. This means, for example, that it must be calculated whether MdLE and ePubLibre agree on their assignment of historical novel for all texts in the corpus, followed by the same process for the romantic novel. After all labels are tested, a new pair of sources is compared for each label in the entire corpus. From these values, the mean Kappa score for the two sources can be calculated. For this process, I only use the semantic-labels obtained in the previous section.

This methodology produces a table with all possible combinations of sources with a mean Kappa for the semantic-labels. The median of the Kappa-values of all the combinations of sources is 0.13, with a variance of IQR of 0.22 (mean of 0.23, standard deviation of 0.26). As stated above, one is the perfect agreement and zero is an arbitrary assignment. But how should a value of 0.13 be interpreted? In Computer Science, an agreement below 0.8 is perceived as tentative, while below 0.67 contains excessive disagreement (Artstein and Poesio 2008, 576). The agreement among sources is generally much lower than this, a reason why it may be convenient to use a more flexible interpretation of the agreement, for instance in the case of a medical diagnosis, in which a Kappa of 0.4 is already a moderate agreement (Artstein and Poesio 2008, 576). In these terms, the sources would regularly have a slight agreement on subgenres. The pairs of sources with mean Kappa-values over 0.4 are presented in the following table:

---

9 I tested the one in <https://github.com/grrrr/krippendorff-alpha> which seems much less performant than the Kappa function in Scikit-Learn.

Table 6: Pairs of sources and mean Kappa over semantic-labels

Source 1	**Source 2**	**Mean Kappa**
Wikidata	subtitle BNE	1
Subtitle	subtitle BNE	0.95
Subtitle	MdLE	0.76
MdLE	subtitle BNE	0.57
HdLE	subtitle BNE	0.5
MdLE	HdLE	0.41

The only pair of sources that agree completely is Wikidata and the covers of the National Library. Consequently, the low amount of information from Wikidata has probably just been automatically extracted from the cover information. Considering them as different sources would mean a duplication of the information and thus it would be counted twice. The second highest agreement confirms one of my expectations: The information from the cover of the digitized texts and the covers at the National Library are in many cases the same. However, the following pairs bring new and unexpected knowledge: The two manuals of literature have a high agreement with the covers (digitized and at the National Library), even higher than that which they share with each other. The mean Kappa-value of 0.41 between the two manuals is relatively low, meaning that even scholars with similar interests in literature tend to share only a weak agreement about their understanding of subgenres.

To examine more possible combinations between the sources, I plot them as a graph in Figure 54, with the sources as nodes and their agreement as edges. The higher the agreement between two sources, the thicker the edge. For a better rendering, I filter out the edges that are below the median of the Kappa-values (0.24). The information in the previous Table 6 becomes apparent in Figure 54 as well. On the one hand, the edges between Wikidata and BNE, and on the other hand, between the BNE and subtitle, are the thickest ones. Also, the edges between the histories of literature (MdLE and HdLE) and the BNE or subtitles are among the thicker edges. As hypothesized in my third expectation, the labels from Amazon are set apart from the rest, and, also as expected, share little with the histories of literature. However, contrary to my expectation, Amazon agrees neither with my own annotation nor with ePubLibre. In fact, the fourth hypothesis, that the labels from ePubLibre

Figure 54: Agreement between sources of semantic-labels

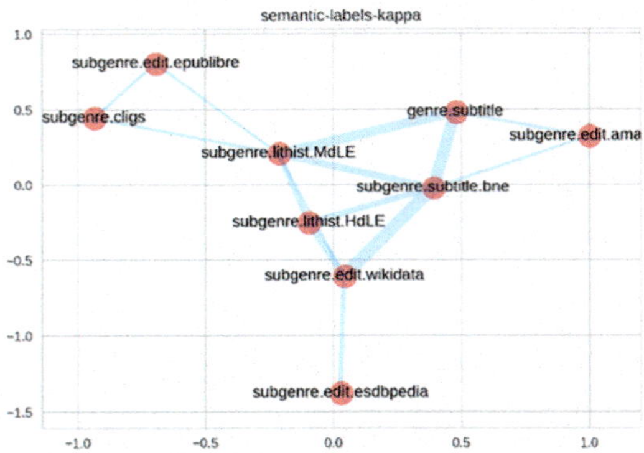

would constitute a bridge between the publishers and the academics, seems erroneous. The most central nodes are actually MdLE and the subtitles from the cover in the BNE, something completely unforeseen (second expectation). This reinforces the idea that, even when it seems trivial which label appears on the cover, it does have a strong influence over time in the study of literature, the automatic extraction of information by resources like Wikidata, and also for the publishers. Other lateral nodes are DBpedia, which is similar to Wikidata, and also my own annotation and ePubLibre. I recognize the influence that both ePubLibre and MdLE had in my own annotation, since many of the texts or the metadata came from these sources (see Chapter 3.2).

The first expectation, that similar types of sources would cluster together, can be confirmed to a certain degree. The agreements between sources like DBpedia and Wikidata, BNE and subtitle, or HdLE and MdLE are among the highest, but it is not the case that the strongest edges between the sources are from similar types of sources. For example, the agreement between MdLE and the cover of the BNE is stronger than between the two manuals of literature. This outlines a fluid panorama of sources of labels without clear clusters but with recognizable patterns:

1. Subgenres from manuals of literature, with a central position.
2. Historical subgenres from the covers, also with a central position.

3. Subgenres from publishers (Amazon).
4. Subgenres from annotation by readers (ePubLibre and my own annotation).
5. Digital sources (Wikidata and DBpedia) that automatically extract labels from other sources.

A significant lesson from this analysis is the fact that, depending on the source of the data, the researcher might be considering very different concepts of genre and subgenre. However, no source is completely isolated from the rest: All of them share a low understanding of subgenres.

At this point, I have to decide which sources should be used for the rest of the work. I could choose only one type of source and remain within a specific area of knowledge. With the cover, my analysis would be closer to the history of literature; with the manuals of literature it would be more relevant to the reception in traditional academic circles; with the labels from Amazon it would belong more to the market; and with my own annotation and the community of users, my investigation would be closer to DH and Computational Linguistics research.

One of my underlying hypotheses in this work is that all areas are able to capture the very complex phenomenon of genre and that some of them grasp this better than others. Therefore, our comprehension of genres and subgenres will profit by combining them in the same analysis. To mention two subgenres, the history of literature might analyze the naturalist novel in more depth, but perhaps the intuition of the publishers in accepting *literary fiction* as a subgenre could be proven beneficial. Since every label for each text still has the information about the specific sources from where it comes, in the sixth section of this research I will construct specific experiments only using particular sources of labels.

The proximity of the different institutions is an argument that not all should have the same status: Some have been verified as not being independent. Wikidata and DBpedia have very few labels, and they seem to depend on the historical sources. Keeping them as references like the remaining sources would lead to unmotivated reinforcement. This is the reason I decide to reject them for the rest of the analysis. As a result, I will only consider the information from the cover from the BNE and not from the digitized text. Without these three references, the remainder of the investigation will consist of six sources of labels: two manuals of literature, own annotation, ePubLibre, Amazon and cover information of the BNE.

5.1.7 Consistent Labels across Sources

After analyzing how the sources classified the texts, the focus now changes to the labels themselves, and the question of which labels are assigned with a minimal consistency by several institutions is asked. This will also establish which terms are applied without any human agreement, being randomly assigned.

To observe the consistency of the labels among sources, I calculate the Kappa-value for each label in all 15 possible combinations of the sources. This gives a table with 109 columns for the semantic-labels and 15 rows for all the pairwise combinations of sources. If a column contains only zeros, no pair of sources uses the label in a minimally consistent manner. In other words, there is no evidence that they were not assigned randomly. This is the case for 77 semantic-labels of all 109 labels: The different institutions treat the labels without any shared understanding on which texts should be included. Even when the inventory is rather large, it is worthwhile listing it in its full extent to better comprehend the importance of this step:

> almacenamiento, americana, animales, antiguo, antireligiosa, antología, autoayuda, biblioteca, borrador, catalán, **ciencia-ficción**, ciudad, clásico, completa, consulta, corta, cortesana, crimen, crítica-social, crónica, cuadro, cuento, culta, cómic, **de tesis**, de-acción, diario, empresa, ensayo, **epistolar**, epopeya, escena, español, **esperpento**, estrategia, etopeya, europea, evocación, familia, ficción, ficción-política, folletín, fábula, híbrido, idiomas, inglés, intriga, irreal, juvenil-infantil, larga, lectura, leyenda, libro de viajes, literatura, marítimo, **moral**, nebulosa, normativa, novela, original, otro, pacifista, periodismo, **picaresca**, **policíaca**, prosa, póstuma, **regeneracionista**, religiosa, saga, sentencias, siglo-xix, suelta, sátira, teatro, teoría literaria, terror

The majority of the labels that were surprising or even strange to find in the sources (*almacenamiento, autoayuda, biblioteca, catalán, español, inglés*, etc.) are from the metadata of Amazon, probably either as a consequence of errors or untypical ways of targeting customers. I have marked in bold some subgenres that can be considered established in Literary Studies, but that do not show any consistency in the corpus: *epistolar, ciencia-ficción, picaresca, policíaca,* etc. These subgenres are probably more solid in former or later periods, in contrast to the analyzed period or in the analyzed sources. The fact that some subgenres that are characteristic for this period (*de tesis, moral, regeneracionista*) also show no consistency is especially surprising, and therefore it is very doubtful that they will show better results in other periods. In addition, there are some one-author-labels: *de acción* (Baroja), *esperpento* (Valle-Inclán), *nebulosa* (Gómez de la Serna), *normativa* (Pérez de Ayala). A label that is also considered to be randomly assigned is *literary fiction,* since a sole source (Amazon) considered it, further analyzed in Chapter 5.3. In this case, it is observed that, even when the label was very common in one source, the methodology proposed in this section requires that labels from a single source be rejected. At least two sources have to agree on the label and use it for similar groups of texts.

On the other hand, there are 32 labels showing a minimal consistency of assignment among the sources. The agreement of each pair of sources for each semantic-label can vary between zero and one. This value can be plotted on the vertical axis, with each subgenre as a single box plot in Figure 55.

Figure 55: Agreement between sources for each semantic-label

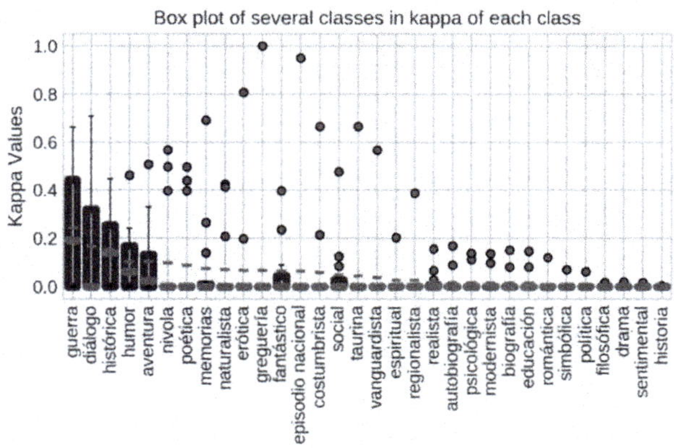

As can be observed, the agreement is very low. The median value (thick line in the box, the thin one represents the mean values) shows values of zero in almost all the medians with only four exceptions: *war, historical, cedy* and *ad-*

venture). If the mean value of all the data points of these 32 labels is calculated, it gives a Kappa-value of 0.02 (with a standard deviation of 0.03). In general, the sources do not agree on the assignment of the subgenres. Almost no pair of sources shows strong agreement for any label (as mentioned before, over 0.8 is considered the typical threshold of strong agreement, cf. Artstein 2017, 302). For the majority of cases, agreement is an exceptional phenomenon, shown as a flier in the box plot (for example the point on the top of *greguería*). Some labels are very close to being randomly assigned since only one pair of sources agrees, and in many cases with a very weak agreement. The labels on the right show agreement for only two pairs of sources with a value lower than 0.1 Kappa. Even when two pairs of sources have agreed on their assignment, should such low values be accepted, and should they be considered *consistent labels*? Should the sentimental novel be treated as a consistent subgenre only because two of the six sources have agreed on it with a Kappa-value of 0.02? Speaking against this is the fact that there are some labels for which only two sources agree, but the values of these are extremely high: *greguería* (perfect agreement in one pair) or *episodio nacional* (0.95). In these cases, only two sources agree on their use, but their assignment is almost identical, which is a very rare outcome.

To achieve a more robust consistency and yet be sensitive to the extremely high cases, I define two criteria for a label to be considered consistent:

- Either two pairs of sources or more have to agree on its assignment,
- Or the Kappa-value of the agreeing pair has to be greater than the accepted threshold of 0.8.

These two criteria filter out those labels that are assigned by only two sources with a very weak agreement: *drama, historia, política, regionalista, romántica, sentimental, simbólica, taurina, vanguardista*. These labels are not completely randomly assigned, but the agreement of only two sources is too weak. This step yields 23 consistent semantic-labels:

> autobiografía, aventura, biografía, costumbrista, diálogo, educación, episodio nacional, erótica, espiritual, fantástico, filosófica, greguería, guerra, histórica, humor, memorias, modernista, naturalista, nivola, poética, psicológica, realista, social

5.1.8 Discussion and Proposal of Subgenre Palette

Chapter 5.1 opened with a list of 292 token-labels and ends with a palette of 23 consistent semantic-labels of subgenre. Considering that the corpus contains 358 texts, I have moved from a ratio of 1.4 texts per label to 15.57. Through the different steps, I have observed that the variance in the labels in different sources is caused to a large degree by superficial linguistic variance such as multilingual, morphological or lexical forms. I subsequently contemplated the agreement of subgenre from distinct sources. Even between similar sources, such as two manuals of literature, this agreement is very weak (median of 0.14 Kappa-values for the different subgenres). These results are far lower than what Computer Science consider usually acceptable. A large proportion of subgenres used by certain sources either did not show any consistency or were extremely low. I have no evidence that humans share a basic concept of many subgenres, even of typical ones for this period such as *de tesis, moral, regeneracionista, sentimental*.

As described in Chapter 2.2 about computational analysis of genres, very few papers have analyzed the agreement on genre between annotators, reporting values of around 0.7 for the novel and 0.5 for different genres. The agreement for finer categories such as subgenres is expected to be lower. We expect humans to have more difficulties distinguishing between the types of novels than differentiating a novel from an essay. In any case, the study on human agreement in subgenres is an interesting area with little research and many questions. Do the annotators need to be specialists? How much text do they have to read to recognize the subgenre? Should it be either a page, a chapter, or do they have to read the entire text? Should they already know the text or anything about the text? Should they be familiar with the author? Should they work with a finite palette or propose their own labels?

As I have pointed out in Chapters 2.1 and 2.3, the opinion that genres do not exist, is at least a century old. The work that computational methods have achieved in the last decades clearly shows that genres and subgenres are labels that can be predicted reasonably well by algorithms using linguistic features. From this chapter, I agree that many literary subgenres do not show any human agreement, and that in general subgenres are only partially recognized by humans.

The final palette of 23 subgenres can be understood as a set of consistent semantic-labels because they have emerged from a semantic mapping and a test of their consistency across several sources. Through these steps, I was not in a position to cherry pick the labels which I found more interesting. However, this methodology has an underlying hypothesis that no single specific source (covers, publishers, literary scholars, annotators) can completely comprehend literary subgenre. Rather, several perspectives need to be reconciled.

In general, the final subgenres show clear differences, while some seem closely related (social-naturalist, naturalist-realist, social-realist). Only one group (autobiographic, biographic, memoir, educational novel) throws doubts on whether a human would be able to distinguish between all of them. The palette still contains some subgenres that are clearly on the frontier between the novel and other genres (dialogue, poetic, autobiographic novel, *greguería*). Contrary to my expectations, three one-author-labels have been confirmed as consistent semantic-labels: *nivola, greguería* and *episodio nacional*, while many others have proved to be inconsistent across the sources. This does not mean that they are truly a phenomenon comparable to subgenres such as dialogue or adventure novel, but it does point out that different actors consider them to be useful categories and that they assign them with a minimal consistency for different texts. Furthermore, some remaining labels in the palette are closely related to specific decades, such as the realist, naturalist or modernist novel.

One of the goals of this chapter was to not only obtain a set for the rest of this research, but also to try to express it in such a way that other researchers can use it for other languages, periods or corpora. For this reason, I have mapped the semantic-labels with the Thema schema whose codes can be used as multilingual bridges. In a perfect scenario, the entire palette could be expressed using the codes of Thema. Sadly, this was not the case for nine of the remaining subgenres, although it was for 14,[10] which accounts for 61% of the palette.

Are the sources applying *wrong subgenres* or is Thema not broad enough? I do not think the role of Thema is to cover one-author-labels such as *nivola* or *greguería*, because that would speak against the very basic purpose of such schemata. On the other hand, it is surprising that subgenres that are very well established in studies of literature, such as *realist* or *naturalist,* are not covered. Going beyond the period analyzed here, I could not find a category

10 The following subgenres are not included in Thema: costumbrista, diálogo, episodio nacional, greguería, modernista, naturalista, nivola, psicológica, realista. The following subgenres are included in Thema: autobiografía, aventura, biografía, educación, erótica, espiritual, fantástico, filosófica, guerra, histórica, humor, memorias, poética, social.

in Thema that would fit historical subgenres such as *picaresque* or *pastoral* novels, *historical plays* or *sonnets*. I understand that romantic stories starring either vampires (Thema code FMR) or protagonists with uniforms (Thema code FRP) currently constitute a larger section of the editorial market than picaresque novels or collections of sonnets, and yet a fraction of the catalogs of specific publishers could be described with more accurate historical terms and, moreover, enable other fields to adopt this schema. Thema is a valuable initiative towards a standardization of textual prose genres and subgenres, but its goal is book trade and therefore important concepts in literary history are ignored.

What is the result for the corpus? How much of the corpus can be described through the analyzed palette? It covers almost the entire corpus, or 98% of the texts. To be more specific, only five novels have lost all their references to subgenres because their labels were not consistent enough: *El primer loco* de Castro, *Contraataque* by Sender, *Doña Inés* by Azorín, and two by Serna (*El chalet de las rosas* and *La mujer de ámbar*). It is interesting that de Castro and Sender are authors that belong to other periods (de Castro to Romanticism, Sender to the post-war period), which is probably the reason why their texts fit better in subgenres that are not (anymore or yet) present in the corpus.

What can other researchers learn from the comparison of the sources? Which were the most useful sources? I have answered these questions for the token-labels in Section 4.1.2, but how do the sources rate when the consistent semantic-labels are observed on their own? How many texts do the sources label? And what is their ratio of texts per subgenre?

Table 7: Summary of tendencies in consistent semantic-labels, grouped by sources

	different labels	labeled texts	ratio
BNE	15	48	3.2
HdLE	16	76	4.75
Amazon	13	68	5.23
MdLE	22	160	7.27
ePubLibre	9	137	15.22
CLiGS	19	350	18.42

Since many labels were deleted because of their inconsistency, the sources have lost a great proportion of their annotation in the corpus. For example, the labels of Amazon have changed from giving information about two-thirds of the corpus to only one-sixth. The coverage of the corpus has dropped to between 25% and 50%, with the exception of my own annotation that still covers the majority of the corpus. Besides this source, none account for more than half of the corpus, with the lowest results from the covers in the BNE. In contrast, the ratio of texts per genre has drastically increased to a median of 6.25, meaning ePubLibre and my own annotation keep clearly higher scores.

Each researcher should consider their specific goals and the amount of time they want to spend in gathering labels. Own annotation or going through large manuals of literature achieve a good coverage of the corpus, but are time consuming. Extracting labels from ePubLibre or Amazon might be a fast path for research with a focus on DH or Computer Science, but these are very heterogeneous (especially from publishers) and will probably be rejected in circles of Literary Studies. Some of these sources, like BNE and Amazon, would be insufficient for analyzing the labels since they cover only around one-sixth of the corpus. This reinforces the idea of considering different sources to better grasp the phenomenon of textual subgenres.

Through this chapter, not only a subgenre palette was conceived, but important effects on the corpus and its metadata about subgenres became blatantly obvious. Before this chapter, each text could belong or not to each subgenre. After the analysis presented here, each of the six independent sources assigns each text to each subgenre. In other words, each text can now belong to each subgenre and this relation is quantitatively expressed from zero to six. These values can be used for measuring whether a text is clearly naturalist (many sources agree on that), only partially naturalist (only one source keeps this assignment) or not naturalist (no sources assigned it to this subgenre). This can change the kind of task for genre analysis from classification to regression, in computational terms; from a taxonomy of subgenres to prototypes of subgenres, from the abstract model. I am now able to analyze not only whether a text belongs to a nominal class or not, but also how clearly (from zero to six) each text belongs to each class. The question changes from "is this text naturalist?" to "how naturalist is this text?" This matter will be analyzed in Section 7.1.6 and represented in the model presented in Chapter 8.

5.2 Analysis of Labels of First Editions

An important distinction in the sources of labels is whether the labels were assigned contemporary to the production of the text or whether they were produced decades or centuries later. Most sources consulted in this thesis were assigned at least half a century after the first publication of the text, more specifically after 1980. The labeling process can be influenced by how the society canonizes and considers the text and author through history.

There are two competing hypotheses about the difference between early and later labels:

1. The early labels (assigned during or soon after the first publication) received less influence from external processes regarding the text and its author; in other words, these labels would have been assigned by internal characteristics of the text, and therefore these labels should be classified more accurately using features extracted from the text.
2. The early labels do not rely more heavily on internal features than the later ones. Both author and first publisher had greater control over the label on the cover, and they used it rather to surprise the public than to catalog the work.

Both hypotheses are reasonable and both outcomes are possible, depending on the languages, tradition, or periods analyzed. On the one hand, a generic label on the cover, such as *novel* or *drama*, is mentioned many times as evidence for the very existences of genres: We found these labels on the cover of many books. On the other hand, it is also common to read the skepticism of scholars about the accuracy of such labels (Garrido Gallardo 1988, 21; Bortrel 2001, 38–45), with clear examples of authors using labels that do not match the book in a traditional way, such as *Divina commedia* by Dante or *Comédie humaine* by Balzac (both mentioned in Petersen 1944, 120). Besides, "some genres are defined only retrospectively, being unrecognized as such by the original producers and audiences" (Chandler 1997, 4), a possibility that I will analyze in detail in Chapter 6.2.

In this chapter, I want to take a closer look at information on the covers of the first edition, and compare its characteristics and performance in classification tests to the rest of the sources of labels.

5.2.1 Description and Comparison of the Labels of the Covers

From the sources presented in Chapter 5.1, only one was assigned contemporary to the publication of the text: the labels on the covers. Nevertheless, these labels might change over time and what a reader can find on the cover of a modern edition might not be what was published in the first place. For this reason, I check all the works with subgenre information on their covers and confirm in the catalog of the Spanish National Library whether the first edition shows a genre label, and if so, which one.

From the 358 texts in the corpus, 131 have some form of genre information on the cover of the first edition. If the label *novel* is deleted, only 79 remain, which represents almost a fifth of the corpus. These texts show 43 different token-labels, which can be summarized in 32 semantic-labels, following the steps in Section 5.1.5. This means that roughly every second work with a label on the cover of its first edition would have a different label. From these, 19 are used for one single work. In summary, the subgenre labels of the first edition are very scarce and specific. In the following bar plot the number of texts per labels can be observed in Figure 56.

Only four labels can be found in more than four texts; two of them cause some kind of a problem. *Historia* ('story') is normally not treated as literary genre, and *episodio nacional* is a one-author-label by Galdós (see Section 2.1.10). In labels with a lower frequency, there are cases that are hardly subgenres of the novels, such as *escena* ('scene'), *borrador* ('draft'), *larga* ('long'), *cuento* ('tale'), *leyenda* ('legend'), or *prosa* ('prose'). The overall picture is that, besides labels as *costumbrista* and *humor*, the rest of the labels were assigned rather with the intention of capturing the attention of the reader or buyer with artistic and surprising terms, and not to group the texts based on internal characteristics.

Figure 56: Bar plot of number of texts per label

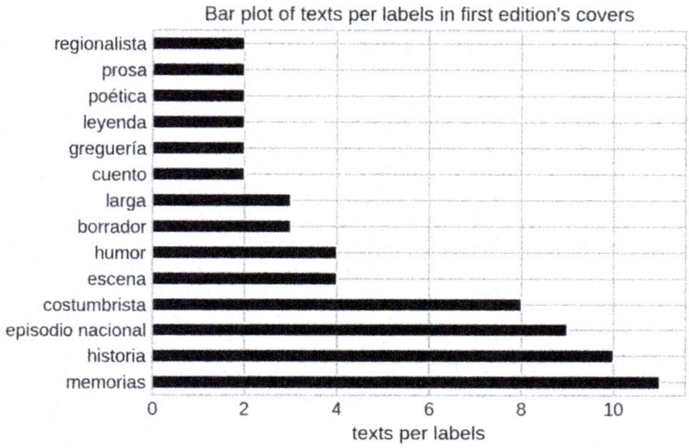

5.2.2 Classification Results Comparing First Publication Labels with other Sources

The first hypothesis proposes that the labels printed on the first edition should describe the text more accurately because the process of canonization and social perception had not started when it was assigned. If these labels were assigned by looking more closely at the textual characteristics of the novel and not at external factors, it would imply that these labels should more predictably apply internal features.

To test this, I run several classification tests with two different data sets:

1. First, only those novels are considered that had a label for their first edition and predict only this label, ignoring the rest of the sources.
2. Second, the entire corpus is considered, predicting the labels obtained in Chapter 5.1. In this case, the information of the first edition is ignored, treating the labels of several editions as one source among others.

The classification set-up relies on the results of Chapter 6.1, which will be used again in Section 5.2.2, and also employed equally in the different tests of this section (see further details in the Jupyter Notebook). In all cases, I only consider labels with more than two texts, obtaining eight subgenres defined and assigned by the cover of the first edition. The results of the classification are shown below:

Figure 57: Box plots of classification results of the labels from the first edition

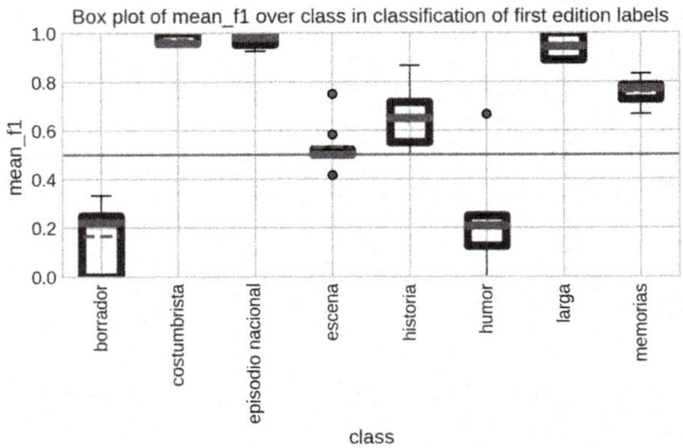

Three of the labels (*borrador*, *humor*, and *escena*) are not classified above the baseline, with two cases clearly below it. What does this mean? It indicates that the algorithm, when considering linguistic features, achieves worse results than those that could be expected in a random process. An interpretation of this could be that these labels were assigned exactly opposite to what the reader could expect from the internal content. On the other hand, three labels achieve an almost perfect classification, with two others between an F1-score of 0.7 and 0.8. In general, the mean F1-score of the different labels is 0.65, with a standard deviation of 0.32. This indicates that the range of prediction of these labels encompasses the whole spectrum, from the worst possible classification (worse than random) to perfect.

To compare these results, I run a second classification test, based on the 23 subgenres assigned by all the sources as explained in Chapter 5.1. Figure 58 shows that, in this case, all boxes of the 23 subgenres are located above the baseline, although the best cases rarely surpass 0.9. In general, the mean accuracy of the prediction of different labels is 0.76, with a standard deviation of 0.11.

Figure 58: Box plots of classification results of the consistent semantic labels

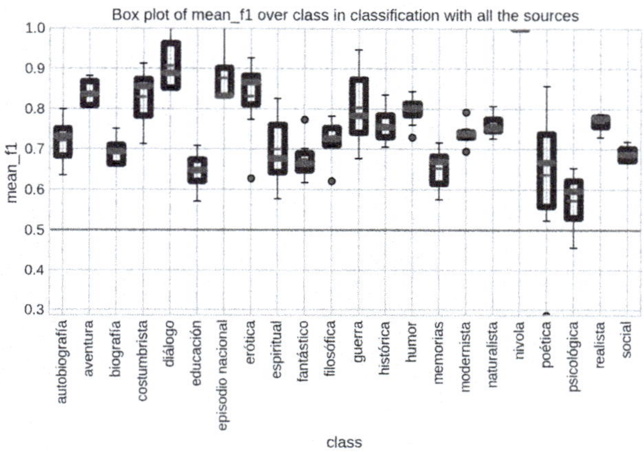

If both tests are compared, the labels on the cover of the first edition generally have lower results and a greater variance in classification than those by different sources. Is this difference statistically significant? Running a Welch's t-test on the mean F1-scores of both variables,[1] the outcome is a p-value of 0.015, which indicates that it is significant. This seems to refute, at least for my corpus, the first hypothesis, that labels contemporary to the first publication would have a higher prediction based on linguistic features. In general, the classification of labels of the first publication's cover yields lower results with a greater variance.

5.2.3 Association between Author and First Edition Label

The second hypothesis on first edition labels considers that these rely more heavily on external information, and that they are more specific to the authors, who used it as part of their artistic means. For this, I want to test

1 The version of the t-test for cases in which the variance of both variables is not equal, as in this case since both variables contain different numbers of observations: 14 different labels in the first edition, and 23 in the second case with all the sources.

whether specific authors tend to use the same label repeatedly on the cover of their first edition, regardless of the content of the book. In this case, since each work of the corpus had a single author and each first edition had only one label, I want to observe the association between two categorical variables: the author's name and the label of the first edition. For this, I run a chi-square test of association on those variables. This is a nonparametric test applicable to categorical data that uses information from a contingency table of several values of both categorical variables (Evans 1996, 453–55). In the following table the "frequency count of outcomes for each possible combination of the levels of two variables" appears (Evans 1996, 453), in this case the number of novels that each author (rows) wrote with each label (columns), highlighting the labels that exceed three books. The last column and the last row represent the sums of both dimensions:

Table 8: Contingency matrix of labels in the first edition and the author's name

author name	**historia**	**memorias**	**episodio nacional**	**costumbrista**	**escena**	**humor**	**total**
Arderius	0	0	0	0	0	1	**1**
Azorin	1	0	0	0	0	0	**1**
Baroja	0	5	0	0	0	0	**5**
Bazan	2	0	0	0	0	0	**2**
Galdos	4	0	9	0	0	1	**14**
Jarnes	0	0	0	0	1	0	**1**
Lorca	1	0	0	0	0	0	**1**
Miro	0	0	0	0	3	0	**3**
Unamuno	1	0	0	0	0	0	**1**
Valdes	0	0	0	8	0	0	**8**
Valle	1	4	0	0	0	0	**4**
WFFlorez	0	0	0	0	0	1	**1**
Zamacois	0	1	0	0	0	0	**1**
total	**10**	**9**	**9**	**8**	**4**	**3**	**43**

Two subgenres seem to be practiced by several authors: *historia* and *humor*. The rest is dominated either by one or two authors: *memorias*, *episodio nacional*, *escena*, and *costumbrista*. The result of this last label is surprising, because it is one of the few that can be related to a semantic feature in the plots and also to the intention of the books. Looking at how it was used on the covers, it is observed that it tends to appear only on the covers of Valdés. In general, in the contingency table one can see that the labels of the first editions are strongly associated with the author. The chi-square test with author name and first edition covers labels gives a p-value very close to zero (1.2e-42[2]), so the association is highly significant. This means that the labels found on the covers are highly depend on the authors who wrote them.

But are the rest of the sources free of this association? Are the current publishers or scholars not influenced by the association of some authors' names with specific labels? As I have demonstrated in the analysis of agreement between sources in Section 5.1.6, covers are a central source of labels when comparing them to the rest. If covers are associated with the author, it is reasonable to expect that others will share it. For this reason, I run the chi-square test, each time comparing each source with the name of the author. From the nine different sources, four of them show meaningful associations with the name of the author (p-value < 0.001): the literary manual MdLE, the first edition, the covers in the National Library, and my own annotation. To better compare the results, the p-values can be plotted as bars in Figure 59, with a logarithmic axis, which shows the probabilities that each source is associated with the name of the author: The larger the p-value, the less probable it is that the label and the name of the author are associated with each other.

The labels provided by publishers on Amazon, ePubLibre, the manual HdLE, DB-pedia, and Wikidata do not seem to have a direct association with the authors. The other four sources show p-values below 0.001, but the distance between them is also notable: The lowest value is for MdLE, followed by the first edition, and then, with many fewer zeros, the information of the covers, and my own annotation. Although the comparison of such small p-values can be problematic, I think there are several aspects that can be read from this. The first edition does have a strong association with the name of the author, even when comparing it to the rest of the sources. Nevertheless,

2 This is common annotation for numbers that are very large, very small, or very close to zero. 1.2e-01 would be equal to 0.12, and 1.2e-02 would be equal to 0.012. In the case of 1.2e-42, there are 41 zeros between the fraction and the value 12.

Figure 59: Bar plot of the p-values of the chi-square test between labels on the first edition cover and the author's name

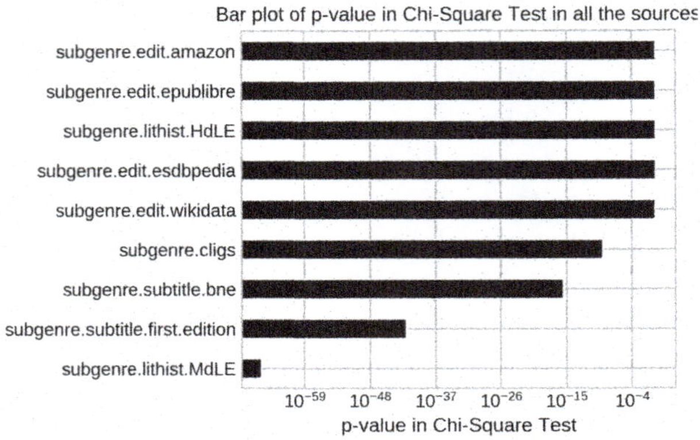

there is another source that is even more likely to have an association with the writer: the manual of literature MdLE. It is interesting that when all the covers are used (and not only that from the first edition), the probability of being associated with the author decreases notably (from 1.2e-42 to 2.8e-16). This indicates that the later a label is assigned, the less affected is it by authorship. However, my data set does not allow testing for this in its complete extension.

An unexpected result is the fact that the labels by the publisher on Amazon or the community of ePubLibre marked a relatively large proportion of the corpus with subgenres when compared to the HdLE, DBpedia, or Wikidata (Section 5.1.3). In addition, the labels from Amazon and ePubLibre do not show an association with the name of the author. This result is difficult to accept from the Literary Studies' perspective. On the one side, these two sources are the ones that would be more easily criticized by literary scholars. On the other side, there is a certain expectation that subgenres should be independent of the author. Yet the results show a very different tendency: The more prestige a source has in Literary Studies, the more likely it is to be influenced by the name of the author.

5.2.4 Conclusions

In this section, I have run several experiments about the status of labels on the cover of the first publication. I have presented and evaluated two competing hypotheses, i.e. that these labels should be either closer to the internal features or to the author.

As a first step, I have observed that the number of works labeled in the first publication is relatively small, with a high tendency to use very specific labels for one or two texts. Those that have a higher frequency present either semantic ambiguity for cataloging novels (*story, tale, legend, scene, long, draft*) or a close association with the author (*episodio nacional, costumbrista*).

As a second step, I have classified these subgenres based on linguistic features before comparing them to the classification of the labels of the rest of the sources. The labels of the first publication achieve lower results and show greater variance than the rest of labels.

As a third step, I have calculated whether the first edition is associated with the name of the author, and I compared it to the rest of the sources. The first edition is one of the sources that shows the strongest dependency on the writer's name.

For this corpus, selecting only the labels from the first edition would cause a strong reduction of the analyzed labels, the researched texts, with lower results in classification using linguistic data, and with a stronger dependency on authorship. That is why I have decided to use information from all covers and not only the first one as a source with the same status regardless of whether they come from publishers, manuals, or my own annotation. However, these can differ greatly in other languages, periods, genres, or levels of descriptions. It is plausible that in specific contexts, the author did not have any influence on what exactly appeared on the cover, but it was rather the publishers who had influence and who might have had a less surprising goal, rather having cataloging in mind. In addition, more generic categories (such as drama and novel) might be more accurate on the cover than more specific subgenres. In any case, this section has raised some interesting questions for which my data set does not allow a deeper analysis: The later a label is assigned, is it more likely to be based on linguistic features? This could be formalized in the question of whether the chronological distance of the assignment of a label would correlate with the classification results. And is the understanding of subgenres in Literary Studies mainly associated with the author?

5.3 The Case of *Literary Fiction*

5.3.1 Introduction

The methodology presented in Chapter 5.1 for the composition of the set of labels imposes one constraint: At least two sources (from publishers, literary scholars, the Spanish National Library, ePubLibre, or annotation) were needed to maintain a label in their palette and to assign it in a minimally consistent manner. But what if only one of these sources tends to frequently consider a specific label to categorize novels? It could have happened that many authors published their works with a specific label on the cover, but that this was not further used by later sources. Only one label showed this kind of exceptionalism in the description of data – *literary fiction* – and was very frequently applied by publishers in their metadata (see Section 5.1.5).

Although the initial instinct can lead to this information which was not sanctioned by other sources being ignored, a recent article by Wilkens concludes that "the sooner we realize that [*literary fiction* is] of the same sort as far as generic specificity is concerned, the better will be our understanding of the system of contemporary fiction" (2016). He and other DH scholars are increasingly using metadata labels about genre from publishers or other platforms (such as GoodReads), including Koolen (2018) or van Cranenburgh, van Dalen-Oskam, and van Zundert (2019), from the *Riddle of Literary Quality* project, in which the term *literary fiction* is also present as a literary genre. Koolen mentions that it is not her choice to use the label (she would have preferred the term *general fiction*), but that she uses it given that she finds it in the metadata of publishers and that the readers can recognize it as a genre (Koolen 2018, 27–28). Publishers and other agents of the book industry do use the label as a genre, and this has become an empirical observation for DH researchers.

But what do publishers want to express with the label *literary fiction*? To answer this question properly, it would be necessary to have a previous definition that the publishers have considered. The Thema taxonomy of shared metadata by publishers (already applied in Section 5.1.5) contains a code (FB) called *Fiction: general & literary*. This code is part of a more general category (F) that stands for *Fiction & Related items*, which should cover all types of prose narrative compositions (drama, lyrical prose, and essay are part of other major categories). The only definition given in Thema is to use this label for "literary & non-genre fiction" and it suggests applying a more exact categorization for works published in the last 50 years (FBA, *Modern & contemporary fiction*) or previously (FBC, *Classic fiction*). The papers mentioned in the previous paragraph do not offer a proper definition and for their analysis they rely on the assignment of this category and the texts. To use the logical terms presented in Section 2.3.1, it is unclear what the intension or internal characteristics of *literary fiction* are, and the researchers are only approaching this label through its extension (through the instances that are part of the category and through the books assigned with this label).

The main question of this chapter is to observe whether *literary fiction* can be understood as a subgenre comparable to erotic, comedy, education novel, or memoir. If the answer is positive, we should expect it to behave similarly to the other types of novels. To find an answer to this question, I will run several tests observing whether this specific label stands out from the rest of the group or not. If it does, I will have to suppose it represents a different type of categorization of texts, such as an operationalization of literariness or a group of genres. If it does show similar characteristics to the other labels, there will be no reason to think that *literary fiction* is anything but a subgenre, as the publishers are treating it.

To be more specific, I will first describe the use of this label applied by the publishers, observing its frequency in sources, its correlation with other approximations of the canon, and general correlations with other metadata. Second, I will apply classifiers on linguistic information to try to predict this particular label and compare the results with the rest of the labels. Third, several types of metadata (especially that regarding only the author, but also metadata internal and external to the text) will be employed to discover whether *literary fiction* depends more heavily on non-linguistic information than the other subgenre labels. Finally, I will argue for adopting *literary fiction* as a hypothetical subgenre of the novel since the data of the publishers and the tests does not suggest otherwise.

5.3.2 Description of *Literary Fiction*

The publishers assigned three labels related to *literary fiction* in Spanish to my corpus: *ficción clásica* (136 novels), *ficción contemporánea* (86), and *novelas y ficción literaria* (1). In general, there is a great overlap between these different labels, with the concept of the label 'classic' being especially frequent in the works published in the 1880s and the 1890s. This means that the labels and the way they were allocated by the publishers do not correspond to different meanings, but are just a matter of chronological distribution: *ficción clásica* for the earlier works, *ficción contemporánea* for the later works. This complementary chronological distribution maps the taxonomy of Thema that I have mentioned previously (codes FBA and FBC). Since I do not consider several subgenres depending on their period of publication in other subgenres, I decide to follow the taxonomy of Thema and use the category hanging a step above, which is *Fiction: general & literary* (FB). But instead of using this specific label, I decide to rather use the shorter term *literary fiction* because it can be related to the papers previously mentioned that also collected metadata from publishers.

The first question I want to focus on is whether this label is assigned with a minimal homogeneity between publishers and, furthermore, to compare it to the other analyzed labels. To do so, I cannot use the methodology applied in Chapter 5.1 comparing different sources, because the term *literary fiction* was allocated by what I considered a single source: the publishers on Amazon. In this case, I am not interested in knowing whether Amazon and the manuals agree on the way they use the label *literary fiction*, or whether several publishers agree on this label for a given work. In contrast, in Figure 60 I calculate the frequency of the label in different sources and calculate the mean for each label. The higher the mean is, the greater the number of sources or publishers that assign it.

The highest values of Figure 60 are occupied by labels like *episodio nacional* or *greguería*; in these cases, around three sources on average tend to agree on assigning them to a text. The lowest values are philosophical, psychological, or autobiographies, labels where only one source tended to assign them to each text, meaning that there is almost no agreement between sources. The label analyzed here, *literary fiction*, has a mean value of 2.51, which means that if a book is considered *literary fiction*, more than two publishers will tend to consider it as such, with values close to other subgenres like poetic or war novel. This shows that *literary fiction* is a term with neither a very high nor very

Figure 60: Bar plot of mean number of sources in texts

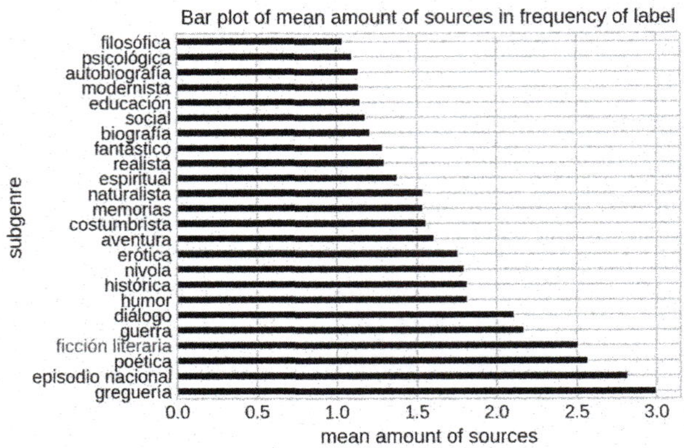

low agreement between publishers in comparison to the rest of the labels. It is rather high, but within the range of the rest of the subgenres.

Is *literary fiction* a subgenre label or is it just another way of expressing something different, like canonization, literary quality, or literariness? This question is clearly beyond the scope of this work and is currently being analyzed by colleagues from the *Riddle of Literary Quality* project. Nevertheless, two proxies for canonization were gathered as part of the metadata, which are the number of pages used by MdLE to describe two instances: the text and its author (see Section 3.2.10). In the scatter plots of Figure 61, the proportion of the frequency of the label *literary fiction* in each work[1] is compared to the two pieces of information about the canonicity of the text (on the left) and its author (on the right).

Both of these indicators of canonicity have positive correlations with statistical significance in a Spearman test (further details in Jupyter Notebook). Nevertheless, it is blatantly obvious that many data points of Figure 61 do clearly deviate from the regression line, meaning that even when there is a

1 More specifically, for each work, the number of times it received the label *literary fiction* was counted, and this number was normalized by the number of publishers that published information about it. In this way, I neutralize the effect that the raw frequency of the labels per texts would have, since the texts published more often would then get higher scores in *literary fiction* as well.

Figure 61: Scatter plots with regression line between proportions of the label literary fiction per text and number of pages in the MdLE used for the text (left) and the author (right)

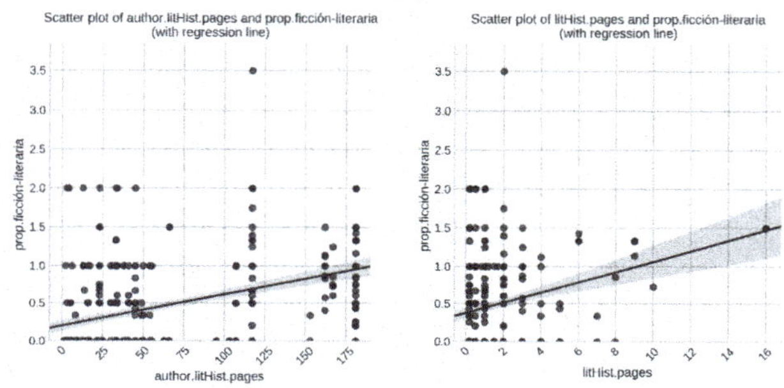

correlation, many other aspects are taken into account when labeling a text as *literary fiction*. Interestingly, the authorial canonicity (right scatter plot) has a stronger correlation with the prevalence of the *literary fiction* label ($\rho = 0.45^{***}$) than the textual canonicity ($\rho = 0.23^{***}$). This seems to show that works of a canonized author are more likely to also be considered *literary fiction*, even when they are per se not treated with as much detail by manuals of Literary Studies like the MdLE.

To obtain a first glimpse of what characteristics are specific for this chapter, I explore metadata and linguistic information that is associated with the texts that have been assigned with this label. The year of birth of the author, the year of publication, and both the mean and standard deviation of the length of sentences correlate negatively and significantly with the frequency of assignment of the *literary fiction* label (details can be read in the Jupyter Notebook). However, the following aspects correlate positively with the label *literary fiction*: the number of publishing houses that have published it, the number of chapters, and the number of interjections and instances of direct speech the work includes.[2] This gives a first broad description about the works labeled as literary fiction: Works published in the first analyzed decades, written by the oldest analyzed generation and published again from several publishers. Their texts tend to be relatively short, with homogeneously short sen-

2 Further internal characteristics of the text will be described in Section 11.4 of the Appendix.

tences, high number of chapters, a higher proportion of direct speech and one of its typographic characteristics: interjections. Further descriptions of this label will be presented in this chapter and in the Section 11.4.

5.3.3 Classification with Linguistic Features

In any research about genre classification, some categories tend to achieve higher outcomes than others: Adventure novels are *easier* to classify than educational novels. Thus, the different categories create a spectrum of classification values. If *literary fiction* is similar to other subgenres, similar results should be expected using linguistic features. In other words, the classification results of *literary fiction* should be in the range of the outcomes of the other subgenres: They should not be higher than the rest, but, more particularly, they should not be lower. Actually, my expectations were that *literary fiction* is a category that relies more heavily on non-linguistic information, such as social perception (of the author, publisher), historical development, etc., and therefore it will be classified with lower results than the rest.

To test this, I run an experiment trying to classify all 23 subgenre-labels plus *literary fiction*. The set-up relies on the evaluation that will be shown in Chapter 6.1. If *literary fiction* has one of the lowest classification scores, I calculate whether its value is in the confidence interval of the rest of the subgenres to test whether this low score is exceptionally low, or only slightly lower than the rest, but still statistically expectable. In the next figure, the outcomes of several tests for each subgenre are shown as box plots, with the mean F1-score in cross-validation steps in the vertical axis (further details about parameters in the Jupyter Notebook).

The results show that the genres tend to be recognized between 0.6 and 1.0 F1-score, with all of them significantly above the random baseline of 0.5. *Literary fiction* is found in the lower half of all subgenres, but not as an extreme low case: 15 subgenres can be better recognized than *literary fiction*, using only linguistic features (among them dialogue, adventure, humor, erotic, or autobiographic). But, surprisingly, nine genres are harder to classify, such as educational, memoirs, or modernist novel. These outcomes are surprisingly high for *literary fiction* and denote that this category is also predictable with only linguistic features, as for the rest of the subgenres.

At this point, it could be argued that any group of texts could be predicted using thousands of linguistic units and thus we could speculate whether *lit-*

Figure 62: Box plots of classification of the different subgenres and literary fiction, using linguistic features

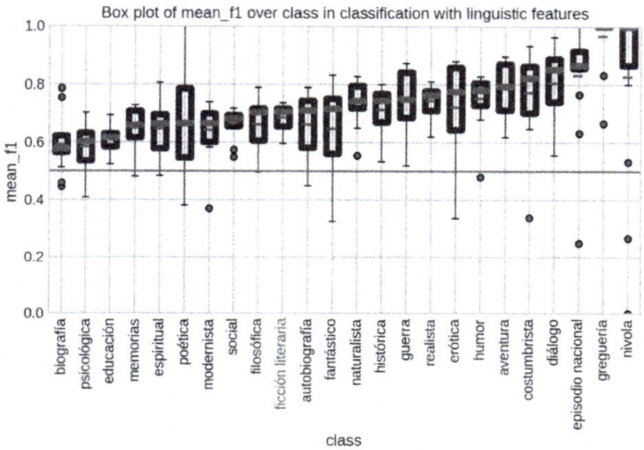

erary fiction is not just a random category assigned by publishers and that our model is simply good at learning ad hoc patterns. In Machine Learning, this problem is known as *over-fitting* and is in fact a very common problem, especially in some algorithms like decision trees or random forests, or when the number of features is greater than the number of classes, as is the case here. To counter this effect, I have used cross-validation in the previous figure, in which the algorithm learns from a section of the data (training set) and is evaluated using a different section of the data (evaluation set), going through this process iteratively. In addition, the data has been statistically compared to the baseline that should be obtained in a random process. However, since the status of *literary fiction* is still in doubt, it could be interesting to compare the results of all subgenres to the classification of artificial random categories. Now the goal is to observe whether the algorithm still recognizes categories that have been composed by random sampling, i.e. if it is too good at recognizing categories – if it is over-fitting.

To test this, I have created ten arbitrary categories sampling texts randomly. To make these categories similar to the rest of the subgenres, each one has a different size within the range of the other categories. Random-genre-1 contains 165 texts (around half of the corpus), with a comparable size to genres like social novel or *literary fiction*. Random-genre-10 contains five novels, with a similar size to other subgenres like *nivola* or poetic novel. The other random-genres increase in steps of roughly 20 works (more details in Jupyter Notebook). In the Figure 63, the 23 subgenres, *literary fiction*, and these ten random categories are again classified with exactly the same set-up.

Figure 63: Box plots of classification of the different subgenres, literary fiction, and ten random labels, using linguistic features

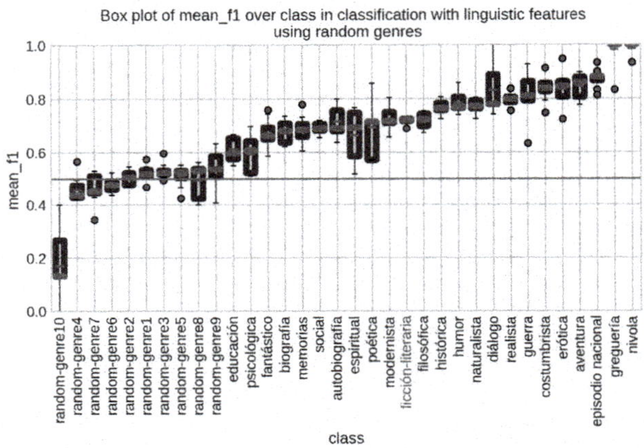

The random categories are in the lowest position in Figure 63, none of them passing the baseline of 0.5 with statistical significance.[3] The rest of the outcomes are very similar to the previous ones, with *literary fiction* again located in the middle of the rest of subgenres, in this case in the upper half. Both tests indicate two facts:

1. *Literary fiction* can be predicted using linguistic features, with a level of success that is similar to the rest of the subgenres.
2. *Literary fiction* does not behave the way random categories do, which are classified as would be expected in a random process.

3 The random-genre-9 has most of its results above the baseline, but its p-value is 0.08. Interestingly, this subgenre is the second smallest of the genres, with 40 texts. This reinforces the idea of the importance of statistical tests especially when it comes to small classes.

5.3.4 Classification with External Metadata

The fact that *literary fiction* can be predicted from the linguistic information to a certain degree does not imply that this category cannot rely more heavily on other information than the rest of the subgenres. As I have already demonstrated, *literary fiction* has a stronger correlation with the literary perception of the author than with that of the text as such, at least in my data set. Perhaps the algorithm uses the linguistic information to reconstruct the personal authorial style and associate specific authorial styles to its reception by publishers and scholars. In other words, perhaps the authorial cue reinforces the classification of *literary fiction*.

In this section, I want to test whether Machine Learning is able to better classify *literary fiction* than the rest of the subgenres when using only non-linguistic information. My expectation is that this label will rely on external information more heavily than other subgenres, especially on information about the author. To test these expectations, I am not using linguistic data as features, but only external metadata about the text (year and decade of publication, importance in the manual of literature) or the writer (name, gender, year of birth, importance in manuals, whether the text is biographical or not), with a total of ten features. The set-up is very similar to the previous one, but instead of logistic regression, I now apply decision trees and random forest algorithms, which are more accurate for working with categorical and ordinal data such as metadata.

The results of Figure 64 confirm my expectations, but again more subtly than I had anticipated. *Literary fiction* can be found in the upper half of the subgenres that are better classified with external information. But again, it is still close to the middle, with eight subgenres whose predictions surpass it, and within the range of other subgenres that could be expected to be more heavily motivated by linguistic features (*more textual*) like the comedy or war novel.

The subgenres that are best classified with external data are two one-author-labels (see Section 2.1.10), i.e. subgenres that were practiced by a single author in several works: *episodio nacional* by Galdós and *nivola* by Unamuno (which have been presented in Section 2.1.10). Interestingly, *greguerías*, another one-author-label by Gómez de la Serna, is actually the worst classified label. Why are *greguerías* not as perfectly recognized as the other two, given that all three share similar associations with their authors? I observe two reasons: First, *episodios nacionales* and *nivolas* comprehend the largest group of

Figure 64: Box plots of classification of the different subgenres and literary fiction, using external metadata

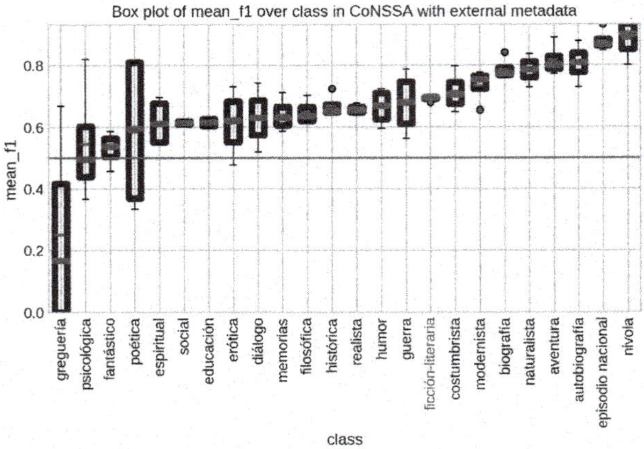

works by Galdós and Unamuno, so the algorithm can predict it as the default whenever the name of the author appears as a feature; this is not the case for *greguerías*, which constitutes a rather small group of works by Gómez de la Serna. Second, *episodios nacionales* are rather unimportant works by Galdós, according to the MdLE (treated normally as a long series instead of independent books), while *nivolas* are the most important by Unamuno. This implies that the algorithm can classify them correctly only by looking at the name of the author and the number of pages in the manuals. The *greguerías* have a similar importance to other works by Gómez de la Serna (at least the ones in the MdLE) and, therefore, the classifiers do not have enough data to recognize them without looking at the text.

In a general comparison, the classification based on linguistic features achieves higher results (mean of 0.71) than with external metadata (0.67). Even though the difference is statistically significant (p-value = 0.01), this is surprisingly close, considering that the first run is based on thousands of linguistic features and the second merely on ten. Further comparisons to the performance of the classification using linguistic and metadata will be undertaken in Section 7.1.5.

This same test has been carried out several times with small modifications with regard to the amount and types of metadata: only looking at the metadata directly related to the author, or applying metadata also concerned with the text (characters, setting, narrator, etc.). The exact results can be observed in the Jupyter Notebook of this chapter, which can be summarized in one sentence: *Literary fiction* does not stand out in comparison to other subgenres. In other words, *literary fiction* does not seem to rely on external data more heavily than the rest of the subgenres.

5.3.5 Conclusions

Does *literary fiction* behave like other subgenres or is it a phenomenon with a distinct nature? In this chapter, I have carried out several tests to observe its characteristics. If a book is considered part of *literary fiction*, it tends to be assigned as such by several publishers, which is a positive sign of agreement among publishers. *Literary fiction* is predictable to a certain degree using linguistic features, with outcomes slightly under average and within the range of the other subgenres. Furthermore, it does not behave like a random category: Its prediction accuracy is clearly above the random baseline. *Literary fiction* also does not rely more heavily on external data than many other subgenres, with results slightly above average and similar to many other subgenre-labels. In fact, the greatest surprise of this chapter is to observe how similar *literary fiction* is to the rest of the subgenres: It never stood out in any of the different tests, its results were never an outlier, and were neither better nor worse but rather behaved very similarly to the rest of the subgenres.

If so, why have Literary Studies ignored this label? Why do we have to take it from publishers, who mark books intensively with it? My explanation is that Literary Studies have mainly used *literary fiction* as a criterion of its object of study. What are we analyzing? The researchers in the field observe mainly sections of *literary fiction:* We mostly remain in the canon, either with a greater or narrower definition of it. The exceptions to this focus on non-literary fiction: the analysis of 21st-century fan fiction, pulp magazines, *Heftromane* (in the German-speaking area), *literatura de kiosco* (in the Spanish one), etc. An article can deal with *literary fiction* (the great majority in Literary Studies) or with non-literary fiction, but it normally does not combine both. It is not a variable in our corpora, it is a constant. Either all works of my collection are literary, or all of them are not. Literariness is a frontier in our field. Normally we pursue analysis inside, sometimes outside, but we do not cross the frontier in a single analysis.

Digital Literary Studies is increasingly working with larger corpora, extending their sizes from a canonical core, as I have done for my corpus. Working with corpus sizes of several hundreds of works, the researcher starts to include works that are part of what could be considered "serious literature," and others that are clearly what many would consider *popular, para-literature*, or plainly *bad literature*. This is the case in the *Riddle of Literary Quality*, analyzing works like *Fifty Shades of Grey* by Erika Leonard James but also highly literary novels such as *The Sense of an Ending* by Julian Barnes (Koolen 2018, 69–70), and also Wilkens (2016) or Jannidis, Konle, and Leinen (2019). In my corpus, the works by Valle-Inlcán or Azorín are clearly literary, but other titles like Ricardo Baroja's adventure novels or the erotic novels are seldom treated in Literary Studies. In my opinion, Digital Literary Studies is increasingly defining a space of work in which *literary fiction* is only a part, completing it with more popular genres.

In this chapter, I have not demonstrated that *literary fiction* is a subgenre of the novel. Instead, I have inductively observed three facts. First, publishers assign *literary fiction* along with other subgenre labels. Second, this makes DH researchers start considering it as a subgenre. Third, I have demonstrated that *literary fiction* does not stand out in comparison to the rest of subgenre-labels in several tests. Even when there is no final proof that this term should be considered an acceptable subgenre, there are also no reasons to think that it is anything different but a subgenre. As a consequence, I add *literary fiction* to the 23 subgenres obtained in Section 5.1 and it will be part of the analysis in the rest of this research study. For example, an empirical description of *literary fiction* will be given (Section 11.4) showing the intension (specific features), extension (texts and prototypical cases), and similarities to the rest of the subgenres.

Nonetheless, *literary fiction* should still maintain a status of hypothetical subgenre and there should be an inquiry into whether it represents another type of category. Perhaps subgenres would be better described in groups of subgenres or macro-subgenres: genre-literature (war, adventure, erotic novel, etc.) against a group of *literary fiction* subgenres (educational, realist, naturalist novel, etc.). This question about how to define macro-models for several subgenres will be explicitly explored in Section 8.6.

6. Feature and Labels Selection

6.1 Feature and Parameter Analysis

6.1.1 Introduction

In the previous chapters I have presented several annotation layers (Chapter 4.1) and transformations (Chapter 4.2). Other researchers have fed similar features into computational methods in order to analyze literary genre (see Chapter 2.2 for more details). In the majority of these works, the researchers applied more than one method and compared their results. The most frequent cases involve applying different algorithms or linguistic annotation layers, while the transformation of the data is rarely a matter of evaluation.

The combination of all the possibilities presented until now leads to many thousands of different results. Just to mention a few: 100 semantic features transformed as tf-idf and analyzed with support vector machines, ten syntactic features transformed as z-scores and analyzed with logistic regression, 1,000 lexical features in their relative frequency analyzed with random forest, etc. The options need to be reduced, and for this the researcher can employ at least three different strategies. First, all possible combinations can be applied in every step of the research (i.e., in all the following chapters). This would lead to excessively long computational times for every section. A second possibility is to argue for using only some possibilities or a few of their combinations and only try those, the preferred strategy in the previous research. However, the foundations for this are based on hypotheses or are not fully tested. A third possibility, common in Computer Science, is to undertake a proper evaluation of parameters as grid search (Müller and Guido 2016, 262–66), trying all possible combinations of parameters in a specific section of the research, comparing the results afterwards, and extracting only a few that remain for the rest of the work.

This last option is the chosen method and represents the core of this chapter. This kind of evaluation delivers empirical results, tests all possible combinations (exploring possibilities that might be overlooked by theoretical arguments) and, although costly in terms of time (when compared to the second strategy), the combinations are measured in only one section and not repeatedly (when compared to the first strategy). Besides, none of the previous works on literary genre have undertaken a comprehensive evaluation of the differences between the results of several parameters; it is still unknown which will lead to higher results.

As previous research has shown, lexical frequencies are one of the best indicators for differentiating genres (see Chapter 2.2). These frequencies of tokens offer a series of advantages: Their extraction from plain text is methodologically trivial and no lexical resources or ad hoc annotation is needed, meaning they can therefore be applied to any language. However, they also present some drawbacks. First, they can only be partially interpreted from a human perspective since it is difficult to comprehend what exactly functional words like *with* or *and* contribute to a genre. Second, they normally compound a very large set of units, often thousands, which again makes it difficult to have an overview of the process. Third, there is little theory about why this basic linguistic information is able to describe literary categories relatively well. In other words, it would be preferable to work with a small set of theory-driven language-independent features that can interpreted.

Besides, in the best case, the same features should be strong indicators for not one, but rather several or all categories. For example, vocabulary about the sea can differentiate several subgenres, since in some categories it is very frequent (*regionalist*, adventure, erotic), while in others it is very infrequent (social, realist, educational novel). Other features are important markers for only one category, while in the rest they are irrelevant. For example, although vocabulary about sentimental relations can be common in erotic novels, some other subgenres also contain texts with this vocabulary, while others do not. The probable result is something intermediary between a very general method for many categories and ad hoc combinations of parameters, each one yielding very high results for one genre and very low results for the rest.

Finally, the speed of the process should also be taken into account, even when it should not be a fundamental criterion. Several parameters can greatly influence the time that a process takes to run, such as the number of features, the span of values of a transformation, or the type of algorithm. A random forest method applied to many thousands of features expressed in relative frequencies predicting several dozens of binary categories could last for hours, while a logistic regression on a dozen binary features is likely to end in less than a second.

This chapter is structured as follows: First, I evaluate which feature combinations achieve higher results in the task of subgenre classification. Second, I inspect the specific features that are more important for the classifier, i.e. that have higher coefficients. Third, several parameters (classifier, transformations, feature combinations and number of features) will be evaluated, with an attempt to explain how the different factors impact the classification process.

6.1.2 Feature Evaluation

In Chapter 4.1, I have described the different textual layers and linguistic annotation applied to the entire corpus. In this section, I evaluate which of these features yield better results in a subgenre classification task. There are two different decisions to be made about the linguistic information. First, the researcher has to decide which type of features should be used: tokens split by a simple tokenizer, idioms treated as a single feature (*multiwords* in FreeLing), information about the tags of the file (how many paragraphs or verses does the document contain?) or lexical (lemmata instead of tokens), grammatical (PoS and morphologica datal), semantic (*lexnames* of WordNet and catalogs of the dictionary by María Moliner) and pragmatic (how many discursive particles the text contains), or textual annotation (narrative or direct speech passage).

The second decision concerns the combination of these features. For example, lexical units can be specified by their PoS, considering different units when the Spanish word *para* is a preposition (*para_preposition*, 'for') or a verb (*para_verb*, 'stop'). Since each sentence is labeled as being part of a narrative or direct speech passage, each token can be treated independently (the word *para* would be split in the features *para_nr* and *para_ds*). Both specifications could be applied to each token, separated by PoS and the narrative passage in four different forms (*para_preposition_nr, para_preposition_ds, para_verb_nr, para_verb_ds*).

I choose to define 20 different combinations of features. The types of linguistic annotations have already been described with examples in Chapter 4.1. For further details, the Jupyter Notebook of this chapter can be consulted. The following list presents them from the most basic (tokens) to the most comprehensive.

1. Tokens
2. Tokens + TEI XML tags
3. PoS differentiated tokens
4. PoS differentiated multiwords
5. PoS differentiated multiwords + ordered entities
6. PoS differentiated multiwords + ordered entities + pragmatic annotation
7. Semantic annotation
8. Linguistic annotation: grammatical annotation + semantic annotation + pragmatic annotation
9. Lemmata
10. Lemmata + linguistic annotation
11. Mean frequency of tokens over chapters
12. Standard deviation frequency of tokens over chapters
13. Mean + standard deviation frequency over chapters
14. Language-zscores of tokens
15. Authorial-zscores of tokens
16. Narrative differentiated tokens
17. Full annotation: narrative and PoS differentiated multiwords + ordered entities + linguistic annotation
18. Full annotation + tags
19. Full annotation + tokens
20. Full annotation + tokens + tags

I expect some of these combinations of features to outperform the option of the raw tokens, although probably some of them lack information (e.g. lemmata and semantic annotation do not contain any grammatical information), or the split of information will create too many features correlating with each other, resulting in useless features.

For this experiment, I choose to apply logistic regression as a classifier since it is one of the best algorithms for this task (as will be shown in Section 6.1.4), it is notably fast and has been used by other researchers for similar tasks (Riddell and Schöch 2014; Underwood 2014). Every transformation presented in Chapter 4.2 has been applied in each combination of features: relative frequency, log, log10, tf-idf, binary, z-scores, log10-zscores, tfidf-zscores, language-zscores and authorial-zscores. Each subgenre is analyzed in a double loop. First, a bootstrap step under-samples the corpus ten times; second, it goes through a ten-fold cross-validation step. From this, I report the mean

F1-scores of this double loop with the aim of obtaining robust results that are not so dependent on the specific texts selected. This setup means a total of more than 30,000 combinations, with almost 3 million iterations.

Which of these combinations of features achieves the highest results in each of the 23 subgenres? Ideally one combination of features performs clearly better than the rest. The bar plot of Figure 65 shows the amount of times that each combination yields the best results for each subgenre.

Figure 65: Best results for each subgenre by feature combinations

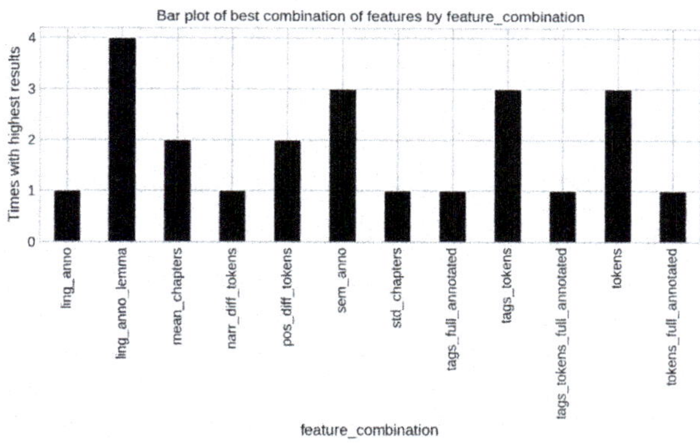

No combination is a clear winner and some features perform better with a specific subgenre. There are four combinations of features with higher results than the rest: linguistic annotation + lemmata, tokens, tags + tokens and semantic annotation. This data is ordered using tokens as the baseline, therefore it can happen that some of these three cases of the tokens are actually not better than the rest, only merely as good as the others. In any case, it is surprising that the apparent difference between linguistic and textual annotation and raw tokens is not greater.

A single value for each subgenre erases much information: In general, a combination of features can have high results even when it does not perform the best in any subgenre. In contrast, some features can be lucky with three or four subgenres, but insufficient for the majority of the rest. The box plots of Figure 66 show the results for all classifications, grouping them by feature combinations.

Figure 66: Mean F1-score by feature combinations

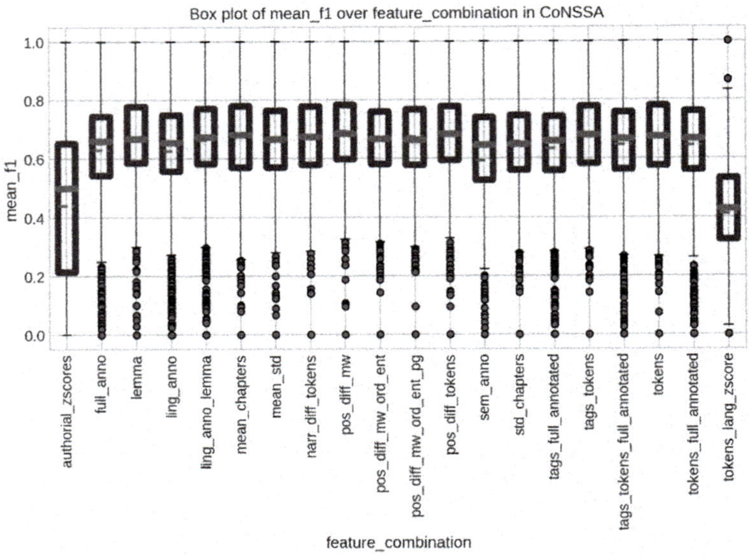

In general, almost all the combinations of features achieve similar results, with the limits of the boxes of Figure 66 around 0.8 and 0.6 mean F1-scores, the median around 0.7, and perfect classification covered by the whiskers. There are two models that clearly function worse than the rest: authorial-zscores and language-zscores. These two representations are based on the frequencies of tokens in the chapters, so in theory their results should be comparable to those of the tokens in order to consider using them in combination with linguistic annotations. It is not surprising that language-zscores function more poorly in a subgenre classification task since a much bigger corpus with many genres was used in its calculation. However, I did not expect the information in the authorial-zscores to become so spoiled that its results are around the baseline.

The box plots of Figure 66 reject the idea that there is one combination of features that clearly works better for all subgenres. For example, the classifiers recognize war novels almost perfectly using semantic annotation, but the results using the same data for social novels are close to the baseline (more detail in the Jupyter Notebook). To better understand the relation between features and subgenres, the facet grid of Figure 67 shows the results in several subgenres using a number of feature combinations.

Figure 67: Facet grid of F1-score for specific subgenres and feature combinations

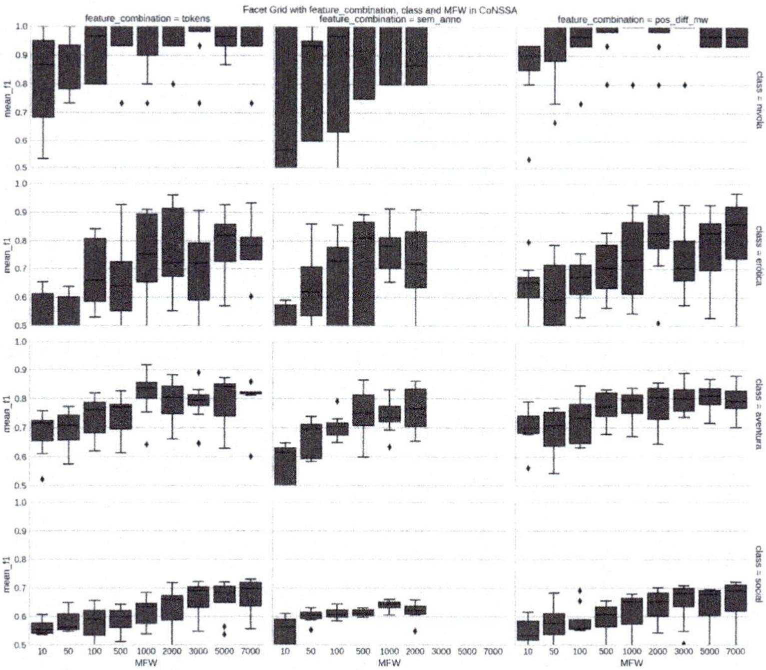

The top row of Figure 67 shows the results for a very distinctive subgenre, *nivola*, which is almost perfectly recognized, regardless of the features and its number. The bottom row plots the results for social novels, which in all cases is relatively close to the baseline. In the middle are the erotic and adventure novels. In general, the variance on the horizontal axis of the facet grid is much smaller than the vertical axis. In other words, the results do not depend so much on the linguistic annotations, but rather on the subgenre. Some subgenres are more difficult to classify than others, and when changing from tokens to specific linguistic annotation, the results remain similar. This effect will be closely analyzed in Chapter 7.2.

Still, it is worth observing more closely which combinations of features have surpassed the single feature of tokens. Tags + tokens, mean frequency in chapters, and the PoS differentiated version of tokens and multiwords generally have slightly higher results than tokens alone, but this difference is only significant in one case: the PoS differentiated multiwords (p-value = 0.004). This confirms what many other researchers have found, i.e. how difficult it is to outperform tokens. A great number of models and annotations do not offer any advantages in this setup, including the division of the tokens depending on whether they are in narrative or direct speech passages, the mean or standard deviation of the frequencies over chapters, or the isolation of the lexical (lemmata) and grammatical data (linguistic annotation) of the tokens. And yet, tokens are not always the very best features, which means that some features are useful for specific subgenres.

6.1.3 Knowledge Extraction about Features

In this section, I analyze more closely some statistical patterns of the linguistic features that are the best predictors of subgenres. First, I look at those features that are stronger cues for differentiating several subgenres. Second, I run a series of experiments concerning hypotheses about which linguistic characteristics these features show:

1. Are the most important features also the most frequent in the text? In other words, does the importance of these features for the classification correlate with their original frequency?
2. Can a set of good predictors be established to achieve high results for not only one category, but for all categories?
3. Are some Parts of Speech (PoS) more important in the classification than others? Are verbs or nouns more necessary for the classification than pronouns and prepositions? Does punctuation play an important role?

In addition, I look more closely at the results of the several layers of the linguistic and textual annotation, particularly in comparison with the more simple tokens.

The question about how important specific words are for groups of texts has been answered through different traditions. Corpus linguistics has implemented measures of keyness, stylometry tends to use Zeta, while Machine Learning uses the weights that some classifiers (for example, support vector machines, logistic regression or decision trees) assign to the features. The question of how they correlate with each other, the parameters and their effects, which one is better for which task, and how they correlate to the human intuition of importance is being currently partially analyzed by other researchers (Schöch et al. 2018). In this section, I use the weight of classifiers to stay within the frame of Machine Learning for this chapter, and to comprehend more deeply the effect of the coefficients in the frame of this parameter evaluation.[1]

I applied a logistic regression classifier since this is an algorithm that obtains high results when classifying texts with linguistic features (in comparison to decision trees that tend to over-fit with many interval features) and assign weights to every feature (in comparison to support vector machines). Other researchers, such as Underwood, have used the coefficients of this algorithm as a metric for the importance of each feature for the classification of each genre (Underwood 2014; 2016) or for other tasks (Rahat and Talebpour 2018; Verhoeven and Daelemans 2018). The matrix of features contains those that showed better results in the previous Section 6.1.2 – tokens, linguistic annotation and TEI-tags, all with their frequencies relative to the number of tokens per text and log transformed, selecting the 3,000 most frequent features (parameters that are in general the most successful, as will be shown in the Section 6.1.4). The classifier is applied to every subgenre in binary form, with a bootstrap step of 100 iterations. From these iterations, the mean coefficient assigned by the algorithm to each feature was obtained. The resulting output is a data frame with the 23 subgenres as rows and the 3,000 features as columns, with negative and positive values (in this case between -0.27 and 0.30), expressing whether the presence of a feature is used by the classifier as a cue to predict a positive or negative category (i.e. whether the text belongs to the genre or not). For example, the word *Madrid* has a coefficient of -0.13 for the philosophical novel, while its coefficient is 0.24 for the realist novel. This means that if the word *Madrid* appears in a text, the classifier will tend to consider it a realist novel and not a philosophical one.

---

1 In other sections, especially in Chapter 8, I argue for the adoption of other measures, such as z-scores, because of their simplicity, lack of parameters, and intuitive metric expressed in standard deviations. In this chapter, since z-scores are one of the analyzed transformations, their use as a measure could lead to circularity.

For now, I do not observe the interaction between features and subgenres, but rather general patterns for all the classes, and therefore I use the absolute values of the coefficients. I calculate the mean of all the subgenres, which expresses the most important features for the entire classification. Following table presents the top 20 features sorted by the mean coefficient:

Table 9: Top 20 features with the highest mean coefficient

features	**mean-coef**	**std-coef**
am.sps	0.054	0.059
madrid_noun	0.047	0.055
..._punctuation	0.046	0.046
etc@type	0.042	0.042
españa_noun	0.043	0.038
am.verses	0.042	0.044
comenzó_verb	0.039	0.035
mar_noun	0.039	0.063
-_punctuation	0.038	0.028
quizá_adverb	0.038	0.036
am.parts	0.038	0.065
rey_noun	0.038	0.054
muchacha_noun	0.038	0.038
maestro_noun	0.037	0.043
papeles_noun	0.037	0.031
am.sections	0.036	0.034
hombre_interjection	0.036	0.064
ésta_pronoun	0.036	0.034
éste_pronoun	0.036	0.032
en_seguida_adverb	0.036	0.035

The tables includes TEI-tags (the top one is the frequency of the tag *sp*, for direct speech presented as for theater plays or dialogue novels, but also the frequency of verses and different divisions like chapters in the novel), punctuation (the sign for ellipsis is in the top three, and the em dash is also present on the list), nouns that refer to places (*Madrid* is in the top two, *España* the fifth, but also the word *mar*), people (*rey, muchaha, maestro, hombre*) and other meanings (*papeles*), adverbs (*etc, quizá, en seguida*), pronouns (*éste, ésta*), and one verbal form (*comenzó*). Further details can be accessed in the Jupyter Notebook.

I could go further and try to group a larger number of lexical units, but this would be limited to a relatively small number of features. At least 1,900 features have relatively high mean coefficients (over 0.01), a number too large to observe manually. Besides, a closer inspection would tend to reinforce the preexisting hypothesis, i.e. that pronouns or nouns are important features for the genre classification. Moreover, this would not contain statistical tests that consider the entire data set. For example, seven nouns are in the top 20 features, which could lead to the idea that this is an important grammatical category. But nouns constitute a very populous group, so, without a statistical test, I cannot be sure of whether a third of 20 is what should be expected.

To control these factors, I run different statistical tests on the mean coefficients. The first question is whether the most useful features are the most frequent ones. This is particularly important because several pre-processing steps tend to erase the most frequent words considering them useless: application of stop-word lists, elimination of words of a single character,[2] or the transformation of the data to tf-idf.[3] To operationalize this question, I have measured the correlation between the mean coefficient and the relative frequency of each feature. The result is a very weak negative correlation (r = -0.2***), i.e. the more frequent a feature is, the lower its coefficient tends to be. This shows that the most useful features tend to have a rather low frequency, but that this tendency is very weak. Therefore, I consider it questionable to erase all the very frequent features in the pre-processing steps. The top 20 list contains words like *éste, ésta* ('this') and the punctuation symbols, and these would be typically erased.

An important question is whether there are features that are important not only for specific subgenres, but rather for many. The word *sea* is an important classifier for genres like adventure novels (because it appears) or so-

2 This astonishing decision is actually set as the default in the scikit-learn tokenizer if the user does not specify a regular expression for the tokenization, meaning that many scripts apply it without knowledge. This deletes words like *I* or *a* in English and *y* or *o* in Spanish.

3 Which, as observed in Chapter 4.2, has a negative correlation with the frequency, meaning it tends to mitigate the influence of the most frequent words.

cial novels (because it does not), but it is irrelevant for others, such as poetic novels (that could either be related or not related to the sea). To observe this more closely, not only the mean coefficients of subgenres are considered important, but also the standard deviation. Do the coefficients deviate strongly? A test shows that the mean coefficient and its standard deviation over subgenres correlates distinctly ($r = 0.94^{***}$), with the standard deviation having a tendency to be even greater than the mean of the coefficients. This correlation seems to point out that the possibilities of finding a set of features that would work well for any subgenre are sadly very limited. Each category is defined by different characteristics, and therefore a classification only achieves good results when specific features are considered.

Nevertheless, I search for the features that are the most stable across subgenres. For this, the standard deviation of the coefficients is subtracted from the mean coefficient. The 20 top more stable features are completely different to those listed previously, with the only exception being the em dash (as the typographical direct speech marker). Many of them are abstract nouns (*nombres, situación, efecto, notas, prisa, sentimiento*), some of them are more concrete nouns (*perro, plata, fiesta, comedor, marido*), two are adjectives (*blancas, antiguo*), there are adverbs and interjections (*rápidamente, sin embargo, ah*), and three are verbs (*esperando* and two forms of the auxiliary verb *haber*: *hubiese* and *has*). In any case, these features seem much harder to group and it is much harder to understand their role in the distinction of the classes.

Besides these statistical tendencies, I want to analyze whether different linguistic categories tend to contain more useful features than would be expected. Are nouns in general good indicators for subgenres in comparison to the other grammatical categories? What would lead to the formalized question of whether the coefficients of the nouns tend to be higher than those of rest of the features. Is the morphological information about verbs (tense, mood, person) used by the classifiers? Are the semantic features of WordNet or the dictionary by Maria Moliner useful in general? Does the strategy of encoding people's names by their ordered frequency (a proxy to encode the protagonist as *0@ord_ent*) result in any gain?

To answer these questions, I consider 24 linguistic categories that will be shown in Table 10 and relate each of them to each feature. I then compare the coefficients of each category with all the others. In the box plots of Figure 68, the coefficients of the TEI-tags and the rest of the features are compared. As is observed, the coefficients of the TEI-tags (box plot on the right) tend to be higher than the rest of the features (box plot on the left). It is not only that some of them are in the top 20, the entire category of the tags tends to be a useful set of features. To evaluate whether the difference in the two groups is statistically significant, I run a Welch's test.[4] Eleven linguistic categories show higher mean coefficients with statistical significance compared to the rest, shown in Table 10.

Figure 68: Mean coefficient of features, grouping by TEI-tags or not

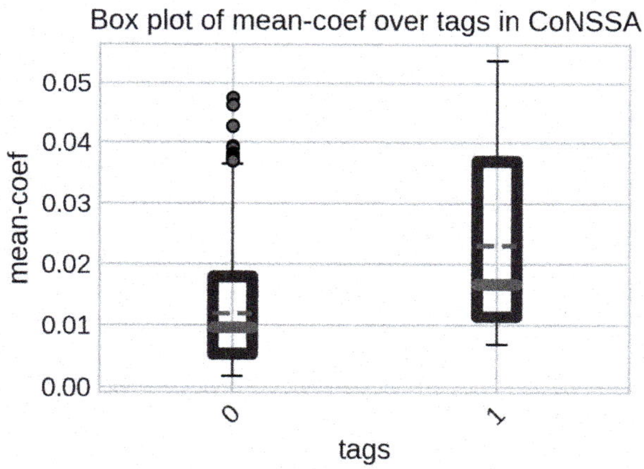

The categories are ordered by how much higher their coefficient is in comparison to the rest. Three linguistic categories with unexpectedly good results are interjections (25.65%***), TEI-tags (20.62%*), and punctuation (12.79%*). Parallel to these are several grammatical categories that are in general useful, including nouns (14.66%***), adjectives (11.93%***), verbs (9.96%***), numbers (8.71%**), adverbs (7.34%***), and pronouns (5.42%**). Overall, tokens tend to have coefficients that are 11%*** higher than the rest (i.e. than the linguistic annotation). Finally, the personal proper names encoded by their ordered frequency have a 5.22%* positive difference. An interesting aspect of these seven categories is that in many typical pre-processing pipelines, some

4 Since the two compared groups do not contain the same number of elements, a t-test is not suitable.

of them (pronouns, tags, punctuation, interjections) would be erased and ignored by the classifier. In other words, pre-processing pipelines do not always improve our data. However, there are some linguistic categories that are in general not useful categories for this task: conjunction, determiners and prepositions.

Table 10: Results of linguistic categories with higher coefficients than the rest

category	**p-value**	**difference**
interjections	< 0.001	25.65 %
TEI-tags	0.029	20.62 %
noun	< 0.001	14.66 %
punctuation	0.048	12.79 %
adjectives	< 0.001	11.93 %
tokens	< 0.001	10.97 %
verbs	< 0.001	9.96 %
numbers	0.009	8.71 %
adverbs	< 0.001	7.34 %
pronouns	0.001	5.42 %
ord. entities	0.035	5.22 %

A surprising negative result is the fact that no linguistic annotation appears as a generally useful set of information. These were also not included in the top 20, and yet linguistic and semantic annotation were two of the feature combinations with the highest results for some subgenres. This means that only specific linguistic annotations are good predictors for some subgenres. If the top 1,000 linguistic annotation features sorted by their coefficients are observed and grouped by their category, 95% are semantic features from the dictionary by María Moliner and WordNet. For example, the semantic feature on vehicles tends to appear in subgenres such as adventure, educational and war novels, it is irrelevant for philosophical or dialogue novels, and it tends to not appear in realist and social novels. The other 5% of the ranked linguistic features are information about frequencies of grammatical subcategories, the types of entities (places, organizations, and people), verbal morphology (tense conditional, future and imperfect, mood gerund, and imperative), morphology of pronouns (number, person, and case), and degree in adjectives. Still, there is some linguistic annotation that is ignored, such as the morphological information about gender and number of articles, the number of the different PoS per text, the discursive particles, or the proverbs.

This list of the 1,000 top linguistic features will be used to enrich what has already been proved to work best, i.e. PoS differentiated multiwords, in an attempt to engineer the best possible features.

A surprising negative result is that the division between direct speech features and narrative features does not bring any advantage, and can even give worse results. To observe this question more closely, I use the narrative differentiated tokens as features, calculating the coefficients for each one. A pattern is observed in the features ranked by their coefficients. The first token would be the ellipsis in direct speech, followed by the ellipsis in narrative passages. The ellipsis feature was split in two, but the coefficients in the different subgenres have a very strong correlation (r = 0.96). This means that the classifier uses these two different features with very similar values. This pattern is observed in the entire data frame. The correlation of the coefficients between the direct speech feature (for example *buscar_ds*) and its counterpart in narrative passages (*buscar_nr*) tends to be very strong or even perfect. In summary, the split of the features by their position in passages has mainly brought redundancy to the table of features, which explains that the results were not improved. The information about direct speech seems to be important for the classification, but apparently the classifiers are able to access it only through the typographical information of the em dashes.

6.1.4 Parameters Evaluation

After analyzing the features in their combinations and linguistic categories, it is necessary to optimize the rest of the parameters. For this, I run a grid search of five different parameters to determine which ones show a better performance. All 23 subgenres were classified in a binary task. Since the previous section did not show a feature combination that worked better in every case, I used five different combinations which had already achieved good results:

- Tokens
- Semantic annotation
- Lemmata + linguistic annotation
- TEI-tags + tokens

- Mixed features: PoS differentiated multiwords + TEI-tags + 1,000 top linguistic features

The last mixed combination of features is based on the best yielding features in the previous sections, so I expect these features to lead to higher results than the rest. The next parameter analyzed is the transformation of the tokens, with nine different ones: relative frequency, log, log10, zscores, binary, tf-idf, log10-zscores, tfidf-zscores (all already presented) plus a logarithmic transformation with base 1,000 (log1000). Each time I extract from ten up to 7,000 features. Finally, four classifiers were applied: support vector machines, logistic regression, decision trees and k-nearest neighbors. All these parameters result in almost 40,000 combinations and each of them is run over a double loop. First the corpus is under-sampled ten times in a bootstrap step, and then a ten-fold cross-validation is applied. The results are ordered with the tokens as the baseline feature, and so that models with fewer features are preferred to more dimensional ones. This means that if two different combinations achieved the same results, the one using fewer features will be preferred. In addition, if tokens and other feature combinations use the same amount and get the same result, the tokens will be taken as winner.

In general, the classification results are relatively high for all subgenres, with F1-scores between 1.0 (poetic, dialogue novels, *nivola*, *greguería*, *episodio nacional*) and 0.74 (social and educational novels), with a mean of 0.89 and a standard deviation of 0.09 for the highest combinations for all subgenres. In other words, the subgenres of the novel are typically recognized with values between 0.98 and 0.8 F1-score. Specific results for the subgenres will be discussed in Chapter 7.1, and in the rest of this chapter I will focus only on the performance of the parameters.

If the feature combinations are observed, tokens are surpassed by the other combinations in nine of the 23 subgenres. The mixed model tags + tokens and the semantic annotation achieved the best results in four subgenres each, and the lemmata + annotation in two cases. If the preference for the tokens as the baseline is ignored, the mixed model achieves better or higher results in nine of the 23 subgenres. Figure 69 shows and compares the results of all possible combinations.

The results of the five combinations are very similar, with the whiskers covering a perfect classification for results clearly under the baseline (of 0.5). If the medians are observed, the mixed model has slightly higher results, and this difference is statistically significant (p-value < 0.001 with semantic anno-

Figure 69: Mean F1-scores by feature combinations

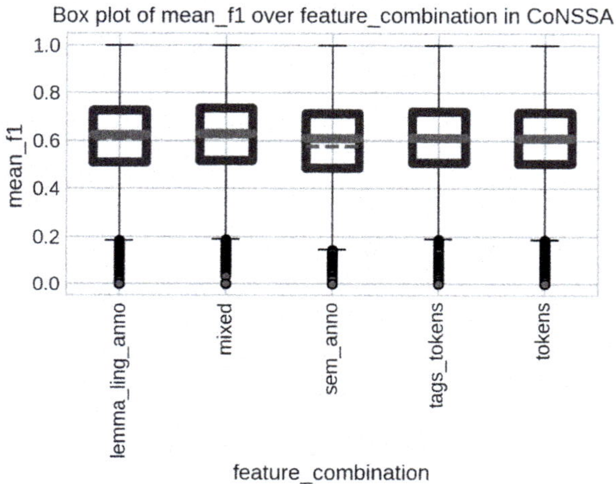

tation, tokens + tags and tokens, p-value = 0.002 with lemmata + annotation). How is it possible that the difference of box plots overlapping so closely could be statistically significant? The reason lies in the large size of the observation: Each type of feature has been applied in 7,500 combinations with different parameters and this large number of observations makes it possible for even small differences to show a statistical significance.[5]

The following box plot shows textual transformation as the analyzed parameter with nine different possibilities. The representation that achieved the highest results in the different subgenres is log10-zscores and natural logarithm (each one with the highest results in six subgenres), followed by log1000 and log10. However, when all combinations are observed, the order of these transformations undergoes small changes.

In Figure 70, two of the transformations yield clearly lower results than the rest: binary and tf-idf (the difference from all the log variants are significant with these two, p-value < 0.001). These are followed by relative frequency and

5 But the size is not so large that any comparison is statistically significant. For example, there is no statistical difference between the results of three of the feature combinations.

Figure 70: Mean F1-scores by transformations

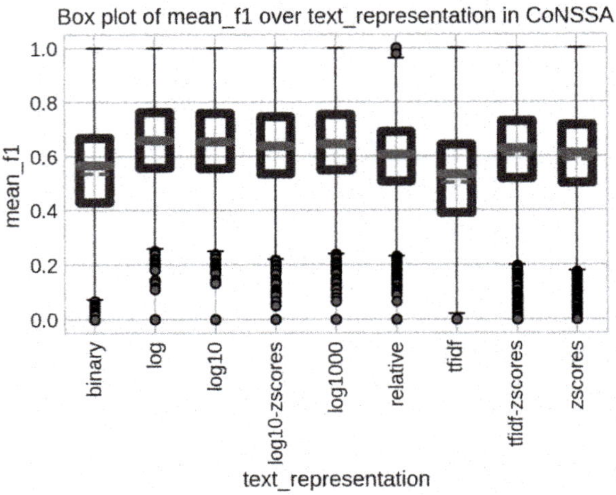

z-scores, results that contradict my expectation of the relative frequency having the lowest outcomes. The transformations with the highest results are the applied logarithmic transformation with different bases, without a statistical difference between them. This shows that, regardless of the base used (e, 10, or 1000), the logarithmic transformation of linguistic data improves the results of the classification for subgenres. The proposed concatenations of steps (tfidf-zscores and log10-zscores) do not seem to result in any improvement.

The third parameter evaluated is the classifiers: support vector machines (SVC), logistic regression (LR), decisions trees (DT) and k-nearest neighbors (KNN). Two classifiers obtain the highest results in nine of the 23 subgenres (SVC and LR), four by DT, and one by KNN. These results are also observed when all combinations are taken in account.

Two classifiers obtain clearly lower results in Figure 71: decision trees (which, in addition, does not cover perfect results within the whiskers) and k-nearest neighbors (with results around the baseline). The differences between these and the other two algorithms are statistically significant (p-value < 0.001), while there is no statistical significance between the results of logistic regression and support vector machines. Besides these four algorithms, several trials were run using random forest, which is notably more time-con-

Figure 71: Mean F1-scores by classifiers

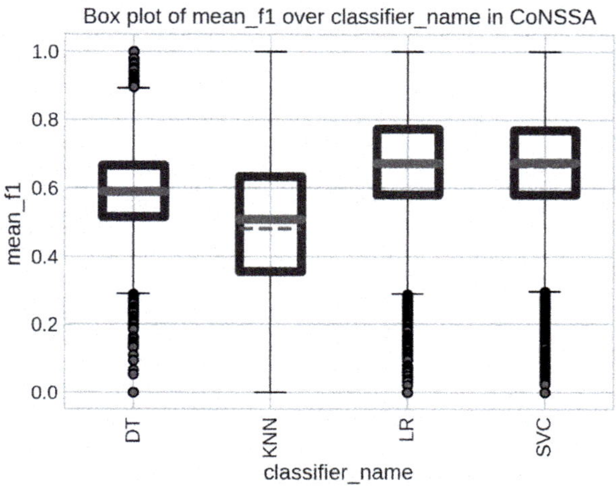

suming than the others. Because its results were very close to those of the decision trees, it was abandoned before all possible combinations were calculated.

A final parameter is evaluated: the number of features. As previously explained, simpler models with fewer features are preferred. This is because if they classify equally well, the influence of the features in the classification is easier to understand and they are faster to compute. For the 23 subgenres, five obtained the highest classification with 7,000 features, four with only ten features, another four with 2,000 and the rest between 50 and 5,000. Which are the subgenres that were best classified with only 10 features? These are *greguerías*, *nivola*, dialogue and poetic novels, very distinctive subgenres that obtain perfect classifications even with so few features, but also with more data. If all combinations are observed, the results are as shown in Figure 72.

The results have a tendency to improve with larger numbers of features. There is in fact a correlation, although very weak, between the results and the number of features used ($r = 0.09^{***}$). The difference between the results in a range and the greater ones is statistically significant until 2,000 (p-value <0.001). After this value, the results remain stable, as is observed in the box plots, without statistical difference.

Figure 72: Mean F1-score by number of features

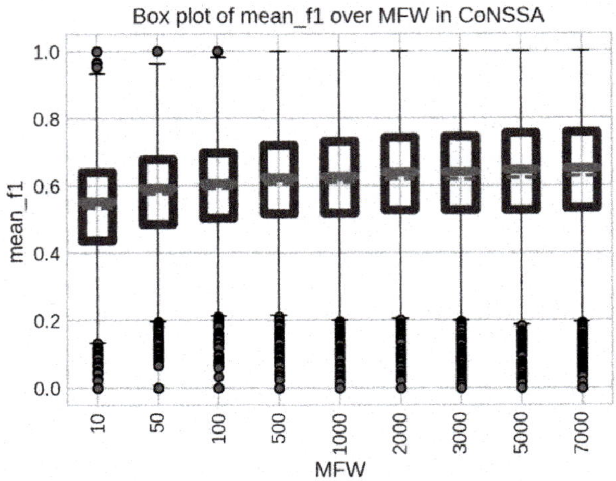

Until now, the various parameters have been observed in isolation, but how do they interact? Are there specific combinations that are in general particularly successful? Can the behavior of some of them be better explained in relation to others? To observe all the parameters together in action, I again use a facet grid. The only parameter not included in this visualization is the classifiers, since its results unmistakably favor LR and SVC, which is the reason why the results of KNN and DT are excluded.[6] In the facet grid of box plots of Figure 73, the columns show the different feature combinations, the transformations are represented by rows, while within each plot the vertical axis has the F1-scores and the horizontal axis the number of features.

Nearly all the possible combinations achieve perfect results in specific combinations (shown in the previous box plots as the upper outliers or the upper whiskers), even with very few features. A group of exception can be

6 An alternative would have been to show scatter plots using hue or color to distinguish the classifiers. Since there are many data points for each combination, the information is much better summarized in the box plots, especially since the results of the classifiers were so clear.

Figure 73: Facet grid of feature combinations and feature transformations

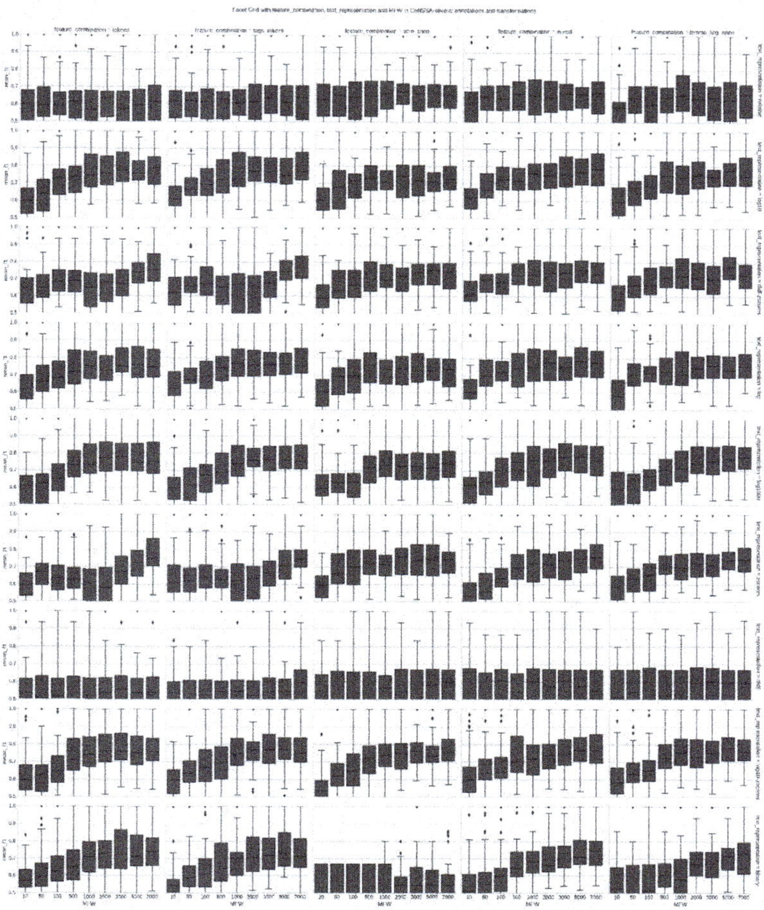

found in the binary transformation of semantic features. These are the previously mentioned very distinctive subgenres (*greguería*, *nivola*, dialogue novel), that are almost always perfectly classified. The very best combinations of all parameters observing the height of the whiskers and the median is the mixed model features, either with a log1000 transformation and 5,000 features, or with log10 and 7,000 features. In these two cases, the medians (shown through a line within the box) are close to 0.74 and the upper whiskers surpass 0.83.

The tendency towards improvement with larger sets of features is observed, except for two of the transformations: relative frequencies and tf-idf. The fact that additional features do not cause an improvement in these results could be the characteristics of their shape, as seen in Section 4.2.2. Since they do not have defined ranges and the shape is extremely skewed, the classifiers tend to ignore all the features that are not the top most frequent. The results of the rest of the transformations (the logarithmic versions, z-scores and binary frequency) improve with a higher number of features.

One hypothesis for this would be that the skewness of the transformation has a clear impact on the results. If the data is very skewed, the classifier will tend to use only those features with the highest values, ignoring the rest, and therefore adding more features will not bring any improvement. If this is the case, the skewness of the transformations and the mean F1-scores should be negatively correlated, i.e. the less skewed a distribution is, the better will be the results. For this, I obtain the skewness of the shape for each transformation,[7] and calculate the correlation with the mean F1-scores. The result is a very strong negative linear correlation ($r = -0.84^{**}$), and therefore the null hypothesis can be rejected: The quality of the classification is explained to a large degree by the skewness of the data. A similar hypothesis would be to test whether the transformation results improve when the shape is closer to a Gaussian distribution. To test this, I use the statistic given by the normality test, and correlate it with the mean F1-score. The result is even clearer: There is an almost perfect negative linear correlation ($r = -0.95^{***}$). It is even surprising that such different measures (statistical normality of linguistic frequencies and F1-scores) have such a strong correlation and that the results are statistically significant with so few data points (nine transformations). The more similar the shape of transformation is to a Gaussian distribution, the better the results in a classification task of subgenres will be.

These two correlations are important findings because they put the statistical description of the transformation of linguistic data in direct relation, and this results in a Machine Learning classification task for genre. The search for more accurate transformations of the data should aim to obtain less skewed and more normal shapes of the data.

7 The Python library *SciPy* has a function for it called *skew*. Further details in the Jupyter Notebook.

6.1.5 Conclusions

Many hypotheses presented in Chapters 4.2 and 4.1 about linguistic annotation and transformations have been proven to not advance the classification of subgenres. The linguistic annotation in several layers offers some advantages, although many others do not seem to make any difference. Tokens are very reliable features that achieve solid predictions. The use of a more accurate conception of lexical units (idioms or multiwords) and the differentiation of lexical units into their PoS (splitting verbs and nouns that have the same form into two lexical units) have given slightly better results. Contrary to my expectations, the differentiation of the tokens by the narrative characteristics of the paragraph has not brought any advantage.

A more in-depth look at the features has highlighted some useful textual features, such as the TEI-tags, punctuation, names of places and the frequencies of the words of many grammatical categories, especially nouns, adjectives and verbs. Some of these features are traditionally erased in typical pre-processing steps, which is an argument for making considered decisions. Two linguistic annotations showed positive results: the semantic features from the dictionary by María Moliner and the encoding of personal proper names through their ordered frequency. Only semantic features achieve good results, in some cases even the best results. These two successful linguistic annotations can be seen as strategies for extracting information about the characters and the meaning of the text that actually improve the classification of subgenres. In my opinion, lexicographic resources such as the catalogs of the dictionary by María Moliner should be more frequently considered for annotating corpora and evaluating their performance in comparison to distributional models such as topic modeling and word embedding. In addition, different morphological data (especially about pronouns and verbs) ranks among the most important linguistic features. From all this data, I have created a mixed model of features whose results are slightly higher than the rest in the majority of the cases.

An important finding is the observation that the standard deviation of the coefficients of the features correlates with its mean. In other words, the features that are very important for the classification of some subgenres are irrelevant for others. This makes it difficult to find a set of features that classify or cluster many subgenres correctly: Each subgenre has its own features that should be considered.

The results for two other parameters are clear: support vector machines and logistic regression give clearly higher results than k-nearest neighbors and decision trees. Nevertheless, these algorithms have been used with their parameters in the default values given by scikit-learn, so further evaluation is necessary. The number of features shows a tendency towards improving the results, with a statistical stagnation over 2,000 features, although some of the best results were achieved with 5,000 and 7,000 features. If even larger vectors were to be considered, I expect the results to deteriorate at some point when several dozens of thousands (or hundreds of thousands) are used. To test this, the computational costs in terms of time should be taken into consideration.

From among the six new transformations proposed in Chapter 4.2, none surpassed the more traditional logarithmic transformations. Actually, logarithmic transformation is clearly the transformation that yields higher results (at least for the classification of subgenres). These results strengthen the argument by Lestrade about the special characteristics of the Zipfian distribution of data after a log-transformation (Lestrade 2017, see Section 4.2.1). Nevertheless, the more traditional transformations in several fields (relative and binary frequencies, z-scores and tf-idf) ranked lower than the logarithmic family. A closer analysis of the combination of parameters showed that the results of the classification when using the different transformations can be explained by the skewness and the normality of the data: The more normal a transformation is (or the less skewed), the better its results in a classification task of subgenre will be. These are probably the most important findings from this chapter because they do not only show specific combinations that work better in some cases, they can also explain the relation between the representation of the text and the results of its classification. These correlations would need to be evaluated with further corpora, languages and especially different tasks (author, genre, subgenre, periodicity, etc.).

6.2 Identification of Hidden Subgenres

6.2.1 Introduction

One of the disadvantages of the classification tasks in Machine Learning is that it requires a closed and clear set of labels. In this way, classification only allows the researcher to inspect already given categories but not detect new ones. In other words, classification presupposes that the genre palette is complete. What if there are subgenres that have not yet been detected? And if so, how can both the process and these hypothetical genres be evaluated?

The standard sources for genre labels are human institutions. The author is often seen as the most accurate source, but others such as publishers, catalogs, readers, or investigators are also considered. This human process of categorizing texts in groups is what Todorov has proposed as a defining criterion for genres: "classes of texts that have been perceived as such in the course of history" (1976, 162).

The task of detecting new genres has been called *genre identification* in Computer Science and, to my knowledge, only one study has addressed it: Santini (2007; 2010; 2011). In her thesis (2011), Santini follows the hypothesis that new genres have been developing on the Internet, groups of texts participating in textual categories that, at the time, had not been labeled by humans. For this purpose, she created two experiments using clustering methods. The first one employs the PCA components as features. The second one uses several syntactic, morphological, and layout features (converting their frequency into z-scores), and then applies k-means as clustering algorithms. In the first experiment, the sites tended to cluster according to discursive patterns, such as informational, instructional, argumentative, descriptive, etc. In the second, she obtained two emerging genres: *contact web pages*, and *fast-effective information delivery* (websites composed by pictures and short texts, heavily hyperlinked, such as in e-shops or galleries of pictures).

The novels of the 19th and 20th centuries are very different materials from those currently found on the Internet. While the literature of the *silver age* has remained mainly as a closed object of analysis for many decades, the Web grows daily. I am not looking for *emerging* genres in the late 19th century or the beginning of the 20th century. As I have shown in Section 2.1.2, Literary Studies have mainly focused on one or a few authors in many of their analysis. Therefore, linguistic or literary similarities could have been overlooked between novels written by authors that do not compound a generation and are normally not analyzed together. My hypothesis for this chapter is that such subgenres exist and that they can be identified through unsupervised Machine Learning methods. This potential clustering should show similar properties to the rest of the subgenres obtained in Chapters 5.1 and 5.3.

Of course, not any cluster grouping a number of texts should be accepted as a hypothetical new subgenre. As Todorov also argued: "one can always find a property common to two texts, and therefore put them together in one class" (1976, 162). To be accepted as possible genres, I propose that the clusters must fulfill three criteria:

1. Recurring: The clusters should be found repeatedly in several attempts, using different combinations of parameters.
2. Not explainable by other subgenres, authorship, or periodization: The texts of the obtained clusters should mainly not belong to the same author, same decade, or be part of a known subgenre. In other words, the clusters should not be explained by already known categories such as authorship, chronology, or other common genre labels.
3. Explainable by complex features: The clusters should show statistical differences in the more complex annotation (textual and semantic) and metadata as a basis for their explanation.

In the sections of this chapter, I will proceed as follows: First, I explore the tendencies of the clustering methods when using literary texts. Second, I present the problem and a possible solution to the authorial cue in clustering literature. Third, I evaluate several parameters, such as the clustering algorithm, the number of features, the transformation of data, and the number of clusters. Fourth, I observe the three criteria previously explained, which means that I look for recurrent clusters across types of features and iterations while evaluating the mentioned criteria, compare them with already known categories (authorship, periods, subgenres), and observe whether they show statistical contrasts in metadata and linguistic annotation. Finally, I discuss the results and consider whether hidden subgenres have been discovered.

6.2.2 Clustering in Stylometry

In Chapter 2.2, the concept of clustering was briefly explained. This is one type of unsupervised task in Machine Learning, meaning that the researcher does not have labels for the instances (in my case, texts), and the algorithm uses the similarities of the features (for e.g. word frequencies) to group the instances (Müller and Guido 2016, 133–34). Clustering is the most applied technique in stylometry, partially due to its visual impact and partially because it is the default option for the results in a very popular tool: *stylo* (Eder, Kestemont, and Rybicki 2016). In a typical stylometric analysis with *stylo*, either for exploratory purposes or for authorship attribution, a number of tokens are transformed to a matrix using a distance measure such as Delta (Burrows 2002) in any of its variants (Evert et al. 2018). This distance matrix is clustered in a hierarchical structure (a dendrogram) and uses the labels of the authors for coloring the names of the texts. The Figure 74 shows the turnout of clustering 42 randomly selected texts from CoNSSA.

As can be observed, some clusters group together texts of specific authors, such as Bazán, Galdós, Fernández Flórez, Valle-Inclán, or Azorín, while many clusters mix works from various authors.

In my opinion, there are several bad practices and misunderstandings in the process described above. The most important error is the fact that the two types of tasks in Machine Learning are being confused. Instead of using supervised methods, unsupervised methods are applied for data sets that do contain specific labels (in this case, about authors). In addition, the clustering algorithm set as default in *stylo* is Ward, an agglomerative method that first links the instances that show a minimal variance, and then this subcluster is linked to a new instance or to a new subcluster, composing a hierarchical tree-like structure. Due to this, a structure without a fixed number of groups is created, which leads the researcher to pick the clusters that best fit their hypothesis. In my case, I can consider that the two texts of Galdós (lower section of the cluster) are separated from those of Baroja, while the three texts of Azorín (upper section) belong to the same cluster. Even when the evaluation of such structures is harder to perform than in a supervised task, the stylo-

Figure 74: Dendrogram of novels produced with stylo with the name of the authors

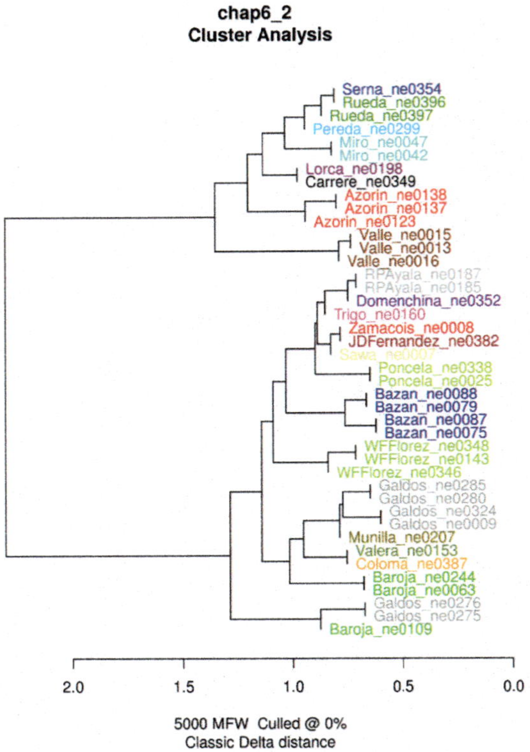

metric community needs to further evaluate their methods and parameters (see Ochab et al. 2019).

These arguments are neither a critique of the pillars of stylometry, nor directed at the developers of stylometric tools. For instance, Burrows did not cluster the outcomes when applying Delta, and *stylo* offers many other outputs of the results apart from the figure of the dendrogram, along with functions for classification. But I do criticize the fact that the stylometric community has established some practices misusing basic concepts of Machine Learning.

In some exploratory works, several researchers have tried to push stylometry beyond authorship, making sense of the clustering output. Normally, it can be observed that within the works of the same author, those that also share the same genre or period are closer in the cluster (Hoover 2014; Jannidis and Lauer 2014; Calvo Tello 2019). If the same subcorpus of 42 novels used in Figure 74 is colored using the subgenre information from my own annotation, the result is as Figure 75 shows. As can be seen, some texts of the same genre are placed together in the same subcluster, such as autobiographical, philosophical, erotic, or dialogue novels. But the majority of them seem to be distributed randomly in an unclear number of subclusters. There are two questions that the stylometric practice normally does not solve. First, how many clusters should be considered? Second, how accurately does the cluster represent the labels?

Figure 75: Dendrogram of novels produced with stylo with the main subgenre

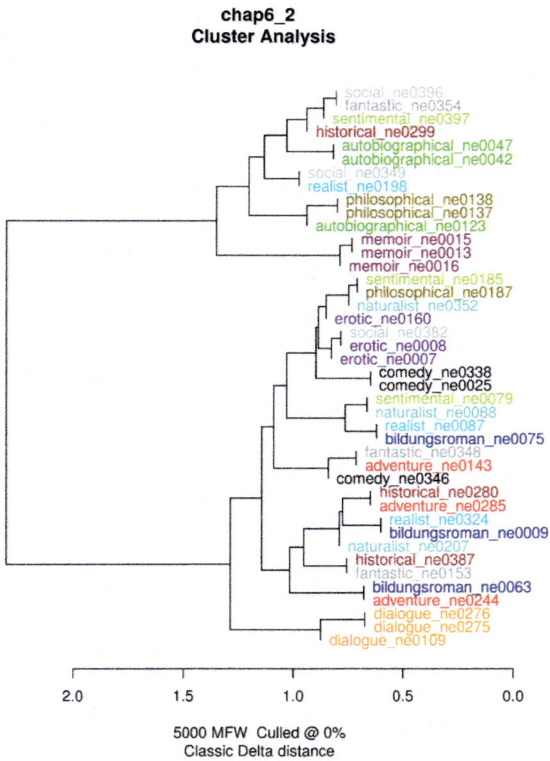

6.2.3 The Authorial Cue Problem when Clustering Literary Works

Many algorithms (such as k-means) require that the researcher defines the number of clusters that should be identified. This depends partially on the researcher's goals: many subclusters with few instances, or a few groups with many instances. This is contingent on the labels that the cluster should fit. In my case, the corpus of novels contains 72 different authors, while I considered 15 categories in the annotation process of the main subgenre for each text, and six decades are represented in the corpus. This means that depending on whether I expect the cluster to represent authorship, decades, or subgenres, I can look for more or fewer subclusters.

The second problem of the stylometric practice of clustering is its lack of evaluation. There are in fact several metrics that compare the clustering with some annotation, which is considered the *ground truth*. In my case, the metadata can be considered as the ground truth, such as the author's name, the decade, and the subgenre of my annotation. The Python library scikit-learn offers several metrics for comparing the cluster results with the ground truth, such as homogeneity, completeness, mutual information score, or adjusted Rand index (ARI). ARI is the most frequently applied in the DH field (Klaussner, Nerbonne, and Çöltekin 2015; Evert et al. 2018; Iosifyan and Vlasov 2019). Its scores vary from one (perfect match) to zero (random assignment), with possible negative values for worse matches than the random label.

In this first step, I apply the clustering algorithm k-means, using the relative frequencies of the 5,000 most frequent tokens, considering the cluster of numbers 2, 6, 10, 15, 20, and then steps of 10 are taken until I get to 72 clusters (which is the number of different authors in the corpus). Since k-means is not deterministic (the initialization of the clusters is randomly declared, causing possible different outputs in equal circumstances), I repeat each combination of parameters ten times. The outcomes are hundreds of clusters that can be mapped to several ground truths from metadata such as the author's name, the decade, or the main subgenre. In each case, I calculate the ARI.

In Figure 76, the three ground truths (the two first box plots and the last one) are clearly above the zero line, which represents random mapping between clusters and ground truth. To confirm whether the values of the decade and main subgenre are not behaving in a completely random manner, I create an extra random category, plotted as the third box plot. This random category has, in fact, a lower value than the rest, which is very close to zero. Consequently, decade and subgenre have a statistically higher ARI score than ran-

Figure 76: Evaluation of the clusters in comparison with several metadata

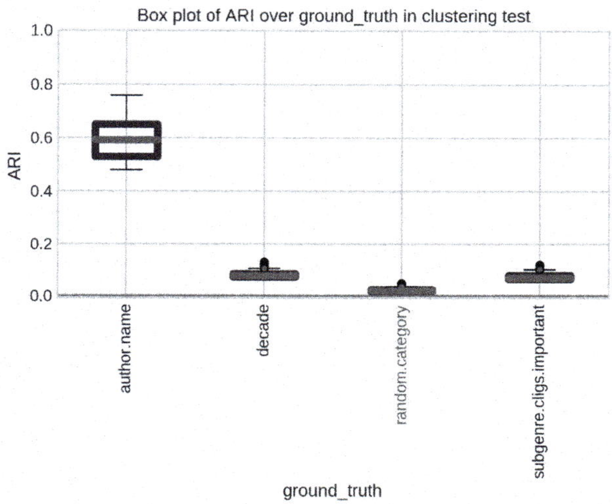

domness (more details in the Jupyter Notebook). There is some information about periodization or genre in the clusters, but how much? The median ARI of authorship for the thousand best combinations of parameters is around 0.6, while the median for the other categories is much lower: 0.08 for decade and 0.07 for subgenre. In this way, I have measured what the stylometric community already knows: The author is dominating the cluster, yet it still shows little information about subgenre and chronology. This is probably the explanation for why clustering has become so popular in stylometric research. When literary texts are clustered, the results tend to show authorship in a much stronger way than any other cue.

There are many options for neutralizing the authorial cue in order to strengthen the other categories, especially subgenre. In Section 4.2.3.6, I have introduced the authorial-zscores, which try to condense the idea of how frequent a feature in a given text is when considering who wrote it, i.e. is the frequency of a word in a novel high, given that it was written by a specific author? In Chapter 6.1, I have evaluated all the proposed transformations in a classification task. The results have blatantly shown that authorial-zscores are in the range of the baseline, which means that the lexical information is spoiled, as will be shown in Figure 79.

I have tried several other transformations besides authorial-zscores to neutralize the authorial cue, such as the normalization of the frequency by subtraction or division against the mean frequency of an author, using the standard deviation of the corpus and not the author, and using medians instead of means. The results when clustering are very similar to the ones obtained when applying classification seen in Section 6.1.2: Either it spoils the information, or the authorial cue remains clearly predominant. Another strategy is to force the selection of texts. The researcher can either take only one text per author or take all texts of each author. This second strategy has been used to analyze and evaluate a specific hypothesis from Literary Studies about the works of Valle-Inclán, with very promising perspectives (Calvo Tello 2019). But these strategies of sampling based on authorship create several problems. The authors who wrote only one text are always represented by the same text in every iteration, therefore, this text becomes very dominant in the sampling method. Moreover, since every iteration changes the selection of texts, the evaluation of clusters becomes even more complicated.

However, using clustering methods to identify one subgenre per text is rooted in the conceptual frame that subgenres are classes in a scholastic-structuralist model: Each novel belongs to only one subgenre. In the previous chapters, I have presented arguments to consider that each text can be linked to many subgenres: from a theoretical point of view (Chapter 2.3), a computational view (Chapter 2.2), the labels (Chapter 5.1), and my own experience with the classification (Chapter 6.1). If this conceptual model is accepted, every text is present in two possible values in all subgenres: Either the novel is part of the category or it is not. I can accommodate the cluster to this model forcing the algorithm to create only two clusters, and try to observe whether they also fit the binary information of each subgenre. Figure 77 shows the results for the different categories and subgenres.

If the researcher forces the process to divide all texts into only two groups, the algorithm is unable to say much about 72 different authors. This is why the authorship (the leftmost box plot of Figure 77) now remains very low, with an ARI of 0.05, while the scores of many subgenres yield higher values – autobiography, biography, dialogue, erotic, spiritual, poetic, psychological, and especially modernist and naturalist. These last two categories yield on average an ARI of 0.24, while the remaining subgenres vary between 0.01 and 0.10. Adjusting the number of clusters to the characteristics of the intended

Figure 77: Evaluation of the binary clusters in comparison with several metadata and subgenres

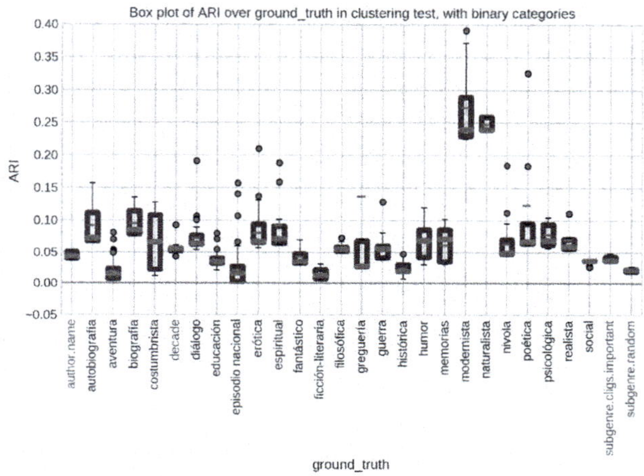

ground truth forces the algorithm to ignore other categories, even the most predominant one: authorship.

I have started this section with two different problems: How many clusters should the algorithm consider? And how can the authorial cue be neutralized? After taking into account several methods, the most promising seems to be a rather simple one. If it is accepted that texts can belong to many subgenres, one difficulty (the number of clusters) turns into the solution for the other problem (predominance of authorial cue). This is a positive finding, but the very best results of subgenres (0.24 ARI for naturalist and modernist novel) are still much lower than the best outcomes of authorship in Figure 76 (0.60). I have managed to cluster the texts avoiding authorship as the strongest cue, but its capacity to find other categories is still limited.

6.2.4 Evaluation of Parameters of Clustering with Linguistic Features

For now, the results shown in this chapter are only based on tokens as features and on a small variety of parameters. The aim of this section is to produce an exact evaluation of parameters and other types of features (both in isolation and combination). Parallel to the evaluation performed in Section 6.1.2 on classification parameters, the following aspects are evaluated:

- *Types of feature combinations*: frequencies of tokens, linguistic annotation, lemmata, semantic annotation, authorial-zscores based on tokens, and the mixed model obtained in Section 6.1.4.
- *Algorithms*: I work with k-means, spectral clustering, and the agglomerative clustering Ward. All these are implemented in the Python library scikit-learn, and allow us to define the number of clusters that should be created.[1]
- *Number of most frequent words (or features)*: 10, 50, 100, 500, 1,000, 2,000, 3,000, 5,000, and 7,000.
- *Transformation of the data*: relative, logarithmic, z-scores, binary, tf-idf, log10-zscores, and tfidf-zscores.

Each combination is repeated ten times, evaluating the results against the subgenres as binary classes, plus the information about authorship, decade, main subgenre, and the random subgenre. This produces more than 250,000 combinations, which will be summarized as box plots for each analyzed parameter. I expect the types of features, number of frequent words, and transformations to perform similarly to the evaluation of classification in Chapter 6.1. In other words, I anticipate that the mixed model will be the best feature type, that logarithmic transformation will yield higher outcomes and that the best range of features will be between 1,000 and 7,000. Concerning the algorithms, it will be interesting to observe whether the stylometric community has good reasons to keep using Ward as a method, or if we should switch to those more commonly used in Computer Science, such as k-means or spectral clustering.

In Figure 78, the 100 best combinations of parameters for each category are selected and presented. In general, the evaluation of subgenres with the best combination of parameters is between 0.10 and 0.80, and the vast majority yields higher scores than authorship or random category (except for three:

1 I also worked with Affinity Propagation, Mean Shift, and Birch, but I decided not to consider them in this section because these algorithms decide on the number of resulting clusters.

Figure 78: Evaluation of the parameters showing results for several categories

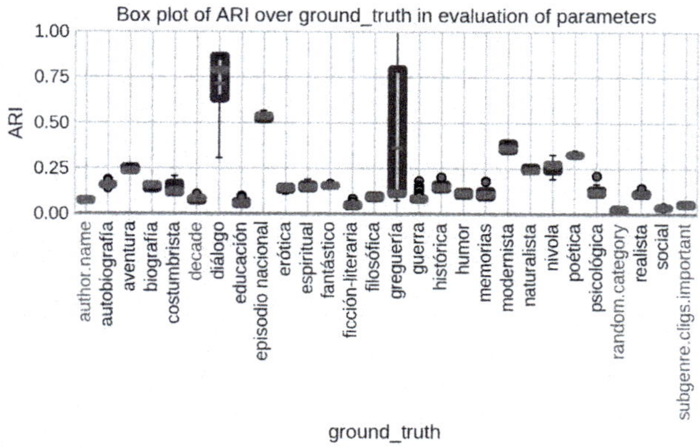

social, educational novel, and *literary fiction*). Using different features and algorithms does improve the results in comparison to those in Figure 77. Still, many of the subgenres show a very low ARI (around 0.15), which means that the clusters do not represent these categories.

The fact that subgenres such as *greguerías*, dialogue, modernist, or poetic novel are among those that best map the clusters suggests that smaller categories (subgenres with fewer texts) rather than larger ones are being recognized. To test this, I run a correlation test between the ARI scores achieved and the number of texts that populate each subgenre (for example, there are nine dialogue novels in the analyzed corpus, and this subgenre obtains a median ARI of 0.77). The outcome of a Pearson's r test is a negative weak-moderate correlation (-0.41***), i.e. the fewer texts a subgenre contains, the more likely it is to be represented in a cluster. This is an interesting effect that gives insight into the characteristics of the clusters that the algorithm proposes: groups with few texts. This tendency of the algorithm is similar to what literary scholars tend to do: find small subgenres with many shared features, populated with few instances. As I will show in Section 7.2.3, similar effects can be observed in the classification results.

Moving on to the next parameter, Figure 79 shows the results of the feature combinations. As expected, the highest results are achieved by the mixed

Figure 79: Evaluation of the feature combinations

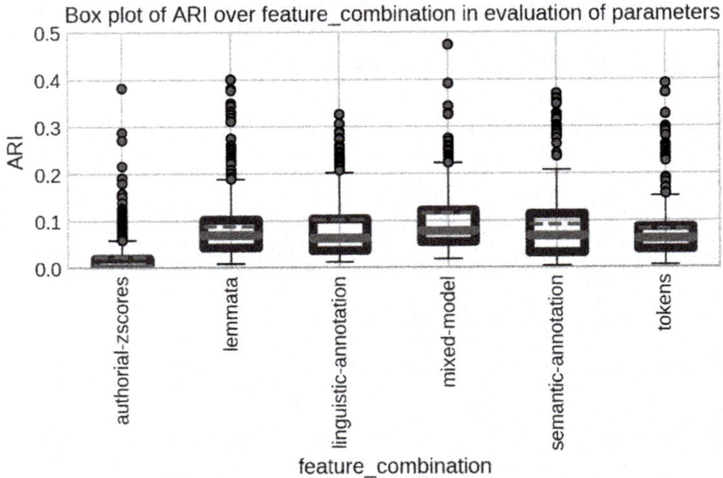

model (which contains the features that were most efficient in the classification task in Section 6.1.4). Even when its box plot overlaps with other combinations of features, the outcomes show statistical significance in a t-test (p-value < 0.001). As mentioned before, the authorial-zscores transformation proposed in Section 4.2.3.6 gives results very close to zero, which represents random clustering. The remaining features yield a similar accuracy in clustering than they do in classification, although in this case, the tokens are below the others (with statistical significance, p-value < 0.01). In other words, the linguistic annotation seems to bring more improvement in clustering tasks than in classifying ones. The following evaluated parameter illustrates in Figure 80 the transformation of the features.

Also, as expected, logarithmic transformation of relative frequencies achieves the highest results on average in Figure 80, with statistical significance in comparison to the other transformations (p-values < 0.001). Besides this and the tfidf-zscores, the rest do not yield higher outcomes than the relative frequency, although the comparison does not obtain statistically significant results in several cases. In other words, except for the logarith-

Figure 80: Evaluation of the feature transformations

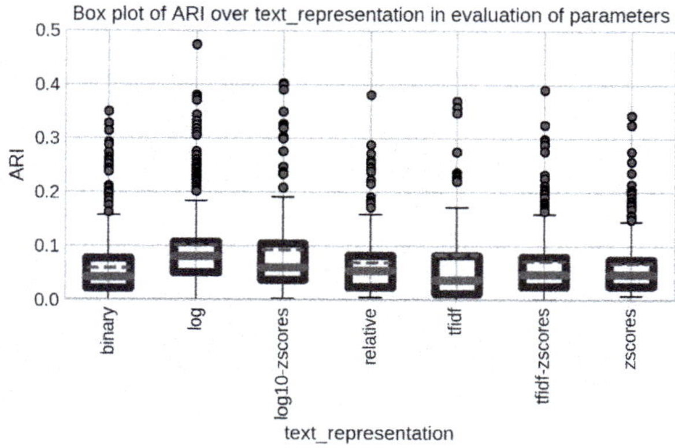

mic transformation and tfidf-zscores, the other transformations could not improve the results when used for clustering.

As far as the other parameters are concerned, there is little distinction between their different values. The agglomerative clustering method Ward does yield slightly higher results than k-means or spectral clustering, although they all lie very close to each other (specific details in the Jupyter Notebook). Moreover, the number of features shows a flat pattern, with high outcomes using very few features (ten or 50), as well as with many (3,000). The tendencies of these two parameters are better observed in combination with the transformation in the facet grid of Figure 81 in which the rows stand for the transformations, the columns are the methods, and each sub-figure represents the number of features with a box plot.

With the three parameters set apart, some tendencies are better observable. In general, the highest results are obtained by log10-zscores, especially with Ward and 3,000 or 5,000 features. Moreover, the outcomes of tf-idf, with rather fewer features, tend to be acceptable. In some cases, the combination of methods and transformation shows a clear tendency of the impact on the size of the vector. When more features are applied, some combinations improve (log10-zscores + Ward, binary + k-means, binary + Ward), under other circumstances the results decrease (tf-idf + Ward, tf-idf + k-means), while others are

Figure 81: Facet grid of algorithms, transformations, and number of features

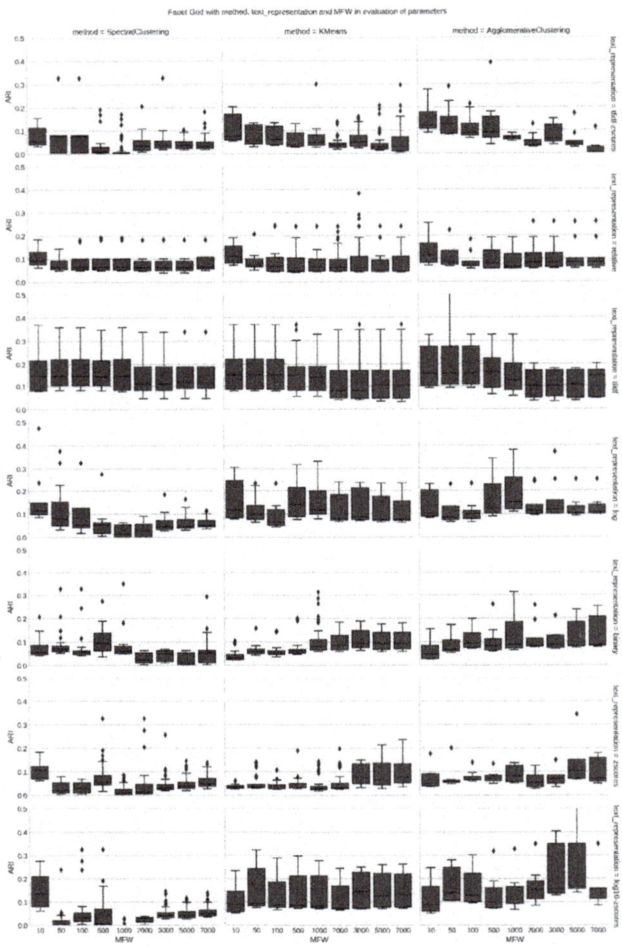

just flat or erratic (relative frequencies and z-scores with any method, tf-idf + spectral clustering, log + k-means).

This analysis gives a fuzzier picture than the evaluation of parameters in the classification in Chapter 6.1. Although logarithmic transformation, Ward,

3,000-5,000 features, and the mixed model show slightly higher results than the rest of the parameters, the differences are insignificant and other combinations also obtain some of the highest outcomes.

6.2.5 Comparison of Clusters and Evaluation with Metadata

The previous evaluation illustrates a series of tendencies across parameters with positive tendencies rather than a clearly optimal combination of them. This means that there is no perfect way of clustering the corpus to find subgenres, but rather several ways. These different combinations of features could be pointing out to the same or to several potential hidden subgenres. In the next step, I apply the different values of the parameters that were most successful and cluster the corpus of novels several times. To be more specific, the features come from the mixed model containing lexical frequencies, TEI-tags, linguistic annotation, and ordered entities, as explained in Section 6.1.4. These features are transformed into four variants with the best results in the facet grid: log, tf-idf, log10-zscores, and tfidf-zscores. Since the algorithms and the number of features have not shown a clear trend as to which of them works better, all of them are applied (except for 7,000 features). The algorithms are set to split the corpus into two clusters, and every combination of parameters is repeated ten times.

This setup produces more than 900 competing clusters: almost a thousand different ways of organizing the corpus in binary groups. This represents nearly a thousand potential new subgenres. Of course, many of them can be very similar, or perhaps even identical. Possibly, there are actually two or three distinct basic clusters, and the remaining 900 show just little differences. To observe the similarity between these 900 competing models, I again use a clustering method. However, instead of using the linguistic information of each text, now the algorithm receives only the information about which texts are part of the clusters. That means that each text now turns into a binary feature of the clusters and this is the underlying data of the next step. This produces a dendrogram of meta-clusters, as observed in the following figure. In this representation, two exact clusters (two clusters with the same extension, i.e. two clusters that contain the same texts) will be tightly grouped together in the meta-cluster, while two clusters that sorted the texts in a completely disjointed manner should hang on branches very far apart from one another. Since it is unclear how many branches this meta-cluster should have, I decide to use the agglomerative method Ward and show the entire structure in Figure 82.

Figure 82: Dendrogram of clusters, using the labels of the texts as features

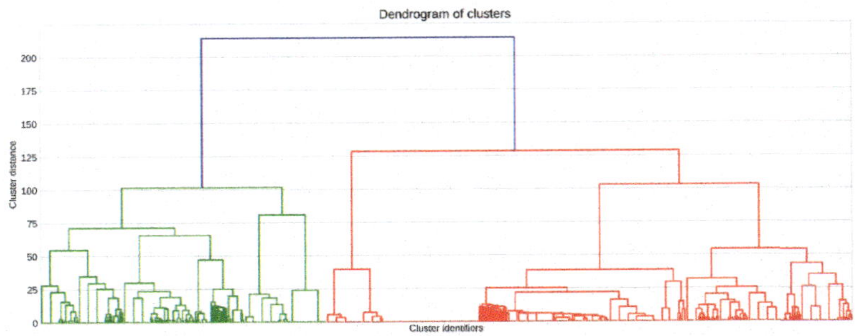

The dendrogram illustrates an open number of meta-clusters, with a minimal number of two large ones (colored in green and red). The y-axis shows the distance between the clusters, where zero represents that two instances are identical. If the dendrogram is read from the top to the bottom, the first division takes place at around 215, while the next is only at around 125; after this, more divisions follow in notably shorter steps: 105, 100, 80, 75, etc. However, the linkage algorithms are designed to show a greater distance between the first clusters. Even when the first division seems more important than the rest, it is worth observing a larger number of the other clusters, which will be inspected later. For the moment, I consider only these two major meta-clusters.

The meta-cluster on the left (meta-cluster 0), represented in green in the previous figure, contains around 300 competing clusters; the red meta-cluster (meta-cluster 1) on the right, contains around 600. As stated before, all these clusters represent almost a thousand competing subgenres. For the rest of the analysis, I need to select a smaller number of clusters to evaluate whether they show similar characteristics to other subgenres. Which specific cluster could be understood as the best candidate for a hypothetical new subgenre? The goal is now to obtain the two clusters that are most similar to the rest from the two branches in the previous figure. To find the similarity between the clusters, I measure the ARI of all clusters pairwise within each meta-cluster. Then, each cluster gets a list of values regarding how similar it is to the rest within the meta-cluster. From these values, I calculate the median ARI.[2] The cluster with the highest median ARI is then the one that is most similar to the rest, and therefore the best representative of the meta-cluster.

Following these steps, the cluster with the highest median ARI for the meta-cluster 0 is cluster 50, with a median ARI value of 0.03. This specific cluster is actually found ten times within the same parameter: logarithmic transformation, Ward, 50 features. This means that repeating the same parameters ten times produces the exact same result, even though the process is not deterministic. This is a positive outcome that shows stability. This cluster assigns 11 works to this category, separating the remaining 341 novels as not participating in it.

For the meta-cluster 1, the cluster with the highest median ARI was the number 217, with a value of 0.14. This means that this cluster does show a larger similarity to the rest of the meta-cluster than the cluster 50 does to the first meta-cluster. In this case, 87 novels are grouped as participating in this cluster, also obtained with logarithmic transformation, k-means, and a much larger number of features (5,000).

The clusters 50 and 217 are potential hidden subgenres that need to be evaluated. The first question is whether they are akin, whether they group the texts in a similar manner? To answer this, I measure their similarity calculating the ARI of both clusters, with a result of 0.05. This low score is a positive outcome: Both clusters are very dissimilar, they point towards two different hypothetical subgenres. This is not surprising since one is based on a few highly frequent features, while the other is obtained with several thousands of units. In the following sections, both are described in detail.

As I have mentioned before, it is necessary to offer further reasons for only considering two clusters (and therefore two possible hidden subgenres) and not more. A criterion for taking this decision can be whether the researcher is interested in analyzing very dissimilar subgenres or nuances of categories that partially show great overlaps. For example, one researcher can decide to coin the terms *historical novels set in Europe* and *historical novels set in the Middle Ages*. These two categories would represent a finer description than subgenre, and they could overlap in their populations (historical novels in the European Middle Ages would belong to both). Since the identification of literary genres

2 The scores are not normally distributed, which is why the median is a better metric of centrality. The mean would favor the clusters that share a high similarity with some other clusters, but that are actually not very similar to the entire group.

is an innovative field, I prefer to consider categories that show great differences between them, and therefore remain with a low number of clusters.

In any case, I have explored three and four subclusters of Figure 82. When more than two clusters are considered, the clusters start having similar extensions of texts with the rest of subclusters when their ARIs are calculated. While the ARI is very low when considering only two clusters (0.05), it increases to 0.34 when considering three clusters, and up to 0.89 ARI with four clusters (more details in the Jupyter Notebook). This shows that the algorithm manages to obtain two very different clusters from Figure 82 that represent two hypothetical subgenres. When attempting to obtain more subgenres, they start to overlap with notable intensity. This empirical argument is a further reason for why only two clusters and therefore only two hypothetical new subgenres are considered in the following sections.

6.2.6 Exploration of Meta-Cluster 0: Cluster 50

After an evaluation of the process, it is necessary now to observe closely the two clusters that are best representatives of the meta-clusters. As a first step of this analysis of these clusters, it is essential to find out whether these groups are identifying the works of a single author, a decade, or an already labeled subgenre. To determine this, I measure the ARI of the cluster while comparing it to subgenres, names of authors, and decades, all of them as binary classes. The metadata that fits the clusters best are two subgenres: dialogue novel (0.57 ARI) and poetic (0.23), followed by authors like Galdós (0.17), Aub (0.16), Benavente (0.16), Chacel (0.16), Azaña (0.14), or Lorca (0.14). Both aspects are easily reconcilable. Galdós and Azaña wrote dialogue novels, and the rest of these authors wrote one or two poetic novels, some of them being epistolary novels. This shows that the cluster somehow mainly recognizes dialogue novels and adds poetic ones to them.

Do these texts share only linguistic features, or do they also show differences in their metadata (described in Chapter 3.2) or semantics (mainly extracted from the dictionary by María Moliner, see Section 4.1.6)? And are these differences statistically significant? To answer these questions, I test the metadata and high-level linguistic annotation of the 11 novels that are part of this cluster opposed to the remaining 341. The categorical information is observed with a chi-square test, while for the numerical data a Mann-Whitney

U test[3] is applied. From 213 distinct fields, 66 reveal significant differences between the two groups (p-value < 0.05; 24 fields with a p-value < 0.001).

Based on these features, what are the dissimilarities between the 11 novels belonging to the cluster and all the others? How can this hypothetical subgenre be explained in literary terms? The greatest difference is that these texts do not contain direct speech as is expected in novels, and the communication is expressed in three manners: as letters, as direct dialogue (like in a theater play), or with a strong autodiegetic narrator. This is related to a statistically higher number of pronouns and adverbs (categories typically correlating with verbs), and a lower relative frequency of articles, prepositions, and adjectives (categories typically correlating with nouns). In addition to the PoS, there are several semantic markers that distinguish both groups – vocabulary relating to body parts, locations, food, animals, contact between people, substances, objects, plants, shapes, processes, artifacts, persons, weather, or motion are statistically less frequent in the 11 novels of the cluster. On the contrary, lexical terms about cognition, emotions, stative verbs, and proper names are higher than in the rest of the corpus. Furthermore, the frequency of the references to the protagonist is lower than in the other group.

Moreover, other metadata about novels and authors allows a differentiation of both groups. The novels are notably shorter (34,072 tokens on average, in contrast to 61,585 for the rest), the action takes place strictly in contemporary times, and the authors in this cluster also used to write theater plays (Galdós, Aub, Benavente), in comparison to the others who tended to write short stories more often (more details in the Jupyter Notebook). In general, the cluster shows statistical differences on many levels of description: closeness to other genres, formal aspects of the text, literary phenomena, grammatical patterns, and semantic annotation.

---

3 The Mann-Whitney U test is a non-parametric test applied to numerical values that are non-normally distributed, as is the case for the ordinal and interval values both of linguistic data and metadata. The disadvantage is that it is less restrictive than the t-test (or its version for vectors of different size, the Welch's test), but this imposes a series of requirements of the data which mine do not fulfill. In these cases, some researchers rather use stricter parametric tests, even when their requirements are being violated. I run the results with both of them, and the U test does in fact show more statistical differences than the Welch's test, although the general results do not change. The two clusters show statistical differences both in the linguistic data and metadata, and the amount of dissimilarities is larger than it could be expected by chance.

6.2.7 Exploration Meta-Cluster 1: Cluster 217

In this section I explore the best representative of second meta-clusters parallel to the analysis in the previous section: the cluster 217, which contains 87 novels. The calculation of the ARI of this cluster regarding authorship, subgenres, and decades shows that the highest value stands for a subgenre, the modernist novel (0.20), followed closely by the author Miró (0.20), a modernist author. After this, the ARI drops by half, with the authors Valle-Inclán (0.10), Azorín (0.09), the biographic subgenre (0.08), the decade of 1900 (0.06), and the philosophical and poetic novel (0.06). The modernist subgenre, modernist authors, and the modernist decade point clearly towards the direction of this cluster.

When the 87 texts in this cluster are contrasted with the rest of the novels, 129 out of 210 textual and metadata fields show a statistical difference. The novels of this cluster tend to be much shorter (22,892 tokens on average versus 68,722) and one of the fields with the strongest association is the author Miró, who wrote 19 novels of the 87, and only his very first novel is placed outside the cluster, a novel (*La mujer de Ojeda*) that the author himself rejected during his life. In the negative group, the author that best fits the group is Baroja, who is mainly found outside the cluster (35 works), except for his three dialogue novels. This could give the impression that this cluster tends to select almost the entire production of several authors. To a certain degree, many authors appear mainly in one cluster, but many others (24 precisely) also have works in both clusters, such as Galdós, Valle-Inclán, Bazán, Unamuno, Blasco Ibáñez, Serna, and even Miró and Baroja. Two authors that are found merely in one cluster are Azorín (inside the cluster of Miró) and Valdés (outside the cluster). In general, the authors of the cluster are more likely to be men and tend to be younger, born around 1879 (specific details in the Jupyter Notebook).

Besides the groups of authors, there is a surprisingly long list of metadata and literary phenomena that differentiate this cluster from the rest of the novels. The 87 works of the group tend to be more autobiographical, are more prone to be vague in their representation of the world, and show a tendency to favor autodiegetic narrators. Furthermore, the protagonists of both groups are different. In the cluster, there is a preference for male protagonists, adult or mature, typically working as artists. Differences in the setting can also be found. Although contemporary times are in general more frequent, the action of texts in cluster 217 are slightly more likely to take place in the past (antiquity, middle ages). The geographical setting shows very distinctive patterns in the cluster. The strongest difference is that the action of the novels of the cluster tends to occur in a rural setting, while the rest of the corpus usually takes place in cities, normally Madrid. More specifically, the novels of this cluster are typically placed in the regions of Castilla, Valencia, an undefined place in Spain, or throughout several places within the country. As is observable, almost all areas of literary metadata allow the novels of this cluster to be described, a very positive sign.

There are also several linguistic elements that differentiate this cluster from the rest of the corpus. Both the mean length of the sentence and its standard deviation is greater in the cluster. These 87 novels tend to have longer sentences, but their length also varies more than it does in the rest of texts. A similar tendency can be observed for the chapters. These are mostly longer on average, but their variance is greater. Regarding the textual and linguistic categories of the tokens, one the one side, the relative frequency of the punctuation is higher. On the other side, the frequencies of the following PoS are lower: adverbs, pronouns, verbs, conjunctions. This seems to point to the fact that verbs and the other PoS that are typically associated with them constitute a smaller proportion of these texts and, therefore, the proportion of nouns (along with adjectives, prepositions, and articles) is higher. The semantic annotation also shows very distinct patterns, with the following being the most frequent semantic areas in the cluster: objects, plants, weather, body, animals, substances, processes, contacts, and perception. On the contrary, the following areas are less frequent: locations, social contact, possessions, cognition, communication, states, acts, groups, competitions, emotions, events, relations, and organizations.

Cluster 217 shows distinct patterns on many levels of description: characteristics about the author, narrator, protagonist, setting, textual features, grammatical patterns, and semantic fields. These 87 novels can be summarized as descriptive novels about a sensitive adult man (to a certain degree a representation of the author) in rural Spain, similar to the novels labeled as modernist or philosophical, with some very good examples in the works of Azorín, Valle-Inclán, Jarnés, and, especially, Miró.

6.2.8 Discussion and Conclusions

The two obtained clusters demonstrate a great number of metadata and complex linguistic annotation that differentiates them from the rest of the corpus

– cluster 50 shows 67 fields out of 210; cluster 217, 129 (in both cases p-values < 0.05). Nevertheless, it would lead to a circular research design to use the linguistic annotation as features for the cluster and use them also for the evaluation. For this reason, I want to look now at the differences in the metadata, information that the clustering algorithm did not have access to. Out of 26 metadata fields, cluster 50 presents statistical differences in five (p-value 0.05; 2 fields with p-value 0.001), while cluster 217 has dissimilarities in 19 (p-value 0.05, 6 fields with p-value 0.001). This means that both clusters show statistical differences in information that was not used by the cluster algorithm (more details in the Jupyter Notebook).

However, any random cluster could show some statistical differences by chance; are these values therefore expected by chance? To test this, I create two iterative null-models of the sizes of clusters 50 and 217 – in other words, a random cluster of the size of 11 texts. Furthermore, I observe how many metadata fields the outcome by chance has a statistical difference in. This process is repeated 100 times for cluster 50. The same process is subsequently undertaken for cluster 217, adapting it to its size (87 novels). After this, I compare whether the number of metadata differentiating clusters 50 and 217 is expected in a random model with a one sample t-test. For both clusters, the results show a statistical difference in the random model (p-values clearly under 0.001). The number of differences in metadata observed in clusters 50 and 217 are not statistically expected by chance.

How do these values stand in comparison to the rest of the subgenres? Do the other subgenres show more differences in the metadata than these two clusters, or are the values similar? If the cluster showed fewer differentiating fields, it could be an argument against them and evince that the clusters are only observable in the textual and linguistic features, but not in more complex ones. To answer these questions, I run a similar experiment observing the amount of metadata differentiating the subgenres in the three standard values for statistical significance (0.05, 0.01, and 0.001), and further, I compare these values to those obtained by the clusters in Figure 83.

The two clusters are close to the extremes of the range. On the one side, cluster 50 is next to the random clusters, but also with similar values to the psychological, erotic, or spiritual novel. On the other side, cluster 217 is in the fourth position with the greatest number of metadata differentiating its novels from the rest, surpassed only by the philosophical, naturalist, and realist novel. This means that cluster 217 can obtain a description in terms of metadata as good as that for these subgenres, a reaffirming cue for this subgenre.

Figure 83: Number of metadata differentiating the subgenres and clusters

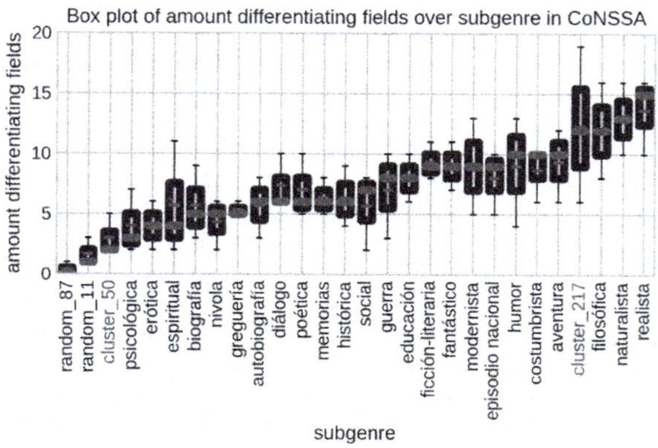

If the statistical significance is set to 0.05, cluster 217 gets the highest value, with 19 metadata fields showing statistical difference; with a lower statistical significance (0.01 and 0.001), this cluster yields very similar results to many other subgenres.

In summary, cluster 50 contains 11 novels, mostly dialogue novels and other marginal texts (epistolary, strongly poetic avant-gardist texts), with direct communication but without direct speech. Their main positive common ground is the lack of narration led by a third-person narrator. The number of metadata differentiating these texts is extremely low in comparison to the rest of the clusters, although it is still higher than what can be expected from randomness. On the other side, cluster 217 seems to be more robust, in extension (87 novels) as well as the intension of a very large number of literary metadata that allows a quite accurate description.

What have I found in this chapter? Several texts whose linguistic similarities lead cluster algorithms to group them repeatedly. The method has been applied in a way that it did not express much information – neither about authorship nor decade, the accepted strongest signals or cues along with subgenre in this kind of analysis of literary corpora. Indeed, the method has been evaluated for binary subgenres and has achieved satisfying results.

How can be these two clusters (or groups) of texts be understood? I have evaluated both of them and they do not show a stronger dependency on authorship or decade than other subgenres – both clusters contain many texts written by several authors in several decades. The clusters fit neither a specific group of authors nor a generational change. Although both clusters show certain similarities to subgenre labels, they do not map an already known subgenre – cluster 217 shows a weak overlap with modernist and philosophical novels; cluster 50 demonstrates a stronger association with dialogue novels, adding other texts with similar direct communication (letters, novels with autodiegetic narrators) to this subgenre.

Are these similarities only observable in the linguistic features? No, both clusters have shown numerous fields in the metadata and annotation that distinguish them significantly. Nevertheless, differences become obvious in both groups. While cluster 50 shows only a few fields differentiating its texts, cluster 217 is definable in terms of protagonist, chronological and geographical setting, narrator, and relationship to the author, showing a great coherence in terms of literary metadata.

Are these clusters subgenres that were hidden until now? This depends on how the researcher defines subgenres and the perspective of their study (see Section 2.3.4). The researcher can undertake a longitudinal perspective, analyzing them as the communicative process between author and reader, which will require observing the clusters under these terms. In my research, I have adopted a cross-sectional perspective, allowing different institutions to modify the list of labels and assign them to texts, also retrospectively. As the results of Chapters 6.1 and 7.1 state, these labels can be predicted by linguistic and literary features. From this perspective, subgenres are groups of texts which share linguistic and literary phenomena and can be identified and labeled retrospectively by other agents (publishers, scholars). These clusters do fit this definition of subgenre, behaving similar to others. They are coherent groups of texts in linguistic and literary terms that do not map authorship, decade, or generation. I do not have a better way of understanding these clusters than to ascribe them to the category of *subgenres*.

What should these clusters be called? What exact label should be used for them? They could be referred to as *cluster 217* (a cold place holder), "somewhat autobiographical novels, normally with a male protagonist traveling through rural Spain, with much description and reflection, and little action and communication" (a long descriptive label), or a label could be coined, such as *mono-dialogue novels* (cluster 50) or *rural-intimist novels* (cluster 217), making clear that they are considered subgenres.[4] However, I am proposing to use the concept of *bucolic* for the last group, which is applied in many European traditions in several periods and in combination with other genres (such as drama and poetry in the historical genres of bucolic poetry or pastoral plays). The concept of bucolic is frequently associated with one of the authors that best represent this subgenre: Miró (Altisent 1988; Fernández Palmeral 2019; Beneyto Pérez 1980; Laín Corona 2009; Baquero Goyanes 1973). If the label is accepted, we could consider that a bucolic novel existed and was practiced mainly between 1908 and 1927, with many examples such as Miró, Valle-Inclán, Azorín, or Jarnés, i.e. the *bucolic novel*. The concept does reflect many characteristics of these novels, such as perception, description of nature, and a rural setting. However, whether the label bucolic novel is really satisfying is a secondary matter. The important finding is the identification of these groups of texts.

In this chapter, I propose that these clusters can be understood as subgenres from a cross-sectional perspective. Nevertheless, they do not have the same status as the rest of the labels given by human sources. They continue to be hypothetical subgenres that have arisen from a clustering process that has been evaluated in several steps. In this way, they are integrated into the subgenre palette, now containing 26 labels,[5] and they will be analyzed in the following chapters, with a special interest in whether they show any abnormality in comparison to the rest. In the future, it would be necessary to discuss both the proposed subgenres in the circles of research on Spanish literature and the methodology in DH conferences. In addition, this innovative method can be applied in the field of Digital Literary Studies to other languages and periods to observe its full capacity.

4 If these clusters are tried to be fitted within Thema (as the rest of the labels were in Chapter 5.1), cluster 217 is partially covered by the tag FXR (fiction, narrative theme: sense of place), while the closest code for cluster 50 seems to be FXM (fiction, narrative theme: interior life).

5 In Chapter 5.1, 23 labels were extracted. *Literary fiction* was added to them in Chapter 5.3.

7. Analysis of Subgenres

7.1 Classification of the Subgenres

After collecting (Chapters 3.1 and 3.2) and filtering the data (Chapter 3.3), extracting features (Chapters 4.1, 4.2, and 6.1), and defining the categories (Chapters 5.1, 5.2, 5.3, and 6.2), all the necessary information is now available to use supervised Machine Learning techniques to classify subgenres of the novel. As discussed in Chapter 2.3 about theory of genre, there are different models and macro-models to understand the relationships between instances (texts), categories (subgenres) and features. The two chapters of this part address the following questions:

Chapter 7.1: How well can the subgenres be classified? Do the results score above the baseline and how high are they?

Chapter 7.2: The classification always yields better results for some subgenres than for others. Why is there variance in the results? What are the variables that explain this?

7.1.1 Introduction

In this chapter, I will show how the different models of subgenre can be formalized in different supervised computational tasks. The goal is to understand what the advantages and disadvantages of each are, as well as what the implications of each are with respect to the theoretical model of subgenres. Important aspects include the specific form in which the labels are required, whether these forms mean an elimination of information, and if so, how strong this is. Specifically, I will apply a multi-class and multi-label classification, a classification of chapters, a classification using metadata as features, and finally I will determine the probabilities of the classification on a numerical scale and compare this to the proportion of labels by several sources.

7.1.2 Subgenres as Classes: Multi-Class Classification from Modal Subgenre

The scholastic-structuralist model (expressed as a taxonomy) understands genres and subgenres as classes (see Sections 2.3.2.1 and 2.3.3.1). In this paradigm, each text belongs to a single subgenre. Metaphorically, the subgenres can be compared to branches of a tree, where each instance is a leaf hanging from a single branch. This abstract model can be fitted to Machine Learning as a multi-class classification task in which the algorithm must predict a single categorical value for each text. This type of classification is more difficult for the algorithm than choosing whether a text belongs or does not belong to any category (multi-label classification). The multi-class approach is more difficult because for every instance, it has to choose one outcome out of a list of several options. In my specific analysis, the algorithm needs to predict a value out of 26 different subgenres for each text.

This task has a strong requirement of the labels: Each text must belong to a single subgenre. This could be a better fit for research with a longitudinal historical perspective (Section 2.3.4), working, for example, with subgenre labels that the same author provided in different para-texts, or from the reception and reviews of the time. My research, however, uses a cross-sectional perspective and, as I have shown in Chapter 5.1, the data gathered does not represent the scholastic model. As a result, is it still appropriate to apply this task to my case? How is it possible to get a single value for each text, since I have observed that the sources tend to assign several subgenre labels to each text and these tend to disagree? One possibility is to choose a single source, for example the labels on the cover, as discussed in Chapter 5.2. Another possibility is to apply my own annotation, using only the subgenre that I believe is the most predominant for each text. Nevertheless, this decision would ignore the rest of the sources, and it is easily arguable that my annotation could have been modified for increased accuracy, since the annotator of the subgenres is the same as the person running the classification, which could result in circular research design. To ensure a more robust methodology, I propose to use the concept of modal value in Statistics as the most frequent categorical value for a given variable. For example, the work *Mister Witt en el cantón*, by Sender, is labeled in the following manner by several sources:

Table 11: Selected labels for Mister Witt en el cantón, by Sender, for the original and modal variants

Labels of *Mister Witt en el cantón*	**ficción-literaria**	**histórica**	**guerra**	**erótica**
Number of sources	1	3	1	0
Modal subgenre	False	True	False	False

There are three different semantic labels used for this novel: historical, war novel and *literary fiction*. I have also added the information of the erotic novel with a zero, in order to precisely describe what happens to those labels that were not assigned by any source. In this data, only one source related the novel to *literary fiction* and one to war novel, whereas three related it to historical novel. There are more sources that consider this text a historical novel rather than *literary fiction* or a war novel. If my goal was to summarize this information, I would search for the modal value of this list, i.e. the value that is most common. In other words, the historical novel is the *modal subgenre* of this text. But what if the text also received a value of three for war novel? In cases where several subgenres share the highest frequency, one could be chosen by chance or the opinion of a specific source could be preferred. An advantage of the modal subgenre is that even when the information is greatly reduced, the final single output for each text is obtained considering all original sources, without relying on only one of them.

I run an initial experiment to evaluate the number of features and the transformations using the mixed model of linguistic annotation obtained in Chapter 6.1 with logistic regression as the algorithm. In this case, the baseline is 0.22, which is the proportion of the most frequent value in the column of modal subgenre (64 realist novels out of 352 texts). In order to obtain sufficient data for each class, I only use those subgenres populated with at least ten texts. The highest results yield a 0.4 F1-score (micro), with statistical significance over the baseline (p-value < 0.001, further details in the Jupyter Notebook). These results are better than chance, but are notably low: More than the half of the texts are being classified incorrectly. A closer look at the evaluation reveals that the most successful parameters are logarithmic transformation and 5,000 MFWs.

Every classification process produces a confusion matrix – a table with true labels on the vertical axis and predicted labels on the horizontal axis. The instances are placed in the table of Figure 84 according to these two variables. In the case of multi-class classification, these matrices allow the researcher to observe which are the classes that have been confused, and those with which they are being confused.

Figure 84: Confusion matrix using classification as multi-class task with 11 classes

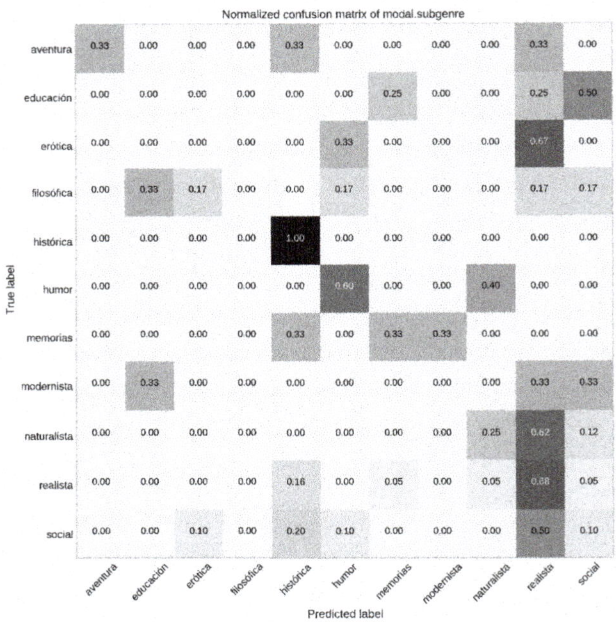

The cells in the perpendicular line of Figure 84 show the proportion of texts that are labeled correctly for each class. For example, 60% of the comedy novels (*humor*) are correctly classified while 33% are recognized as erotic, and 17% as philosophical novels. If the multi-class classification could predict the majority of the texts correctly, the perpendicular lines in the matrix would show very high proportions, and this is not the case. Many of the subgenres are completely mismatched, with some of them even being completely confused with other subgenres, such as the erotic novels being classified mainly as realist novels. In general, the algorithm tends to rely on the most populated classes: realist, historical, adventure and comedy novels.

But these errors are not randomly distributed, they show specific tendencies and it can be interesting to observe the associations among them. Realist, naturalist and social novels tend to be confused with one another, and other subgenres like educational or erotic novels are grouped together. Adventure novels and memoirs tend to be labeled as historical novels, while philosophical and partially erotic novels tend to be recognized as comedy novels. In summary, the classification groups the texts into three macro-subgenres: historical, comedy and realist-naturalist-social.

Following this, a further multi-class classification test can be performed using only the three subgenres that would include the rest: historical, comedy and naturalist. Using logarithmic transformation and the 5,000 MFW again, the F1-score (micro) of the classification now increases to 0.70 (over the baseline of 0.56 with statistical difference, p-value < 0.001) and the confusion matrix shown in Figure 85 is generated. When using only these three major subgenres, the perpendicular lines have the greatest values of the matrix, although many texts are still strongly mismatched. Roughly a third of the texts are misclassified, even when the algorithm has only three different classes.

The multi-class classification approach would be the most fitting task for researchers with a single and highly qualitative label for each text, which can be a better fit for a longitudinal historical perspective. The confusion matrices produced allow one to observe which subgenres tend to be mismatched. These errors can be understood as similarities between the categories in gradual macro-models such as the one by Petersen (1944, see Section 2.3.3.3). There are two main disadvantages of the multi-class task. The first is the necessary reduction of information when the sources apply more than one label per text, which is the normal situation for subgenres. The second is the low results, which can be understood as proof that the subgenres of this period cannot be correctly classified, as many authors and literary scholars of the period have revealed (see Chapter 2.1).

7.1.3 Subgenres as Categories : Multi-Label Classification

The next way to operationalize subgenres would be to consider that each text can participate in several subgenres. From a theoretical perspective, this task

Figure 85: Confusion matrix using classification as multi-class task with three classes

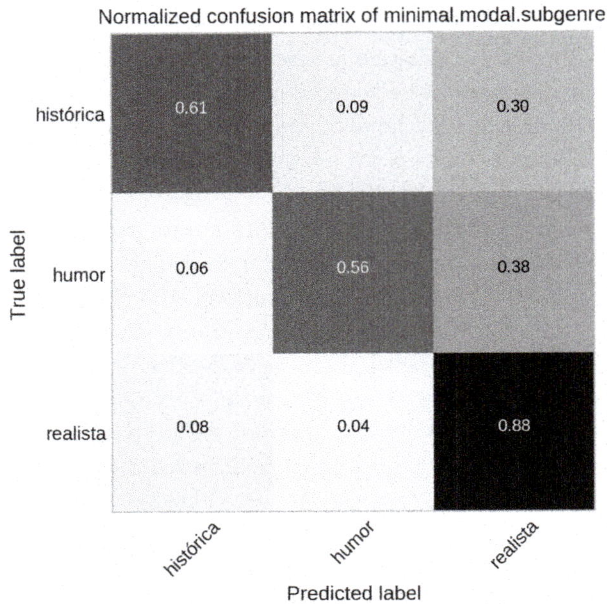

better fits the understanding of genre as a textual category. Similar to how a person can participate in several social institutions (participate into one or two families, a political party, a religious group, a sport association), each text can participate in several subgenres. From a computational point of view, this would be seen as a multi-label classification: Each instance is related to several categories. In this kind of task, the algorithm needs to predict whether each text participates in each subgenre or not. This means that it has to make a binary decision for each category and each instance.

As in the case of multi-class classification, the labels about subgenre gathered from the sources are not in binary form. How can the semantic labels be transformed to meet the requirements of this task? Each label needs to be transformed into binary values (typically zero for negative values and one for positive values). For example, I could implement the rule that if any source has labeled the text with a subgenre, this subgenre should have the positive value of one, while if none of the sources did this, the subgenre has a value of zero.

Table 12: Selected labels for Mister Witt en el cantón, by Sender, for the original, modal and binary variants

Labels of *Mister Witt en el cantón*	**ficción-literaria**	**histórica**	**guerra**	**erótica**
Number of sources	1	3	1	0
Modal subgenre	False	True	False	False
Binary	1	1	1	0

The binary values of these labels could be used to train a classification algorithm and measure its reliability. This is the most frequent manner of applying Machine Learning to subgenres (see Chapter 2.2). Still, I would like to highlight that the binarization of the frequency of labels on the sources also implies a reduction of information. The binary vector for a multi-label classification does not represent the fact that a large number of sources assigns the labels historical for this text. The elimination of information is not as strong as the modal value of the previous section, since each text may still be related to several subgenres, but these have become flat.

With the binary labels, I run a multi-label classification using the parameters from Chapter 6.1 that showed higher results, i.e. logistic regression as an algorithm, several ranges of MFW (from 100 up to 7,000) and the transformation with the highest results (log, log10-zscores and tfidf-zscores). The corpus is under-sampled for each category creating equal sub-corpora, and the process is repeated 10 times using cross-validation (ten-fold). The top ten results of this for each category are shown in Figure 86.

The results are clearly higher than the baseline of 0.5 for all subgenres, with many of them (bucolic, dialogue, *episodios nacionales*, erotic, *greguerías*, mono-dialogue, *nivola*) having results close to a perfect classification. The general median of these top ten F1-scores for all subgenres is 0.79 (standard deviation of 0.11), but this increases to 0.84 when the best result of each category is considered (standard deviation of 0.10). These outcomes surpass my original expectation for a medium-sized corpus, such as the CoNSSA, and for so

Figure 86: Best results for each subgenre using linguistic features

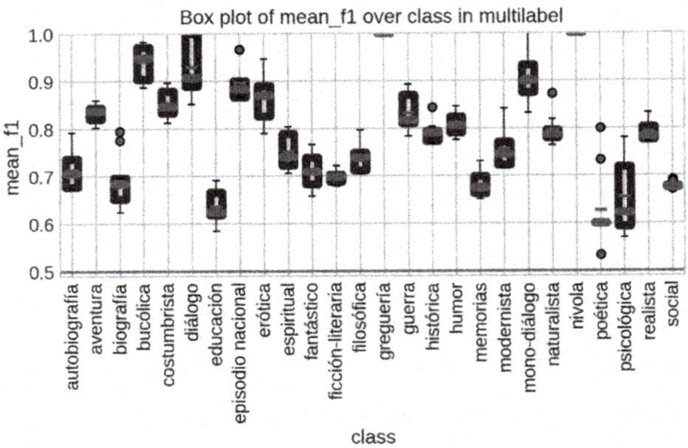

many and highly literary subgenres such as the autobiographic, poetic novel or *literary fiction*. These high results are one of the reasons why this task is frequently used in Computer Science: It allows for the reporting of high scores, a desirable goal in several computational areas. In fact, the results could be easily improved if the researcher eliminated some subgenres from the analysis, such as biographic, educational, *memoir*, poetic, psychological or social novels (all of them with F1-score values between 0.6 and 0.7). This is one of the reasons why a clear selection of the labels, as per Chapter 5.1, is vital: It takes away the possibility of the researcher pre-selecting only those labels that will be better classified.

One of the leading goals of this research study is to observe whether genre classification is possible in a period in which authors, readers, literary scholars and others agents did not expect them to be categories that truly expressed much about the content of their texts (see Section 2.1.3). The low results of the multi-class approach of the previous section can be seen as computational proof for this. However, the multi-label approach of this chapter shows that these literary categories can be predicted correctly in the majority of the cases. This points out in two directions. First, literary categories can be predicted by algorithms to a certain degree, even when they have access only to linguistic information. In other words, that subgenres of the novels are expressed in linguistic and textual features. Second, the literary categories can be better predicted if it is accepted that any text can belong to any number of subgenres.

One of the unanswered questions is why there is a clear variation in the results of the classification of the different genres that is repeatedly observed in other papers: Erotic and adventure novels (easy genres) are more accurately classified than social or educational novels (difficult genres). The traditional response to this is that the easy genres have a larger number of good indicators on the surface of the text (this will be further discussed in Section 7.1.5). Words about sex or pirates are clear indicators for erotic and adventure novels, while the vocabulary of society and personal development is not as distinct. But this is mainly due to the fact that the researcher takes features from the surface. If more complex features were to be used, the variance would be eliminated and those difficult-to-classify categories would achieve higher results. Would this also be the case when the literary metadata is used as features?

7.1.4 Subgenres of Chapters

Before I answer the previous question, I would like to address another issue. In the majority of the papers on the topic, the subgenre label is predicted at the volume level: Each novel belongs to one or several subgenres. Alternatively, in Underwood (2014), this information is predicted at the page level in order to distinguish whether a page was part of the main text (and if so, to which genre) or of the para-text (title page, publishing information, advertising, indexes, etc.). To train the algorithm, they manually annotate several thousand pages for each category.

From the perspective of literary scholars, it is easily acceptable to imagine a novel that begins as an adventure novel and ends as a romantic one. This hybridism over the development of the plot of the novel can be formalized in many ways, some of them being:

1. The text belongs to both subgenres (without specifying which parts belong to which subgenre).
2. The first half of the novel belongs to a subgenre, the second one to another.
3. The first chapters of the novel belong to a subgenre, the last ones to another.
4. The first 50 pages belong to a subgenre, the last 50 to another.

5. The first 100 chunks belong to a subgenre, the last 100 to another.
6. The first 1,000 paragraphs belong to a subgenre, the last 1,000 to another.

From the above list, the first option is what the majority of projects and institutions would use, and it is also what the previous section used in the multi-label task. The second option would correctly classify novels that are divided into two halves, but not with narrower or uneven divisions. Separating the text into smaller units, such as chapters, pages (as Underwood did), chunks, or paragraphs, would allow more accurate information about specific units to be provided and, in addition, the number of observations would multiply, since each novel typically contains several dozen chapters, hundreds of pages, and thousands of paragraphs. A larger number of observations could lead to an improvement in classification without the cost of digitizing thousands of texts. However, this strategy of splitting a larger unit into smaller parts could also lead to disadvantages. On the one hand, shorter textual instances contain fewer linguistic features and therefore make the classification more difficult. Even for humans, it would be a challenge to recognize subgenres in a single paragraph or a short chapter. On the other hand, the classification system could reinforce the recognition of subgenres only by identifying the volume, i.e. that two instances (chapters, pages or paragraphs) belong to the same text. This is similar to what happens between the texts of the same author (see Section 6.2.3). Two texts of the same subgenre written by the same author are more likely to be classified together than two texts of the same subgenre but written by different authors. The effect of this association will be further analyzed in Chapter 7.2. A similar effect is seen when two texts come from the same series or collection in the popular genres, such as western or science fiction (Jannidis, Konle, and Leinen 2019). Either way, the classification of smaller units is not a new type of problem, it just augments the number of categorical variables being associated with the subgenre.

Ideally, carefully annotated labels about the subgenres of each chapter should be designated by human annotators after reading them. These labels could not be gathered nor found. For this reason, each chapter inherits all the subgenre-labels from the novels it belongs to. i.e., all the chapters of an adventure and erotic novel will also be associated with these two labels. The number of instances is now much greater, but the accuracy about the description of the genre is lower. For this reason, there are two competing hypotheses about the results of this set-up:

1. The accuracy of the classification of chapters improves in comparison to using the complete novel, due to an increase of instances and the similarity between them.
2. The accuracy of the classification of chapters decreases in comparison to using the complete novel, due to a reduction in the linguistic features per instance and inadequate volume labels applied to chapters.

If an improvement is observable, a way of accessing larger corpora with real texts produced by humans (in comparison to synthetic texts or strategies of over-sampling) would be found, without further costs relating to digitization.

For this, I separate the novels into their chapters using the manually assigned boundaries in the TEI *div* elements (see Section 3.1.8). This produces a total of 10,780 chapters. Around 400 of them are abnormally short, with less than 100 tokens, and this is the reason why these have been left out of the corpus. After this, 10,306 chapters remain as instances, which means that in this section I am working with a corpus 29 times greater than the original one, composed of 352 complete novels. The frequencies of both tokens and linguistic annotation are considered features. The parameters include most frequent features, the most successful transformations from Chapter 6.2 (log, log10-zscores and tfidf-zscores) and logistic regression as the algorithm. As in the previous section, I under-sample the corpus for each category ten times to get equal size sub-corpora, and apply a ten-fold cross-validation. The results of the top ten combinations of parameters per subgenre are shown in the figure below.

The box plots show results clearly above the baseline, with almost all F-1 scores above 0.8, and a median of 0.89 from all subgenres when taking the best results. In comparison to the classification at the volume level (which had a median of 0.84), the results of using chapters are statistically higher (using a t-test, p-value = 0.03, further details in the Jupyter Notebook). This means that even when the labels of subgenre are not meant to describe the chapters, and even when the instances contain fewer features, a far larger number of analyzed texts improve the classification's results. When looking at each subgenre, the accuracy improves by 10% of the F1-score on average. The subgenres that benefit the most from the classification of chapters are poetic (improvement of 30%), psychological (21%), educational (16%), biography (15%), and fantasy novel (15%). Interestingly, with chapters, two subgenres achieved slightly lower results: *greguerías* (-2%) and *nivolas* (-1%).

Figure 87: Best results for each subgenre on chapters

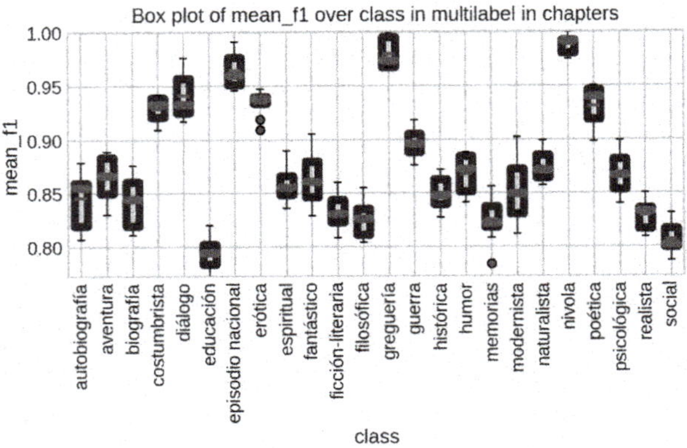

Even when labels are not assigned to the chapters, and even when chapters contain fewer features, the task improves notably using chapters instead of complete novels. This could be seen as a method of gathering corpora of greater size, taking texts produced by humans and using frontiers that are relevant to literature, such as chapters. The question of whether this improvement was only the result of a larger number of texts, or the reinforcement of subgenre through the recognition of the text, remains unanswered. To fully answer this question, it would be necessary to use a corpus in which it is possible to access thousands of novels separated into chapters and then test the two possible variables in isolation. For now, I do not have access to such a corpus. However, a similar hypothesis will be addressed in the following Chapter 7.2.

7.1.5 Subgenres as Linguistic and Literary Categories

Literary phenomena encoded as metadata have, until now, played a small role in the analysis of genre in Digital Literary Studies. Some researchers have added some information to the algorithms (Riddell and Schöch 2014; Underwood 2016; Wilkens 2016). The reason for not using more metadata is probably not a lack of interest, but rather the cost of encoding it in relatively large corpora. Researchers use frequencies of linguistic features as an easy but efficient proxy for more complex phenomena: Exotic settings should be expressed through verbs related to boats and names about plants, animals, or food, a child protagonist should be verbalized to a certain degree with vocabulary about siblings and school, etc. (Allison et al. 2011, 24; Jockers 2013, 92; Underwood 2016; Schöch 2017b).

In this section, I apply the literary metadata about the content of the novel, presented and described for the entire corpus in Chapter 3.2. This contains manually annotated information about the protagonist, the geographical and temporal setting of the plot, the narrator, the relation to the author, the ending, etc. All this data will here be called *literary characteristics of the novel* and this section will be treated as *literary features*. In contrast, the several linguistic annotations (presented in Chapter 4.1) will from now on be called *linguistic features* or *characteristics*, such as the frequencies of tokens, grammatical information, TEI-tags, sentence length, etc.

Nominal definitions of subgenres are normally expressed in a combination of literary characteristics (protagonist, setting, plot, end) and some characteristics about the structure, style, theme or aim (see Chapter 2.1). For example, historical novels could be nominally defined as being a novel set in the past and with a realistic representation of the world. If metadata about all historical novels is available, would it really be the case that all novels follow this pattern? The use of literary phenomena encoded as metadata and passed on to the algorithm as features is a bridge between two tasks that have been considered until now to be very different: the classification and the definition of subgenres.

This section has three goals:

1. Evaluate whether literary metadata used as features can yield higher results in a classification task than linguistic features.
2. Observe whether the subgenres that are correctly classified with linguistic features yield similar results with literary metadata.
3. Establish whether there is less variance in the results of the classification than when using linguistic features.

In Chapter 3.2 the different types of metadata relating to the internal content of the text were explained. These are now split by type from an informational point of view:

- *Categorical fields*: narrator, gender and profession of the protagonist and information about the setting (continent, country, territory, whether it exists, the real setting being represented).
- *Ordinal fields*: such as the size of the setting, its chronological period, the age and sociological level of the protagonist, the type of ending, the representation of reality, or the relation between the text and the author's life.
- *Interval fields*: chronological span in days.

In order to pass this kind of information on to the algorithm as features, all of them have to be converted to numerical values. The ordinal fields, originally encoded as alphabetical strings, were recoded as numerical ordinal values. For example, clearly sad endings were encoded as zero (actually 0), while clearly happy endings were encoded as four (4). The categorical fields were transformed following the one-hot encoding process (VanderPlas 2016, 376), in which each value of each field becomes a new column, assigning either one or zero to each text. In this step, the categorical column of the protagonist gender becomes three columns, one for each different value: female, male and other. When a text has a male protagonist, it contains a one in the male column and zeros in the female and other columns. The interval information of the chronological span of the action does not require transformation since it was originally encoded as a numerical value.

From the steps described in the previous paragraph, all metadata fields now contain only numerical values. Nevertheless, there was an extreme divergence in the ratios that would affect the results of the classifiers: While many are between zero and one, others achieve values of four, and the span of the action achieved around 25,550 for novels whose actions last 70 years. To homogenize these values, a min-max transformation was applied to each column, converting all maximum values to one, and all minimum values to zero.

The one-hot transformation for categorical metadata multiplies the number of columns since every categorical column is replaced by several new ones. Especially in fields without a closed list of possible values, this number explodes into hundreds of new columns, producing, in this case, 409 new metadata features. The information about the geographical setting is particularly profuse, with numerous columns of names of countries, territories or places for each novel. I expect much of this information to be useless for the classification, cause noise and reduce the accuracy of the classification: When a novel takes place in Madrid, the fact that it also takes place in Spain is irrelevant. To explore whether a shorter list of metadata would actually benefit the classification, the columns of the metadata are sorted by the mean value in all columns. In this way, the recurring features of many novels are at the beginning of the data frame, and the sparser columns are arranged at the end.

Besides the steps undertaken until now, several other types of transformations are also tested, such as z-scores, binary and tf-idf. Logistic regression is again chosen for the algorithm, and different numbers of features are used: 10, 25, 50, 75, 100, 200, 300, and 400. The results are shown in Figure 88.

Figure 88: Best results for each subgenre using metadata

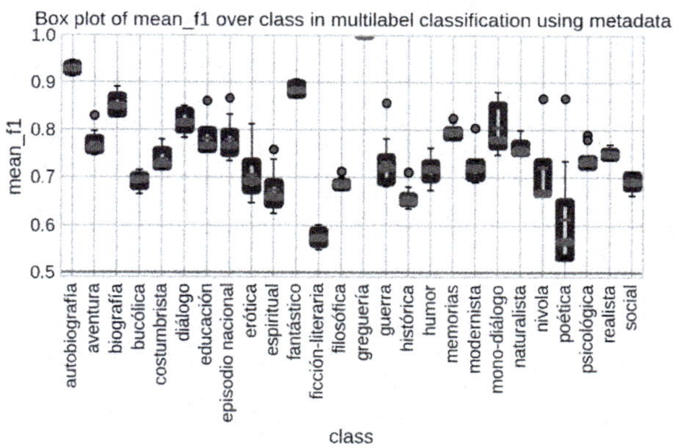

The classification results using metadata achieve results above the baseline. The median classification for the best results of each subgenre is 0.82, a surprisingly low result in comparison to the 0.84 achieved by linguistic features. Even when so much literary metadata has been manually annotated, this does not improve the classification, it actually delivers lower results.

What about the parameters that were evaluated? As I mentioned previously, the literary features are first treated with the min-max transformation, sorted by frequency and then transformed in different ways. The z-scores and binary transformation tends to achieve slightly higher results, although they overlap to a large extent with tf-idf and even with no transformation. In terms of the number of features, the highest scores are achieved with between 100 and 300 literary features, although these results overlap greatly with those using only 20 features. As expected, many of the more seldom features cause noise in the results. Further details can be observed in the Jupyter Notebook.

An important outcome of this test is related to the variance of the results. As I noted previously, the variance of the classification when using linguistic features is normally explained by the fact that linguistic features are better approximations of the defining features in some subgenres. However, my results show that the subgenres are again distributed within a large range of accuracy in the classification. While some subgenres are close to or above the 0.8 F1-score (dialogue, educational, memoir, autobiographic, fantasy novel, and *greguería*), others yield much lower results (*nivola*, poetic, spiritual, historical novel, or *literary fiction*). As happens when using linguistic features, some subgenres yield higher results than others. However, the same explanation used for the variance of the classification using linguistic features cannot be applied to literary metadata. In this case, I am not using features on the surface of the text, but rather abstract concepts annotated after understanding the plot of the text. Therefore, the lack of complex features cannot be the reason why some subgenres are still better classified than others. Is perhaps the lack of linguistic features the reason why the classifier cannot now achieve better results? This seems to be the case for subgenres such as the poetic novel or *literary fiction* where it is easily acceptable for linguistic style to play an important role.

A comparison of the results of the classification using linguistic features on the one hand, and literary metadata on the other shows some surprising outcomes.

In the bar plot of Figure 89, it can be observed that some subgenres are classified with values over 0.7 F1-score with both types of features, such as dialogue novel or *greguería*. On the contrary, other subgenres achieve lower results than 0.7 F1-score with both types of features (social novel, *literary fiction*). However, some subgenres yield low results with linguistic features, but high with literary information (educational, fantasy novel), or the other way around (historical novel). This seems to show that the accuracy of both types of features is not correlated: Some subgenres are better classified by linguistic features (erotic), some by literary metadata (fantasy), some by the both (*greguería*), and some by neither (poetic). In the Figure 90, the mean accuracy of the top ten combinations of each type of feature for each subgenre is plotted on a different axis.

Figure 89: Bar plot of the comparison of the results using literary or linguistic features

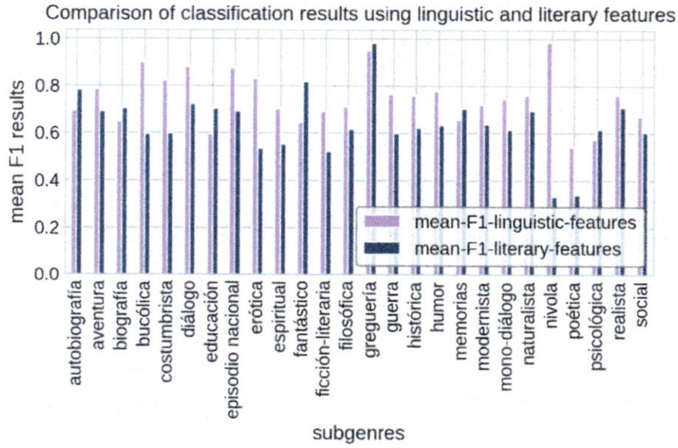

It can be seen in Figure 90 that there is no correlation whatsoever. A high classification based on linguistic features does not represent a high classification based on literary metadata. In other words, linguistic features are not being used as a proxy for more complex literary phenomena, or at least not for those that have been encoded as literary metadata for this corpus. There are also not two clear groups of subgenres (one being defined exclusively by linguistic features, another by literary features). Some subgenres are better classified by linguistic features, others by literary features, and all lie in continuity without a correlation of the variables.

A further step is to combine both types of information in the same data frame and pass literary and linguistic features at once to the classifiers, trying to get the best possible results. This means that the algorithm is receiving hundreds of data points of information about specific aspects of the text and the plot. My expectation is to surpass both types of classification using only one of the types of features. To homogenize the information, I transform the linguistic features logarithmically with a base of 1,000, which sets the minimal values close to minus one, and the maximum values to zero. Then the absolute value is taken, making zero the absence of the feature in the text, and one its maximum frequency. Subsequently, I merge the data frames of

Figure 90: Scatter plot of results using literary and linguistic features

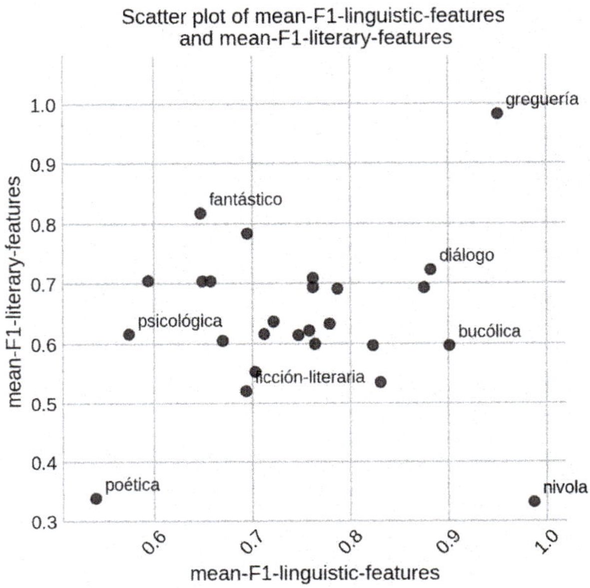

literary features and linguistic information (more details in the Jupyter Notebook).

This combined feature table is passed on as features to a logistic regression algorithm, with several further transformations (raw, z-scores, tf-idf and binary), and a range of number of features, from ten up to 7,000 (based on the results of the Chapter 6.1). The top ten results for each subgenre are summarized in the box plot of Figure 91.

Now all subgenres are not only above the baseline, but also around or above the 0.7 F-1 score. In fact, the median of the top results is 0.86 (standard deviation of 0.09). Does the concatenation of literary and linguistic features lead to higher scores than only linguistic information? In other words, do the algorithms take advantage of accessing both qualitative and quantitative features? The mean top ten results with linguistic features in Section 7.1.3 achieved a mean F1-score of 0.79, while the combination now yields 0.83, which is statistically significant (p-value < 0.001, details in Jupyter Notebook).

Figure 91: Best results for each subgenre using linguistic and literary features

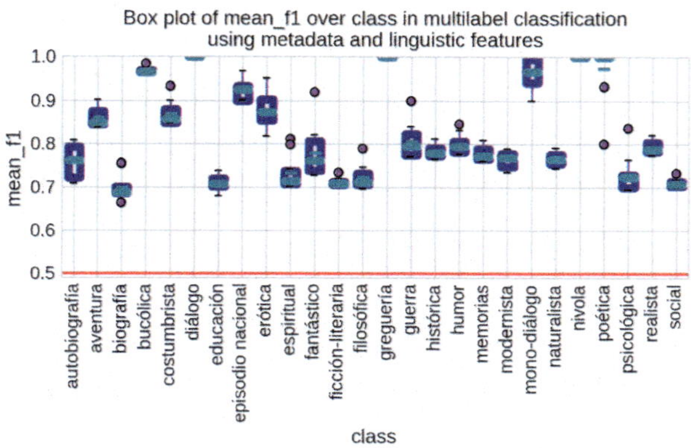

In short, yes, the combination of literary and linguistic features does improve the results of the classification, although the difference is lower than I expected.

In any case, the subgenres still show a variance in their scores, even when literary and linguistic features are used. The classic answer to this variance points out that the linguistic features better cover the necessary complex phenomena to correctly define each subgenre (Allison et al. 2011, 24; Jockers 2013, 92, further discussed in Section 7.2.1). This explanation would mean that when using more complex features, the results should be homogeneous and all subgenres would yield similar scores. This is not the case, regardless of the type of features used (linguistic, literary or both). A series of hypotheses to explain this variance will be tested in the Chapter 7.2.

7.1.6 Subgenres as Gradual Categories: Probabilities of Classification

Before I move to the question about the variance, I want to model subgenres in a final manner. Both the modal subgenres of the multi-class and the binary subgenres of the multi-label undergo a simplification of the underlying label in the several sources. The first strategy only takes one label while the second strategy ignored the frequency of the labels in the sources. Going back to the example of *Mister Witt en el cantón*, five different sources in total provided information about the subgenre of this novel. The frequency of the labels is set in relation to the total number of sources showing the values for the labels in the table below:

Table 13: Selected labels for Mister Witt en el cantón, by Sender, for several variants

Labels of *Mister Witt en el cantón*	**ficción-literaria**	**histórica**	**guerra**	**erótica**	**Total number of sources**
Number of sources	1	3	1	0	5
Modal subgenre	false	true	false	false	5
Binary subgenre	1	1	1	0	5
Proportional subgenre	0.2	0.6	0.2	0	5
Ordinal (str) subgenre	minority	majority	minority	none	5
Ordinal (nr) subgenre	1	2	1	0	5

The proportional subgenre (fifth row of the previous table) is obtained by dividing the number of sources (second row) by the total number of sources which provides labels for that text (last column). Its possible values lie between zero (no sources applied this semantic label to the text, as in erotic novel) and one (all sources used this semantic label for the text, which in this case does not occur). The row of the proportional subgenre data does not contain any simplification of the original frequencies. A transformation has been performed, but the difference between the positive labels remains. Besides, the original row of the number of sources can be recreated by multiplying the values by the total number of sources, which is not the case for the rest of the transformations of the labels.

This is similar to a very common way of communicating relations between texts and subgenre in which literary scholars describe a text belonging mainly to subgenre x, but also containing traces of subgenres y and z. This can be expressed in linguistic form (as ordinal strings) or in numerical encoding (as ordinal numbers). In other words, belonging to the subgenres is being reported in an ordinal way, i.e. one of them has greater importance than the others. This is the core idea of the prototype theory, in which the belonging of instances to a category is not expressed in categorical terms, but in Hempfer's words "a matter of gradience" (Hempfer 2014, 411, see Section 2.3.2.4). Even when similar expressions are both in common language and Literary Studies, I have not found any sources in which the annotators or the institutions assigned the subgenre labels in degrees.

For both the proportial subgenre and the ordinal subgenre, I propose to use the number of institutions assigning each label as a proxy for more accurate labels about subgenre. I am aware that to test this properly, a number of annotators should assign labels to all texts, expressing them numerically. Additional questions would arise from this process which would surpass the limits of this research: What should the background of the annotators be? How much text should they read to label the novel? Should all annotators label all texts? Is this feasible? What should their guidelines be? Which subgenre palette should be considered? How exactly should the numerical value for each subgenre be encoded?

From a computational perspective, *regression* would be considered the type of task that predicts a floating number from an instance (Müller and Guido 2016, 28), such as the proportional subgenre. In cases where the labels are understood as ordinal, the task would fall within *ordinal classification*. The advantage of these two types of tasks for subgenre is that the value the algorithm tries to predict is more precise than the binary labels of the classification. Nevertheless, the data for the labels is too sparse and the values are too low to use these techniques properly. When the data is split into the different possible values, the algorithm does not have enough material to correctly learn the differences between, for example, a highly spiritual, a medium spiritual, and a less spiritual novel. Several attempts of using regression and ordinal classification were undertaken and can be observed in the Jupyter Notebook of this chapter.

However, there is another way to compare these numerical labels to the output of Machine Learning. Some classification algorithms can also express how clearly an instance belongs to the different categories. More exactly, they express what the probabilities are for the instance to be part of the different categories. This is done, for example, by logistic regression, the algorithms that have being used in the previous sections based on the positive results of the evaluation in Chapter 6.1. In the Figure 92, the information about the subgenre of a single novel (*Gerifaltes de antaño*, by Valle-Inclán) is expressed in two ways: the proportion of sources (proportional subgenre) and the predicted probabilities of belonging to each subgenre.

Figure 92: Bar plot of proportion of sources and predicted probabilities for each subgenre in the case of Gerifaltes de Antaño, by Valle-Inclán

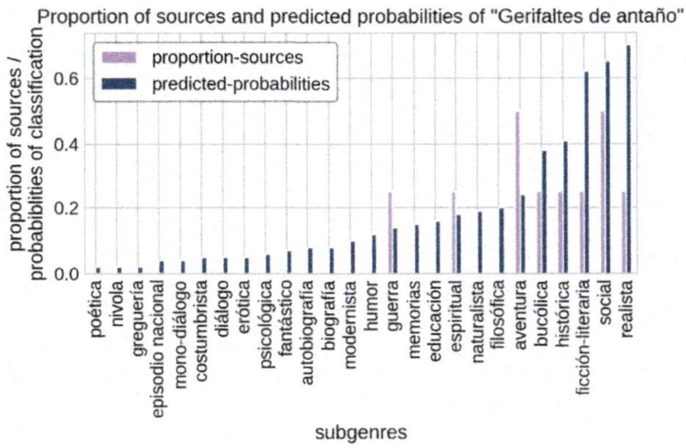

All subgenres can have values from zero to one in Figure 92, both in the proportional subgenre and in the predicted probabilities. I expect both variables to correlate, meaning that when a larger proportion of sources agree on the text belonging to a category, the algorithm will also very probably predict that the texts belong to the subgenre. For this novel, they do correlate strongly (r = 0.73***). Still, there is some discrepancy in the previous figure. In some cases, it is clearer to human sources than to the algorithm that the text belongs to a subgenre, as in the case of the adventure novel which achieves a higher score by human sources (a proportion of 0.5) than by the algorithm (probability of 0.24). In other cases, it is clearer to the algorithm that the text belongs to the category, like the realist novel, with the highest probability (0.72) and few human sources assigning it (a proportion of only 0.25).

To observe this in the entire corpus, I run a logistic regression classifier on the binary results. In this case, the division of training set and test set is restricted by the scarcity of the number of sources that assign the different range of values to every text. For this reason, I observe the probabilities of the classification based only on the train set. The problem when measuring accuracy in the training set, is that the algorithm has too many features to define each category. It learns the category too well, and this is called overfitting. To solve this, I decide to work with fewer features than instances. More specifically, I decompose the concatenated data-frame of linguistic and literary features using principal component analysis (PCA). This technique creates a number of synthetic dimensions that try to maintain the variety of the original data. In my case, the original data frame of 7,000 features is decomposed into 200 components, which is a number considerably lower than the number of texts in the corpus.

After running the test, the algorithm gives the probabilities of each text belonging to each subgenre. These probabilities can then be compared with the proportional subgenre assigned by the sources and its correlation measured with Pearson's r. This gives a correlation coefficient for each subgenre between the proportional subgenre and the predictions, shown in Figure 93.

Figure 93: Bar plot of the correlation between predicted probabilities and proportion of sources using label

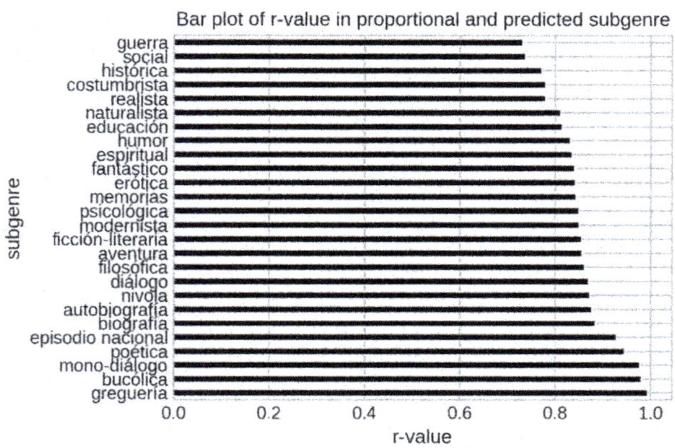

The data lies between 0.73 and 0.99, with a median of 0.85. Hence, all cases show either a strong or a very strong correlation. This confirms my hypothesis: The predicted probabilities of the algorithm follow the proportion of human sources that assign the subgenre to each text. In other words, the idea that a text belongs more to one subgenre than to another is based not only in how literary scholars typically express these relations, this is also observable in the assignment of human institutions and in the predictions of the algorithms. The basic idea of the prototype model, where some instances belong more tightly to a category, finds several forms of evidence when applied to literary genre.

7.1.7 Conclusions

In this chapter, I have applied several tasks to computationally analyze subgenre. Each of these makes certain assumptions about the main model of the genre, and therefore expects the labels to be transformed in a specific manner. As a consequence, they offer answers to different types of questions.

The first was the multi-class task, in which each text belongs to a single subgenre and the goal of the algorithm is to predict a single categorical value for each text of the entire label palette. From a logical point of view, this task quite accurately reflects the classic scholastic-structuralist model. From the perspective of Literary Studies, it can better accommodate longitudinal historical studies in which the researcher has a single label of high quality, a kind of ground truth label about the subgenre, for example from the author. In general, this is not what is found in real labels, not even when one reads the author's opinion on their work. Because of this, the majority of the cases require an important reduction of the information and retain a single label for each text. Because this research study has assumed a cross-sectional synchronic perspective, the labels available are not of such a nature. Nevertheless, I have considered the modal subgenre, taking for each text the label with the highest number of sources labeling it. Depending on the number of labels analyzed, the F1-score yields values of 0.4 and 0.52, both statistically higher than the baseline (0.22 in the first case, 0.42 in the second), but nevertheless rather unimpressive scores.

These low scores mean the algorithm was not able to find the necessary features to distinguish the categories, or, in other terms, was not able to find the necessary and sufficient conditions. That can be seen as a failure for conceptualizing genre with the classic scholastic-structuralist model. Of course, this failure could be explained by other factors, like insufficient features or, more importantly, a lack of labels of sufficiently high quality. An advantage of this kind of task is the possibility of creating confusion matrices, in which the researcher can observe which subgenres are being mislabeled. In my case, the algorithm has distinguished three main subgenres: historical, comedy and realist-naturalist-social novels. This can help to define the model of genres and to respond to the categories that are more similar between them.

The second type of task is the multi-label classification, which is most frequently used for analyzing genre, in which any text can participate in one or more categories. The following table shows an over-view of the most important results of the different tests using multi-label classification in this chapter.[1]

Table 14: Overview of the results when applying multi-label classification

	median F1-score (all subgenres)	std F1-score (all subgenres)	baseline	median F1-score (lowest subgenre)	median F1-score (highest subgenre)
multi-label with linguistic features	0.84	0.1	0.5	0.6	1.0
multi-label (chapters) with linguistic features	0.89	0.05	0.5	0.79	0.99
multi-label with literary features	0.82	0.09	0.5	0.57	1.0
multi-label with literary and linguistic features	0.86	0.09	0.5	0.7	1.0

When multi-label classification is applied to the entire novels using linguistic features, the F1-scores for all the subgenres were between 0.60 and

1 The reason why this table does not offer the results from the multi-class tests is that this information is not directly comparable, since the multi-class classification does not allow the calculation of an F1-score for each subgenre, as the multi-label classification does.

1.0 (with a baseline of 0.50), and a median of 0.84. This improves to 0.86 when linguistic and literary features are concatenated, and up to 0.89 using chapters instead of entire volumes as instances. This means that the results are acceptably high, but still far from being perfect. However, this lack of perfection is not a problem in Digital Humanities research. In comparison, the classic scholastic-structuralist model does require finding the necessary and sufficient conditions to correctly classify all instances. In computational terms, this would mean that a series of features has to be present in all instances of a category, and be absent in all instances that do not participate in the category. These expectations are much higher than those for Machine Learning, in which acceptably high scores (around 0.9 F1-score) are positively evaluated and, in some cases, perfect results are viewed with a certain skepticism. Besides, there is no expectation of finding the necessary and sufficient conditions, but rather that different features define whether different instances are part of the category or not. In other words, Machine Learning (and specifically the use of multi-label tasks) more accurately fits the looser expectation of the family resemblance model (see Section 2.3.2.3).

However, both the multi-label classification task and the family resemblance model require the instance to participate in the category in categorical terms, not in degree. A person either belongs or does not belong to a family, a text either belongs or does not belong to a subgenre. Nonetheless, scholars tend to describe these relations in degrees: The text belongs *mainly* to one subgenre. Since the labels were originally gathered from several sources, this number can be used as the base for ordinal labels. These have been compared with the probabilities of the classification for each category. The correlations range from strong to very strong, meaning that both humans and algorithms have similar manners of assigning the information about subgenre, not in categorical terms but in degrees. These results fit the prototype theory, in which some instances are better representatives of a category.

In any of the tasks, there is always a variance in results: Some subgenres are clearly better classified than others. The traditional explanation is that the linguistic features are better proxies for some subgenres than for others (Allison et al. 2011, 24; Jockers 2013, 92). A classification run using complex literary metadata shows similar variances. Even the concatenation of both types of features still shows a variance in the results. These results contradict the idea that superficial features are not able to correctly map complex features, but rather that some subgenres just have more accurate features than others. Either way, this requires another explanation for the reasons the classification yields better results in some categories. This will be discussed in the following chapter.

7.2 Easy Genre, Difficult Genre: Why is there Variance in the Results of the Classification?

7.2.1 Introduction

In the previous chapter I have used several methods of classification to analyze subgenres. In all instances, a pattern appears: Some categories yield much higher results than others. As discussed in Section 7.1.5, a traditional explanation in computational analysis has been to consider the indicators for the subgenre as more or less present in the surface of the text. Allison et al. describe the frequencies of tokens as dependent traits that are "mere consequences of higher-order choices. [...] They are the effects of the chosen narrative structure" (2011, 24). Jockers mentions that with "plot conventions come stylistic constraints" and "these constraints exist at the level of the most common linguistic features" (2013, 92). In other words, in both papers, the linguistics features are consequences of information about the plot, encoded in CoNSSA as metadata. Even when vocabulary describing exotic plants or weapons is not a defining feature of the adventure novel, at the lexical level it maps the exotic setting and physical danger of the protagonist, which are the defining literary components of this genre.

If this were the reason for the variance of the classification results, having abstract literary features about the plot should lead to a homogeneous level of classification with all categories possibly very close to a perfect classification. In Section 7.1.5, I have passed literary metadata as features along with linguistic information, and this was not the case: Some subgenres are still much better classified than others. One of the reasons could be the lack of certain metadata important to some subgenres, such as the deeper attributes of the main characters (e.g. particularities of their political positions, beliefs, or sexuality) to correctly classify specific subgenres (spiritual, erotic novel). But perhaps other reasons could better explain these differences. Possibly more complex texts express their subgenres in a more subtle way, which should lead to lower classification results. Subgenres that were written by only one or a few authors should be more easily recognized since the author's style reinforces the classification. Numerous texts populating a subgenre could well lead to both outcomes: either an increase in accuracy due to more data, or a decrease due to a greater variance.

To test these possible causes of variance, each is tested as a hypothesis and is described in the following sections. For this, the variable was first operationalized in a quantifiable manner. For example, to observe whether the genres become more difficult to predict over time, all texts belonging to a genre were selected and then the median year of publication for each genre was calculated. Thus, a value is assigned to the time of publishing for each genre. These values are then compared to the F1-scores obtained from the combination of linguistic and literary features[1] and the applied regression analysis. After interpreting the results, I move on to the next hypothesis and measure a further characteristic of the subgenre, such as its median text length in tokens, its median number of chapters, the total number of texts populating the category, or the number of authors contributing to it.

In this chapter, I use two kinds of features, as I did in Section 7.1.5: linguistic features (superficial cues, linguistic annotation, frequency of TEI tags; for further details, see Chapter 4.1) and literary features (annotated as descriptive metadata after an understanding of the plot; for further details, see Chapter 3.2).

7.2.2 Year of Publication

As discussed in Chapter 2.1, a traditional hypothesis for this period expresses that the subgenres of the 19th century (naturalist, realist) novel are more distinct than those from the latter decades of the period (Mainer, Alvar, and Navarro 1997, 557; Longhurst 1999, 3; Ródenas de Moya 2000, 89–90; Aubert 2001, 14; Altisent 2008, 2–3; Buckley 2008). The change of century could have awakened a tendency to write contrary to expectations, which would contribute to lower results in the classification. If this is the case, the chrono-

1 I also compared these values with the results of the classification using only linguistic and literary features in the Jupyter Notebook software. In general, the correlations were very similar between the three data sets.

logical tendency of classification should decrease over time, obtaining higher scores in the first decades and lower scores in the latter decades. In the following scatter plot, each subgenre is a data point and its position is defined by the median year of publication (horizontal axis) and the mean F1-score of using a combination of the two features (linguistic and literary data).

Figure 94: Scatter plot of year of publication and results of the classification

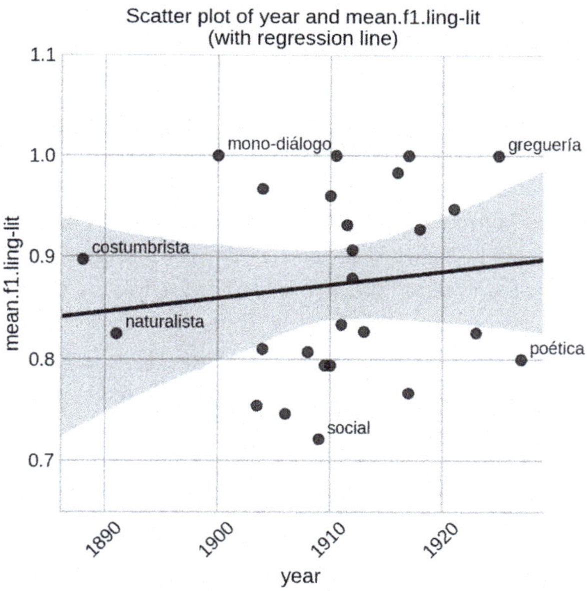

The above figure does not show any tendency towards a decrease or increase, but rather a random distribution. The regression analysis falsifies any statistical pattern of the data points (p-value 0.53). Very similar results appear when only linguistic or only literary features are used for the classification (visualizations and values in the Jupyter Notebook). This means that the data falsifies the hypothesis that the genres of the 19th century can be better classified than those from the latter decades.

7.2.3 Number of Texts and Authors

An interesting variable is the number of texts populating the subgenre. In Machine Learning there is a certain expectation that classes having many instances should yield higher results than those with fewer instances because the algorithm has more data to learn from (VanderPlas 2016, 363; Müller and Guido 2016, 31). Nevertheless, in the several runs up until now, some subgenres with very few texts obtained virtually perfect scores, such as *greguerías*, *nivolas* or dialogue novels, while the realist novel (the largest group) was located in the lower section of the results. Similar results have been observed when clustering techniques were evaluated, in which subgenres with fewer texts mapped the clusters more accurately (Section 6.2.4). This tendency is also observable in human annotators, who tend to use a ratio of only three texts per subgenre (Section 5.1.3). This seems to point out, at least in this case, that more novels also bring more variance to the category, making it more difficult to determine a shared set of features to identify them. In other words, both outcomes are plausible: A larger number of texts might lead to an increase or to a decrease in the accuracy of the classification. To show this, the data is plotted in Figure 95 as for the previous scatter plot, but with the horizontal axis representing the new analyzed variable: the number of texts per subgenre.

In Figure 95, small subgenres (in terms of number of texts) can achieve a perfect classification (*greguería*), but they can also be some of the subgenres with the lowest scores in the classification (like spiritual below 0.8). On the other hand, the largest subgenres also achieve low results, between 0.7 and 0.81 (social, realist novel). A regression analysis on the data shows a slope of -0.001***, meaning that for each additional text, the results for the classification of the subgenre are slightly lower. In general, large subgenres tend not to obtain these spectacularly high classification scores, while the classification of small subgenres is completely open: They vary between perfection and some of the lowest results.

The number of texts per subgenre is one way of measuring the variance, but as I have discussed in Section 6.2.3, in stylometry the author's style is also a strong cue (Argamon et al. 2003; Oakes 2009; Riddell and Schöch 2014; Calvo Tello et al. 2017). Since many authors wrote several works in the same subgenre, the classification of some subgenres might be reinforced by association with the author. For example, if an author wrote all his works in a subgenre, with no other author writing in this category, then the task of classifying this

Figure 95: Scatter plot of number of texts per subgenre and results of the classification

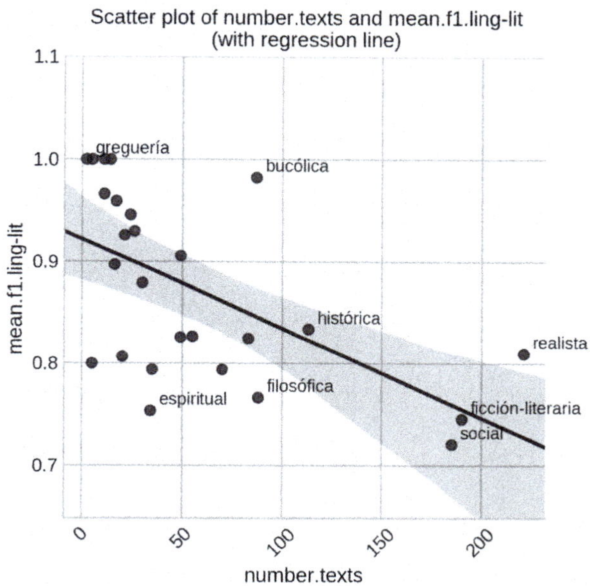

subgenre would not differ from classifying this author. To measure this influence, the number of authors per subgenre is counted and used as the x-axis of Figure 96, and compared to the results of the classification.

The results in Figure 96 are similar to the ones with the number of texts in Figure 95, but the correlation between both variables is stronger, with one exception: The subgenres written by fewer than ten authors tend to have scores of over 0.89. As the number of authors increases, the classification becomes less precise, with scores between 0.85 and 0.65 (with a single exception, the bucolic novel, that will be discussed below). The regression analysis shows a slope of -0.004**, i.e. for each second additional author in a subgenre, the classification of this category tends to be almost 1% lower.

In the top right corner of Figure 96, the scatter plot shows a subgenre written by many authors that is very accurately classified: the bucolic novel. This is one of the two hypothetical subgenres detected through the clustering

Figure 96: Scatter plot of number of authors writing in a subgenre and results of the classification

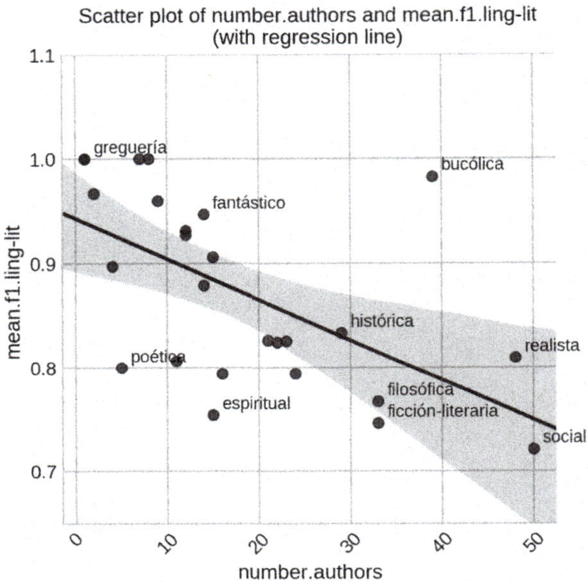

methods that are described in Chapter 6.2. This is highly suggestive because it shows that this category is an outlier in this case: It has higher classification results than the subgenres with a similar number of authors. This can be interpreted as a positive (it is a highly coherent subgenre in terms of internal characteristics) or a negative sign (its results are too high in comparison with similar subgenres, i.e. it performs too well). However, this is the only hypothesis in this chapter in which this subgenre is an outlier. Other categories also show exceptions for values in either the previous or following scatter plots. In other words, many subgenres show surprising results when analyzing specific variables, including the bucolic novel.

Returning to the main question in this section, it was shown that the influence of the number of texts and authors cannot be falsified by the data: Both variables influence the results, however to different degrees. It seems that the authorial cue is capable of explaining the data better than only the number of texts. At the end of this chapter, I will measure which of the variables correlate with the others.

7.2.4 Length of Novels

A further hypothesis is to observe whether the length of the text influences the classification results. As in the case of the number of texts, both outcomes are arguable. On the one hand, longer novels contain more words, which means that their features are less sparse (they contain fewer features assigned with zero), which should lead to a more exact classification. On the other hand, shorter novels could possibly be defined with a sharper set of features, while longer novels tend to participate in several genres blurring their relationship to each single genre. In this case, the x-axis of the scatter plot is the median length in tokens of the subgenre.

Figure 97: Scatter plot of length of text (in tokens) and results of the classification

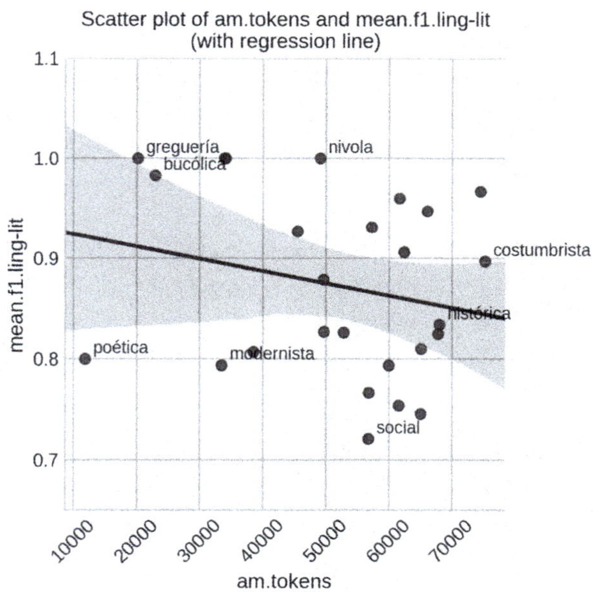

As can be observed, there is no clear tendency for the results, with similar results arising when using only either linguistic or literary features. It is true that the subgenres with 40,000 tokens or fewer achieve higher results on average (between 0.8 and 1), while novels with more than 50,000 tokens are between 0.7 and 0.95. Nevertheless, the data points are too spread out and the tendency is too flat to obtain a statistical value on a regression analysis (p-value of 0.26). However, it could be worth examining this hypothesis with larger collections of texts or non-literary genres.

7.2.5 Canonicity of the Texts

The next hypothesis relates to the degree of canonicity of the text. In the French tradition, there is a common differentiation between *littérature blanche* (literary 'white literature', with a similar meaning to the concepts of *high-brow literature* or *literary fiction*) and *genre literature* (also called *para-literature*). These concepts could explain the observed results that some highly canonized subgenres (realist, naturalist, *literary fiction*) tend to be classified with a lower accuracy than more popular subgenres, such as adventure or erotic novels. In other words, a correlation could exist between the canonicity of the text and the classification results.

To measure this, the number of pages in the manual MdLE is again used as a formalization of the canonization, with possible values of between 0.2 pages (a paragraph) and any number of complete pages, to calculate the median of all texts that populate the genre. All are between 0.2 and one page, with one exception – the *nivolas* tend to have three pages. This is mostly in two single texts (*Niebla* with ten pages, and *San Manuel bueno, martir* with eight pages). This category is removed from the calculations for this hypothesis for two reasons. First, the correlation analysis is sensitive to outliers, and second, the extreme value of the subgenre is mainly based on a couple of outlying canonized novels. The correlation of the rest of the subgenres is shown in the scatter plot below.

The genres that occupy fewer pages in the manual (*greguería, episodio nacional*, erotic, and war novels) tend to have a classification result of over 0.95, the middle range tends to lie between 0.95 and 0.82, and those subgenres populated by texts that typically occupy a page in the manual lie between 0.93 and 0.72 (with the only exception being the dialogue novel). A regression analysis gives a statistical tendency (p-value 0.005), i.e. the more canonized a subgenre

Figure 98: Scatter plot of number of pages in literary manual and results of the classification

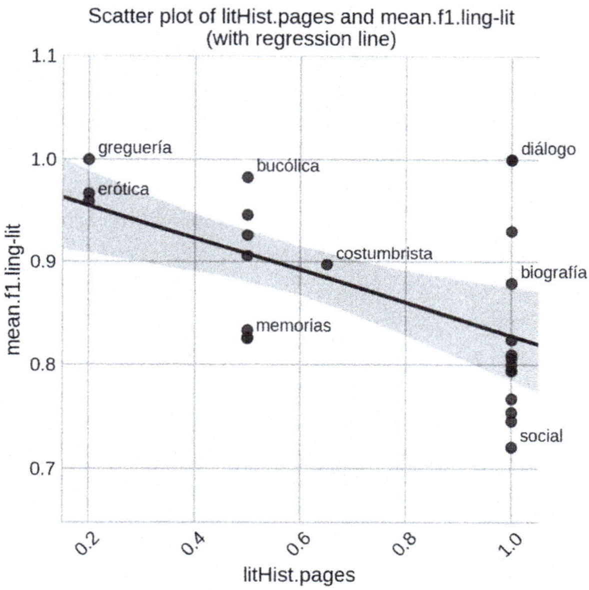

is, the lower its classification results will tend to be.[2] The results for this hypothesis show that when a subgenre is populated by texts that the history of literature considers important, this subgenre will be difficult to classify.

7.2.6 Disagreement on Human Sources

In the hypotheses tested so far in this chapter, the premise has been that if the algorithms do not perfectly classify the subgenres, this is because a part of the experiment has some caveats: complex features are missing, the composition of the corpus (in terms of number of texts or authors) is not optimal,

2 Interestingly, these results apply when using both types of features or only the linguistic features, but not when using only the literary metadata as features. Specific values in the Jupyter Notebook.

the algorithms are not sufficiently accurate, etc. But the reason is potentially different. Perhaps some subgenres are just difficult to distinguish, regardless of whether the task is undertaken by a human or a machine. Perhaps some subgenres represent more coherent groups of texts. Using the examples and terms of Underwood, some categories such as detective fiction would be more "tightly knit" than others, such as the Gothic novel (2016). It is possible that some groups of texts have no clear set of features defining them, and therefore neither humans nor algorithms are able to find these patterns.

To test this hypothesis, the Kappa scores for the agreement between the institutions obtained in Chapter 5.1, is used.[3] This variable was set as the x-axis in the scatter plot of Figure 99. It shows a correlation between both variables: The subgenres that tend to have a lower mean Kappa (with low human agreement), also tend to get lower scores (between 0.7 and 0.95). When mean Kappa scores are above 0.2, the results improve and lie between 0.8 and one. A regression analysis gives a p-value of 0.003, meaning that when humans have a strong agreement on the label, the algorithms also tend to achieve a higher classification. This tendency is even stronger with linguistic features (p-value < 0.001) but weaker with literary features (p-value 0.015). This means that the accuracy of the results is closer to the discrepancies among humans when looking at the linguistic features rather than the literary features. Contrary to a shared intuition, this could lead to the conclusion that humans rely more heavily on linguistic features than on complex literary phenomena (acquired after understanding the text) when assigning subgenre labels. In any case, the difficulties that the algorithm faces when classifying subgenres might not lie in the design of the experiment, but rather on the fuzzy nature of the phenomenon analyzed.

3 This means that the subgenres that emerged in previous chapters, such as *literary fiction* in Chapter 5.3 and bucolic and mono-dialogue novels in Chapter 6.2, have been excluded for this specific hypothesis. The reason for that is that the Kappa scores calculated for the rest of the subgenres is based on the labeling of the several before mentioned sources (cover, manuals of literature, ePubLibre, Amazon, own annotation). There is no comparable information for the labels *literary fiction*, bucolic and mono-dialogue novel.

Figure 99: Scatter plot of agreement on labels (mean Kappa values) and results of the classification

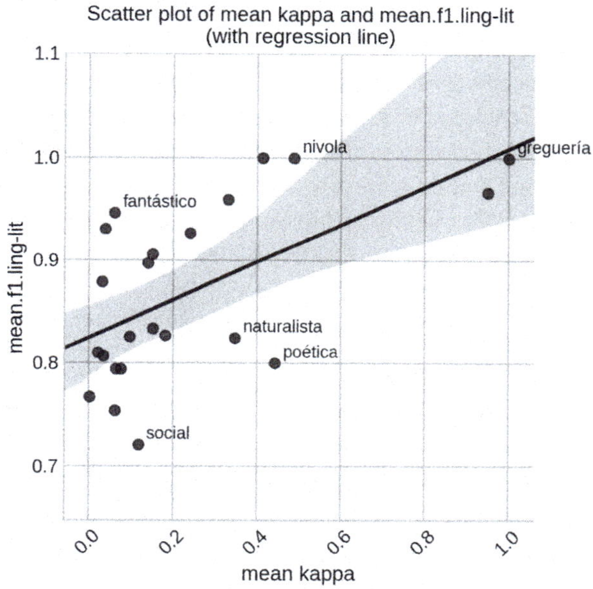

7.2.7 Specificity of the Features

But why is that? What makes a subgenre difficult to distinguish, either by humans or by algorithms? Perhaps some subgenres are too similar to the other categories and it is more difficult for both humans and machines to separate them. To formalize this question, I attempt to first determine what the distinctive features of each subgenre are. The question of how to measure distinctiveness is an open question that normally finds its solution in each research field (Schöch et al. 2018): coefficients or weights of classifiers in Machine Learning (Müller and Guido 2016, 61–64), log-likelihood in linguistics (Brezina 2018), z-scores in Statistics (Evans 1996, 102–4), Zeta values in stylometry (Burrows 2007), etc. In Section 8.3, I will argue for using z-scores for answering this question, because they are simple statistical measures that do not have parameters, are expressed as standard deviation, and have a simple statistical interpretation (absolute values over two are statistically overrepresented).

To identify how distinctive the features of each subgenre are, I first summarize each subgenre with the mean values of each feature (both linguistic and literary). From this data, the z-scores of each feature are calculated, and the distinctiveness of each feature for each subgenre is obtained. The z-scores then express the difference between the value of this subgenre in comparison to the rest of the subgenres, expressed as standard deviations. For example, the war novel assigns a z-score of 4.16 to the feature that the protagonist is a military character, and a z-score of 2.53 to the frequency of the word *hombres* ('men'). This shows that the means of these features in this category are greater than in other subgenres, or, in other words, that they are overrepresented in these categories, i.e. these are distinctive features for this subgenre.

The next step is to obtain a single value for each subgenre that represents the variation of the values in those z-scores. To obtain this, the standard deviation of the z-scores of all features was calculated. A large standard deviation represents features with larger differences in comparison to the other subgenres, as is the case with *greguerías* (2.08), *nivola* (1.47), and the poetic novel (1.34). A low standard deviation in the z-scores represents less differences in the features of the subgenre in comparison to the others, as is the case in *literary fiction* (0.34), the realist novel (0.39), and the social novel (0.4). This is a way of formalizing the distinctiveness of the features using simple statistical concepts such as the mean, standard deviation, and z-scores. This variable is set as the x-axis and compared to the accuracy of the classification as shown in the scatter plot of Figure 100.

This plot shows a linear correlation of the data, in which the subgenres are able to yield a perfect classification score only when the standard deviation of the z-scores is 1.00 or greater. A regression analysis gives a p-value of 0.0005, i.e. algorithms fail to correctly separate some subgenres because their features are not specific enough and they are too similar to other subgenres to be correctly identified. This could not only be the reason why the algorithms find some subgenres difficult, but also explain the discrepancies in human sources, as I will show in following section.

Figure 100: Scatter plot of year of specificity of features (standard deviation of z-scores) and results of the classification

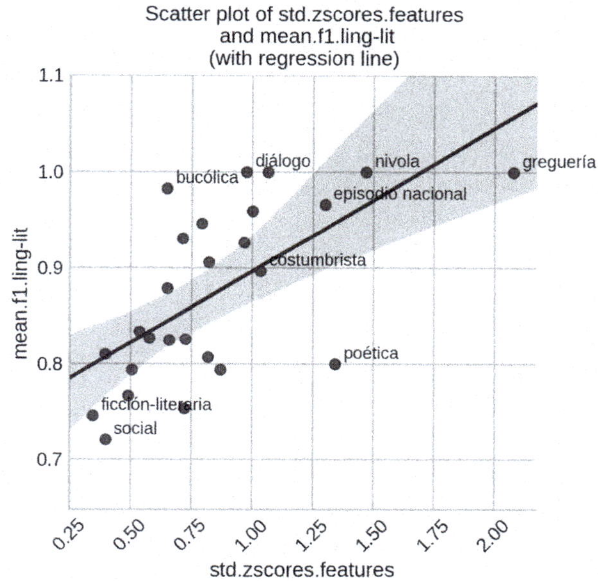

7.2.8 Correlation and Regression of Variables

Until now, several variables correlate with the results of the classification: number of texts, number of authors, agreement of labels, canonicity, and specificity of features. However, it is expected that some of these will correlate with each other. It is very likely that a shared increase in the number of authors and the number of texts in a genre will be found. For this reason a correlation test is carried out on all possible causes, leaving out the three subgenres that did not contain data in all fields, such as the hypothetical subgenres obtained through clustering (which do not have information on the agreement on sources), and the outlying value of *nivola* for the canonization. The absolute values of these correlation tests are plotted as a heat map in Figure 101, where lighter colors represent a weak correlation, while darker colors represent a stronger correlation.

Figure 101: Heat map of correlation of variables and results of the classification

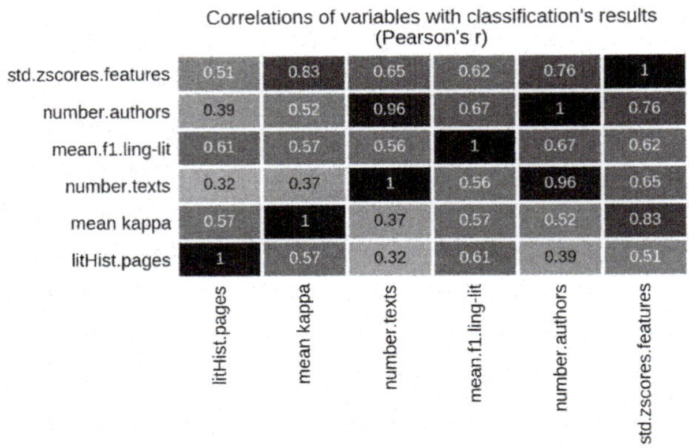

This heat map shows that all variables correlate with each other, although the number of pages in the manual as proxy for the canonization shows lower values. The two variables with the strongest correlation are the number of texts and number of authors ($r = 0.96^{***}$), an expected result. This is followed by the correlation between the agreement of the sources (mean Kappa) and the specificity of the features (std.zscores.features, $r = 0.83^{***}$). The variable with the strongest mean correlation with the others is the specificity of the features, with values from moderate to very strong. In other words, the specificity of the features is strongly related to all the other possible explanations.

Even when two variables correlate to a certain degree, they can also express different nuances about the classification. For example, although the specificity of the features correlates with the number of texts, each one could be covering specific aspects in the variety of the classification results. To measure this more accurately, a regression analysis was performed with classification scores as the dependent variable and the five numerical variables as independent variables, using the data from all subgenres (with the three exceptions mentioned above). The result of this regression analysis yielded an R^2 of 0.56 (p-value of F-statistic < 0.01), a relatively high result (the maximal value is one) which shows that these variables explain the majority of the variation in the classification results. This is a important outcome because it offers an explanation for the variation in the classification of the subgenres, the easy-genre-difficult-genre question: Why do some subgenres yield higher results? These results show that once the five characteristics of the categories are obtained (the canonicity of the text, the number of authors, the number of texts, the agreement of the labels in several sources, and the specificity of the features), the researcher can predict almost perfectly how accurately an algorithm will be able to classify the subgenre.

The regression analysis also gives a coefficient for each independent variable, which expresses their effect on the regression, shown in the table below.

Table 15: Coefficients of the regression analysis to predict results of the classification

independent variables	coefficient
mean kappa	0.063
number.texts	0.006
litHist.pages	-0.006
number.authors	-0.008
std.zscores.features	-0.011

The greater the coefficient is in absolute terms, the greater its effect is on the regression analysis, and therefore the greater impact it has on the results of the classification of subgenres. Thus, the positive or negative sign does not only reflect the direction of the correlation. Two variables stand out clearly: the agreement in sources (mean Kappa) and the specificity of features (std.zscores.features). These are the variables with the strongest effect on the classification result. These two variables with high coefficients correlate strongly as can be seen in Figure 101, while the canonicity has the weakest correlation with the others. In other words, the agreement of the labeling may have a strong effect solely because it correlates with the specificity of the features. This is why I run a second regression analysis leaving the agreement of the labeling and using the remaining four variables as independent variables (i.e. canonicity, number of texts, number of authors and specificity of the features). By doing this, I am attempting to predict the classification results with one fewer data point for each category, therefore expecting a lower result. However, this analysis yields a higher R^2 of 0.63 (p-value of F-statistic < 0.01). The results of the regression analysis improve when one of the correlating variables is ignored.

An interesting fact is that some of these five variables are not based on the text and are easy to obtain without digitization: canonicity and number of authors. This means that I could have predicted to a certain degree how high the results of classification would be, even before having the actual texts. When running the regression with only these two variables, the R^2 value is 0.48 (p-value of F-statistic < 0.01), which is a rather high result when considering the simplicity of the data used.

7.2.9 Conclusions

In any paper on computational analysis of genre, it can always be observed that some categories achieve a much higher result than others. I have conducted a series of hypotheses tests to try and explain this variation and find the possible reasons for it. In each instance, I have measured the correlation between the classification results of the subgenre and a second variable. Five of these variables are statistically associated with the classification results: the agreement in the sources, canonicity, number of texts per subgenre, and especially number of authors, and the specificity of their features. When regression analyses are run, the results account for the majority of the variation of the classification results, up to 0.63 R^2. Subgenres are not more difficult to predict because their defining features are not expressed at the linguistic surface, but rather because they contain many texts written by many authors, because their features are not distinctive enough to separate them from other categories, and these tendto be the same texts that are difficult for humans to classify.

8. Discussion of Tripartite Graph for Genre

8. Discussion of Tripartite Graph for Genre

8.1 Introduction

The previous chapters of this research study have focused on a single aspect of genres, either in summarizing previous research, presenting data, or analyzing specific questions. In contrast, the goal of this chapter is to combine the most important findings into a single model for genre. As Raible states in his article about literary genres:

> We work neither in the area of our sensory perception, nor in what we call originals, which in their diversity would not be conceivable, but rather with models of these originals. A model, like a map of a city as opposed to the original "city," is created through reproduction and reduction. Certain features from the original "city" will be emphasized as relevant in the map, others disappear. (Raible 1980, 322, my translation).

Following this author, my goal in this chapter is to present not the city, but a map of the city; I do not represent the "genres" here, but a model for them, explaining exactly how this is composed and what can it be used for. This theoretical model for genre unifies core ideas of the family resemblance and the prototype theory (discussed in Chapter 2.3), which have been already mentioned in the works of scholars working on genre (Fricke 2010a; Santini 2011; Hempfer 2014; Underwood 2016; Henny-Krahmer et al. 2018; Schröter 2019).

However, what are the characteristics that a scientific model (a reduced representation of an analyzed object) should fulfill? The philosopher of science Michael Weisberg (cited by Zweig 2016, 366) distinguishes two main components: the structure (or formalization) of the model (2013, 24–31) and the *construal* component (39–42). In Section 8.3 I will argue for graphs as the formalization of this model. Related to the construal component of a scientific model, Weisberg differentiates three parts:

1. The *assignment*: the mapping between the elements of the model and the real object.
2. The *intended scope*: the application of the model.
3. The *fidelity criteria*: measurable principles that should answer whether the model is a good representation of the complex system.

Following Weisberg, the model presented here is composed as follows:

1. The *assignment* of the model will be based on seven observations made in the different chapters of this book, which I will summarize in Section 8.2. These observations are operationalized in the components of the genres (features, instances and categories, see Section 2.3.2 for a theoretical discussion) and their interaction. This will be assembled in Section 8.3.
2. The *intended scope* of the model can be decomposed in four aspects: First, to fit several observations about the entire corpus into a single model. Second, to reproduce several observed effects, such as the variance of the classification results (discussed in Chapters 7.1 and 7.2). Third, to quantify and operationalize, through the mathematical properties of the networks, certain expectations about genres, particularly the macro-model of subgenres (Is a subgenre another type of subgenre? Are they merely similar? Do they overlap? See Section 2.3.3 for a theoretical overview). This will be observed in Section 8.6 Ultimately, the model will be used as the basis for empirical descriptions of subgenres (Section 8.7 and Appendix).
3. The *fidelity criteria* of the model will be presented in Section 8.5 as an evaluation of whether the model can reproduce the similarity and the classification results with statistical significance.

8.2 Characteristics of the Genres

To construct this model, I follow Wittgenstein's inductive suggestion of observing the characteristics of the analyzed phenomenon: "Don't think, but look!" (Wittgenstein and Schulte 2013, 36e). In this publication, I observe the following aspects relating to subgenres:

1. Several human agents (such as authors, printing houses, libraries, readers, researchers) assign genre labels to texts. The way these are encoded

has been presented in Chapter 3.2, compared in Chapter 5.1, and closely analyzed in Chapters 5.2 and 5.3. In addition, in Chapter 6.2 I have used clustering techniques to discover two hypothetical subgenres hidden until now.

2. A text can belong to any number of genres: one, several, or even none, as was shown in Chapter 5.1. This fact is at the core of the zero-to-multi genre classification scheme of Santini (2011).
3. Some texts belong more clearly to one genre than to others. This can be observed in different ways: in the recurrent mentioning of specific works as classic examples of a category by previous researchers (see Chapter 2.1), in the fact that some texts are related to some categories by a larger proportion of human sources (Chapter 5.1), or in the probabilities assigned by algorithms (Section 7.1.6). In other words, the prototype theory (Rosch 1975) can describe how texts participate in the categories.
4. Texts can be described using their specific internal features, as shown for example in Chapter 4.2. In some texts, specific linguistic, textual, or literary features are more dominant than in other texts.
5. These internal features can be used to classify texts into genres. They can be of a linguistic (Chapter 4.1 and Section 7.1.3) or literary nature (Chapter 3.2), or a combination of both (Section 7.1.5). The classification results are clearly better than what would be expected in a random process, as seen in Chapters 6.1 and 7.1. In other words, internal features do play an important role in the genres. This is the premise for the computational analysis of genres and subgenres, summarized in Chapter 2.2.
6. However, the results of the classification are rarely perfect, both in my own and previous research. There is no evidence that the texts of a category have to share a set of necessary and sufficient conditions (Chapter 7.1), as the scholastic model requires (Section 2.3.2.1). The features that are overrepresented in a novel could be specific or not specific to their category, or could even be specific cues for other categories. This is the core of the prototype family model (Wittgenstein and Schulte 2013, discussed in Section 2.3.2.4), in which a member of a family does not have to share the traits of the family and may actually show some traits that are related to other families.
7. Genres are not isolated phenomena. Some genres show greater similarity than others, for example naturalist and realist novels. This can be observed in previous research, which tends to relate specific categories like adventure and historical novels (see Chapter 2.1.). Certain hypothetical similar-

ities can be observed in the confusion matrix of the results of the multi-class classification carried out in Section 7.1.2. How these relations can be measured or whether some categories are sub-categories of others as part of a taxonomy (Section 2.3.3.1), a gradual model (Petersen 1944, see Section 2.3.3.3), or just similarity still needs to be addressed.

8. Some categories achieve higher classification results, as observed in Chapters 6.2 and 7.1, regardless of whether the features applied were of a linguistic or literary nature, or a combination (Section 7.1.5).
9. This variance in the classification results can be predicted to a certain degree based on the agreement in the sources, the canonicity of the works, the number of texts per subgenre, the number of authors, and the specificity of their features, as observed in Chapter 7.2.
10. In Chapter 2.1, I have collected a series of descriptions of genres based on previous research. These often contain:
    a. Information about their total extension (the number of texts populating it) and the most prototypical cases.
    b. Their intension in terms of specific literary and linguistic (with a special interest in semantics) patterns.
    c. Their relation towards other genres.

The goal of this chapter is to find a theoretical and computational model that can explicitly represent all these observations. This should be the base for a visualization and an interpretation of the categories analyzed. In other words, it should constitute a reduced representation of the genres that allows a better understanding of what genres are.

8.3 Assembling the Graph Model for Genre

In this section, the assignment of the model (following Weisberg's terminology) is undertaken. I build up the assignment of the genres step-by-step, either by adding new data or new relations. The fundamental form of this model is a graph which is currently used in several research areas due to its capacity in representing scientific models (Zweig 2016, 366). There are several reasons for using this formalization: its flexibility, scalability, and its mathematical properties (such as the fact that it permits calculation of centrality, distances, or communities). In addition, it is implicitly mentioned in Wittgenstein's family resemblance model. In several DH areas, graphs have been extensively applied to show stylometric similarities between texts or to formalize networks of literary characters. However, they often lack a formal evaluation. In this section, I give exact information about the composition of the edges and in the following section I will evaluate the model.

In order to achieve a clearer presentation, I start with relatively few genres and texts, increasing the number until all subgenres are fed into the model. Besides, each step will be presented with a visualization of the graph. It is necessary to consider that these illustrations are merely one possible visualization of the underlying model, which are intended to serve as a visual aid for the reader.

The first of the ten observed characteristics listed in the previous section states that texts can be grouped into genres. These relations can be formalized in a bipartite graph, which is a graph "that can be split in two parts such that all known relationships are only between entities from different parts" (Zweig 2016, 8). In my case, the bipartite graph is composed of two partitions of nodes: texts (shown with the color green in following illustration) and genres (shown with the color purple). The nodes of both partitions are connected when any institution has labeled the texts in a category. For the visualization of Figure 102, I only consider three subgenres – adventure, historical, and war novel – each of them associated with 25 texts.

In Figure 102, each subgenre has several texts associated with it, and these are not isolated. Three novels have been labeled both as adventure and war novel. This same number joins war and historical novels, while four are labeled as both historical and adventure. In addition, *Zalacaín el aventurero* belongs to all the three subgenres and is plotted in the center of the network. The illustration shows that the second observation of the list is valid: A text can belong to any number of categories, from zero to *n*. Potentially, a text can belong to all subgenres, or to none, as is the case for some novels of the corpus (Section 5.1.8), which will be discussed in Section 8.6.

In the graph of Figure 102, the edges represent the third observation: Some texts belong more clearly to one genre than others. To quantify this, I use the proportion of sources (publishers, literary scholars, readers, CLiGS annotation, as explained in Chapter 5.1). To illustrate this better, the following illustration retains the two types of nodes (texts in green, genres in purple), but changes the perspective. In Figure 103, I look at three specific novels that were included in the previous graph: *La media noche* by Valle-Inclán, *Zalacaín el aventurero* by Baroja, and *Paz en la guerra* by Unamuno.

Figure 102: Bipartite graph with three subgenre-labels and their texts

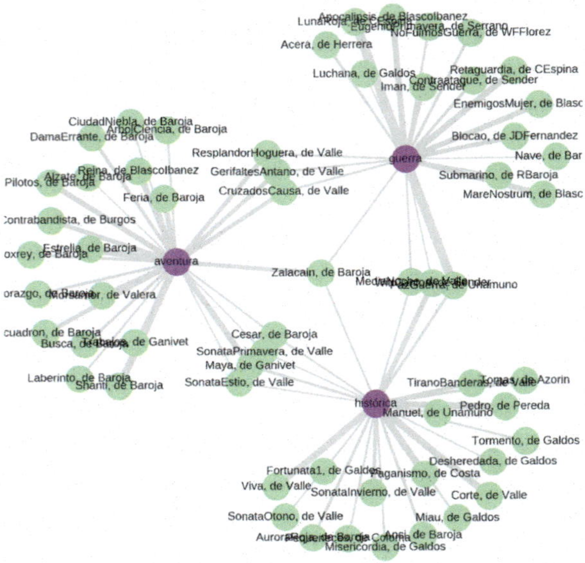

The novel by Unamuno (on the right of Figure 103) is labeled as a war novel by all sources, and therefore is a good representative of the genre. This gives this edge a value of 100% or a proportion of one. In addition, a third of the sources have also assigned the labels historical and modernist novel to this text. The text also belongs to these categories, but their connections are not so strong (33% or a proportion of 0.33). The quantification of the participation of a text in a genre is expressed as a weight of the edges, which is visualized as thickness. The three novels are connected by the labels war and historical novel, and these appear in the middle of the figure. The thickest edge in the graph is that connecting *Paz en la guerra* and war novel, because, as explained, all sources applied this label to this text. *Zalacaín el aventurero* is connected to five subgenres in total, but its thickest edge is to the adventure novel, a label that half of the sources assigned to this text. This gradual participation has been already used and compared to the probabilities of a classifier (Section

Figure 103: Bipartite graph with three novels and their subgenre-labels

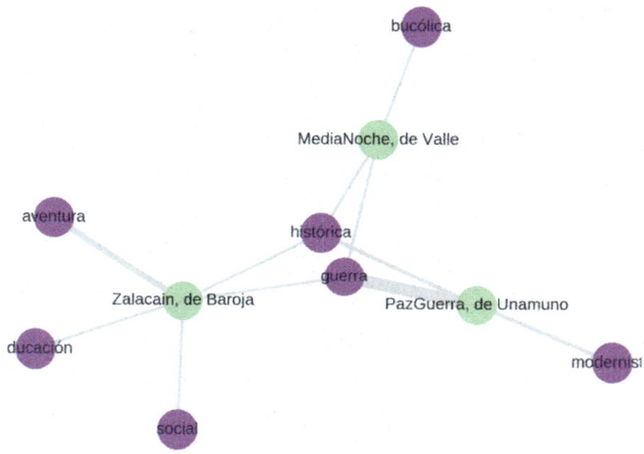

7.1.6). The weighted edges formalize the main idea of the prototypes in which an instance does not belong to a group in categorical terms, but rather in terms of degree.

To operationalize this prototypicality, I have used one of the possible operationalizations. However, at least two other operationalizations of the prototypicality of genres are possible. The first is to adopt a more historical perspective and consider the center of the prototype of the works that were published first or that had a greater influence in later works (Henny-Krahmer et al. 2018). The second is to obtain qualitative labels from annotators in which they can express the subgenres to which the text belongs and how clearly the text belongs to this subgenre (discussed in Section 7.1.6). The option chosen here is coherent with the cross-sectional perspective using several already existing sources.

The fourth observation of genres states that texts can be described by their specific internal features. For now, the model has only considered two types of instances: genre categories (expressed through the labels) and texts. Now, the third main element is added: internal features (introduced in Chapters 3.2 and 4.1, and evaluated in Chapter 6.1 and Section 7.1.5).

But, how can it be determined whether a feature is distinctive to a text? Several traditions formalize distinctiveness using different metrics, such as weights of features of classifiers in Machine Learning, Zeta values in stylometry, log-likelihood in Linguistics, z-scores in Statistics, etc. I use z-scores (described in depth in 4.2.2.6.) for several reasons:

1. A z-score is a standard and simple measure from Statistics.
2. It does not have any parameters.
3. Its calculation is deterministic (meaning that none of the steps of its calculation uses randomness).
4. The scores are expressed in standard deviations, which is a more intuitive metric than the other measurements.
5. These are not only a normalization of the data, but can be understood as a statistical test for whether a feature is overrepresented in an instance in comparison to the rest of the data set.

In any case, other numerical metrics can be applied if other traditions or arguments are preferred.

The texts mentioned above can be described with those features that have a high z-score.[1] This can be formalized in a bipartite graph, shown in Figure 104, composed of two partitions of nodes: features (shown in the illustration as blue nodes) and texts (green). Two nodes of both partitions are connected when their z-scores are high enough, in other words, over a given threshold (for example higher than 1.5 standard deviations, which also keeps the number of features acceptable for the size of the following visualizations). The edge is weighted with the exact z-score, which is shown as the thickness. To reinforce a later interpretation of this model and its application for descriptions, I only use relatively abstract features, such as textual features (number of verses, proportion of direct speech), semantic features (from WordNet and the dictionary by María Moliner), grammatical annotation, and literary metadata.

The three novels of Figure 104 show distinctive features: Cues that are overrepresented in these texts in comparison with the rest of the corpus. In other words, these are features that have higher z-scores in these texts than

1 The features with negative z-scores will be discussed in Section 8.8.

Figure 104: Bipartite graph with three novels and their specific features

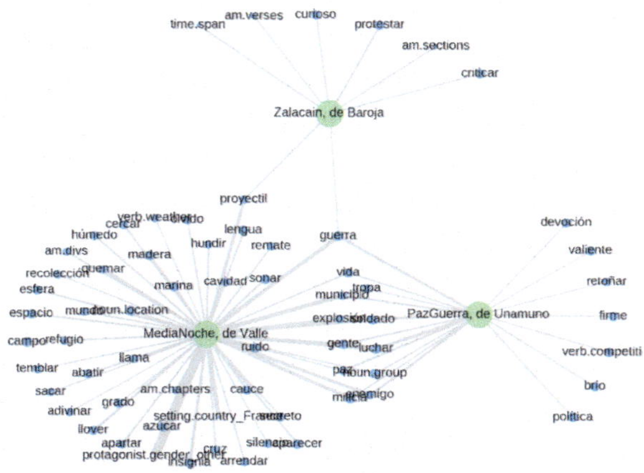

for the defined threshold. One of the texts, *La media noche* (on the left in the figure), has more distinctive features than the rest, meaning that it shows many particularities (mainly semantic) in comparison to the rest of the corpus.

A number of the features are distinctive for not only one, but for two or three novels, i.e. shared particularities. For example, the two novels at the bottom of the previous figure, *La media noche* and *Paz en la Guerra*, share many distinctive semantic fields about life, troops, people, fighting, peace, enemies, etc. On the left, *Zalacaín el aventurero* shares vocabulary about projectiles with *La media noche*, while on the right, it does not share any other distinctive vocabulary with *Paz en la guerra*. These three war novels have a single semantic field in common: vocabulary about war, which appears in the middle of the figure.

Even in these cases, the features can be more characteristic for one novel than for another. This difference is kept in the edges through the z-scores, which are visualized through the thickness of the edge. For example, the edge between the semantic feature of war (in the middle of the network) for the novels *La media noche* (z-score of 4.41) or *Paz en la guerra* (3.13) is thicker than that between either of these novels and *Zalacaín el aventurero* (1.56).

The fifth observation points out that it is not only texts that have distinctive features, but also genres, and this is the basis for classifying results over a baseline of randomness. In the previous figures, graphs always contained texts, combining them with either genres or features. In contrast, the following graph does not include novels, and only the categories (purple) and features (blue) remain. For this, I first gather all novels that are part of each category. From here, I calculate the mean value for each feature. Finally, I again calculate z-scores for each subgenre, obtaining the features that are distinctive not for a specific text, but for the entire group of texts, i.e. the specific linguistic or literary characteristics for the subgenre. The exact steps can be observed in the Jupyter Notebook.

Figure 105: Bipartite graph with three subgenres and their specific features

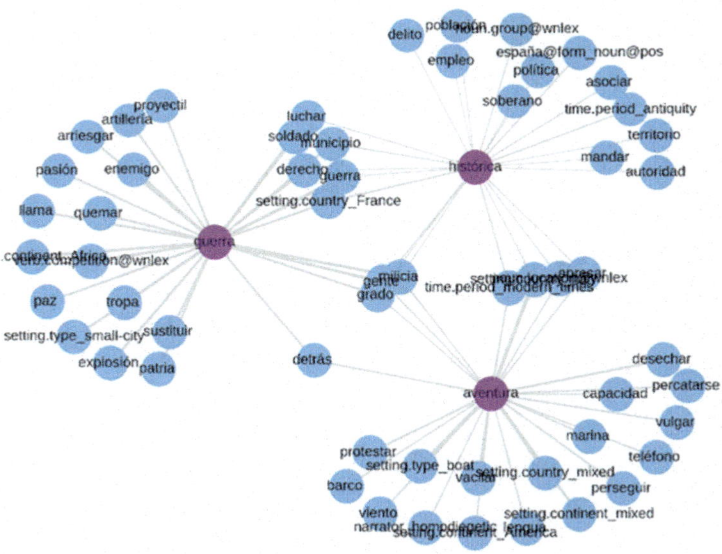

The three subgenres in Figure 105 have many features that are specific to each subgenre: vocabulary about passion and peace for the war novel, a homodiegetic narrator and settings in a boat for the adventure novel, settings in antiquity and vocabulary about sovereignty for historical novels, to mention a couple of examples for each category. But they also share a number of features. Historical and adventure novels share geographical (Italy) and chronological (modern times) settings. Historical and war novels share France as a typical setting, as well as vocabulary about soldiers, war, or fighting. The three subgenres share semantic features about militia, people, and rank (the three blue nodes in the middle). All these features are distinctive to a different degree for each category. The z-score for militia in war novels is higher than for the other two, which can be seen in the thickness of the edges. This means that subgenres share features to different degrees.

The sixth observation states that perfect classification is very rare, which leads to the idea that the texts do not hold a set of necessary and sufficient conditions to be considered part of a genre. If this was the case, computational methods working on complex features would identify these conditions and achieve perfect results. Texts only have to show a certain number of features to belong to a genre, just as people do not have to share all the traits to belong to a family.[2] To observe this, the three nodes are added in Figure 106 to a single tripartite graph of texts (green), features (blue), and genres (purple). Each edge is weighted as previously explained.

Figure 106: Tripartite graph with three subgenres, their texts and features

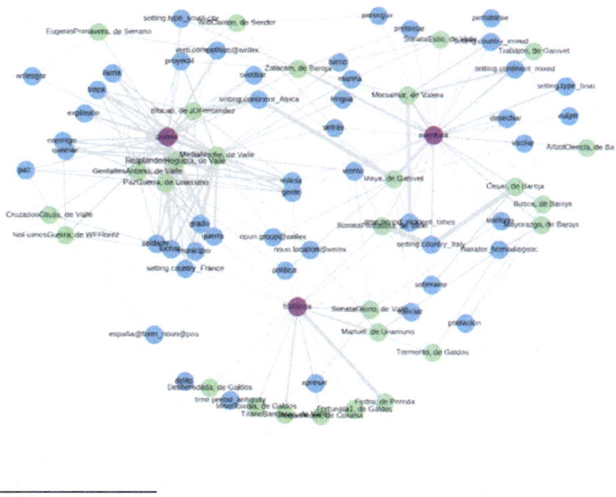

2 Or to participate in social institutions, in the terminology of Wellek and Warren (1956), as opposed to Todorov's or Voßkamp's. See Section 2.3.2.3.

The model of Figure 106 and the subsequent visualization connects the three main components of the analysis of genres. This visualization illustrates the lack of necessary and sufficient conditions, and instead shows a criss-cross of shared features. For example, vocabulary about language is a specific feature of adventure novels. However, it is also a distinctive feature of the text *La media noche*, even though it is not part of the adventure genre. It belongs, among other categories, to war novels, sharing with it many semantic features, such as vocabulary about soldiers, peace, or fighting. In a sense, this is a visualization of the criss-crossed characteristics described by Wittgenstein in the family resemblance model or Wellek and Warren's social instituions. In addition, the model describes the participation of the instances in the subgenres not in categorical terms, but rather in ordinal terms, as in the prototype theory. Through this, the model unifies elements of the family resemblance and prototype theory into a single formal model.

Until this point, the several steps of this section have assigned and delivered new data to the model. The four observations that will follow are an essential part of the scope of this model (following Weisberg's terminology 2013). From now on, I do not deliver new kinds of data to the model, I just add more examples of categories, features, and texts. The model is now expected to either reproduce the rest of the observations, or allow responding aspects that have not found a proper quantification.

The seventh observation states that some genres are more similar to one another than to other genres. Similarity can be understood as the number of shared features and texts across genres. Therefore, two genres that are more similar would share more connections to features and texts and this can be visualized as closed nodes in the illustration.[3] To observe this more clearly, in Figure 107 I add a subgenre to the network, the dialogue novel, which is very dissimilar to the categories analyzed until now in this chapter.

War, adventure, and historical novels share more features and texts between them, and therefore Figure 107 shows them closer together in the lower section. These three genres have a shared continuity of nodes of texts or features. In contrast, there is a visible gap of features and texts between these three subgenres and the dialogue novel at the top. This gap is caused by the lack of shared features and texts between this subgenre and the rest.

3 The layout algorithm effects only the visualization and not the evaluation that will be carried out in the following sections. This will be discussed in more detail in the sections regarding evaluation and limitations.

Figure 107: Tripartite graph with four subgenres, their texts and features

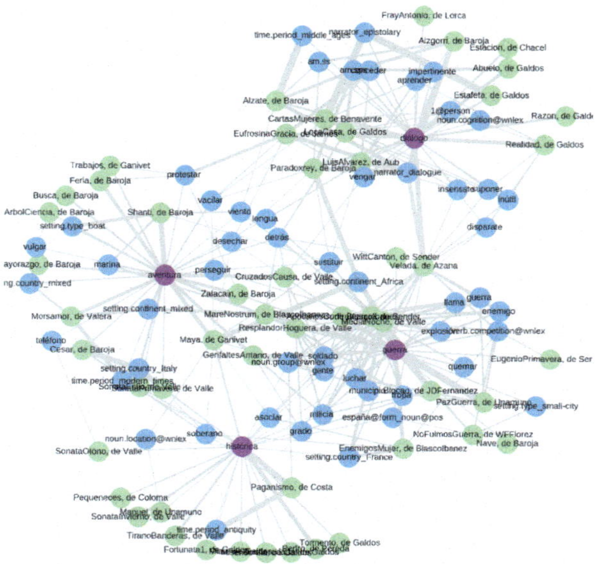

More specifically, the texts labeled as dialogue novels rarely participate in any other genre, they tend to participate only in this category. In addition, this atypical type of novel does share some features with other novels, such as vocabulary about cognition, disorientation, or numerous divisions in text.[4] But actually, the majority of the features of this category are exclusive, i.e. they are not shared with any other nodes – among others, the grammatical information about the first person, narrators in epistolary style, the em dash, the TEI element *sp*, or vocabulary about optics, to learn, to attenuate, to suppose, or to revenge. In the previous figure, these nodes pull the dialogue subgenre out of the rest of the nodes of the graph, which can be observed in the mentioned gap between the nodes around the dialogue category and the rest of

4 These divisions are textual units that contain chapters. The exact taxonomy about the kind of encoded units in the novel is found in Section 3.1.8.

the network. In fact, none of the specific features of this genre are shared with any other of the three categories. In terms of graph theory, the node of the dialogue novel does not have any common neighbor with the three others subgenres. In contrast, the other three do have some common neighbors (shared features and texts): between 10% and 27%. This point will be an object of closer evaluation in Section 8.5.2.

The eighth observation declares that the classification results typically show variance: Dialogue novels are better classified than genres like the social novel. The ninth observation contains the reason for this variance: canonicity of the genres, number of authors, agreement on the labels, and specificity of the features. This last aspect is reproduced in the model through its centrality. The genres that are easily recognized are those that are being pulled out of the network. This is what happens with the dialogue novel, which is normally almost perfectly classified by classification algorithms (Section 6.1.4 and Chapter 7.1). This aspect will be formally evaluated in Section 8.5.1.

Finally, the tenth observation states that researchers have an interest in describing the characteristics of the genres. The three components mentioned are already formally part of the model. The extension of the genre is described through the number of edges to the texts, and the most prototypical cases are the ones with a larger proportion of sources assigning them. The intension of the genre can be summarized through its most distinctive features. Lastly, the similarity of the genres can be formalized through the number of shared features. In Section 8.7 I will show how this can be applied to a selection of subgenres, while the Appendix contains description for all the 26 analyzed subgenres of the novel.

8.4 The Complete Tripartite Graph Model of Genre: Principles

In the inductive process of the previous section, a theoretical model of genre has been composed, which can be summarized in the following six principles:

1. The model contains three partitions of nodes: categories-labels (subgenres), features (linguistic and literary), and instances (texts).
2. Each node of each partition can be connected to any number (from zero to *n*) of nodes from the two other partitions (edges label-text, text-feature, label-feature).
3. The edges are weighted:

a. Between text and feature: How specific is the feature for the text (expressed in z-scores)?
b. Between subgenre and feature: How specific is the feature for the subgenre (expressed in z-scores)?
c. Between subgenre and text: What is the proportion of sources relating the text to the subgenre?

These six points respond to the main questions about genres mentioned at the beginning of Chapter 2.3, such as whether texts can belong to several subgenres, whether they do this in discrete or gradual terms, whether texts without subgenres are possible, etc.

Until now, the model has only been fed with a reduced number of subgenres. Potentially, the model can contain all categories, instances, and features, creating a graph with thousands of nodes. This causes problems, not only for the visualization, but also for the question of whether all extracted features should be part of the model or if they duplicate information (as seen in the parameter analysis of the classification and clustering in Sections 6.1.4 and 6.2.4). In the following visualization of the graph, the model contains all subgenres, and these are associated with 20 distinctive features and their five most representative texts.

The visualization of the graph[6] in Figure 108 contains more than 400 nodes from three partitions, and almost 700 connections between them, each of them weighted. This means that there are thousands of categorical and numerical values being plotted simultaneously. The visualization of the graph allows the reader to remain at a distant reading level, observing only the macromodel of the subgenres, such as their relations to other categories. But it also makes it possible to view the more in-depth details of any nodes (features, subgenres, and texts) and their connection to the other elements, showing the assignment between subgenres and texts, or the specificity of features for both novels and subgenres. However, perhaps there is too much information. Some labels are difficult to read because they overlap, or the origin and ending of many edges is not clear. To solve this, individual networks for each subgenre as in Figure 112 can be observed in the Jupyter Notebook.
The visualization of this graph in Figure 108 can be understood as a visual

5 The sizes of the nodes will be explained in the last paragraphs of the Section 8.5.1.
6 The original figure can be found in https://github.com/cligs/scripts-ne/blob/master/visualizations/thesis/figure_108.png.

Figure 108: Tripartite graph with all subgenres, five of their texts, and 20 most distinctive features.[5]

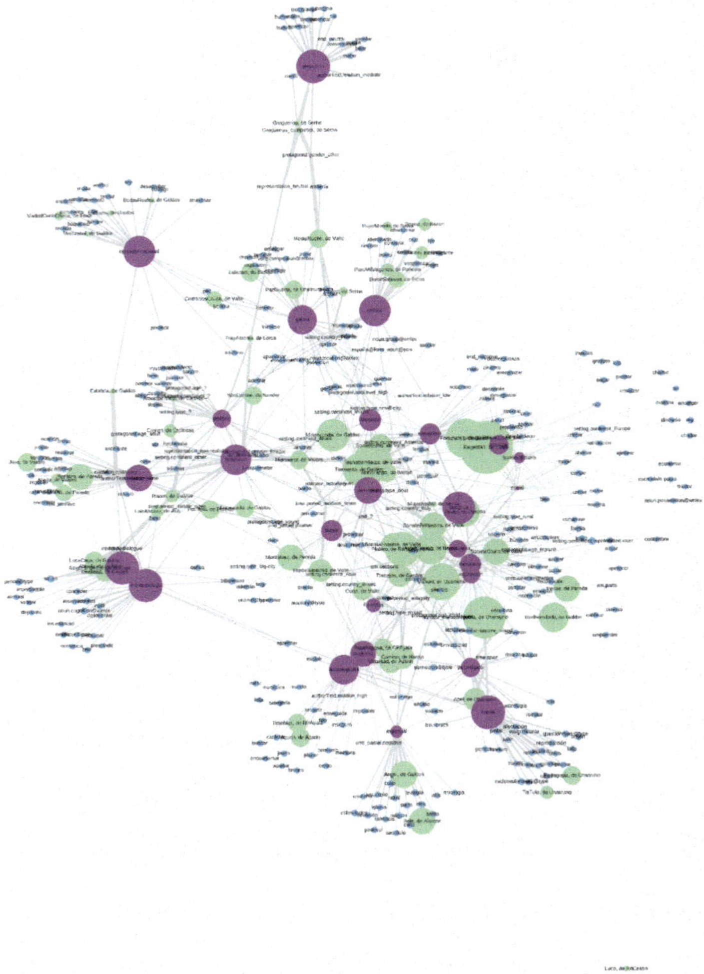

summary of the entire book. It is the plot of a theoretical model for genre (as discussed in Chapter 2.3), through digital means (Chapter 2.2) using texts from the Spanish literature of the *silver age* (Chapter 2.1) which is based on the corpus (explained in Chapter 3.1 and filtered in Chapter 3.3) explicitly showing the metadata (Chapters 3.2) and linguistic annotation (described in 4.1, transformed in Chapter 4.2, and evaluated in Chapter 6.1), with the genres emerging through the comparison of the sources (in Chapters 5.1, 5.2, and 5.3) or clustering techniques (Chapter 6.2), showing the most important results of the classification (Chapter 7.1) and, as I will evaluate in the next paragraphs, the factors involved in this variance (Chapter 7.2).

8.5 Evaluation and Interpretation

Due to their spectacular visual aspect and scientific charm, networks are highly popular in many fields, particularly in DH. However, several works that have evaluated the use of networks for capturing literary information have shown that they are far less successful than expected (Hettinger et al. 2016; Krautter et al. 2018; Santa María, Calvo Tello, and Jiménez 2020). These papers have shown that the previous use and interpretation of the networks could have been misleading. The information that the community thought the networks were bringing does not seem to be there. This is why, before I begin with interpretation of the network, it needs to be evaluated.

Following Weisberg's terminology (2013), it is necessary to assess the fidelity criteria of the model. In Section 8.3 I have stated that the first six observations are part of the assignment of the model, while the last four should be reproduced or enabled by the model. Trying to measure the fidelity of the first six observations would lead to circular arguments. For example, the first observation states that texts are grouped into genres and the information about the labels of the texts is passed on to the model. Since the labels are already part of the model, trying to evaluate them would be circular.

In contrast, the last four observations are well suited to the evaluation, since they have not been delivered to the model. For example, the last observation states that genres can be described, and expects the model to supply these. These descriptions could be compared to previous research that has described these genres. However, in order to obtain comparisons of scientific value, several aspects of the descriptions should be controlled, such as their language, style, treated features, analyzed epoch, or the period when it was produced. Besides, it would be necessary to evaluate the comparison itself: How can the researcher be sure that the method recognizes that two different descriptions are written differently but highlight the same basic information? Still, in this chapter, a series of descriptions will be presented and their acceptability and limitations discussed.

For these reasons, I evaluate the seventh, eighth and ninth observations of the genres in following section, using two mathematical characteristics of the graphs: centrality and distance of the subgenres.

8.5.1 Evaluation of Centrality

An aspect that is more suitable for a formal evaluation is the classification results. In Section 8.3, I have suggested that the genres that have more distinctive features (specific features not shared with other genres) are being pulled out of the network, as in the case of the dialogue novels, which is a genre that yields very high results in the classification. From this, the hypothesis follows that the genres with low results should be at the center of the network, while those with high results should be placed in the periphery.[7] There are several ways in which the centrality of nodes in a graph can be measured. My interest is not in measuring how many edges each node has, but rather in capturing whether the neighbors of the nodes (novels and features) are isolated (as is the case for the peripheral nodes) or linked to other nodes (which is expected in the central nodes). This is what the eigenvector centrality measures (Bonacich 1987), and is defined as follows: "the centrality of a node should be the sum of the centralities of its neighbors, normalized by some factor λ" (Zweig 2016, 248). This centrality measure has already been applied to measure centralities in bipartite graphs (Faust 1997), and from this point, when I refer to centrality in the graph, I refer to this operationalization. In the previous graph, subgenres like *greguerías, episodio nacional,* or erotic novels stand clearly in the periphery of the graph (observed with several layout algorithms), and they also have some of the lowest eigenvector centrality values. In other words, the perceived centrality in the figure correlates strongly with the eigenvector centralities.[8] The exact values for all subgenres are shown in Figure 109.

---

7 I use the term periphery merely in contrast to centrality: a non-central node is a peripheral node.

8 This is not the case for formalizations such as betweenness centrality. If the eigenvector and the betweenness centralities of the previous network are measured, it is clear that some subgenres that are visibly in the periphery of the network do not show a low betweenness centrality, although they do show a low eigenvector centrality value. For example, in the previous plot, the greguerías shows an outlying peripheral position, which correlates with a very low eigenvector centrality, while its betweenness centrality is in the middle range.

Figure 109: Eigenvector centrality values for each subgenre

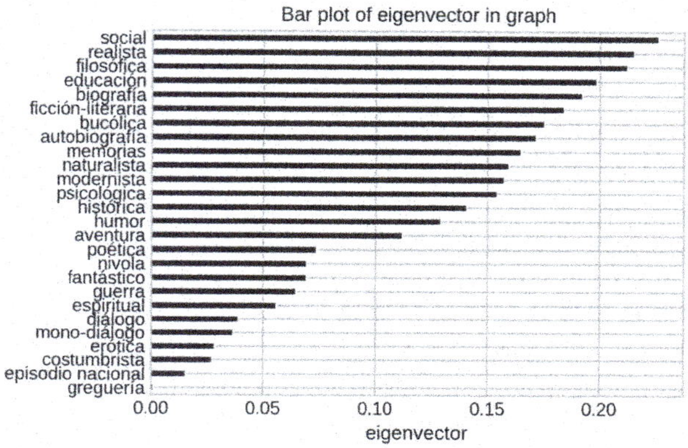

The subgenres with a higher eigenvector centrality (social, realist, philosophic, educational novel) are more central in the graph, while the ones with the lowest values (*greguería, episodio nacional, costumbrist,* or erotic novels) are peripheral.

Each subgenre now has two numerical values: the centrality in the network and the results in the classification (obtained in Section 7.1.5). Now the question is whether they correlate, and if so, to what degree. The previous network shows a strong negative correlation (r = -0.65***) between these variables. The higher the results of the classification, the lower the eigenvector centrality, the less central the genre is in the graph.

Even when this positive evaluation is a first step to sustain the interpretation, there are at least two problems that need to be observed more closely. The first problem involves the parameters of the model: What if more features or texts are taken into account than those of the previous figure? In other words, what is the impact of the parameters of the model in this correlation? Does the statistical effect described in the previous paragraph depend on pure luck in tuning the parameters?

The main parameter of the model is the number of nodes in each partition, particularly texts and features. The extension of each partition can be defined in two ways: either by a fixed number of texts and features per partition, or by defining how strong the association to the genre has to be. For example, in Figure 104, a fixed number of features per text was not defined, but rather that the features should have z-scores over 1.5 standard deviations. This means that one text (*La media Noche*) shows a much larger number of overrepresented features than the other two novels. Similarly, it can be observed how overrepresented the features need to be in relation to the categories. All these possibilities are evaluated to monitor the impact of using different numbers of nodes in the three partitions. The details of the tests can be seen in the Jupyter Notebooks and their results show that the number of texts per genre is the factor with greater influence. Figure 110 shows the correlation between the centrality and the classification results on the vertical axis, while the horizontal axis shows a selection of the number of nodes in the partition of texts.

Figure 110: Effect of the number of texts in correlation to centrality and classification results

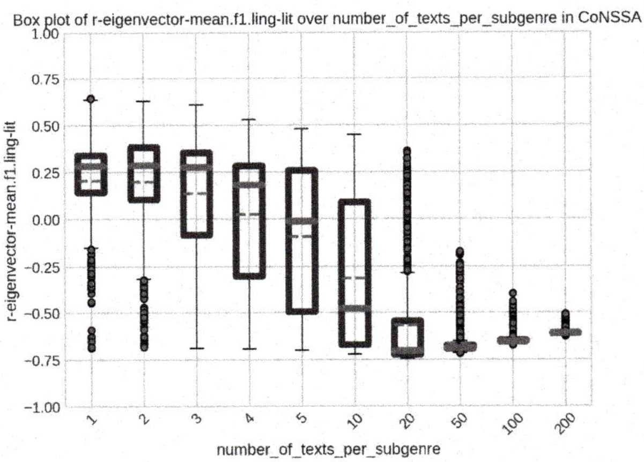

When only a few texts are placed in the network (between one and five), the medians of the correlation in Figure 110 tend to be very weak. In other words, with few texts, the subgenres are not distributed in the network as stated previously. However, when more texts enter the partition, the correlations tend to be negative and strong, and the variance is reduced (the box plots on the right are flat). This means that the evaluated characteristics of the model do not appear only with a lucky selection of the parameters, but in general whenever numerous texts per subgenres are considered. This reinforces the quantitative distant reading approach using a larger number of novels than what is common in Literary Studies: The position of the subgenres in the network is erratic when only a few texts are considered.

The second difficulty of the entire evaluation until now relates to whether it is acceptable to measure the centrality of the nodes in a multipartite graph, even when the work of Faust shows that this can be accepted for bipartite graphs (1997). Why can it be problematic? One of the simplest measures for centrality is the degree to which the number of edges a node is connected to (Zweig 2016, 63). However, in a multipartite graph with ten nodes in each of the three partitions, a node cannot be connected to the other 29 nodes of the network, but only to the nodes of the two other partitions, i.e. to 20 nodes. For this reason, the library NetworkX contains specific functions for bipartite graphs that normalize the centrality values of each node with the size of the other partition, but not for graphs with more partitions. Applying the function without normalization would cause the centrality values to be rather low, meaning they are not able to achieve the maximum values. In other words, the range of possible values remains relatively close to zero, as observed in Figure 109, with values varying from zero to 0.25. In any case, since these values are used to calculate correlations with the classification scores, it is irrelevant that these do not cover the full theoretical span up to one.

Nevertheless, I follow the strategy to observe these categories in a simpler structure: a *one-mode projection*, i.e., a graph with only one partition (Zweig 2016, 137). In my case, the graph will now only contain subgenre nodes. I decide to follow the simplest projection in which two subgenre nodes are connected when having common neighbors, shared texts or specific features (see Zweig 2016, 137–39 for a discussion about further possibilities). Two subgenres sharing 80% of the texts and features in the tripartite graph, are connected in the one-mode projection with an edge with a value 0.8. In other words, two of the partitions of the tripartite graph (features and texts) now become the edges of this simpler one-mode projection of subgenres in Figure 111.

This network retains several characteristics to those in Figure 108, such as the peripheral position of categories like *greguerías*, dialogue, erotic novel, or *episodio nacional*. The question that needs to be answered is whether a similar effect to the tripartite graph can be observed, and that the subgenres with higher results in the classification are in the periphery. A correlation test between the eigenvector centrality of this one-mode projection and the classifi-

Figure 111: One-mode projection graph of subgenres

cation results gives a very similar result with a strong negative correlation (r = -0.61 ***). Not only the eigenvector centrality, but also other more basic operationalizations of centralities, such as degree, show very similar results in this case. Furthermore, the eigenvector centralities of the tripartite graph are very similar to the degrees and eigenvector values from the one-mode projection (with very strong correlations; for more details see the Jupyter Notebook).

These results are important because they support the interpretation of the centrality of the graph model. The central genres tend to obtain low classification results, while the peripheral ones are those with very high scores. In addition, the tripartite graph plots the major reason for the variance of results in the classification, as obtained in Chapter 7.2: the specificity of the features. The subgenres with high results in the classification tasks (the *easy genres* such as *greguerías,* dialogue, or the erotic novel, the ones that already yield perfect results with ten features, see Section 6.1.4) are peripheral in the graph because they have many distinctive features which pull them out. The subgenres with lower results (the *difficult subgenres* such as the educational and social novel) are more central because they share many features with the other categories.

Because the evaluation of the centrality is crucial, I run two further experiments trying to falsify it. First, I generate a statistical null-model of the graph using the same components, structure, and parameters. However, in this null-model, the weights of the edges are replaced with random values within the range of the graph analyzed up to this point. As expected, the centrality of the null-model does not correlate with the classification results.

In a further test, I analyze whether the composition of the corpus leads to these results. Perhaps the use of other texts could lead to opposite results. To test this, I sample the corpus 20 times, each time randomly selecting half of the texts in the CoNSSA. With each sample, the same correlation test between the centrality and the classification results is run. The results of the various samples show strong correlations (Pearson's r between -0.62 and -0.7, p-value < 0.001) close to the above reported r of -0.65.

In any case, for now this sampling process is being run with the texts of the same corpus. It is necessary to test this on other corpora and languages. This question leads to a general problem in the DH: the lack of standard corpora with rich metadata published without restrictions to which different algorithms and models can be applied. However, in a recent paper I have applied the tripartite graph model to two other well-known corpora with genre information (Calvo Tello 2020): on the one side, to classical French drama; on the other side, to the genres of the Bible such as letters, gospel, and prophetical and historical texts. The correlations between the centrality and the classification results are similar to the ones reported for the Spanish literature of the period analyzed here.

The positive results of the different tests allow for the use of concepts such as central and peripheral for genre categories in an innovative and very specific way. But this is not limited to the genres. As observed in Section 7.2.5, there is a moderate correlation between the canonicity of genre and the results in the classification. This suggests the hypothesis that the position on the graph does not only have a meaning for the categories, but also for the texts. More canonical texts should be in the center, populating genres that are difficult to classify. To evaluate this, I run a correlation between the canonicity (in pages of the MdLE) and its eigenvector centrality, which results in a strong positive correlation ($r = 0.74^{***}$), i.e. the more important to literary history a text is, the more central it is in the graph.

These correlations are strong, but not very strong, nor perfect. Some exceptional subgenres, such as the bucolic genre, are very well classified. Based on this, this category should be peripheral in the network, yet it is rather central. Likewise, the spiritual novels are in the periphery of the network, but are considered one of the hardest subgenres to classify.[9] For this reason, the actual data of canonicity and classification results are used as the size of the textual and genre nodes in Figure 108.[10] This means that the size and the positions are to a certain extent redundant. The sizes of the difficult subgenres in the center tend to be small due to their F1-scores while the sizes of canonical texts in the center are greater. The position and the size correct the exact results. Although the centrality of the bucolic subgenre gives us to understand that its classification should be low, the size of the node corrects that.

8.5.2 Evaluation of Distance

A second important aspect that can be evaluated is whether the similarity of two genres is represented through their distance on the graph. Are similar genres really closer on the visualization of the graph? As in the case for centrality, there are several ways to formalize the distance between nodes in a network. One of the most intuitive and basic ways is to simply count the number of common neighbors, the number of shared nodes. In my case, this translates into the intuitive idea of how many features and texts two subgenres share.

To formally evaluate this, it would be necessary to possess information about the perceived similarity between genres from annotators, literary scholars, or institutions. Sadly, I was not able to find such information, and the process of annotating such abstract information was not feasible.

Rather, I have observed some subgenres that are traditionally treated together by literary scholars (as described in Chapter 2.1), such as the realist and naturalist novel; the historical novel, adventure novel and war novel; or autobiographies, memoirs, and educational novels. In addition, the two hypothetical subgenres obtained by the clustering analysis in Chapter 6.2 are compared to the subgenres that overlapped to a greater extent (see Section 6.2.5): on the one side are the mono-dialogue and dialogue novels, and on the other side bucolic and modernist novels.

9 In Section 11.17 of the Appendix I will propose an explanation for this low results.

10 This means the sizes of the nodes are incomparable across sets, and comparable only within the set. In other words, the size of a novel does not relate in any respect to the size of a subgenre. However, the different sizes of the novels do represent their different levels of canonicity.

When observing the common neighbors, all these subgenres are indeed among the five closest categories to the others. In many cases, they are the closest, and if not, then less prototypical subgenres occupy the first position, but they are clearly very similar. For example, the naturalist novel is the third category with the larger number of common neighbors (shared features and texts) with the realist novel. Ahead of this, are the social novel and *literary fiction*, two categories that are arguably very similar to the realist novel.

Although a more formal evaluation could be possible, the relations observed do not falsify the hypothesis, and the distance (formalized as the number of common neighbors, shared texts and features) can be interpreted as similarity between genres. This similarity across subgenres has not been properly formalized in computational works until now due to the flat macro-model that the labels are transformed into multi-label tasks (see Sections 2.3.3.2 and 7.1.3). However, this model now offers a way of measuring it as a proportion, and allows the identification of the exact features and texts that are shared (or not) by each pair of genres.

8.5.3 Summary of Evaluation and Interpretation

In concluding the evaluation, it has been shown that there are four aspects that can be interpreted from the model:

- Central genres (measured through the eigenvector centrality) achieve low classification results in contrast to the peripheral genres.
- Central texts are more canonical in contrast to the peripheral texts.
- As a consequence, central genres are more canonical, with less canonical categories in the periphery.
- The distance between genres (measured through common neighbors, shared nodes) corresponds to a similarity between genres.

8.6 Further Properties of the Tripartite Graph Model

I have already used two mathematical properties of the graphs to evaluate the model for genres: the centrality and the common neighbors of the nodes. But there are at least two further possibilities.

The first is that the tripartite graph model is able to accommodate cases of texts without being assigned to any analyzed subgenre – *genreless texts* in

Derrida's terms and zero assignment according to Santini. In Section 5.1.8 I have mentioned that five texts remained without any information about genre after the comparison steps of the analysis. However, two of these texts have been associated to the labels coined in Chapters 5.3 and 6.2. Thus, there are still three examples of *genreless texts*:

1. *El primer loco* by de Castro, which in Figure 108 is observable as a disconnected node in the bottom right corner of the graph. In Section 3.1.3 on the description of the corpus, it has been already stated that the texts of this specific author could rather relate to previous periods of literature, as this particular situation now seems to indicate. The reason for this complete isolation is that the text is neither connected to any node of the subgenres, nor it is connected to the nodes of the features, since the novel does not have any feature with a z-score greater than the threshold. More nodes or a lower threshold would connect this novel to some features, but it would not be linked to any subgenre because no source used any of the semantic labels for this text.
2. This is actually the case for the two other novels, both by Serna.[11] They do not have any links to labels, but they do to features, more specifically to the setting of the action in France and Italy. These novels are connected to the rest of the network through the shared features with other texts and subgenres. This can be used to calculate which subgenres would be closer to them, even though no human sources have assigned them: the philosophic and historical novel for *La mujer de ámbar*, and *literary fiction* for *El chalet de rosas*. In other words, the model allows texts to be assigned both with a subgenre but also without a subgenre, and from these *genreless* texts it is possible to predict the closest subgenres, even when no label is available.

The second further possibility of the model is the detection of internal structures: groups of features, texts, and subgenres that can be identified as communities. This is a way of observing the macro-model of the genres (discussed in Section 2.3.3), evaluating whether there are groups of elements that could be identified as macro-genres, i.e. groups of subgenres that are tightly joined by their sharing of texts and features. In Chapter 5.3, I have mentioned the

---

11 Both texts are more in the center of the network. *El chalet de rosas* is between the philosophical and war novel. *La mujer de ámbar* is between the war and historical novel.

hypothesis of whether *literary fiction* should be understood not as a genre but as a group of genres (and within the realist, naturalist, and social novels) in contrast to genre literature (adventure, erotic novels). The structure of Chapter 2.1 suggests that some subgenres belong to hypothetical macro-genres: realist-naturalist, historical-adventure, historical-war novel, *nivola-greguería*, etc. In Chapter 6.2, one of the identified hypothetical subgenres (the mono-dialogue novel) could be a macro-genre grouping the dialogue and the poetic novel. Can the network sustain all these hypothetical groups of genres, these macro-genres?

There are several algorithms for detecting communities in graphs. One of the few that does not require any parameters (such as the number of communities, its minimal sizes, or the starting point) is the Girvan-Newman algorithm (Newman and Girvan 2004).[12] When this is applied to the previous graph, it results in three communities: one with the isolated text by de Castro, a second one with the *greguerías* and its specific features, and a third large community containing all the rest. The elimination of the isolated text does not affect the rest of the results. When deleting the text by de Castro, the *greguerías* are again differentiated from the rest of the network without smaller communities. If the process of deleting the smaller community is continued, the algorithm tends to isolate one subgenre and keep the rest in a very large community. After deleting the *greguerías*, the algorithm isolates the spiritual novel. Taking it one step further, it differentiates the *nivola* from the rest.

These results highlight two facts: First, the *greguerías* (presented in Section 2.1.10) are something clearly different to the rest of the categories of the network (even though they could not be related clearly to any other genre in Chapter 3.3). Second, there is no clear taxonomy for the rest of the subgenres. The algorithm does not distinguish two groups, one populated by literary genres, the other with popular literature. War and historical novels, or dialogue and mono-dialogue novels are not so close that they constitute a group of subgenres of novels. They are categories that share numerous features with specific subgenres, but each also shares features with other subgenres. The war novel is closer to the adventure novel, while the historical novel is closer

12 Of course, other community detection algorithms different to Girvan-Newman can be applied and evaluated (see Traag, Waltman, and Eck 2019 for a discussion about this specific algorithm).

to *literary fiction*. This is not well described in a hierarchical taxonomy, but rather in a network of criss-crossed nodes, as in the model.

In any case, these are the results for this corpus. In other periods or genres, it could be the case that communities would be observed. This is actually the case for the two other corpora analyzed in Calvo Tello (2020). The Bible shows two communities: one with the gospel and the letters, the other one with the rest of the biblical genres. These communities could be seen as macro-genres of the Bible which relate clearly to the historical divisions of the Old and New Testament. The classical French drama also shows two communities: the first one grouping the comedy and related labels (*comédie, comédie-ballet, farce, parade,* etc.), the second with the labels closer to the tragedy (*tragédie, tragédie-lyrique, tragicomédie, drame, opera, pastorale*). In any case, the tripartite graph model is flexible enough to fit categories that could constitute macro-genres, but these are not forced as in the taxonomic macro-model.

8.7 Using the Tripartite Graph Model of Genre for Descriptions

As for any model, this one aims to contain the most important characteristics of the object represented. A good model for genre should be able to provide the basic information for adequate descriptions. How descriptions of genres can be measured and evaluated is an open question that is not going to find an answer in this work. However, any literary scholar has certain expectations of what should be included in a definition of a genre. In this section, I present a series of *real definitions* (Pawłowski's terminology, 1980, see Section 2.3.1) of some subgenres based on empirical data. A complete list of the 26 categories can be accessed in the Appendix of this work.

In general, these descriptions provide a short paragraph summarizing the most important information of each subgenre in terms of their characteristics in the graph, extension, intension, and similarity. First, some characteristics of the categories in the graph are described, such as their centrality, specificity of the features, or canonicity. The intension is expressed through their distinctive semantic, textual, and literary features, which are all highly interpretable. These features are distinctive not only in the larger version of the corpus, CoNSSA, but also in its canonized version, CoNSSA-canon, which represents a controlled statistical population (see Section 3.1.6). This means that these features are distinctive not only for the representations of these subgenres in this corpus, but in a representative sample of canonical texts. Thereafter, the extension is expressed through the number of texts in the corpus and its best representatives (i.e. the texts to which the largest proportion of sources assigned a label). Finally, I state the similarity to other subgenres in terms of common neighbors (shared features and texts).

All this data is derived only from the tripartite graph in different ways: by the size of the nodes, the values of the edges, the number of nodes with specific characteristics, by calculating the eigenvector centralities, or the common neighbors. In other words, the following paragraphs are textual paraphrases of what has already been plotted as the entire network of subgenres, texts, and features. In this section, I describe four different subgenres: the realist novel, *literary fiction*, the historical, and the erotic novel. These are the same descriptions contained in the Appendix, which also offers definitions of all the other categories. In addition, in the repositories and Jupyter Notebooks there are visualizations of sections of the graph,[13] where each time a single subgenre can be seen, as shown in the Figure 112 for the realist novel.

In the center of the network there are three subgenres with an eigenvector centrality of 0.26. One of them is the realist novel, a subgenre that does not have many specific features (standard deviation of z-scores of 0.32). The subgenre covers 221 novels in CoNSSA, 103 novels in CoNSSA-canon, which makes it the largest subgenre in terms of instances. In general, the novels of this genre are highly canonized, with a mean of 1.5 pages per novel in the manual MdLE. The low specificity of the features explains a relatively low classification result of 0.81 mean F1-score. The features that show higher distinctiveness for this subgenre are linguistic ones, such as vocabulary about negative actions or characteristics (such as the semantic features from the dictionary by María Moliner *desobedecer, zaherir, criticar, abusar, avergonzar, descortés, grosero*, or negations), as well as words about the economy (*propiedad, pagar, retribución, prestar, lujo, lucir,* or *bien*, although this last one is highly ambivalent), health (*salud*), and words that are difficult to interpret (*impulso, comprometer*, and *ensalzar*). From a literary metadata perspective, the strongest feature is a protagonist from lower classes of the society, followed by a realistic setting in Europe (mainly in Spain), with a heterodiegetic narrator. Some of the texts that have a large proportion of sources relating them to this subgenre are by Valera (*Genio y figura…, Juanita la Larga*), Galdós (*El doctor Centeno, Miau, Lo prohibido*), Valdes (*José*), or Azaña (*El jardín de los frailes*). The most similar subgenres (in

13 https://github.com/cligs/scripts-ne/tree/master/visualizations/appendix.

Figure 112: Graph with the realist novel, five novels, and its most distinctive features

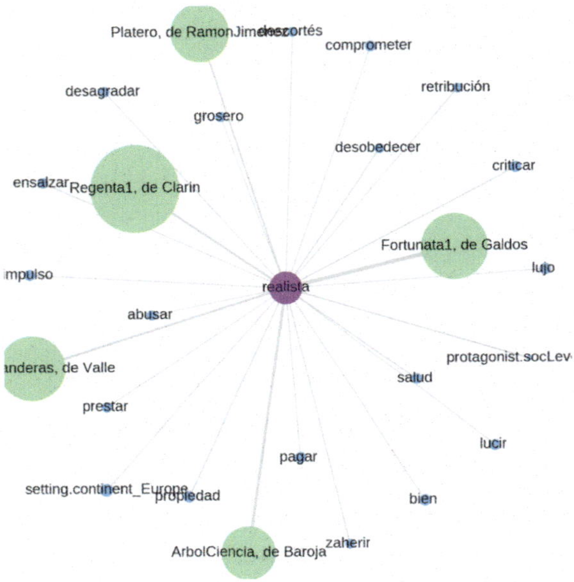

terms of shared features and texts) are the social novel (63% of features and texts shared), *literary fiction* (59%), and the naturalist novel (46%).

The same central position has *literary fiction*, a special case of the subgenre palette which has been found in a single source: the publishers on Amazon (see Chapter 5.3). This subgenre has the lowest specificity of features of all subgenres (standard deviation of z-scores of 0.28). It contains 190 novels in CoNSSA, 94 in CoNSSA-canon. The novels are, unsurprisingly, highly canonized, with 1.64 pages in the manual on average. All this explains a low classification result of 0.75 F1-score. The strongest feature of this subgenre would be a protagonist of lower classes of the society, followed at a distance by a setting in France, and, surprisingly, that the story does not reflect the author's life. From the linguistic perspective: communication (*criticar, discurso, oratoria, charlar*), money and work (*ajetrear, bien, propiedad, encargar, función, pagar*), royalty (*soberano, rey, linaje*), and other fields (*familia* and negations) are distinctive.

Publishers use this label to assign several texts by authors like Baroja (*Mala hierba, La busca*), Valle-Inclán (*Baza de espadas, La media noche*), Galdós (*El doctor Centeno, Lo prohibido*), Azorín (*Tomás Rueda*), or Unamuno (*Paz en la guerra*). The most similar subgenres are the two other most central ones: the realist (59% of shared features and texts) and the social novel (56%).

The historical novel is in the middle range of centrality of the network (eigenvector of 0.18), with a relatively low specificity of features (standard deviation of z-scores of 0.48). It contains 113 novels in CoNSSA, 59 in CoNSSA-canon. Its novels are relatively highly canonized, with 1.46 pages of the manual on average. The most distinctive feature, unsurprisingly, is a setting in the antiquity, followed by geographical settings in Italy or America, and a protagonist of the higher classes of society. An interesting aspect is that, even though the setting in Spain is not very distinctive for this subgenre, the references to Spain are. In other words, historical novels do not take place more often in Spain than the rest, but they do mention Spain by name more frequently. Besides this, vocabulary about groups (*gente, asociar, población*, and nouns about groups marked by WordNet), military and war (*milicia, soldado, luchar, grado, guerra, delito, apresar*), politics (*soberano, política, empleo, autoridad, mandar*), and places (*municipio, territorio*, and nouns referring places marked by WordNet) are specific for this subgenre. Some novels frequently associated with this category by several sources were written by Baroja (*Los últimos románticos, La feria de los discretos, La ciudad de la niebla*), Coloma (*Jeromín*), Costa (*Último día del paganismo*), Valle-Inclán (*Viva mi dueño, La corte de los milagros*), Pereda (*Pedro Sánchez*), or Sender (*Mr. Witt en el Cantón*). The most similar subgenres are *literary fiction* (33% of shared elements), followed by adventure (29%), social (22%), war, and realist novel (both with 21%).

In the periphery of the network is the erotic subgenre, with an eigenvector centrality of 0.03 and a relatively low specificity of features (standard deviation of z-scores of 0.81). This subgenre comprehends 17 novels in CoNSSA, and only four novels in CoNSSA-canon. Its texts are normally not strongly canonized (0.5 pages in the manual on average). That explains a rather high classification score of 0.96 F1-score. This category has very distinctive features (with values over two z-scores) like type of relationships (*novio, matrimonio*), sentimental verbs or actions, mainly positive (*admirar, caricia, enamorar, encantar, apasionar, abandonar*), personal qualities (*vergüenza, sincero, extravagante, feo, antipatía*), gender and sexual orientation (*mujer, afeminado*, which was a historical manner of referring to homosexuality), and others (*convertir, suelto, sal, espina*). It is interesting that the only semantic field in the top 20 about physical relations is *caricia* ('caress'), and none of them is related to sexual practices or body parts. The protagonist is typically an adult woman of the higher classes of the society. Even more distinctive is the fact that stories do not represent the author's life. Other distinctive literary metadata are urban settings, in some cases traveling through different countries, in a contemporary realistic world, with a heterodiegetic narrator. Many of these features are not explicitly mentioned by the two monographs about the erotic novels that I have summarized in Section 2.1.8. However, some of the characteristics that they mention are confirmed in this analysis, like a middle-class female protagonist, urban settings, or trips. Other like references to interior spaces, underwear, or female body parts do not stand out in my analysis. The texts most frequently assigned with this label are many by Trigo (*Del frío al fuego*, *Mi media naranja*, *En la carrera*), but also from other authors like Bacarisse (*Los terribles amores de Agliberto y Celedonia*), Picón (*Dulce y sabrosa*), or Serna (*El gran hotel*, *La viuda blanca y negra*). The closest subgenre is the comedy (10% of shared texts and features), followed by others subgenres at around 5% and 6% (*costumbrist*, poetic, naturalist, fantasy novel).

Are these four empirical definitions of subgenres adequate? They do provide an overview of several internal and external aspects, as well as their status in the computational analysis and its reception in the history of literature. However, it can be argued that there is important information missing, such as the development of the protagonist, the authors that wrote in the category, or the decade in which it was mainly produced (1880 for naturalist novel, 1900 for erotic novel, 1920 for historical novel, see Section 3.1.5). This is partially a result of the cross-sectional interest of this research, which does not try to observe the chronological development of the genres. However, some of these aspects could be fixed by using this information as features if they are considered important characteristics for the descriptions of genres.

8.8 Limitations of the Tripartite Graph Model for Genre

Despite its advantages and possibilities, the model proposed here has a series of limitations. First, I will present those relating to the formal aspect, moving on to its implementation in this corpus, and finally the visualization.

The first absent formal aspect is the fact that the authors are not explicitly a part of the model (neither which texts they wrote, nor how they labeled the texts). In the visualization, their names appear as part of the textual nodes, making this information available to the reader. Although the author is a pertinent category whose number per subgenre explains the classification results to a certain degree, it does not map the three basic elements of the classification tasks (labels, features and instances). In any case, its representation as a fourth partition of nodes with links to the text nodes is arguable. Another important category that could be appended as a further partition of nodes is the source of the label, i.e. which labels did each source use and which source labeled which texts. Nevertheless, with further partitions of nodes, the edges between the other partitions are questionable. Is it sensible to connect sources of labels and features? The addition of this type of partition would require the position of the rest of the elements to be defined.

A second limitation of the formal aspect is the fact that I have defined several formalizations, such as using z-scores for the edges (and not other distinctiveness measures, such as the weights in a classification algorithm, log-likelihood scores, or Zeta values) or the parameters of the number of nodes that should be fed to the model. All these decisions were well thought through, evaluated, and discussed, but they might not ultimately be optimal. Nevertheless, these can be understood as parameters of the model that can undergo even more exhaustive evaluations.

A limitation of the model resulting from its later visualization is the fact that it does not contain negative features, i.e. features that are distinctive for *not* appearing in a subgenre. For example, the erotic novel is typical for its *lack* of vocabulary about workers or dust, for *not* having an infant protagonist, or because the story *does not* take place in rural areas. These negative features are also used by the algorithm to correctly classify the texts. Its representation in the network could be possible in different ways: normalizing the data leaving all the features with positive values, duplicating features (one with positive values, one with negative ones), or through negative edges. This final possibility is sometimes used in graph theory, but that would make the model considerably more complex. In any case, many of the negative features correlate strongly with positive features (if the action of a novel takes place in a city, it does not take place in rural areas).

There are at least two limitations relating only to the visual aspect of the model. The most important one is that the figures cover all the subgenres which are the main research object of this work, but do not show all features or texts. This results in a reduction of the information, but only visually and not in the computational model. Actually, as I have shown in the evaluation of Section 8.5.2, the correlation between centrality and classification results becomes stronger and more stable with more texts. Besides, the use of a larger visualization or interactive formats could better fit a larger proportion of the corpus.

A second issue of the visualization is that the influence of the layout in the graphical visualization of the networks should not be ignored. In this case I have used the *spring* layout, although in the Jupyter Notebook I have also used *neato* with very similar results. However, other layouts arrange the elements differently. This needs to be considered before making statements about the network based on the visualizations. In any case, the layout only influences the visualization and not the other particularities of the graph model, such as the calculation of the centrality of the nodes, the common neighbors, or the detection of communities. Therefore, the layout does not have any influence in the entire evaluation of the model.

Finally, the model proposed here has a more general limitation, which is related to the fact that in this work I am offering the results for the period of the Spanish literature presented in Chapter 2.1. For example, I only analyze subgenres of the novel, and not several genres (plays, poems, novels, essays) and their subgenres. As mentioned before, the results in corpora of classical French drama or the Bible show very similar results (Calvo Tello 2020).

Besides, the model has been applied to only several decades of Spanish literature. Even if the data was gathered for longer periods of centuries, the current model would only show a static overview of the entire period. A further development could be the implementation of chronological networks that would show the historical development of the genres. Hypothetically, this could show how some genres become central or peripheral over time, how some genres become closer or drift further apart in specific decades or centuries, or how some features gain or lose distinctiveness.

8.9 Conclusions

This list of limitations shows that I do not consider this model as the ultimate way of describing genres. Nevertheless, having a single formalized model for genre which can be visually plotted can help to explain several characteristics of the complex system of genres in one specific period and language. It summarizes many of the most important elements (features, labels, and texts), defining exactly how they can be related. The centrality of the categories in the graph correlates with the results of the classification and the canonical status of the texts in the history of literature. It unifies aspects of other abstract models, such as the prototype theory, the family resemblance model,[14] or the zero-to-multi genre classification scheme. Furthermore, it has already been applied to real data in a relatively large number of texts, features, and categories.

Genre theory is heavily discussed in many linguistic and scholarly traditions. These interact with each other only in limited terms, partially because they are unintelligible due to different languages and jargons. Abstract models that can be formalized and visualized, such as this tripartite graph model, can help enclose, formalize, and visualize many details, and enable a more specific and fruitful discussion about the very complex phenomenon that is genre.

14 Also applicable to the social institutions of Wellek and Warren (1956), see discussion in Section 2.3.2.3.

9. Conclusion

9. Conclusion

As mentioned in the introduction, genres are constantly used either to define research objects (in academic circles) or to structure cultural products (libraries, bookstores, digital platforms). However, specific questions about the abstract principles of genres, their realization in specific periods and languages, or the particular definitions of categories find little consensus. In other words, society agrees on the utility of genres, but disagrees on how to exactly model these categories.

In this research study, I have answered in each chapter one main research question about genre. For this, I have taken literary works of the challenging period of the Spanish modernism, the so-called *silver age* (1880-1939), in which many authors explicitly tried to escape the classic genres and subgenres. Independently of the specific epoch, it has to be considered that, apart from the papers and contributions originating from the CLiGS project, Spanish literature has received little attention from quantitative approaches concerning genre. For the analysis, I have chosen a series of computational techniques, mainly supervised but also unsupervised Machine Learning methods, as well as graphs for the final model. In this conclusion, I summarize the answers obtained throughout this research study to the five main questions raised in the introduction, stating limitations and possible future paths.

I would like to remind readers that this research is highly interdisciplinary. It is rooted in the Digital Humanities, but also considers theories, data, and methodologies from Literary Studies, Computer Science, and Linguistics. Although interdisciplinarity seems highly attractive nowadays, it does come at a price: One researcher is never able to delve into the different disciplines as much as they would do when working in a single field. For this reason, I consider this book as one research step, to be continued in the best case by research performed by interdisciplinary teams.

One of the most important aspects is that this project adopted a cross-sectional and synchronic perspective on subgenres of the Spanish novel of the *silver age*. This decision was taken mainly because of the digitization state of Spanish texts, but also because of my interest in the period. On the one hand, this has the advantage that the conclusions cover many subgenres of these decades. On the other, the conclusions do not analyze the development of the genre chronologically.

The first main question of this book is how to achieve representativeness in a data set, more specifically in a literary corpus. Since the Humanities are increasingly working with larger data sets, one must realize that obtaining acceptable conclusions regarding the analyzed object requires clarity in what the data set represents. Currently, the computational approaches on genre have preferred to work with large but opportunistic corpora, rather than try to assemble mid-sized corpora that were gathered following more strict criteria. In Chapter 3.1, I have shown how the traditional method coming from Statistics (random sampling), often applied in Life Sciences and Social Sciences, cannot be applied in the Humanities in many cases. In our field, the complete population if often not available or even known, sections of the data are not digitized, or worse, they are lost. For this reason, I have not tried to achieve the largest possible population of novels (population in its statistical meaning, see Section 3.1.3 and 3.1.6), but considered smaller populations that are based on considerably stricter criteria derived from literary manuals and that I was able to obtain in their full size. In this manner, the *Corpus of Novels of the Spanish Silver Age* (CoNSSA) is designed as two nested sub-corpora: a smaller sub-corpus that maps a literary population, and a second sub-corpus that is larger but opportunistic. This double structure has provided me with the possibility of testing hypotheses in both of them (see Section 3.1.9). In this structure of corpus, any test can have one of the following outcomes:

1. First, the hypotheses can be observed only in the larger sub-corpus, meaning that the result might be based on bias related to digitization.
2. Second, the hypotheses can be observed only in the smaller sub-corpus of what literary scholars traditionally tend to consider the relevant novels of this period, meaning that the results can be observed only in canonical texts.
3. Third, the hypotheses can be observed (or falsified) in both sub-corpora, and therefore this phenomenon might not depend on the specific corpus,

meaning that it is a result that can likely be generalized for larger data sets of this literary period.

The corpus has been annotated with several layers of literary metadata and linguistic information. All these annotations were placed in a single TEI file per novel that contains all the types of data (original text, genre-labels, literary metadata, linguistic annotation), allowing the researcher to extract only the specific intended element every time. For the annotations, apart from some Natural Language Processing tools, I have applied lexicographic tools that were not meant for quantitative goals and that are not part of the tool box of Digital Humanities, as explained in Chapter 4.1. The semantic features of the catalogs of María Moliner's dictionary have shown to be of great benefit, both for the classification results (Chapter 6.2) and especially for the description of the genres (Chapter 8 and Appendix). An important conclusion therefore is that semantic features coming from dictionaries should be explored further, with special interest regarding their performance in comparison to distributional models (like topic modeling or word embeddings), both for classification results and description of categories.

A current limitation of working with Spanish literature is the culture of not sharing data openly, a tendency that is still dominant. Nevertheless, the situation is improving thanks to some institutions with a more open strategy as far as sharing data openly (e.g. the Spanish National Library) or on request (e.g. the Real Academia) is concerned, and thanks to researchers who are openly publishing their data. This research also wants to contribute in this manner, making available all the texts which are currently in public domain, extracted data for an ever larger portion of the corpus, and the metadata for the entire corpus (see further details in Section 3.1.11).

The second major goal was related to the labels and their sources. Computational approaches on genre have mainly used only a single source of labels from several possibilities: authors, publishers, first edition covers, or metadata from previously composed corpora, etc. In many cases, researchers decide to employ a source mainly because of its availability. In contrast, in this research study I have collected metadata from several sources, coming from very different institutions, such as publishers, the covers of editions held by the National Library, literary manuals, digital platforms of readers, or my own annotations. The labels originally assigned by these sources were first semantically standardized, and in a second step compared for consistency among them (steps undertaken in Chapter 5.1). This analysis has shown that the different sources share little as far as the extension of the genres is concerned (which texts populate which genre), even among similar sources such as two literary manuals. However, none of these sources is so particular that it has no similarity to the rest: They all seem to share a very basic understanding of what constitutes the genres. The results support this for the labels that have been analyzed in the rest of the work. A series of labels has shown statistical agreement across several institutions, and these constitute the basis of the genre palette of this publication. These labels were not only expressed in Spanish, but also employ the terms of a multilingual taxonomy of genre labels collected by publishers (called Thema, see Section 5.1.5). In contrast, a great number of the subgenre-labels (a total of 77 different ones) did not show any evidence that humans share a basic concept (such as *novela de tesis, moral, regeneracionista, sentimental*), at least for the literature of this period.

Two further questions about labels have been analyzed. Chapter 5.2 examines whether using the labels on the cover of the first edition leads to higher classification results than using other labels, following the hypothesis that the original labels could be more influenced by textual internal characteristics and not by external factors. The results have shown the opposite: The labels on the covers of the first editions have a stronger association with the author's name, and lead to a lower classification result than the labels from the rest of the sources. In Chapter 5.3, a specific case has been analyzed: *literary fiction*, a label that is frequently assigned by publishers along with other more accepted subgenre terms. In several tests, *literary fiction* behaved just like the rest of the subgenres. Publishers seem to understand this label as part of their genre palette and nothing could be found that proves that its characteristics differ from the other labels.

The third major goal was the identification of subgenres, that is, the use of algorithms to find subgenres that have not been considered before as such. Previous research has only observed this possibility in non-literary texts, such as Web documents. Several researchers have used unsupervised methods (clustering or dimensionality reduction) to analyze subgenres (see Chapter 2.2 for an overview). However, these methodologies have not been previously used for genre identification due to several difficulties, such as the dominance of the authorial cue in the clusters, or the open question about how many genres the process should identify. The analysis in Chapter 6.2 has shown that understanding subgenres as binary categories and consequently requiring the clustering algorithm to create binary groups, makes it possible to silence the authorial cue. In this way, two different clusters of texts were found which cannot be explained by other categories like authorship, chronology, or previously assigned genres. In order to find out what forms the coherence of these groups, I ran a series of statistical tests, showing that both groups of texts can be defined through literary metadata and semantic features. Besides, further tests were carried out to find out whether they behave differently from the other of categories: It turned out that they in fact behave very similarly to the others. Although it cannot be proven that they constitute subgenres, it was also impossible to prove the contrary. The better explanation for these groups is to consider them as subgenres, at least hypothetical ones, which have not been recognized as such until now. The labels I coined for these hypothetical new subgenres are the *mono-dialogue* and the *bucolic novel*. This last category constitutes a particularly interesting case because it can be defined from all the important literary aspects of the action, such as the setting, the narrator, or protagonist – strong signs to understand it as a subgenre. Of course, these should be revised by other scholars from a longitudinal diachronic perspective, observing more closely why these groups of texts have not received a label until now. These analyses should address the two sides of communication between the actors: On the one side, whether the writers of the texts of these clusters were aware of these similarities and knew they were writing alike and creating a new tradition; and on the other side, whether the public and critics perceived this similarity at the time and already understood these texts as a group.

The fourth main goal was to apply supervised Machine Learning methods (classification) to respond to several questions, each one analyzed in a specific chapter:

1. Before questions about the type of novel (subgenre) could be answered, it was necessary to establish which texts are considered novels, which in many cases is unclear in the literary manuals. This question has been analyzed in the highly interdisciplinary Chapter 3.3. In this chapter, I have employed a section of the Spanish diachronic reference corpus CORDE (with almost 7,000 texts) to classify which works of my corpus belong to the category of novel and which do not. This corpus is a standard tool for researchers of Spanish, especially in Corpus Linguistics. Nevertheless, until recently, the Real Academia has been reluctant to offer this data in other forms than queries on the Web interface, and therefore it has not

been previously used in this manner. The results show that some works clearly belong to the category of the novel,[1] some are clearly part of other subgenres,[2] and some remain in a gray area.[3]

2. The second question about classification is very simple: Does it work, especially in a challenging period like this one? Although the answer to this question could be seen as obvious from the tradition of computational approaches on genre, my case presents several aspects that make it especially challenging: First, its moderatly large size of *only* several hundreds of instances; second, the fact that the corpus is composed by literary works; third, the relatively high canonical status of many of these texts; fourth, the fact that the authors tried to escape the classic genre categories (discussed in Section 2.1.3); and fifth, the relatively large number of analyzed categories (more specifically, 26 different labels). In Chapter 7.1, several classification tasks have been implemented, such as multi-class and multi-label classification, using the probabilities of the classification, predicting the subgenres of chapters, and using literary metadata as features. All of them showed results that were significantly higher than the baseline that would be expected from a random process. Several specific tasks depend on the theoretical model of genre that is applied, on how much information of the labels the researchers are willing to lose, and on their research goals. The highest results were between 0.7 and 1.0 F1-score for the different subgenres, with a median of 0.86 (standard deviation of 0.09). These results show that the classification of subgenres is definitely possible and the scores can be relatively high. Even when authors tried to escape these categories, subgenres can be predicted quite accurately.
3. The third question about classification is what exact parameters should be used to obtain optimal results. Although previous computational approaches did vary the algorithms or the kind of features (lexical frequencies, linguistic annotation, topics, characters), none of them undertook a comprehensive evaluation of parameters. In Chapter 6.1, I have tried

1 *Aviraneta: o la vida de un conspirador* by Baroja, *Luis Candelas, el bandido de Madrid* by Antonio Espina and *La novela de un novelista* by Valdés.

2 *La lámpara maravillosa* by Valle-Inclán, *Cartas finlandesas* by Ganivet, *Juan de Mairena* and *De un cancionero apócrifo* by Machado, *Diario de un poeta recién casado* by Ramón Jiménez and *La vida de Rubén Darío* by Darío.

3 *La media noche* by Valle-Inclán, the two editions of the *Greguerías*, *Tomás Rueda* by Azorín, and especially *Platero y yo* by Ramón Jiménez.

several thousands of combinations of multiple parameters, with a special focus on the features, i.e. their linguistic type, their combination, their number, or their transformation. In addition, I have also observed the influence of the classification algorithms. Many hypotheses about which parameters should lead to higher results were proven wrong, such as the information about the direct speech passages, or the standardization of data through other corpora. This once again reinforces the idea that a very solid and plausible hypothesis can be falsified by the evaluation of real data and that these parameter evaluations are an important aspect of our work. However, other features did perform well, such as the basic tokens, the TEI-tags,[4] punctuation, names of places, semantic features from WordNet and the dictionary by María Moliner, and the categories of nouns, adjectives, and verbs. An improvement in the results can be seen up to 2,000 features; after this, the results remain mainly stable. As far as the algorithms are concerned, support vector machines and logistic regression yield the highest results. Particularly interesting is the evaluation of the transformations, with very clear results favoring the logarithmic transformation of relative frequencies, a transformation that until now was rarely applied in comparison to other, more frequently used ones, like tf-idf or z-scores (see Chapter 2.2). Moreover, I have managed to find an explanation for this: The normality of the data after the transformation correlates with the classification results (see Section 6.1.4). Still, this evaluation has not covered other options, such as parameters that are specific to each algorithm, or neural networks for classification.

4. An important question about the classification of genres is concerned with the theoretical grounds of using linguistic information to distinguish literary categories such as subgenres. Linguistic annotation can be perceived as a superficial cue that represents only indirectly the true defining characteristics of genres, such as abstract information about the intention of the author, the plot, or the protagonist, which is normally not available. Hypothetically, the low classification results of some categories (educational or social novel) could be explained by the fact that their defining characteristics are not represented on the surface of the text. What would the results of the classification be if the algorithm had access to this complex information? Would every subgenre achieve a homogeneous

4 Such as the relative frequency in texts of number of verses, chapters, paragraphs, dialogue in the form of theatre, etc.

and similarly high result? Some previous papers have provided a few fields of metadata to the algorithm as features. In my research study, literary metadata has great importance as a controlled path of distant reading in order to obtain both more reliable evaluations and descriptions based on complex features, explained in more detail in Chapter 3.2. In Section 7.1.5, this literary metadata was passed on to the algorithm as features in several forms. But almost all the results failed to fulfill my expectations: Many of the subgenres with low results showed similar results; the overall classification did not improve in comparison to using linguistic features; and neither did the variance of the results decrease. However, a combination of linguistic and literary features did bring slightly higher results. These results should not be an argument against literary metadata, but rather function as proof that many of our current intuitions about genres are wrong. As is shown in Section 3.2.11 and in the definition of subgenres in the Appendix, these literary metadata operate as an intermediary step between the basic linguistic information and the complex literary genres. They can be used to better understand the development of the history of literature, building bridges between Literary Studies and Computer Science. A current limitation is the lack of standardization for this type of information. I have undertaken a first step towards this goal: encoding it in TEI. However, much of the information does not have specific elements or attributes. It requires greater consensus in the community as far as specific information that should be marked is concerned, as well as the standards and formats that should be used.

5. If the variance of the classification results is not caused by an unequal distance between the superficial linguistic features and the deep literary characteristics, what is it caused by? What *exactly* is the reason for the fact that the realist or social novel constantly obtain lower results than the erotic or adventure novel, regardless of the features? To answer this, in Chapter 7.2, I have evaluated a series of hypotheses about why some subgenres seem to be easier for the algorithms. The results contradict the plausible hypothesis that the 19th-century subgenres should achieve higher results. Instead, five variables show correlations with the results: the number of texts and authors per category, their canonicity, the human agreement on them, and the specificity of the features. These variables explain the majority of the variation of the results of the classification (0.63 R^2). The specificity of the features in particular shows the strongest influence on the results and the strongest correlation with the rest of variables.

> The easy subgenres tend to be the ones that have features that are more distinct, i.e. that are not shared with other categories. Vocabulary about eroticism or adventure are only frequent in erotic and adventure novel, while rare in other categories, i.e. they are very specific for their subgenres. In contrast, social or realist topics are present in many subgenres, they are not specific enough to distinguish the social and realist novel from the rest. Thus, I have shown that Machine Learning methods cannot only be applied to literary genres, their results can be also explained by combining literary data and statistical methods.

All these questions distributed across separate chapters resemble the parable about the blind men and the elephant. In this story, the blind men encounter for the first time a pachyderm, and each one touches a part of it and describes what they experience: A part of the elephant feels like a snake (trunk), a spear (tusk), a fan (ear), a tree (leg), a wall (gut), or a rope (tail). All these descriptions are unconnected to the rest and it is unknown how they should fit together, what the elephant in its integrity should look like. Similarly, the individual chapters do not offer a comprehensive picture of the analyzed object: literary genre.

In the classic theoretical scholastic model, each text belongs to a genre based on a series of necessary and sufficient conditions. From this model, a taxonomy emerges in which a genre (for example, war novel) belongs to a more general category or *genus proximum* (historical novel) based on its *differentia specifica*. This elegant and intuitive model is rooted in the way our society and a section of current research comprehends genres, but it fails when we try to add real examples. Proposing an alternative and comprehensive model for genre is the goal of Chapter 8, where the main elements used for the classification of subgenres are tied together: features (linguistic and literary ones), texts (instances), and genre-labels (categories). The model is ruled by the four following principles:[5]

1. Texts participate in any number of genres (from zero to multiple genres).
2. Some texts participate more intensely in some genres than in others (a relation which can be formalized using the proportion of sources assigning each label).

5 See Section 8.4 for further details.

3. Texts hold distinctive features, overrepresented in comparison to the rest of the corpus. This distinctiveness can be formalized in the calculation of z-scores.
4. The genres also show distinctive features in comparison to the rest of the genres. Again, this can be measured through the z-scores of the mean values of all texts belonging to the category.

This abstract model can be expressed in a tripartite graph in which all labels, features, and texts correspond to separate but connected partitions of nodes. All the connections (edges) are weighted: Some texts belong more clearly to a label than others. This is the main novelty of the prototype theory, i.e. that some instances are better representatives of a category than others. The texts assigned with a given subgenre label tend to share a series of features, which constitute the distinctive features of the subgenre, but not all texts of the subgenre present all these features. It happens that texts also present some distinctive features of other subgenres, even though they do not belong to them. This complex criss-cross pattern of features, categories, and instances is better described by the family resemblance model, in which not all members of the family have to share all physical traits, and in which these traits can also be found in other families. Only by combining the prototype and the family resemblance theories can an alternative model to the scholastic model emerge which can accurately represent the data obtained throughout all chapters (Figure 113).

This model is not only able to fit hundreds of instances of the three different types of elements and their interactions, it also is able to reproduce or quantify other aspects of genre. The evaluation of the model (Section 8.5) has shown that the centrality of the network[6] has an intuitive interpretation both for the genres and the texts. The subgenres in the center of the graph tend to yield lower results in the classification. The explanation for this is that these central subgenres share many features with the rest of the categories, and therefore the algorithm is not able to distinguish them correctly. In addition, these central subgenres are populated by literary works that tend to

6 Which is measured through the eigenvector centrality of the nodes.

Figure 113: Tripartite graph with three subgenres (purple), their texts (green), and features (blue)

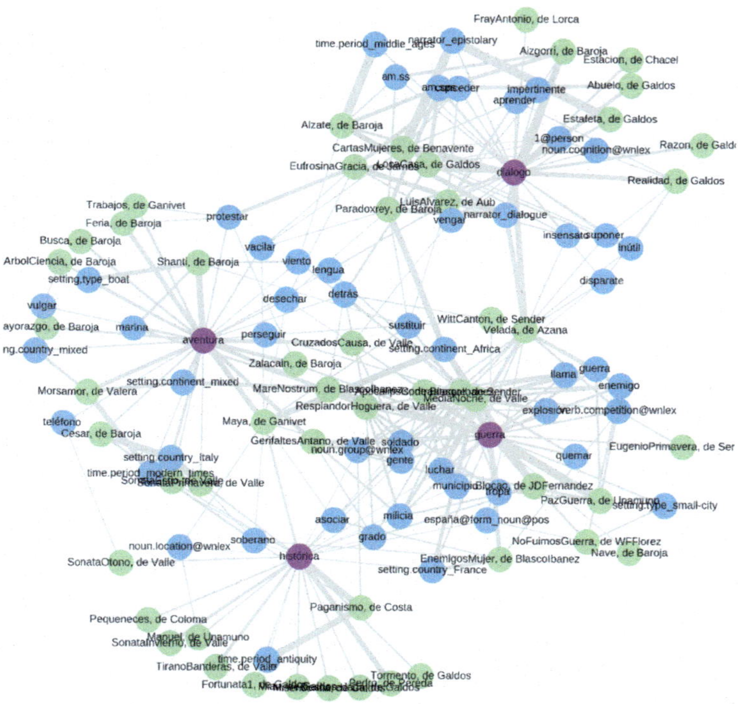

be highly canonized (realist, educational novel, *literary fiction*). In the periphery of the graph are the subgenres with very specific or distinctive features that are not shared with other categories. This high specificity allows the algorithm to classify them almost perfectly. The peripheral subgenres are either popular subgenres (war, erotic, *costumbrist* novels) or produced by one or only a few authors (*episodio nacional*, *greguerías*, *nivola*, dialogue novel).

Another possibility of the model that has been evaluated is its capacity to measure the similarity between pairs of subgenres. When two category nodes have many common neighbors, it means that they share many features and texts, and therefore they are more similar. When the networks are visualized, this similarity is shown as proximity: If two subgenres are close in the network, they are similar.

In addition, the graph gives rise to further mathematical possibilities that can be applied to answer new questions about genres. For example, the question of whether some categories constitute intermediate groups of genres (macro-genres) can now be answered through community detection in the network. A first attempt shows that, apart from the case of the *greguerías*,[7] the subgenres of this period do not show any groups of genres. There is no evidence that canonical subgenres (educational, realist, naturalist novels, *literary fiction*) cluster more tightly together, nor are there other such groups, like the adventure-historical macro-genre. Even though these subgenres share similarities, they are not separated enough from the rest to constitute their own category at a higher level. However, other periods or languages could show these intermediate groups of genres, as the classical French drama or the genres of the Bible do (see Section 8.6 and Calvo Tello 2020). In other words, the tripartite graph model is able to find these macro-genres, but it does not impose them as the scholastic taxonomy does. In this way, the researcher can maintain a descriptive attitude towards genres, rejecting prescriptive aims about how they should be structured.

The results have led me to be very critical with taxonomies as a model for genres. However, it is only fair to admit that, at the beginning of this project, I implicitly accepted the taxonomy of genres and this skewed the gathering of the data and the research questions. My goal has been to analyze subgenres of the novel, i.e. categories, such as the adventure novel, connected to a more general category, the novel. On the one hand, this helped me to structure the phases of my work. On the other hand, this limited the results of my research. In any case, the taxonomies as a complete model for genre are not able to fit the texts in them: As observed again and again in the different chapters, texts can belong to any number of categories and this relation is better described in ordinal terms rather than categorical ones. These two characteristics are hard to model in a taxonomy. However, taxonomies can only be useful as macro-models for genres, i.e., they can only be used to describe the relations between different categories.

7 See Section 2.1.10 for the reasons why this category was considered for this research, and Chapter 3.1 to observe that it was not possible to relate it to other genres more clearly than to the novel.

In Section 8.7, I have extracted information from the tripartite graph model in order to define four subgenres (realist, historical, erotic novel and *literary fiction*) in empirical terms. More specifically, the data in these descriptions comes from either the attributes of the nodes and edges, the calculations in the model, or the semantic and literary features used as a partition of nodes. The Appendix contains a comprehensive list of definitions for all 26 subgenres analyzed. These descriptions represent a solid step towards more accurate empirical descriptions about how the subgenres of this period can be understood. Other researchers can contrast them with previous or future research. In any case, these descriptions should not be understood as final definitions, since the use of other texts, sources, labels, features, or parameters can change them. They are a solid step towards more exactitude in definitions, but just one step.

As mentioned before, this research takes a cross-sectional perspective and data was collected for this purpose. Therefore, the conclusions do not try to reflect any aspect of the historical development of these categories. This constitutes one of the greatest challenges for further research: to add a chronological dimension to the analysis. This research study contributes to this in two ways. First, the publication of the CoNSSA makes more data available for future investigators. Second, from the methodological point of view, the tripartite graph could be enriched with the characteristics of temporal graphs, in which the genres and the texts would evolve dynamically through time.

More access to texts could lead to more comprehensive projects, but the publication of other types of data would also represent important milestones. Scholars from Literary Studies could publish formalized annotations about literary phenomena, which could be used by other scholars as literary features to analyze them through computational means. The digitization of historical sources such as catalogs could be used to reconstruct the history of the reception of specific genres and constitute a source for historical labels. Full access to newspapers published during the authors' life, journals, essays, and personal documents from the authors could lead to the retrieval of the subgenre that the author intended for a text, and how it was received by the public.

Another aspect that would be positive is more frequent access to the code used by researchers. In the past years, publishing scripts or Jupyter Notebooks have become an increasingly normal practice for sharing code in the frame of conference papers or journal articles. Still, they are rarely present in more comprehensive works, such as monographs[8] or PhD theses (cfr. Dombrowski, Gniady, and Kloster 2019). In my case, any person can have access to the repositories containing the Python scripts with the functions. In addition, every chapter has a Jupyter Notebook companion in which it is documented what functions were called, the exact parameters, and the actual results. However, this does not imply that the entire research study can be replicated at any moment. Some data is still protected by copyright. Another aspect is related to the fact that the libraries and the programming languages are constantly being developed, causing conflicts and differences in the results over time. Scientific research needs to explore more user-friendly ways to archive software for future decades that are suited for personal projects such as dissertations. In addition, more radical forms of integration between scientific prose and coding should be explored. Perhaps future dissertations with a computational interest should be written directly in formats similar to a Jupyter Notebook.

As in the majority of studies about literature, this work analyzes one period of the literary texts of one language. As described before, I have already begun applying the tripartite graph model for genre in other corpora, such as classical French drama and the genres of the Bible, with very similar results (Calvo Tello 2020). If the model is flexible enough to accurately describe many properties of the problematic subgenres of the Spanish novel between 1880 and 1939, I do not have any reason to think that it would not be possible to do it with data from other periods or languages. There is no evidence that would suggest that the features and texts of other genres would create anything different from a complex criss-cross pattern. However, as I have experienced many times throughout the elaboration of this book, real data can always falsify very plausible and solid intuitions. A more radical challenge would be to try to fit cases from other media into this model, such as paintings, music, comics, or video.

Considering again the parable of the blind men and the elephant, this book would be an interdisciplinary blind man, perched on the neck of the animal. From here, he reaches with his hands the parts that he has access to. He still does not reach the legs or tails, which hinders an accurate, complete sense of the pachyderm. The combination of disciplines has enabled me to obtain results that would not have been possible otherwise: that literary genres rely

8 See (VanderPlas 2016) for an example in Computer Science, and (Dobson 2019) for an example in the DH field.

heavily on linguistic information and that literary metadata makes possible the better comprehension of genres and can explain the results of Machine Learning techniques. I stated in the introduction that genres were useful but fuzzy categories for many purposes. This research study has shown that genres are useful even when the authors tried to avoid them – and thanks to the model they are less fuzzy than before.

10. References

10. References

Abad Nebot, Francisco. 2007. "La 'Edad de Plata' (1868-1936) y las generaciones de la Edad de Plata: cultura y filología." *Epos: Revista de filología* 23: 243–56.

Agenjo, Xavier. 2015. "Las bibliotecas virtuales españolas y el tratamiento textual de los recursos bibliográficos." *Ínsula: revista de letras y ciencias humanas*, no. 822: 12–15.

Aitchison, Jean. 2012. *Words in the Mind: An Introduction to the Mental Lexicon*. Chichester, West Sussex; Malden, MA: Wiley-Blackwell.

Allison, Sarah, Ryan Heuser, Matthew L. Jockers, Franco Moretti, and Michael Witmore. 2011. "Quantitative Formalism: An Experiment (Stanford Literary Lab, Pamphlet 1)." Stanford: Stanford Literary Lab.

Alonso, Cecilio. 2010. *Historia de la literatura española: 5. Hacia una literatura nacional. 1800-1900*. Edited by José-Carlos Mainer and Gonzalo Pontón. Madrid: Crítica.

Alpaydin, Ethem. 2010. *Introduction to Machine Learning*. Cambridge MA: MIT Press.

Altisent, Marta Eulalia. 2008. *A Companion to the Twentieth-Century Spanish Novel*. Colección Támesis 263. Woodbridge: Tamesis.

Altisent, Marta Eulalia. 1988. *La narrativa breve de Gabriel Miró*. Anthropos Editorial.

Altszyler, Edgar, Mariano Sigman, Sidarta Ribeiro, and Diego Fernández Slezak. 2017. "Comparative Study of LSA vs Word2vec Embeddings in Small Corpora: A Case Study in Dreams Database." *Consciousness and Cognition* 56 (November): 178–87.

Álvarez, Blanca. 2000. "Corín Tellado: mantilla y matrimonio." In *La novela popular en España*, edited by Fernando Martínez de la Hidalga, 147–54. Madrid: Ediciones Robel.

Antoniak, Maria, and David Mimno. 2018. "Evaluating the Stability of Embedding-Based Word Similarities." *Transactions of the Association for Computational Linguistics* 6: 107–19.

Argamon, Shlomo, Moshe Koppel, Jonathan Fine, and Shimoni Anat Rachel. 2003. "Gender, Genre, and Writing Style in Formal Written Texts." *Text and Talk* 23: 321–46.

Artstein, Ron. 2017. "Inter-Annotator Agreement." In *Handbook of Linguistic Annotation*, edited by Nancy M. Ide and James Pustejovsky. Dordrecht: Springer Netherlands.

Artstein, Ron, and Massimo Poesio. 2008. "Inter-Coder Agreement for Computational Linguistics." *Computational Linguistics* 34 (4): 555–96.

Atkins, B. T. S., and Michael Rundell. 2008. *The Oxford Guide to Practical Lexicography*. Oxford, New York: Oxford University Press.

Aubert, Paul, ed. 2001. *La novela en España, siglos XIX-XX*. Collection de la Casa de Vélazquez 66. Madrid: Casa de Velázquez.

Bacarisse, Mauricio. 2005. *Los terribles amores de Agliberto y Celedonia*. Alicante: Biblioteca Virtual Miguel de Cervantes.

Baquero Goyanes, Mariano. 1973. "'Las Cerezas Del Cementerio', de Gabriel Miró." In *El Comentario de Textos*, 285–304. Madrid: Castalia.

Baroja, Pío, and Pío Caro Baroja. 1985. *El árbol de la ciencia*. Letras hispánicas 225. Madrid: Cátedra.

Basili, Roberto, Alfredo Serafini, and Armando Stellato. 2004. "Classification Of Musical Genre: A Machine Learning Approach." In *ISMIR*.

Baßler, Moritz. 2010. "Gattungsmischung, Gattunsübergänge, Unbestimmbarkeit." In *Handbuch Gattungstheorie*, edited by Rüdiger Zymner, 52–54. Stuttgart: Verlag J.B. Metzler.

Becker, Martin G. 2013. *Einführung in die spanische Sprachwissenschaft*. Stuttgart: Metzler.

Beneyto Pérez, Juan. 1980. "Miró, viajero bucólico." *Ínsula: revista de letras y ciencias humanas* 400 (12).

Berninger, Vera, Yunhyong Kim, and Seamus Ross. 2008. "Building a Document Genre Corpus: A Profile of the KRYS I Corpus." In *BCS-IRSG Workshop on Corpus Profiling*. London.

Beyrie, Jacques, and Paul Aubert. 2001. "Novela e Historia en el siglo XIX." In *La novela en España, siglos XIX-XX*, 23–34. Collection de la Casa de Vélazquez 66. Madrid: Casa de Velázquez.

Biber, Douglas. 1988. *Variations across Speech and Writing*. Cambridge: Cambridge University Press.

———. 1992. "The Multidimensional Approach to Linguistic Analyses of Genre Variation: An Overview of Methodology and Finding." *Computers in the Humanities* 26 (5–6): 331–47.

———. 2009. *Register, Genre, and Style*. Cambridge Textbooks in Linguistics. Cambridge: Cambridge Univ. Press.

———. 2014. "Using Multi-Dimensional Analysis to Explore Cross-Linguistic Universals of Register Variation." *Languages in Contrast* 14 (1): 7–34.

Blank, Andreas. 2001. *Einführung in die lexikalische Semantik für Romanisten*. Romanistische Arbeitshefte 45. Tübingen: Niemeyer.

Blei, David M. 2012. "Probabilistic Topic Models." *Communications of the ACM* 55 (4): 77–84.

Bonacich, Phillip. 1987. "Power and Centrality: A Family of Measures." *American Journal of Sociology* 92 (5): 1170–82.

Bortrel, Jean-François. 2001. "La novela, género editorial (España, 1830-1930)." In *La novela en España, siglos XIX-XX*, edited by Paul Aubert, 35–52. Collection de la Casa de Vélazquez 66. Madrid: Casa de Velázquez.

Bradbury, Malcolm, and James McFarlane. 1978. "The Name and Nature of Modernism." In *Modernism: 1890-1930*, 19–56. Pelican Guides to European Literature. Hassocks: Harvester Pr.

Bretz, Mary Lee. 1992. *Voices, Silences and Echoes*. Colección Támesis 149. London: Tamesis Books.

Brezina, Vaclav. 2018. *Statistics in Corpus Linguistics: A Practical Guide*. Cambridge: Cambridge University Press.

Briz, Antonio, Salvador Pons Bordería, and José Portolés. 2008. *Diccionario de Partículas Discursivas Del Español*. www.dpde.es.

Bru, Sascha. 2009. "Introduction." In *Europa! Europa?, The Avant-Garde, Modernism and the Fate of a Continent*, 3–17. Berlin, Boston: De Gruyter.

Brunner, Annelen. 2015. *Automatische Erkennung von Redewiedergabe*. Narratologia. Berlin: de Gruyter.

Buckley, Ramón. 2008. "Tales from the Avant-Garde." In *A Companion to the Twentieth-Century Spanish Novel*, edited by Marta E. Altisent, 45–59. Colección Támesis 263. Woodbridge: Tamesis.

Burguera Nadal, María Luisa, and Santiago Fortuño Llorens, eds. 1998. *Vanguardia y humorismo: la otra Generación del 27*. Summa 10. Castelló de la Plana: Universitat Jaume I.

Burnard, Lou. 2004. "Metadata for Corpus Work." In *Developing Linguistic Corpora: A Guide to Good Practice*, edited by Martin Wynne. Oxford: AHDS Literature, Languages and Linguistics.

Burrows, John. 2002. "'Delta': A Measure of Stylistic Difference and a Guide to Likely Authorship." *Literary and Linguistic Computing* 17 (3): 267–87.

———. 2007. "All the Way Through: Testing for Authorship in Different Frequency Strata." *Literary and Linguistic Computing* 22 (1): 27–47.

Calinescu, Matei. 1987. *Five Faces of Modernity: Modernism, Avant-Garde, Decadence, Kitsch, Postmodernism*. Durham: Duke University Press.

Calvo Tello, José. 2017. "Estado de la digitalización de la Edad de Plata: un análisis cuantitativo." *Revista de Humanidades Digitales* 1 (October): 76–95.

———. 2019. "Delta Inside Valle-Inclán: Stylometric Classification of Periods and Groups of His Novels." In *Romanische Studien Beihefte*. Vol. 6. Romanische Studien Beihefte. München: AVM.edition.

———. 2020. "What Is a Genre? A Graph Unified Model of Categories, Texts, and Features." In *Carrefours / Intersections*. Ottawa: ADHO.

Calvo Tello, José, and Gonzalo Castillo. 2011. *Refranario.Com*. Madrid: Molino de Ideas. http://www.refranario.com/acerca.html.

Calvo Tello, José, Ulrike Henny-Krahmer, and Christof Schöch. 2018. "Textbox: análisis del léxico mediante corpus literarios." In *Historia del léxico español y humanidades digitales*, edited by Dolores Corbella, Alejandro Fajardo, and Jutta Langenbacher-Liebgott, 223–51. Berlin: Peter Lang.

Calvo Tello, José, Daniel Schlör, Ulrike Henny-Krahmer, and Christof Schöch. 2017. "Neutralising the Authorial Signal in Delta by Penalization: Stylometric Clustering of Genre in Spanish Novels." In *Access/Accès*, 181–83. Montréal: ADHO.

Carstensen, Kai-Uwe, Christian Ebert, Cornelia Ebert, Susanne Jekat, Hagen Langer, and Ralf Klabunde. 2009. *Computerlinguistik und Sprachtechnologie: Eine Einführung*. Heidelberg: Spektrum Akademischer Verlag.

Castañar, Fulgencio. 1992. *El compromiso en la novela de la II República*. Lingüística y teoría literaria. Madrid: Siglo Veintiuno Editores.

Cerviño Beresi, U., José Juan García Adeva, R. A. Calvo, and Hermenegildo Alejandro Ceccatto. 2004. "Automatic Classification of New Articles in Spanish." In *X Congreso Argentino de Ciencias de La Computación*.

Chandler, Daniel. 1997. "An Introduction to Genre Theory." http://visual-memory.co.uk/daniel/Documents/intgenre/chandler_genre_theory.pdf.

Chiang, Holly, Yifan Ge, and Connie Wu. 2015. "Classification of Book Genres By Cover and Title." Stanford.

Combet, Louis. 1996. "Los refranes en la literatura." *Euskera: Euskaltzaindiaren lan eta agiriak. Trabajos y actas de la Real Academia de la Lengua Vasca. Travaux et actes de l'Academie de la Langue basque* 41 (3): 821–39.

Coseriu, Eugenio (1921-2002). 2007. *Textlinguistik*. Tübinger Beiträge Zur Linguistik. Tübingen: Narr.

Cranenburgh, Andreas van, Karina van Dalen-Oskam, and Joris van Zundert. 2019. "Vector Space Explorations of Literary Language." *Language Resources and Evaluation*, February.

Croce, Benedetto. 1902. *Estetica come scienza dell'espressione e linguistica generale*. Milano, Italy.

Dendle, Brian J. 1992. *Galdós y la novela histórica*. Ottawa Hispanic studies 10. Ottawa: Dovehouse Ed.

Derrida, Jacques. 1980. "The Law of Genre." *Critical Inquiry* 7 (1): 55–81.

Díez Taboada, Juan María. 1965. "Notas sobre un planteamiento moderno de la Teoría de los géneros literarios." *Homenajes. Estudios de Filología Española* 2: 11–20.

Dobson, James E. 2019. *Critical Digital Humanities*. Topics in the Digital Humanities. Urbana, Chicago, and Springfield: University of Illinois Press.

Dombrowski, Quinn, Tassie Gniady, and David Kloster. 2019. "Introduction to Jupyter Notebooks." *The Programming Historian* 8. https://programminghistorian.org/en/lessons/jupyter-notebooks.

Dufter, Andreas, and Elisabeth Stark. 2003. "La variété des variétés: combien de dimensions pour la description?" *Romanistisches Jahrbuch* 53: 81–102.

Dunst, Alexander, Jochen Laubrock, and Janina Wildfeuer. 2018. *Empirical Comics Research: Digital, Multimodal, and Cognitive Methods*. New York: Taylor & Francis Ltd.

Echeverría Pazos, Rosa María. 1987. *Wenceslao Fernandez Florez: su vida y su obra (Creación, humor y comunicación)*. A Coruña: Deputación Provincial da Coruña.

Eder, Maciej, Mike Kestemont, and Jan Rybicki. 2016. "Stylometry with R: A Package for Computational Text Analysis." *The R Journal* 16 (1): 1–15.

Eisenstein, Jacob. 2019. *Introduction to Natural Language Processing*. Adaptive Computation and Machine Learning. Cambridge, MA: The MIT Press.

Escandell Vidal, María Victoria. 2012. *Apuntes de semántica léxica*. Madrid: Universidad Nacional de Educación a Distancia.

Escobar Bonilla, María del Prado. 1997. "La presencia del narrador en las novelas dialogadas de Galdós." In *VI Congreso Internacional Galdosiano*, 290–300. Las Palmas de Gran Canarias: Ediciones del Cabildo de Gran Canaria.

Espina, Antonio. 2004. *Prosa escogida*. Edited by Gloria Rey Faraldos. Alicante: Biblioteca Virtual Miguel de Cervantes.

Estévez, Francisco. 2013. "Galdós frente a la novela histórica." *Anthropos. Cuadernos de cultura crítica y conocimiento* 240: 159–66.

Evans, James D. 1996. *Straightforward Statistics for the Behavioral Sciences*. Pacific Grove: Brooks/Cole Pub. Co.

Evert, Stefan, Thomas Proisl, Fotis Jannidis, Isabella Reger, Steffen Pielström, Christof Schöch, and Thorsten Vitt. 2018. "Understanding and Explaining Delta Measures for Authorship Attribution." *Digital Scholarship in the Humanities* 32 (2): ii4–16.

Faust, Katherine. 1997. "Centrality in Affiliation Networks." *Social Networks* 19 (2): 157–91.

Fernández Cifuentes, Luis, and José Esteban Gonzalo Santonja. 1984. "La novela social." In *Historia y crítica de la literatura española. 7*, edited by Francisco Rico and Víctor García de la Concha. Páginas de filología. Barcelona: Editorial Crítica.

Fernández Palmeral, Ramón. 2019. *Buscando a Gabriel Miró en Años y leguas*. Lulu.

Ferreras, Juan Ignacio. 1987. *La novela en el siglo XIX (hasta 1868)*. Historia crítica de la literatura hispánica 16. Madrid: Taurus.

———. 1988. *La novela en el siglo XIX (desde 1868)*. Historia crítica de la literatura hispánica. Madrid: Taurus.

Finn, Aidan, and Nicholas Kushmerick. 2006. "Learning to Classify Documents According to Genre." *Journal of the American Society for Information Science and Technology* 57 (11): 1506–18.

Flores Requejo, María José. 2000. "Ramón Gómez de la Serna, humor, incongruencia y ludus: 'Las Novelas de la Nebulosa.'" In *Ludus, cine, arte y deporte en la literatura española de vanguardia.*, 89–108. Pre-textos.

Fricke, Harald. 2010a. "Definieren von Gattungen." In *Handbuch Gattungstheorie*, edited by Rüdiger Zymner, 10–12. Stuttgart: Verlag J.B. Metzler.

———. 2010b. "Definitionen und Begriffsformen." In *Handbuch Gattungstheorie*, edited by Rüdiger Zymner, 7–10. Stuttgart: Verlag J.B. Metzler.

Frye, Northrop. 1957. *Anatomy of Criticism*. Princeton, NJ: Princeton University Press.

Gabriel Fernández, Narciso de. 1997. "Alfabetización y escolarización en España (1887-1950)." *Revista de educación* 314: 217–43.

Gálvez Vidal, Alba María. 2014. "Las paremias como recurso literario y su traducción." *Paremia* 23: 45–55.

García Berrio, Antonio, and Javier Huerta Calvo. 1992. *Los géneros literarios: sistema e historia (una introducción)*. Crítica y estudios literarios. Madrid: Cátedra.

García de Nora, Eugenio. 1963. *La Novela Española Contemporánea*. Biblioteca Románica Hispánica: 2, Estudios y Ensayos. Madrid: Ed. Gredos.

García Lara, Fernando. 1980. "El lugar de la novela erótica: Felipe Trigo." In *Historia y crítica de la literatura española. 6. Modernismo y 98*, edited by Francisco Rico and José-Carlos Mainer, 212–18. Barcelona: Crítica.

———. 1986. *El lugar de la novela erótica española*. Biblioteca de bolsillo 8. Granada: Diputación Provincial de Granada.

Gardt, Andreas. 2012. "Textsemantik. Methoden der Bedeutungserschließung." In *Geschichte der Sprache - Sprache der Geschichte: Probleme und Perspektiven der historischen Sprachwissenschaft des Deutschen*, edited by Jochen Bär, 61–82. Lingua historica germanica 3. Berlin: Akademie Verlag.

———. 2013. "Textanalyse als Basis der DiskursanalyseTheorie und Methoden." In *Faktizitätsherstellung in DiskursenDie Macht des Deklarativen*, edited by Ekkehard Felder. Berlin, Boston: De Gruyter.

Garrido Domínguez, Antonio. 2009. "El texto narrativo." In *El lenguaje literario: Vocabulario crítico*, edited by Miguel Ángel Garrido Gallardo. Madrid: Síntesis.

Garrido Gallardo, Manuel Angel. 1988. "Una vasta paráfrasis de Aristóteles." In *Teoría de los géneros literarios*. Madrid: Arco/Libros.

Garrido Medina, Joaquín. 2009. *Manual de lengua española*. Madrid: Castalia.

Genette, Gérard. 1988. "Géneros, 'tipos', modos." In *Teoría de los géneros literarios*, edited by Manuel Angel Garrido Gallardo, 183–233. Madrid: Arco/Libros.

Gómez de la Serna, Ramón. 1923. *El novelista*. Valencia: Sempere.

González García, José Enrique. 2005. "Consideraciones sobre la influencia de Walter Scott en la novela histórica española del siglo XIX." *Cauce: Revista de filología y su didáctica* 28: 109–20.

González, Juana María. 2021. "Análisis cuantitativo de la revista Índice Literario (1932-1936)." *Artnodes* 27.

Gries, Stefan Thomas. 2008a. "Dispersions and Adjusted Frequencies in Corpora." *International Journal of Corpus Linguistics* 13 (4): 403–37.

———. 2008b. *Statistik für Sprachwissenschaftler*. Studienbücher zur Linguistik 13. Göttingen: Vandenhoeck & Ruprecht.

———. 2009. "Dispersions and Adjusted Frequencies in Corpora: Further Explorations." *Language and Computers*, 197–212.

Gullón, Germán. 1994. "Limites de la novela moderna." In *Historia y crítica de la literatura española*, edited by Francisco Rico, 6/1:199–207. Barcelona: Crítica.

Haslwanter, Thomas. 2016. *An Introduction to Statistics with Python*. Statistics and Computing. Cham: Springer.

Hempfer, Klaus W. 1973. *Gattungstheorie. Information und Synthese*. München: Fink.

———. 2014. "Some Aspects of a Theory of Genre." In *Linguistics and Literary Studies/Linguistik Und Literaturwissenschaft. Interfaces, Encounters, Transfers/Begegnungen, Interferenzen Und Kooperationen*, edited by Monika Fludernik and Daniel Jacob, 405–22. Berlin: De Gruyter.

Henny-Krahmer, Ulrike. 2017. *Bib-ACMé. Bibliografía Digital de Novelas Argentinas, Cubanas y Mexicanas (1830-1910)*. Würzburg: CLiGS.

———. 2018. "Exploration of Sentiments and Genre in Spanish American Novels." In *Puentes/Bridges*. México DF: ADHO.

Henny-Krahmer, Ulrike, Katrin Betz, Daniel Schlör, and Andreas Hotho. 2018. "Alternative Gattungstheorien: Das Prototypenmodell am Beispiel hispanoamerikanischer Romane." In *Kritik der digitalen Vernunft*, 105–12. Köln: DHd.

Henny-Krahmer, Ulrike, and Frederike Neuber. 2017. "Criteria for Reviewing Digital Text Collections, Version 1.0." *A Review Journal for Digital Editions and Resources* 6.

Hettinger, Lena, Isabella Reger, Fotis Jannidis, and Andreas Hotho. 2016. "Classification of Literary Subgenres." In *Digital Humanities Im Deutschsprachigen Raum Konferenz*, 154–58. Leipzig: Universität Leipzig.

Hoover, David L. 2014. "A Conversation Among Himselves: Change and the Styles of Henry James." In *Digital Literary Studies*, edited by David L. Hoover, Jonathan Culpeper, and Kieran O'Halloran, 90–119. New York & London: Routledge.

Iosifyan, Marina, and Igor Vlasov. 2019. "And Quiet Flows the Don: The Sholokhov-Kryukov Authorship Debate." *Digital Scholarship in the Humanities*.

Isasi, Jennifer. 2017. "Posibilidades de la mineria de datos digital para el analisis del personaje literario en la novela española: El caso de Galdos y los 'Episodios Nacionales.'" Ph.D. Thesis, Lincoln: University of Nebraska - Lincoln.

Jackson, Tom, ed. 2016. *Mathematik: 100 Meilensteine in der Welt der Zahlen*. Kerkdriel: Librero.

Jaime Gómez, José de, and José María de Jaime Lorén. 1997. "Índice de las obras clásicas de la literatura española del siglo XIX, en cuyos títulos figuran refranes y frases hechas I." *Paremia* 6: 343–48.

Jaime Lorén, José María de, and José de Jaime Gómez. 2004. "Índice de la obras clásicas de la literatura española del siglo XIX, en cuyos títulos figuran refranes y frases hechas II." *Paremia* 13: 43–51.

Jannidis, Fotis, Leonard Konle, and Peter Leinen. 2019. "Makroanalytische Untersuchung von Heftromanen." In *Digital Humanities: Multimedial & Multimodal*, 167–73. Mainz-Frankfurt: Dhd.

Jannidis, Fotis, and Gerhard Lauer. 2014. "Burrows's Delta and Its Use in German Literary History." In *Distant Readings. Topologies of German Culture in the Long Nineteenth Century*, edited by Matt Erlin and Lynne Tatlock, 29–54. Rochester: Camden House.

Jannidis, Fotis, Isabella Reger, Markus Krug, Lukas Weimer, Luisa Macharowsky, and Frank Puppe. 2016. "Comparison of Methods for the Identification of Main Characters in German Novels." In *Digital Identities: The Past and the Future*, 578–82. Kraków: ADHO.

Jannidis, Fotis, Albin Zehe, Andreas Hotho, and Markus Krug. 2018. "Analysing Direct Speech in German Novels." In *Book of Abstracts: DHd-Jahrestagung 2018, Kritik Der Digitalen Vernunft*. Köln: DHd.

Jauß, Hans Robert. 1970. *Literaturgeschichte als Provokation*. Frankfurt am Main: Suhrkamp.

Jockers, Matthew L. 2013. *Macroanalysis - Digital Methods and Literary History*. Champaign, IL: University of Illinois Press.

Johnson, Roberta. 2008. "From the Generation of 1898 to the Vanguard." In *A Companion to the Twentieth-Century Spanish Novel*, edited by Marta E. Altisent, 155–71. Colección Támesis 263. Woodbridge: Tamesis.

Kabatek, Johannes. 2007. "Las tradiciones discursivas entre conservación e innovación." *Rivista di filologia e letterature ispaniche* 10: 331–48.

———. 2011. "Diskurstraditionen und Genres." In *Rahmen des Sprechens. Beiträge zu Valenztheorie,Varietätenlinguistik, Kreolistik, Kognitiver und Historischer Semantik.*, edited by Sarah (197X-) Dessì Schmid, Ulrich Detges, Paul Gévaudan, Wiltrud Mihatsch, and Richard Waltereit, 89–100. Tübingen: Narr.

———. 2015. "Warum die „zweite Historizität" eben doch die zweite ist – von der Bedeutung von Diskurstraditionen für die Sprachbetrachtung." In

Diskurse, Texte, Traditionen: Modelle und Fachkulturen in der Diskussion, edited by Franz Lebsanft and Angela Schrott, 49–62. Göttingen: V&R unipress.

Kabatek, Johannes, and Claus D. Pusch. 2011. *Spanische Sprachwissenschaft: eine Einführung*. Bachelor-Wissen. Tübingen: Narr.

Kessler, Brett, Geoffrey Numberg, and Hinrich Schütze. 1997. "Automatic Detection of Text Genre." In *Proceedings of the 35th Annual Meeting of the Association for Computational Linguistics and Eighth Conference of the European Chapter of the Association for Computational Linguistics*, 32–38. ACL '98. Stroudsburg, PA: Association for Computational Linguistics.

Kestemont, Mike, Kim Luyckx, Walter Daelemans, and Thomas Crombez. 2012. "Cross-Genre Authorship Verification Using Unmasking." *English Studies* 93 (3): 340–56.

Klaussner, Carmen, John Nerbonne, and Çağrı Çöltekin. 2015. "Finding Characteristic Features in Stylometric Analysis." *Digital Scholarship in the Humanities* 30 (suppl_1): i114–29.

Klinke, Harald. 2017. "Information Retrieval." In *Digital Humanities: Eine Einführung*, edited by Fotis Jannidis, Hubertus Kohle, and Malte Rehbein, 268–78. Stuttgart: Metzler.

Koch, Peter. 1997. "Diskurstraditionen: zu ihrem sprachtheoretischen Status und ihrer Dynamik." *Script Oralia* 99: 43–79.

Koch, Peter, and Wulf Oesterreicher. 1985. "Sprache der Nähe — Sprache der Distanz. Mündlichkeit und Schriftlichkeit im Spannungsfeld von Sprachtheorie und Sprachgeschichte." *Romanistisches Jahrbuch* 36: 15–43.

———. 2011. *Gesprochene Sprache in der Romania: Französisch, Italienisch, Spanisch*. Berlin: De Gruyter.

Koolen, Cornelia Wilhelmina. 2018. "Reading beyond the Female: The Relationship between Perception of Author Gender and Literary Quality."

Krautter, Benjamin, Janis Pagel, Nils Reiter, and Marcus Willand. 2018. *Titelhelden und Protagonisten - Interpretierbare Figurenklassifikation in deutschsprachigen Dramen*. Pamphlete des LitLab 7. Digital Humanities Cooperation.

Laín Corona, Guillermo. 2009. "Raíces picarescas de la novelística de Gabriel Miró." *Espéculo* 42.

Landeira, Ricardo. 1985. *The Modern Spanish Novel*. Twayne's World Authors Series; 764. Boston: Twayne.

Lara, Luis Fernando. 2016. *Teoría semántica y método lexicográfico*. Ciudad de México: Colegio de Mexico.

Lara López, Alfredo. 2000. "La novela de aventuras." In *La novela popular en España*, edited by Fernando Martínez de la Hidalga, 97–120. Madrid: Ediciones Robel.

Lawrence, Mark. 2014. *Spain's First Carlist War, 1833-40*. Springer.

Lebsanft, Franz, and Angela Schrott. 2015. "Diskurse, Texte, Traditionen." In *Diskurse, Texte, Traditionen: Modelle und Fachkulturen in der Diskussion*, edited by Franz Lebsanft and Angela Schrott, 11–46. Göttingen: V&R unipress.

Leech, Geoffrey N, and Mick Short. 2007. *Style in Fiction: A Linguistic Introduction to English Fictional Prose*. London; New York: Longman.

León Pacheco, Pablo. 2017. "Extracción de características de textos y clasificación según género literario mediante redes neuronales." Master Thesis, Madrid: Universidad Carlos III de Madrid.

Lestrade, Sander. 2017. "Unzipping Zipf's Law." *PLOS ONE* 12 (8).

Lewis, Pericles, ed. 2011. *The Cambridge Companion to European Modernism*. Cambridge Companions to Topics. Cambridge, New York: Cambridge University Press.

Lissorgues, Yvan. 2001. "Hacia una estética de la novela realista (1860-1897)." In *La novela en España, siglos XIX-XX*, edited by Paul Aubert, 53–72. Collection de la Casa de Vélazquez 66. Madrid: Casa de Velázquez.

Lojendio Quintero, María Pilar. 2011. "Los animales en la comedia latina: aproximación a un análisis fraseológico." *Paremia* 20: 161–68.

Longhurst, Carlos Alex. 1999. "The Turn of the Novel in Spain: From Realism to Modernism in Spanish Fiction." In *A Further Range*, edited by Anthony H. Clarke, 1–43. Exeter: Univ. of Exeter Press.

———. 2008. "The Early Twentieth-Century Novel." In *A Companion to the Twentieth-Century Spanish Novel*, edited by Marta E. Altisent, 30–44. Colección Támesis 263. Woodbridge: Tamesis.

Lozano Marco, Miguel Ángel. 2002. "La formación de la novela lírica (1901-1910)." In *Gabriel Miró, novelista: actas del II Simposio Internacional "Gabriel Miró,"* 9–20. Alicante: Caja de Ahorros del Mediterráneo.

Lukács, Georg. 1955. *Der Historische Roman*. Berlin: Aufbau-Verlag.

Mainer, José-Carlos. 1975. *La edad de plata (1902-1931): ensayo de interpretación de un proceso cultural*. Ediciones Asenet.

———. 2009. *La edad de plata (1902-1939). Ensayo de interpretación de un proceso cultural*. Madrid: Cátedra.

———, ed. 2010. *Historia de la literatura española*. Madrid: Crítica.

Mainer, José-Carlos, Carlos Alvar, and Rosa Navarro. 1997. *Breve historia de la literatura española*. Madrid: Alianza.

Mainer, José-Carlos, and Gonzalo Pontón, eds. 2010. *Historia de La Literatura Española*. Madrid: Crítica.

Manning, Christopher D., and Hinrich Schütze. 1999. *Foundations of Statistical Natural Language Processing*. Cambridge, Mass: The MIT Press.

Martínez Cachero, José María. 1984. "Novela: los años estériles de la guerra civil." In *Historia y crítica de la literatura española. 7*, edited by Francisco Umbral and Víctor García de la Concha. Páginas de filología. Barcelona: Editorial Crítica.

Martínez de la Hidalga, Fernando, ed. 2000. *La novela popular en España*. Madrid: Ediciones Robel.

McEnery, Tony, and Andrew Wilson. 2001. *Corpus Linguistics: An Introduction*. Edinburgh Textbooks in Empirical Linguistics. Edinburgh: Edinburgh University Press.

Mikolov, Tomas, Kai Chen, Greg Corrado, and Jeffrey Dean. 2013. "Efficient Estimation of Word Representations in Vector Space." *ArXiv*.

Millares, Selena. 2013. *Prosas Hispánicas de Vanguardia*. Letras Hispánicas; 729. Madrid:Cátedra.

Moliner, María. 1966. *Diccionario de uso del español*. Madrid: Gredos.

Montesinos, José Fernández. 1980. "Modernismo, esperpentismo, o las dos evasiones." In *Historia y crítica de la literatura española* 6, 298–303. Barcelona: Crítica.

Moretti, Franco. 2000. "Conjectures on World Literature." *The New Left Review*, 2000.

———. 2005. *Graphs, Maps, Trees: Abstract Models for a Literary History*. London: Verso.

Mosteller, Frederick, and David L. Wallace. 1963. "Inference in an Authorship Problem." *Journal of the American Statistical Association* 58 (302): 275–309.

Mowat, Barbara, and Paul Werstine. 2010. *Shakespeare Folger Library*. Washington: Folger. https://www.folgerdigitaltexts.org.

Müller, Andreas C., and Sarah Guido. 2016. *Introduction to Machine Learning with Python: A Guide for Data Scientist*. Beijing, Boston: O'Reilly.

National Information Standards Organization (NISO). 2004. *Understanding Metadata*. Bethesda, MD: NISO. http://www.niso.org/publications/press/UnderstandingMetadata.pdf.

Navajas, Gonzalo. 2008. "The Spanish Novel in the Twentieth Century." In *A Companion to the Twentieth-Century Spanish Novel*, edited by Marta E. Altisent, 17–29. Colección Támesis 263. Woodbridge: Tamesis.

Newman, M. E. J., and M. Girvan. 2004. "Finding and Evaluating Community Structure in Networks." *Physical Review E* 69 (2).

Nielsen, Lars Holm. 2013. "ZENODO - An Innovative Service for Sharing All Research Outputs."

Novillo-Corvalán, Patricia. 2018. *Modernism and Latin America: Transnational Networks of Literary Exchange*. Routledge Studies in Twentieth-Century Literature. New York, NY: Routledge.

Oakes, Michael. 2009. "Corpus Linguistics and Stylometry." In *Corpus Linguistics: An International Handbook*, edited by Anke Ludeling and Merja Kyto, 2:1070–90. Mouton de Gruyter.

Ochab, Jeremi, Joanna Byszuk, Steffen Pielström, and Maciej Eder. 2019. "Identifying Similarities in Text Analysis: Hierarchical Clustering (Linkage) versus Network Clustering (Community Detection)." In *Complexities*. Utrecht, Netherlands: ADHO.

Oddo Bonnet, Alexandra. 2011. "Influencia del refrán en las intrigas de comedias del Siglo de Oro español." *Paremia* 20: 169–78.

Ortega y Gasset, José. 2009. *La deshumanización del arte, ideas sobre la novela*. Castalia didáctica. Madrid: Castalia.

Øveraas, Anne M. 1993. *Nivola contra novela*. Biblioteca Unamuno 15. Salamanca: Editorial Universidad de Salamanca.

Padró, Lluís, and Evgeny Stanislovsky. 2012. "FreeLing 3.0: Towards Wider Multilinguality." In *Proceedings of the Language Resources and Evaluation Conference (LREC 2012) ELRA*, 2473–79. Istanbul, Turkey: ELRA.

Pattison, Walter T. 1965. *El naturalismo español*. Biblioteca románica hispánica. Madrid: Gredos.

Pawłowski, Tadeusz. 1980. *Begriffsbildung und Definition*. Berlin, Boston: De Gruyter.

Pearson, Norman Holmes. 1940. "Literary Forms and Types or a Defense of Polonius." *English Institute Annual* 2: 61–72.

Pedraza Jiménez, Felipe B., and Milagros Rodríguez Cáceres. 1980. *Manual de literatura española*. Pamplona: Cénlit Ediciones.

———. 1982. *Manual de literatura española. 6: Época romántica*. Pamplona: Cénlit Ediciones.

———. 1983. *Manual de literatura española. 7: Época del realismo*. Pamplona: Cénlit Ediciones.

———. 1986. *Manual de literatura española. 8: Generación de fin de siglo: introducción, líricos y dramaturgos*. Pamplona: Cénlit Ediciones.

———. 1991. *Manual de literatura española. 10: Novecentismo y vanguardia: Introducción, prosistas y dramaturgos*. Pamplona: Cénlit Ediciones.

Percillier, Michael. 2017. "Creating and Analyzing Literary Corpora." In *Data Analytics in Digital Humanities*. Multimedia Systems and Applications. Cham: Springer International Publishing.

Pérez, Roberto. 1993. "Humor y sátira en las novelas de Jardiel Poncela." In *Jardiel Poncela, teatro, vanguardia y humor: actas del VI Congreso de Literatura Española Contemporánea*, edited by Cristóbal Cuevas García and Enrique Baena, 33–64. Contemporáneos 19. Barcelona: Anthropos.

Petersen, Julius. 1944. *Die Wissenschaft von der Dichtung*. Berlin: Erich Trunz.

Petrenz, Philipp, and Bonnie Webber. 2011. "Stable Classification of Text Genres." *Computational Linguistics* 37 (2): 385–93.

Pueo Domínguez, Juan Carlos. 1994. "Humor y misoginia en las novelas de Enrique Jardiel Poncela." In *Actas del IX Simposio de la Sociedad Española de Literatura General y Comparada: Zaragoza, 18 al 21 de noviembre de 1992, Vol. 1, 1994, ISBN 84-920044-1-X, págs. 313-322*, 313–22. Sociedad Española de Literatura General y Comparada.

Pustet, Regina. 2004. "Zipf and His Heirs." *Language Sciences* 26 (1): 1–25.

Rahat, Mahmoud, and Alireza Talebpour. 2018. "Parsa: An Open Information Extraction System for Persian." *Digital Scholarship in the Humanities* 33 (4): 874–93.

Raible, Wolfgang. 1980. "Was sind Gattungen?" *Poetica*, no. 12: 320–49.

———. 1983. "Von der Allgegenwart des Gegensinns." In *Zur Semantik des Französischen*, edited by Romanistentag (1981, Regensburg) and Helmut (1917-1987) Stimm, 1–24. Zeitschrift für französische Sprache und Literatur. Wiesbaden: Steiner.

Ramsay, Stephen. 2005. "In Praise of Pattern." *Faculty Publications – Department of English*, January.

Rauber, Andreas, and Alexander Müller-Kögler. 2001. "Integrating Automatic Genre Analysis into Digital Libraries." In *Proceedings of the 1st ACM/IEEE-CS Joint Conference on Digital Libraries*, 1–10. JCDL '01. New York, NY, USA: ACM.

Riddell, Allen, and Christof Schöch. 2014. "Progress through Regression." In *Digital Humanities 2014: Conference Abstracts*. Lausanne: UNIL/EPFL.

Rivalan Guégo, Christine. 2008. *Fruición-ficción: novelas y novelas cortas en España (1894-1936)*. Biblioteconomía y administración cultural 180. Gijón, Spain: Ediciones Trea.

Rochat, Yannick. 2014. "Character Networks and Centrality." Ph.D. Thesis, Lausanne: Université de Lausanne.

Ródenas de Moya, Domingo. 1998. *Los espejos del novelista: Modernismo y autorreferencia en la novela vanguardista española*. Historia, ciencia, sociedad 274. Barcelona: Ed. Península.

———, ed. 2000. *Prosa Del 27: Antología*. Colección Austral; Prosa Literaria 504. Madrid: Editorial Espasa Calpe.

———. 2009. *Travesías vanguardistas*. Devenir ensayo 18. Madrid: Devenir.

Rodríguez Molina, Javier, and Álvaro Sebastián Octavio de Toledo y Huerta. 2017. "La imprescindible distinción entre texto y testimonio: el CORDE y los criterios de fiabilidad lingüística." *Scriptum digital: revista de corpus diacrònics i edició digital en llengües iberoromàniques* 6: 5–68.

Rodríguez, Valentina Marta. 2013. "Ideología religiosa en la lexicografía francesa y española: el 'Petit Robert' frente al 'DRAE.'" *Hesperia: Anuario de filología hispánica* 16: 45–62.

Román Gutiérrez, Isabel. 1988. *Persona y forma, una historia interna de la novela española del siglo XIX. I: Hacia el realismo*. Colección Alfar/universidad 34. Sevilla: Ediciones Alfar.

Romero López, María Dolores. 1997. "Hispanic Modernismo in the Context of European Symbolism — Towards a Comparative Dekon-Struction." *Orbis Litterarum* 52 (3): 194–210.

———. 1998. *Una relectura del "fin de siglo" en el marco de la literatura comparada: teoría y praxis*. Perspectivas hispánicas. Bern: Peter Lang.

———. 2012. *Mnemosine. Biblioteca Digital de La Otra Edad de Plata*. Madrid: Grupo LOEP, Universidad Complutense de Madrid.

———. 2014. "Hacia la Smartlibrary: Mnemosine, una biblioteca digital de textos literarios raros y olvidados de la Edad de Plata (1868-1936)1. Fase I." In *Humanidades Digitales: desafíos, logros y perspectivas de futuro*, 411–22. A Coruña: SIELAE.

Rosch, Eleanor. 1973. "On the Internal Structure of Perceptual and Semantic Categories." In *Cognitive Development and the Acquisition of Language*, edited by Timothy E. Moore, 111–44. New York: Academic Press.

———. 1975. "Cognitive Representations of Semantic Categories." *Journal of Experimental Psychology: General* 104 (3): 192–233.

Rubio Jiménez, Jesús. 1998. "Novela, relato breve y drama en el cambio de siglo: Una aproximación." *Insula: revista de letras y ciencias humanas* 614: 20–22.

Sánchez Sánchez, Mercedes, and Carlos Domínguez Cintas. 2007. "El banco de datos de la RAE: CREA y CORDE." *Per Abbat: boletín filológico de actualización académica y didáctica*, no. 2: 137–48.

Santa María Fernández, Teresa, José Calvo Tello, and Concepción María Jiménez Fernández. 2020. "¿Existe correlación entre importancia y centralidad? Evaluación de personajes con redes sociales en obras teatrales de la Edad de Plata." *Digital Scholarship in the Humanities*.

Santa María, Teresa, Elena Martínez Carro, Concepción Jiménez, and José Calvo Tello. 2018. "¿Existe correlación entre importancia y centralidad? Evaluación de personajes con redes sociales en obras teatrales de la Edad de Plata?" In *Puentes/Bridges*, 494–98. México DF: ADHO.

Santini, Marina. 2004. "State-of-the-Art on Automatic Genre Identification." In *Technical Report ITRI-04-03*.

———. 2007. "Automatic Identification of Genre in Web Pages." Ph.D. Thesis, Brighton, United Kingdom: School of Computing, Engineering and Mathematics, University of Brighton.

———. 2010. "Cross-Testing a Genre Classification Model for the Web." In *Genres on the Web: Computational Models and Empirical Studies*, edited by Alexander Mehler, Serge Sharoff, and Marina Santini. Text, Speech and Language Technology 42. Dordrecht: Springer.

———. 2011. *Automatic Identification of Genre in Web Pages: A New Perspective*. Saarbrücken: LAP Lambert Academic Publishing.

Schaeffer, Jean-Marie. 2006. *¿Qué es un género literario?* Madrid: Akal.

Schöch, Christof. 2013. "Fine-Tuning Our Stylometric Tools: Investigating Authorship and Genre in French Classical Theater." In *Digital Humanities 2013: Conference Abstracts*. Lincoln: UNL.

———. 2017a. "Aufbau von Datensammlungen." In *Digital Humanities: eine Einführung*, edited by Fotis Jannidis, Hubertus Kohle, and Malte Rehbein, 223–33. Stuttgart: J.B. Metzler Verlag.

———. 2017b. "Topic Modeling Genre: An Exploration of French Classical and Enlightenment Drama." *Digital Humanities Quarterly* 11 (2).

Schöch, Christof, José Calvo Tello, Ulrike Henny-Krahmer, and Stefanie Popp. 2019. "The CLiGS Textbox: Building and Using Collections of Literary Texts in Romance Languages Encoded in XML-TEI." *Journal of the Text Encoding Initiative*.

Schöch, Christof, Frédéric Döhl, Achim Rettinger, Evelyn Gius, Peer Trilcke, Peter Leinen, Fotis Jannidis, Maria Hinzmann, and Jörg Röpke. 2020.

"Abgeleitete Textformate: Text und Data Mining mit urheberrechtlich geschützten Textbeständen." *Zeitschrift für digitale Geisteswissenschaften* 5.

Schöch, Christof, Ulrike Henny, José Calvo Tello, Daniel Schlör, and Stefanie Popp. 2016. "Topic, Genre, Text. Topics im Textverlauf von Untergattungen des spanischen und hispanoamerikanischen Romans (1880-1930)." In *Modellierung, Vernetzung, Visualisierung. Die Digital Humanities als fächerübergreifendes Forschungsparadigma*, 235–38. Leipzig: nisaba verlag.

Schöch, Christof, Daniel Schlör, Stefanie Popp, Annelen Brunner, Ulrike Henny, and José Calvo Tello. 2016. "Straight Talk! Automatic Recognition of Direct Speech in Nineteenth-Century French Novels." In *Digital Identities: The Past and the Future*, 346–53. Kraków: ADHO.

Schöch, Christof, Daniel Schlör, Albin Zehe, Henning Gebhard, Martin Becker, and Andreas Hotho. 2018. "Burrows' Zeta: Exploring and Evaluating Variants and Parameters." In *Puentes/Bridges*, 274–77. México DF: ADHO.

Schröter, Julian. 2019. "Gattungsgeschichte und ihr Gattungsbegriff am Beispiel der Novellen." *Journal of Literary Theory* 13 (2).

Schrott, Angela. 2015. "Kategorien diskurstraditionellen Wissens als Grundlage einer kulturbezogenen Sprachwissenschaft." In *Diskurse, Texte, Traditionen: Modelle und Fachkulturen in der Diskussion*, edited by Franz Lebsanft and Angela Schrott, 115–46. Göttingen: V&R unipress.

Senabre, Ricardo. 1984. "Técnica de la greguería." In *Historia y crítica de la literatura española. 7*, edited by Francisco Rico and Víctor García de la Concha. Páginas de filología. Barcelona: Editorial Crítica.

Shaw, Donald L. 2010. "Hispanic Literature and Modernism." In *The Oxford Handbook of Modernisms*, edited by Peter Brooker, Andrzej Gąsiorek, Deborah Longworth, and Andrew Thacker. Oxford, New York: Oxford University Press.

Sigley, Robert. 1997. "Text Categories and Where You Can Stick Them: A Crude Formality Index." *International Journal of Corpus Linguistics* 2: 199–237.

Sinclair, John. 1991. *Corpus, Concordance, Collocation*. Oxford: Oxford University Press.

Söll, Ludwig. 1985. *Gesprochenes und geschriebenes Französisch*. Grundlagen der Romanistik. Berlin: Schmidt.

Spang, Kurt. 2009. "Géneros literarios." In *El lenguaje literario: Vocabulario crítico*, edited by Miguel Ángel Garrido Gallardo. Madrid: Síntesis.

Stamatatos, Efstathios, Nikos Fakotakis, and George Kokkinakis. 2000. "Automatic Text Categorization in Terms of Genre and Author." *Computational Linguistics* 26 (4): 471–97.

———. 2001. "Automatic Text Categorization in Terms of Genre and Author." *Computational Linguistics* 26 (4): 471–97.

Swanepoel, Piet. 2005. "On Defining 'Imaginary' Beings and Attributes: How Do Lexicographers Cope with Culturally Determined Differences in Beliefs about Cosmology, Ontology and Epistemology?" *Lexikos* 15 (0).

Todorov, Tzvetan. 1976. "The Origin of Genres." *New Literary History* 8 (1): 159–70.

Traag, V. A., L. Waltman, and N. J. van Eck. 2019. "From Louvain to Leiden: Guaranteeing Well-Connected Communities." *Scientific Reports* 9 (1): 1–12.

Trilcke, Peer, Frank Fischer, Mathias Göbel, and Dario Kampkaspar. 2016. "Dramen als small worlds? Netzwerkdaten zur Geschichte und Typologie deutschsprachiger Dramen 1730-1930." In *DHd 2016 Modellierung, Vernetzung, Visualisierung*, edited by Elisabeth Burr, 254–57. Leipzig: Dhd/nisaba.

Umbral, Francisco. 1984. "Los géneros fingidos de Ramón." In *Historia y crítica de la literatura española. 7*, edited by Francisco Rico and Víctor García de la Concha. Páginas de filología. Barcelona: Editorial Crítica.

Unamuno, Miguel de, and Mario J. Valdés. 1982. *Niebla*. Letras Hispánicas 154. Madrid: Cátedra.

Underwood, Ted. 2014. "Understanding Genre in a Collection of a Million Volumes, Interim Report." https://figshare.com/articles/Understanding_Genre_in_a_Collection_of_a_Million_Volumes_Interim_Report/1281251.

———. 2016. "The Life-Cycle of Genres." *Journal of Cultural Analytics* 1.

———. 2018. "Why Literary Time Is Measured in Minutes." *English Literary History* 85 (2): 341–65.

———. 2019. *Distant Horizons: Digital Evidence and Literary Change*. Chicago: The University of Chicago Press.

Utrera Torremocha, María Victoria. 1999. *Teoría del poema en prosa*. Sevilla: Universidad de Sevilla.

VanderPlas, Jake. 2016. *Python Data Science Handbook: Essential Tools for Working with Data*. First edition. Beijing, Boston: O'Reilly.

Verhoeven, Ben, and Walter Daelemans. 2018. "Discourse Lexicon Induction for Multiple Languages and Its Use for Gender Profiling." *Digital Scholarship in the Humanities*.

Villanueva Prieto, Dario, ed. 1983. *La novela lírica*. Madrid: Taurus.

Vivas, Eliseo. 1968. "Literary Classes: Some Problems." *Genre* 1: 97–105.

Voßkamp, Wilhelm. 1977. "Gattungen als literarisch-soziale Institutionen. Zu Problemen sozial- und funktionsgeschichtlich orientierter Gattungstheorie und -historie." In *Textsortenlehre, Gattungsgeschichte*, edited by Alexander von Bormann. Medium literatur 4. Heidelberg: Quelle & Meyer.

Weisberg, Michael. 2013. *Simulation and Similarity: Using Models to Understand the World*. Oxford University Press.

Wellek, Rene, and Austin Warren. 1956. *Theory of Literature*. New York: Harcourt, Brace and World.

Wilkens, Matthew. 2016. "Genre, Computation, and the Varieties of Twentieth-Century U.S. Fiction." *Cultural Analytics* 1.

Willows, Howard, Graham Bell, Alex Ingram, and Chris Saynor. 2018. "Thema Version 1.3 Basic User Instructions." London: EDItEUR. https://www.editeur.org/files/Thema/20180426%20Thema%20v1.3%20Basic%20instructions.pdf.

Wittgenstein, Ludwig, and Joachim Schulte. 2013. *Philosophische Untersuchungen*. Bibliothek Suhrkamp 1372. Frankfurt am Main: Suhrkamp.

Wynne, Martin, ed. 2004. *Developing Linguistic Corpora: A Guide to Good Practice*. Oxford: AHDS Literature, Languages and Linguistics.

Yu, Bei. 2008. "An Evaluation of Text Classification Methods for Literary Study." *Literary and Linguistic Computing* 23 (3): 327–43.

Zipf, George. 1932. *Selected Studies of the Principle of Relative Frequency in Language*. Cambridge, MA: Harvard University Press.

Zweig, Katharina A. 2016. *Network Analysis Literacy: A Practical Approach to the Analysis of Networks*. Lecture Notes in Social Networks. Vienna: Springer Vienna.

Zymner, Rüdiger. 2003. *Gattungstheorie. Probleme und Positionen der Literaturwissenschaft*. Paderborn: mentis.

11. Appendix

11. Empirical Description through the Tripartite Graph Model

11.1 Introduction

Finally, this Appendix aims at offering empirical descriptions (or *real definitions* following Pawłowski's terminology 1980, see Section 2.3.1) of each subgenre using the model presented in Chapter 8. The aim is to provide several short paragraphs summarizing the most important information about each subgenre, such as the results on classification, its canonicity, its main distinctive semantic, textual, and literary features (intension), the number of texts in the corpus (extension) and its best representatives (the ones that are most frequently assigned to it), and its similarity to other subgenres in terms of shared features and texts (common neighbors). All this information has been extracted or can be calculated from the tripartite graph in different ways: by the size of the nodes, by counting nodes with specific characteristics, by observing its eigenvector centrality, or by obtaining the shared neighbors in the graph. In other words, the following paragraphs are mainly textual paraphrases of what has already been plotted as the entire network of subgenres, texts, and features.

The intension of every subgenre is defined by the top specific features, both linguistic and literary, mentioning every time which of these two types is more specific for the subgenre. Thus, the reader has access to the information of whether the category is defined rather by linguistic or literary information (see Section 7.1.5). The semantic features are grouped together to give a more coherent overview, but the specific data from the dictionary by María Moliner or Wordnet are listed in parenthesis in their original language. These are sorted following their distinctiveness for the genre. Furthermore, I do not pick only the information that fits my concept of the genre correctly, but all the top features, in many cases indicating that their interpretation is unclear.

In any case, readers have access to the online repositories and the Jupyter Notebooks, in which the exact values for each subgenre can be observed, in addition to graphs as the one shown in Figure 112.[1]

To provide more robust descriptions, two parallel graphs have been calculated, one based on the larger but opportunistic CoNSSA, and the other one on the more accurate but smaller CoNSSA-canon (see Section 3.1.6). Unless I make it explicit, all the information from the descriptions is based on observations from both corpora. In that manner, these descriptions are controlled against the possible bias of the composition of the corpus, and based on a statistical population based on manuals of literary history.

The descriptions given in this Appendix can be contrasted with the conclusion from other scholars, summarized in Chapter 2.1. The subgenres are sorted according to their centrality, starting with the central subgenres, moving step by step towards the periphery.

11.2 Realist novel

In the center of the network there are three subgenres with an eigenvector centrality of 0.26. One of them is the realist novel, a subgenre that does not have many specific features (standard deviation of z-scores of 0.32). The subgenre covers 221 novels in CoNSSA, 103 novels in CoNSSA-canon, which makes it the largest subgenre in terms of instances. In general, the novels of this genre are highly canonized, with a mean of 1.5 pages per novel in the manual MdLE. The low specificity of the features explains a relatively low classification result of 0.81 mean F1-score.

The features that show higher distinctiveness for this subgenre are linguistic ones, such as vocabulary about negative actions or characteristics (such as the semantic features from the dictionary by María Moliner *desobedecer, zaherir, criticar, abusar, avergonzar, descortés, grosero*, or negations), as well as words about the economy (*propiedad, pagar, retribución, prestar, lujo, lucir*, or *bien*, although this last one is highly ambivalent), health (*salud*), and words that are difficult to interpret (*impulso, comprometer*, and *ensalzar*).

From a literary metadata perspective, the strongest feature is a protagonist from lower classes of the society, followed by a realistic setting in Europe (mainly in Spain), with a heterodiegetic narrator.

1 https://github.com/cligs/scripts-ne/tree/master/visualizations/appendix

Some of the texts that have a large proportion of sources relating them to this subgenre are by Valera (*Genio y figura…*, *Juanita la Larga*), Galdós (*El doctor Centeno, Miau, Lo prohibido*), Valdes (*José*), or Azaña (*El jardín de los frailes*).

The most similar subgenres (in terms of shared features and texts) are the social novel (63% of features and texts shared), *literary fiction* (59%), and the naturalist novel (46%).

11.3 Social novel

The second subgenre in the center of the graph (eigenvector centrality of 0.26) is the social novel, also with a low specificity of its features (standard deviation of z-scores of 0.29). This subgenre covers 185 novels in CoNSSA, 89 in CoNSSA-canon. The texts of this subgenre are relatively highly canonized, with 1.6 pages on average in the manual. These variables bring about the lowest classification result of all analyzed subgenres: 0.72 F1-score.

From the linguistic perspective, the vocabulary is marked by negative fields (*desobedecer, criticar, inmoral*), crime (*cruel, delito, abusar, traidor*), economy and poverty (*retribución, pobre, bien, economía, propiedad, ahorrar, ajetrear, esforzar, pagar*), and others (*salud, niño, costumbre*). However, the most specific feature comes from the metadata: a protagonist from lower classes. Other aspects, also specific but to a lesser degree are a geographical setting in Europe (mainly Spain), no representation of the author's life (see Section 3.2.6 for an explanation about the author-text relation field), and a heterodiegetic narrator.

Some instances with larger proportions of sources assigning them to this subgenre are texts by Valle-Inclán (*Gerifaltes de antaño, Los cruzados de la causa, Baza de espadas*), Baroja (*César o nada, Mala hierba*), or Unamuno (*San Manuel Bueno, mártir*).

The most similar subgenres are the realist novel (63% of shared features and texts), *literary fiction* (56%), and the naturalist novel (43%).

11.4 Literary Fiction

The third subgenre in the center of the network is *literary fiction*, a special case of the subgenre palette which has been found in a single source: the publishers on Amazon (see Chapter 5.3). This subgenre has the lowest specificity of features of all subgenres (standard deviation of z-scores of 0.28). It contains 190 novels in CoNSSA, 94 in CoNSSA-canon. The novels are, unsurprisingly, highly canonized, with 1.64 pages in the manual on average. All this explains a low classification result of 0.75 F1-score.

The strongest feature of this subgenre would be a protagonist of lower classes of the society, followed at a distance by a setting in France, and, surprisingly, that the story does not reflect the author's life. From the linguistic perspective: communication (*criticar, discurso, oratoria, charlar*), money and work (*ajetrear, bien, propiedad, encargar, función, pagar*), royalty (*soberano, rey, linaje*), and other fields (*familia* and negations) are distinctive.

Publishers use this label to assign several texts by authors like Baroja (*Mala hierba, La busca*), Valle-Inclán (*Baza de espadas, La media noche*), Galdós (*El doctor Centeno, Lo prohibido*), Azorín (*Tomás Rueda*), or Unamuno (*Paz en la guerra*).

The most similar subgenres are the two other most central ones: the realist (59% of shared features and texts) and the social novel (56%).

11.5 Educational Novel

The next subgenre is the educational novel, with an eigenvector centrality of 0.22. It contains 70 texts in CoNSSA, 39 in CoNSSA-canon. These novels are highly canonized, with an average of 1.66 pages in the manual (2.35 for CoNSSA-canon). The specificity of the features is the fifth lowest (standard deviation of z-scores of 0.36), which in general explains a poor classification result, being also in the fifth position with a 0.79 F1-score.

The most distinctive features are a child or very young protagonist at the beginning of the text, and a rather long chronological span of the action. The mix of values in several metadata fields are also noticeable literary features, such as the change between rural and urban spaces, and different narrators. As far as linguistic features are concerned, vocabulary about institutional education (*colegio, educar, universidad, enseñar, estudiar, convento*), family (*familia, padre, linaje*), life (*emprender, alojar, protestar, grosero, crear*), or typical Spanish themes (*España, cuerno, toro*). Besides, the semicolon and a larger proportion of parts (groups of chapters) are overrepresented.

The clearest examples are *El jardín de los frailes* by Azaña, *El torero Caracho* by Serna, *Genio y figura...* by Valera, several works by Pérez de Ayala (*La pata de la raposa, A. M. D. G.*), or Baroja (*El árbol de la ciencia, Camino de perfección*).

The most similar subgenres are the realist novel (31% of shared features), followed closely by *literary fiction* and the social novel (30%), philosophical novel and memoir (29%).

11.6 Philosophical Novel

The philosophical novel has an eigenvector centrality of 0.19, which is produced by a relatively low specificity of the features (standard deviation of z-scores of 0.34). This category is populated by 88 texts in CoNSSA, 45 texts in CoNSSA-canon, with a relatively high canonization status (1.35 pages in the MdLE, 1.99 in CoNSSA-canon). All this explains the low classification result of 0.77 F1-score.

The features that are the most specific for this subgenre are semantic features about cognitive (*vacilar, desechar*) and social processes (*estudiar, enseñar, protestar, imitar, describir*), school (*colegio, universidad*), relatively general concepts (*mundo, literatura, mecánica, categoría, lista*), or qualitative adjectives (*imposible, exacto, extravagante*), besides the quotation mark and a large number of sections (divisions inside a chapter). Furthermore, a series of literary characteristics are specific for them, such as a setting in Italy or Africa, either with the plot taking place completely in towns or several types of settings (for example, the start in a city and the continuation in rural places). The narrator tends to be homodiegetic, the protagonist male, and the ending tends to be either uncertain or partially negative.

Some of the texts identified as such with higher frequency are *La pata de la raposa* and *Troteras y danzaderas* by Pérez de Ayala, *Un intelectual y su carcoma* by Verdaguer, *Locura y muerte de Nadie* by Jarnés, *Cinematógrafo* by Carranque, or *La piedra angular* by Bazán.

The subgenres that share a larger proportion of features and texts with the philosophical novels are the educational novel (29%), and a clear step behind the social novel (21%), the comedy novel (20%), *literary fiction*, and memoir (both with 20%).

11.7 Naturalist Novel

The naturalist novel (along with the subgenre that will be described in the next section) can be found in the value 0.18 eigenvector centrality. The naturalist novel shows a relatively high specificity of features (standard deviation of z-scores of 0.51), higher than any of the values seen in the previous subgenres. It is composed by 83 texts (in CoNSSA, 50 in CoNSSA-canon). They are highly canonized (2.24 pages in the MdLE in CoNSSA, 3.39 in CoNSSA-cannon). The classification result is slightly higher than the ones previously seen, with a 0.83 F1-score.

The following semantic features are overrepresented in this category: health (*salud*), negative interactions (*desagradar, avergonzar, desobedecer, abusar, deshonrar*), negative personal attributes (*descortés, malo, inmoral, cinismo, cruel, desvergüenza, grosero*), childhood (*pequeño, travieso, niño*), economy (*propiedad*), and others (*esforzar, zaherir, suelto*).

However, the most specific feature for this group is not a linguistic one, but literary information: that the protagonist belongs to lower classes of the society, with a z-score over three. Besides, the text tends to have a clearly negative ending, the protagonist tends to be young and female, and the settings is typically in Spain or Europe (all these features have a z-score over one).

Some of the texts that are related to this category by a large proportion of sources are *Boy* by Coloma, *Cleopatra Pérez* by Munilla, *La espuma* and *Tristán o el pesimismo* by Valdés, *Los pazos de Ulloa* by Bazán, or several works by Gadlós (*Miau, Lo prohibido, La de Bringas, Fortunata y Jacinta*).

Two subgenres show a great affinity to the naturalist novel: the realist (46% of shared texts and features) and the social novel (43%). After that, *literary fiction* (28%), educational (17%), and *costumbrist* novel follow (15%).

The naturalist novel is a category that raises some doubts among many researchers when it is mentioned as an analyzed as a literary subgenre. The fact that there is a period in many national literatures called *naturalism* can give the impression that the naturalist novel is not the same kind of category as the erotic or adventure novel. The analysis of this category in the different sections shows that this category is not dissimilar to the rest. It does show a preference for specific decades, but so do other subgenres like the historical or erotic novel (see Section 3.1.5). Besides, it does show literary characteristics such as a poor protagonist with a story ending sadly. Throughout the several steps that were analyzed in this research study, the naturalist novel behaves just as the rest of the categories, which are perceived as more typical subgenres of the novel.

11.8 Historical Novel

The historical novel is in the middle range of centrality of the network (eigenvector of 0.18), with a relatively low specificity of features (standard deviation of z-scores of 0.48). It contains 113 novels in CoNSSA, 59 in CoNSSA-canon. Its novels are relatively highly canonized, with 1.46 pages of the manual on average.

The most distinctive feature, unsurprisingly, is a setting in the antiquity, followed by geographical settings in Italy or America, and a protagonist of the higher classes of society. An interesting aspect is that, even though the setting in Spain is not very distinctive for this subgenre, the references to Spain are. In other words, historical novels do not take place more often in Spain than the rest, but they do mention Spain by name more frequently.

Besides this, vocabulary about groups (*gente, asociar, población*, and nouns about groups marked by WordNet), military and war (*milicia, soldado, luchar, grado, guerra, delito, apresar*), politics (*soberano, política, empleo, autoridad, mandar*), and places (*municipio, territorio*, and nouns referring places marked by WordNet) are specific for this subgenre.

Some novels frequently associated with this category by several sources were written by Baroja (*Los últimos románticos, La feria de los discretos, La ciudad de la niebla*), Coloma (*Jeromín*), Costa (*Último día del paganismo*), Valle-Inclán (*Viva mi dueño, La corte de los milagros*), Pereda (*Pedro Sánchez*), or Sender (*Mr. Witt en el Cantón*).

The most similar subgenres are *literary fiction* (33% of shared elements), followed by adventure (29%), social (22%), war, and realist novel (both with 21%).

11.9 Memoir

The memoir (*memorias*) shows an eigenvector centrality of 0.16 and a relatively low specificity of features (standard deviation of z-scores of 0.39). This category is composed by 55 texts (20 in CoNSSA-canon). The texts are relatively canonized (1.17 pages on average in the MdLE, 2.25 in CoNSSA-canon). The classification result is of 0.83 F1-score.

The most specific features of this genre are literary ones, especially with the protagonist being at the beginning of the novel either a child (2.01 z-scores) or a mature person (1.83). The narrator varies between autodiegetic, homodiegetic, or a mix. Besides, the texts only in CoNSSA (and not in CoNSSA-canon) show a low level of autoreference to the author's life, and the setting mixes usually several types of places (cities, towns, rural areas).

The linguistic characteristics with values over one z-score are a large proportional number of chapters, vocabulary about the passage of time (*conservar, viejo*), cognitive processes (*enseñar, describir, calificar*), education (*convento, literatura, ensayar, lengua, educar*), family (*familia, linaje*), positive vocabulary (*apetecer, curioso, extravagante, generoso*), and pronouns and verbs in first person (information extracted from Freeling).

Works frequently assigned with this label are works by Valdes (*La novela de un novelista*, *Papeles del doctor Angélico*), Baroja (*El sabor de la venganza*, *El aprendiz de conspirador*, *Crónica escandalosa*, *El escuadrón del Brigante*, *Los amores tardíos*), and others (*Doña Milagros* by Bazán, *La quinta de Palmyra* by Serna, *La tragedia de Calisto* by Hernández).

The most similar category is the educational novel (29% of shared features and texts), followed by philosophical, biographic, and adventure novel (20%).

11.10 Bucolic Novel

This category is the first of the two that do not come from human-annotated labels, but from the evaluated process of using clustering techniques to identify categories that show consistent patterns of overrepresented literary and linguistic characteristics. As discussed in Section 6.2.7, the exact label that is being used here, *bucolic novel*, is only a way of describing this group and is the final step of a series of evaluations and comparisons. The groups of novels here described show numerous differences with the rest that can be easily understood in literary terms. Whether the community is more satisfied with calling this group *intimist novel*, *bucolic novel*, or *cluster 217*, is a secondary matter. This category has been already described in Section 6.2.7, although in that Section the description did not follow the methodological steps presented in Chapter 8, nor both version of the corpus were contrasted. For this reason, both description of the subgenre show certain variance.

This category is still in the middle range of the centrality (eigenvector centrality of 0.14) but shows a relatively high specificity of the features (standard deviation of z-scores of 0.66). This category is populated by 87 texts (30 in CoNSSA-canon). The books are relatively highly canonized (1.1 pages in the MdLE, 2.18 in CoNSSA-canon). Even though the works show a relatively central position in the network, the classification yields almost perfect results (0.98 F1-score).

The vocabulary overrepresented in this category are related to the mind (*secreto, arrepentirse, memoria*), sounds (*ruido, silencio*), natural elements (*llama, quemar, madera, mojar, húmedo, fuente*, and vocabulary about weather from WordNet), landscape (*cercar, cauce, campo*), others (*escultura, fecundar*), and there is a large proportion of chapters and divisions.

The literary metadata that are specific for this category are a setting in rural environment or towns, in some cases in the antiquity, a mature and male protagonist. Besides, the texts of this category in CoNSSA show an unclear ending.

Some texts in this category are novels by Francisco de Ayala (*Cazador en el alba, Erika ante el invierno*), Miró (*Los pies y los zapatos de Enriqueta, Nómada*), Clarín (*Cuesta abajo*), Azorín (*Tomás Rueda*), Chacel (*Estación*), or Antonio Espina (*Luna de copas*).

The closest category is clearly the modernist novel (42% of shared texts and features), followed by historical, philosophical novel, and memoir (all three with 16%).

11.11 Adventure Novel

The adventure novel shows an eigenvector centrality of 0.13, and a relatively high specificity of the features (standard deviation of z-scores of 0.79). It is populated by 49 texts (16 in CoNSSA-canon). The books typically occupy less than one page in the MdLE (0.97, 1.97 in CoNSSA). The classification results are relatively high (0.91 F1-score).

The most specific features of this genre are related to the setting of the text, such as a boat, a trip within continents or countries, Italy, America, or Africa. Besides, the action normally takes place in modern times, it has a homodiegetic narrator and the protagonist is a male adult.

The overrepresented vocabulary is related to interactions (*vacilar, protestar, percatarse*), some of them physical (*perseguir, apresar, desechar, apresar, arriesgar*), places (*detrás, patria*), boats (*marina, viento, barco*), communication (*teléfono, lengua*), army (*milicia, grado*), others (*vulgar, gente, capacidad*), and references to places.

Works referenced by several sources as part of this category were written by Baroja (*Las inquietudes de Shanti Andía, La estrella del Capitán Chimista,*

La feria de los discretos, Los pilotos de altura), Blasco Ibáñez (*El paraíso de las mujeres, La reina Calafia*), Ganivet (*La conquista del reino de Maya*), Ricardo Baroja (*Aventuras del submarino alemán U, La nao «Capitana»*), or de Burgos (*El último contrabandista*).

The most similar categories are the historical novel (29% of the shared texts and features), followed by memoir (20%), philosophical, and war novel (18%).

11.12 Biographic Novel

The biographic novel shows an eigenvector centrality of 0.11, and a relatively low specificity of features (standard deviation of z-scores of 0.50). The subgenre is populated by 30 novels (14 in CoNSSA-canon), relatively well canonized (1.44 pages in the manual MdLE, 2.12 for the cases in CoNSSA-canon). Its classification is relatively high (0.88 F1-score).

The features most overrepresented are literary ones, such as a close relation between the text and the author, endings that are either partially positive or partially negative (i.e., the ending is neither clearly positive, nor negative, nor neutral), settings that mix several types (for example, city and town) and countries, and a male protagonist from the middle class.

The linguistic vocabulary represented in this category are about time (*enseguida, joven*), education and childhood (*colegio, resumir, inseguro, memoria, pequeño*), food (*estómago, cerdo*), positive vocabulary (*benévolo, placer, dócil*), others (*tipo, espacio, silencio, modo, escaso*), besides the presence of poems in the text.

Some frequently assigned texts with this label are *Papeles del doctor Angélico* and *Sinfonía pastoral* by Valdés, *Niño y grande* and *Amores de Antón Hernando* by Miró, *El novelista* and *La quinta de Palmyra* by Serna, *Erika ante el invierno* and *Cazador en el alba* by Francisco de Ayala, or *La pata de la raposa* by Pérez de Ayala.

The most similar subgenres are the autobiography (60% of shared texts and features), memoir (20%), philosophical, and psychological novel (19%).

11.13 Modernist Novel

The modernist novel shows also an eigenvector centrality of 0.11, even though the specificity of its features is much greater than the previous case (standard deviation of z-scores of 0.88). This category is populated by 35 novels (15 in

CoNSSA-canon) and is rather canonized, occupying on average 1.61 pages of the manual MdLE (2.6 for the cases in CoNSSA-canon). The subgenre achieves rather low values of classification (0.79 F1-score).

The most specific features are linguistic, especially vocabulary about communication and sounds (*secreto, silencio, ruido, sonar*), natural elements (weather marked by WordNet, *húmedo, frío, quemar*), descriptions (*observar, cavidad*), emotions (*temblar, insensible, emoción, arrepentirse*), food (*azúcar, recolección, cosecha*), and others (*sostener, buscar, pintar*).

The most distinctive literary metadata are plots in several geographical settings: other continents (especially America and Asia, this last case only in CoNSSA and not in CoNSSA-canon), rural places, trips, Italy. In addition, previous periods of history are slightly overrepresented. The protagonist tends to be young and male, and there is a certain relation between the author and the text.

Texts frequently labeled as modernist novels are *El novelista* and *Cinelandia* by Serna, *Nomada* by Miró, *La quimera* by Bazán, *La cópula* by Rueda, *Paz en la guerra* by Unamuno, *Romance del fantasma y doña Juanita* by Pemán, *Historia vulgar* by Lorca, *Escenas junto a la muerte* by Jarnés, or *Locuras de Carnaval* by Baroja.

The most similar category to this one is the bucolic novel (42% shared texts and features), followed at a distance by autobiographic (15%), biographic, and psychological novel (14%).

11.14 Autobiographical Novel

This category shows an eigenvector of 0.10 and a rather low specificity of the features (standard deviation of z-scores of 0.59). The category is populated by 26 instances in CoNSSA, 11 in CoNSSA-canon. The novels are relatively canonized, with 1.28 pages on average in the manual MdLE (1.68 for CoNSSA-canon). The results of the classification are relatively high: 0.93 F1-score.

Two literary features are notably distinctive for this category: The first is, unsurprisingly, a strong relation between the author's life and the plot of the text (3.08 z-score). However, the second one is less obvious: the mix of several kinds of types of places (2.19 z-score), meaning a change of setting from a town to a city, for example. The protagonist tends to be a child at the beginning of the text from the middle classes of society and the endings tend to be either partially or clearly positive.

The overrepresented vocabulary in this category is about childhood (*niño, joven, pequeño*), personal descriptions (*carácter, inseguro, dócil, brusco, benévolo*), food (*estómago, digerir*), time (*enseguida*), cognitive process and education (*resumir, encuadernar, colegio*), and others (*tipo, buscar, sutil, apartar*).

Texts frequently assigned with this label are works by Valdés (*Papeles del doctor Angélico* and *Sinfonía pastoral*), Francisco de Ayala (*Cazador en el alba* and *Erika ante el invierno*), Serna (*El novelista*), Miró (*Amores de Antón Hernando* and *Niño y grande*), and Pérez de Ayala (*La pata de la raposa* and *Troteras y danzaderas*).

Similar subgenres are the biographic novel (60% of shared features and texts), followed at a distance by memoir (18%), psychological (17%), modernist (15%), and educational novel (14%).

11.15 Comedy Novel

As the previous one, the comedy novel (*novela de humor*) has an eigenvector centrality of 0.10 and a lower specificity of the features (standard deviation of z-scores of 0.54). The category is populated by 49 texts in CoNSSA, 14 in CoNSSA-canon. The works show a rather low canonicity with one page on average in the manual MdLE (2.29 for CoNSSA-canon). The classification results are relatively low (0.83 F1-score).

The most distinctive features of the category are linguistic, concerning information or lack thereof (*exacto, vacilar, percatarse, confirmar, fingir, protestar*), education (*colegio, universidad*), crime (*delito, policía*), physical descriptions (*ademán, óptica, fotografía*), relations (*matrimonio, prometer*), and others (*desechar, imposible*). Besides auxiliary verbs, numbers, and sections (divisions within chapters) are also overrepresented. Relating the literary features, the action of some novels ocurrs in America or Africa, being frequently in cities. In addition, the protagonist comes from the upper layers of society, the narrator is heterodiegetic, and the endings tend to be either negative or neutral (this last case only in CoNSSA, not in CoNSSA-canon).

Some novels frequently assigned to this subgenre are works by Jardiel Poncela (*¡Espérame en Siberia, vida mía!*, *Amor se escribe sin hache*), Fernández Flórez (*El malvado Carabel*, *Relato inmoral*, *El hombre que compró un automóvil*), Pemán (*De Madrid a Oviedo pasando por las Azores*), Serna (*El doctor inverosímil*, *El caballero del hongo gris*), Baroja (*Aventuras, inventos y mixtificaciones de Silvestre Paradox*), or Carrere (*La torre de los siete jorobados*).

In comparison with the previous subgenres, this one shows little similarity with the rest. However, the ones sharing a larger number of texts and features are philosophical (20%), adventure (14%), and fantasy (12%).

11.16 Psychological Novel

The psychological novel is the first one with a value of eigenvector lower than 0.10, more specifically 0.09, with a rather low specificity of the features (standard deviation of z-scores of 0.60). This category is populated by 20 texts, ten in CoNSSA-canon. The novels are relatively well canonized, with 1.58 pages in the manual MdLE on average (1.8 when only CoNSSA-canon is observed). The classification results are relatively low (0.81 F1-score).

However, some semantic features show relatively high z-scores over two. The most distinctive semantic fields are about knowledge and education (*astrología, enseñar, educar, convento*), descriptions (*describir, retratar, pequeño, espacio, silencio*), art (*arte, escultura, pintar, teñir*), sentiments (*afectación, maduro*), and others (*escaso, insignificante, estómago, perfecto*).

One literary feature holds a very high z-score (3.71): a mixed narrator. This means that the change of narrator (for example from a heterodiegetic to an autodiogetic one) would be a very distinctive feature of this subgenre. Other literary top features are settings in Europe, Spain, and rural areas, a partially negative ending, and a male protagonist from the middle class.

Some texts frequently associated with this subgenre are works by Valdés (*La alegría del capitán Ribot*), Salaverría (*La Virgen de Aránzazu*), Bazán (*Morriña, La quimera*), Ganivet (*Los trabajos del infatigable creador Pío Cid*), Baroja (*Camino de perfección, El cura de Monleón, Susana*), or Azaña (*El jardín de los frailes*).

The closest categories are the biographical (19%), philosophical (18%), autobiographical (17%), educational novel, and memoir (both with 16%).

11.17 Spiritual Novel

The spiritual novel (*novela espiritual*) also has an eigenvector centrality of 0.09, with a rather low specificity of the features (standard deviation of z-scores of 0.61). This category is populated by 34 novels (18 in CoNSSA-canon) with values about canonicity in the middle range (1.36 pages on average in the manual

MdLE, 2.15 for CoNSSA-canon). The classification result is among the lowest ones with a 0.75 F1-score.

The distinctive vocabulary of this category is clearly religious, relating church (*culto, iglesia, religión, eclesiástico, altar, misa*), theology (*teología, Jesucristo, cristiano, Dios, cielo, mitología) or religious practices (rezar, devoción, santo, virtud, sacrificio*), and negative vocabulary (*susto, farmacia*).

Besides, some of the plots of these works take place in biblical times and settings (Italy, Asia), mainly in towns that represent a real place in the world. The protagonist tends to be young and female, and the narrator tends to be homodiegetic.

Some works frequently assigned with this label are works by Galdós (*Ángel Guerra, Halma, Torquemada en la hoguera, Nazarín*), Miró (*El hijo santo, Figuras de la Pasión del Señor*), or Salaverría (*La Virgen de Aránzazu*).

Some similar subgenres are the educational novel (19% of shared texts and features), followed by the bucolic, social (13%), and the *nivola* (12%).

The relatively low results are surprising if one takes into account the fact that some literary and linguistic features have values over two or even three z-scores. This can be explained by the fact that the previously mentioned vocabulary is very infrequent in the corpus. When a number of features is selected, such as 3,000, many of these features would be deleted from the matrix that is passed onto the algorithm.

11.18 Fantasy Novel

A step further towards the periphery is the fantasy novel (*novela fantástica*), with an eigenvector centrality of 0.06, and a middle range of specificity of features (standard deviation of z-scores of 0.64). This category is populated by 24 texts (only eight when considering CoNSSA-canon). Their canonicity is relatively low, with less than a page (0.92) on average in the manual MdLE (2.12 in CoNSSA-canon). The classification achieves an almost perfect result (0.95 F1-score).

However, this positive result is mainly caused by a very specific literary feature that achieves z-scores over four: that the plot does not take place in a realistic world. Following this, with values over two z-scores, is information about the period (past eras) and settings, such as non-existing continents, Africa, or France (this last one only in CoNSSA). The protagonist tends to be an adult, the endings are partially positive, and the texts do not represent the opinion or experiences of the author.

From the point of view of linguistic information, one semantic area is clearly overrepresented: magic (*adivinar, hechicería, predecir, encantar*). Besides, other areas that appear frequently are qualifications (*excelente, falso*), danger and movement (*refugio, imprevisión, destreza, adelantar, imposible*), social interactions (*preguntar, confesar, chisme*), very general words (*ser, cosa*), and others (*soberano, empleo, óptica*).

Some works frequently associated with this category are *La jirafa sagrada* by Madariaga, works by Fernández Flórez (*El secreto de Barba Azul, Las siete columnas, El hombre que compró un automóvil*), *El profesor inútil* by Jarnés, *Morsamor* by Valera, *La torre de los siete jorobados* by Carrere, *El secreto del Acueducto* by Serna, *La "tournée" de Dios* by Jardiel Poncela, or *La última fada* by Bazán.

The most similar subgenre is the adventure novel (15% of shared features and texts), followed by the historical, comedy (12%), and philosophical novel (10%).

11.19 War Novel

A step further away from the center is the war novel, with an eigenvector centrality of 0.05, and relatively high specificity of the features (standard deviation of z-scores of 0.94). The subgenre is populated by 21 novels (only six when considering CoNSSA-canon), and these are works that hold a relatively low canonization status (0.77 pages in average in the manual MdLE, 1.58 when considering only CoNSSA-canon). The classification results are relatively high, with a 0.93 F1-score.

The most specific features of this subgenre are linguistic and closely related, unsurprisingly, to the topic of war (*enemigo, luchar, guerra, paz*), army (*tropa, milicia, soldado, grado, artillería*), fire and weapons (*llama, explosión, quemar, proyectil*), but also to people and social interactions (*gente, sustituir, arriesgar*), and space (*municipio, detrás, patria*).

The literary features distinctive for this category are settings in towns, in Africa, France, or several countries (these last two only observed in CoNSSA). The ending tends to be either partially positive or partially negative (only in CoNSSA). Also only in CoNSSA, the information about the protagonist tends to be blurred (in some cases because there is not a single clear protagonist, but a group of soldiers). An interesting aspect is that these novels tends to take place in contemporary times in a realistic world. This is noteworthy because, as seen in Section 3.2.11, the enormous majority of plots of the corpus share these characteristics. In order for these features (contemporary times, realistic world) to be distinctive for this subgenre, an even larger proportion than the rest of the texts has to contain them.

Texts assigned frequently with this label are works by Concha Espina (*Luna roja*, *Retaguardia*), Unamuno (*Paz en la guerra*), Blasco Ibáñez (*Los cuatro jinetes del apocalipsis*, *Los enemigos de la mujer*, *Mare nostrum*), Sender (*Imán*, *Contraataque*), Díaz Fernández (*El blocao*), or Herrera (*Acero de Madrid*).

The closest subgenre is the historical novel, but with a lower percentage than expected: only 21%. This is followed by historical (18%), bucolic (10%), *literary fiction* (6%), and social novel (5%).

11.20 Dialogue Novel

The dialogue novel shows an eigenvector centrality of 0.05, with a relatively high specificity of the features (standard deviation of z-scores of 0.95). This subgenre is populated by 14 texts (seven when considering only CoNSSA-canon), with a middle range of canonicity on average (0.95 pages of the manual MdLE, 1.14 when considering only CoNSSA-canon). The classifiers yield perfect results (1.0 F1-score).

Although the top feature is a literary one, in general the linguistic and textual characteristics are more specific for this genre, especially the TEI-tag *sp*, typically used for encoding theater plays, but also for these texts (see Sections 2.1.4 and 3.1.8). However, other linguistic information is less obvious and still very specific, such as the forms of pronouns and verbs in first person (annotated by Freeling), the short length of the sentences, many divisions, or the frequency of the typographical sign of period. Besides, some semantic features are overrepresented, such as social interaction (*conceder*, *simpatía*), negative vocabulary (*impertinente*, *inútil*, *insensato*, *vengar*, *disparate*, *desorientar*, *insustancial*), cognitive verbs (*suponer*, *aprender*, *atenuar*, and cognitive verbs marked by WordNet), and others (*óptica*, *ser*).

However, the most predominant feature is the lack of a narrator either in the first or third person. The geographical settings show several possibilities such as Africa, non-existing continents, cities, or rural areas. The plots tend to end happily and the texts do not tend to be autobiographical. Many protagonists are adults, female characters are slightly overrepresented, commonly from the middle class.

Novels frequently assigned with this label are works by Azaña (*La velada en Benicarló*), Baroja (*La casa de Aizgorri, Paradox, Rey, La leyenda de Jaun de Alzate*), Galdós (*Realidad, El abuelo, La loca de la casa, La razón de la sinrazón*), or Benavente (*Cartas de mujeres*).

The clearly most similar subgenre is the mono-dialogue novel (43% of shared features and texts), followed at a distance by the philosophical, fantasy (9%), comedy (7%), and bucolic novel (6%).

11.21 Mono-Dialogue Novel

This subgenre is the third exceptional case analyzed in this research study, obtained in Chapter 6.2 through unsupervised methods (along with *literary fiction* and bucolic novel). This category has an eigenvector centrality of 0.04 and a relatively high specificity of the features (standard deviation of z-scores of 1.11). It is composed by only 11 texts (six when considering CoNSSA-canon). The works in this category show a middle range of canonicity (1.05 pages in manual MdLE on average, 1.17 for CoNSSA-canon). As in the previous case, the classifiers yield perfect classification.

Also, as in the dialogue novel, the most distinctive features are forms that do not have a narrator in the first or second person, but are written in epistolary or dialogue form. After these, the most specific features are the frequency of the TEI-tag *sp*, negative vocabulary (*inútil, desorientar, prescindir, excluir, insensato, disconforme, insustancial, tímido, sentencia, impertinente, disparate*), cognitive verbs (*preocupar, suponer, aprender, conceder*, and cognitive verbs marked by WordNet), and others (*brío*). Besides, pronouns and verbs in the first person and a large proportion of divisions are overrepresented.

In addition to the narrator, other literary features are overrepresented in this category, such as a positive ending, several possible settings (non-existing continents, a trip through several countries, rural areas, and cities), and female protagonists are overrepresented in comparison to the rest of the corpus.

Texts assigned with this label are works by Benavente (*Cartas de mujeres*), Chacel (*Estación*), Aub (*Luis Álvarez Petreña*), Azaña (*La velada en Benicarló*), Lorca (*Fray Antonio*), or Galdós (*Realidad, La razón de la sinrazón*).

The most similar subgenre is the dialogue novel (43%), followed by poetic (7%), naturalist, realist, and social novel (this last three with 5%).

11.22 *Costumbrist* Novel

The *costumbrist* novel also has an eigenvector of 0.04, with a relatively low specificity of the features (standard deviation of z-scores of 0.82). The genre is populated by 16 texts (six when only CoNSSA-canon is considered) of low canonization status (1.06 pages in the manual MdLE in average, 1.95 for CoNSSA-canon). The results of the classification are relatively high, with a 0.90 F1-score.

In this subgenre, the top features are a mix of linguistic and literary characteristics. Specific vocabulary for this category are about relations (*comprometer, reservar, comedir, admirar*), descriptions (*suelto, breve, remate, encontrar, ocasión, propio, ceñir*, and a larger proportion of adjectives), positive (*solución, regocijo, risa*) but also negative vocabulary (*pinchar, chocar, desvergüenza*), and others (*muchacho, café*).

The literary metadata that are overrepresented in this group are female and young protagonists, who, when only looking at CoNSSA, tend to be from higher classes of society. The ending is usually partially or clearly positive, the narrator is heterodiegetic, and the authors do not try to represent their life in the text. The settings are normally rural areas or towns in Spain.

Texts who receive this label frequently are works by mainly two authors: Valdés (*Los majos de Cádiz, Sinfonía pastoral, Marta y María, Tristán o el pesimismo*) and Pereda (*Sotileza, La puchera, De tal palo, tal astilla, El sabor de la tierruca*), but also other authors such as Rueda (*La reja*) or Serna (*La Nardo*).

The most similar category is the naturalist novel (15% of shared texts and features) followed by the realist (6%), erotic, comedy, and spiritual novel (5%).

11.23 *Nivola*

The *nivola*, a one-author-label coined by Unamuno and introduced in Section 2.1.10, also has an eigenvector of 0.04. This category has a high specificity of the features (standard deviation of z-scores of 1.79) and only five texts which are highly canonized (4.8 pages on average in the manual MdLE). This very small category associated with only one author can be classified with perfect results (1.0 F1-score).

Although both the literary and linguistic features show high z-scores (over two), the strongest ones are linguistic. They can be mainly organized in negative vocabulary (*hundir, anular, excluir*), life and childbirth (*retoño, destino, crear, reproducción, útero, aprender, vida, origen*), poverty (*mendigo, limosna*), and objects (*canal, tallo, cuerno*). Besides, several typographical signs are overrepresented, such as question, exclamation, and quotation marks.

Nonetheless, the literary features also show some high values, such as a very long span of the plot, a homodiegetic narrator, a high identification of the author in the text, a partially or clearly negative ending, and a setting in unspecific towns of Spain.

The five works by Unamuno assigned with this label are *Niebla*, *Abel Sánchez*, *San Manuel Bueno, mártir*, *La tía Tula*, and *Amor y pedagogía*.

The most similar categories are the spiritual (12%), the educational (11%), and the philosophical novel (8%).

11.24 Erotic Novel

In the periphery of the network is the erotic subgenre, with an eigenvector centrality of 0.03 and a relatively low specificity of features (standard deviation of z-scores of 0.81). This subgenre comprehends 17 novels in CoNSSA, and only four novels in CoNSSA-canon. Its texts are normally not strongly canonized (0.5 pages in the manual on average). That explains a rather high classification score of 0.96 F1-score.

This category has very distinctive features (with values over two z-scores) like type of relationships (*novio, matrimonio*), sentimental verbs or actions, mainly positive (*admirar, caricia, enamorar, encantar, apasionar, abandonar*), personal qualities (*vergüenza, sincero, extravagante, feo, antipatía*), gender and sexual orientation (*mujer, afeminado*, which was a historical manner of referring to homosexuality), and others (*convertir, suelto, sal, espina*). It is interesting that the only semantic field in the top 20 about physical relations is *caricia* ('caress'), and none of them is related to sexual practices or body parts.

The protagonist is typically an adult woman of the higher classes of the society. Even more distinctive is the fact that stories do not represent the author's life. Other distinctive literary metadata are urban settings, in some cases traveling through different countries, in a contemporary realistic world, with a heterodiegetic narrator. Many of these features are not explicitly mentioned by the two monographs about the erotic novels that I have summarized in Section 2.1.8. However, some of the characteristics that they mention are confirmed in this analysis, like a middle-class female protagonist, urban settings, or trips. Other like references to interior spaces, underwear, or female body parts do not stand out in my analysis.

The texts most frequently assigned with this label are many by Trigo (*Del frío al fuego*, *Mi media naranja*, *En la carrera*), but also from other authors like Bacarisse (*Los terribles amores de Agliberto y Celedonia*), Picón (*Dulce y sabrosa*), or Serna (*El gran hotel*, *La viuda blanca y negra*).

The closest subgenre is the comedy (10% of shared texts and features), followed by others subgenres at around 5% and 6% (*costumbrist*, poetic, naturalist, fantasy novel).

11.25 Episodio Nacional

This one-author-label coined by Galdós (see Section 2.1.10) also has an eigenvector of 0.03, and a relatively high specificity of the features (standard deviation of z-scores of 1.08), although not as high as the other two similar labels: *nivola* and *greguería*. In this corpus, this subgenre is populated by 11 texts. The texts are treated very briefly in the manual MdLE, occupying only a fifth of a page. The subgenre yields almost perfect classification results (0.97 F1-score). Because of its canonical status, this genre is not present in CoNSSA-canon, and therefore its following description is only based on CoNSSA.

The most specific features of this subgenre are clearly linguistic, with semantic fields being overrepresented such as the transmission of information (*intrigar, predecir, citar, enviar, recado, teléfono, recado, verdad*), social relations (*desaprobar, corregir, extrañar, imponer*), danger (*baquetear, atravesar, travieso*), politics and society (*ley, política, heredar, moda*), and others (*elemento, perseverar*).

Literary features that are specific for this subgenre are related to the setting: The plots tend to take place in cities, trips through several continents, in boats, or in Spain, being typically realistic. However, some novels do depict a non-existing world (especially the later works). The protagonists are normally adults from the middle class, the narrator is usually autodiegetic or the text is in epistolary form, and the ending is rather partially or clearly positive (with some neutral exceptions).

Works populating this category were written by Galdós, such as: *Mendizábal, Luchana, Bodas reales, Narváez, O'Donnell, La vuelta al mundo en la «Numancia», Amadeo I, La Primera República, Cánovas,* or *La estafeta romántica*.

As expected, the most similar categories of this subgenre are the historical and the adventure novel, although the percentage of shared features and texts is lower than expected: only 7%. Besides, this same number is shared with *literary fiction*, while the fantasy novel shares 6% of features.

11.26 Poetic Novel

Close to the limits of the network is the poetic novel, with an eigenvector centrality of only 0.02, and a relatively high specificity of the features (standard deviation of z-scores of 1.56). The category is populated by only five texts, a number that is reduced to two when CoNSSA-canon is considered (that is why the following description is based only on CoNSSA), but the texts have a high canonical status (1.88 pages on average in the manual MdLE). For a category with so few instances, it yields a low classification result of 0.80 F1-score.

It is rather astonishing that the features that are most distinctive for this category are not linguistic, but literary information. More specifically, there is a distinct lack of definition of several fields caused by a general lack of plot or vagueness in the story, for example, regarding the type of setting or the identification of the protagonist (see Section 3.2.5 to see how uncertain metadata was encoded). Besides, the narrator tends to be autodiegetic, the protagonist male and mature, it has a negative ending, and the author is clearly represented in the text.

Nonetheless, many linguistic and textual characteristics are also very distinctive, such as vocabulary about feelings (*enamorar, apasionar, ilusión, compadecer, pasmar*), personal characteristics (*valiente, firme, dócil, insignificante*), descriptions (*desierto, parecer, espina*), body (*sangre, nervio*), or negative vocabulary (*injustificado, abatir, confundir*). Besides, there are large proportions of chapters and sections.

The five texts assigned to this category are *Fray Antonio* by Lorca, *Amor de sacrificio* by Carrere, *Luis Álvarez Petreña* by Aub, *Crimen* by Espinosa, and *Platero y yo* by Ramón Jiménez.

This category shares only a few features and texts with any other category, being the closest mono-dialogue (7%), bucolic, psychological, erotic, and modernist novel (each time 6%).

11.27 Greguería

Finally, the *greguería* is the least central category, with an eigenvector centrality very close to zero, and a very high specificity of the z-scores (standard deviation of z-scores of 2.16). This category is populated only by two editions in my corpus, and they are treated rather scarcely in the manual MdLE (five pages altogether for all the different editions). The classifiers tend to achieve perfect results, even with very few features. The reasons why this label has been analyzed throughout this research study have been discussed in detail in Sections 2.1.10, 3.1.4, 5.1.7, and especially in Chapter 3.3, in which it has not been possible to prove that these texts are not somehow related to the novel when compared to the CORDE. As it happens with the *episodio nacional*, the description of this genre is based only in the CoNSSA and not in the CoNSSA-canon.

The most distinctive features of this genre are its lack of definition of many aspects, such as the protagonist, the type of representation of the world, the setting, etc. This is due to the lack of plot in the *greguerías*. However, these are not the only cues that the classifier can use to sort this subgenre correctly. Many semantic features show z-scores over four, such as movement (*aparecer, sacar*), objects (*huevo, trampa, esfera, cal, caja, billar, insignia*), body (*cuello, matar, biología*), animals and nature (*llover, astronomía*, animals marked by WordNet), negative vocabulary (*convencional, manía*), humor (*humor*), and others (*arrendar, simular*).

As mentioned before, only two texts written by Serna are part of this category. The most similar subgenre shares only 3% of the features, and that is the comedy novel, followed only by the poetic and psychological novel (1%).